MW01592877

Agency, Partnership, and the LLC

**SELECTED STATUTES AND
FORM AGREEMENT**
1997 Edition

J. DENNIS HYNES
Professor of Law
University of Colorado

MICHIE
Law Publishers
CHARLOTTESVILLE, VIRGINIA

1177813

Preface

This statutory supplement makes available to the reader the complete text of the statutes essential for a study of the law of partnership, the limited liability partnership, and the limited liability company. This edition includes the 1996 amendments to the Uniform Partnership Act (1994) ("RUPA") that incorporate limited liability partnership act provisions into RUPA, creating the Uniform Limited Liability Partnership Act ("ULLPA"). Also, the 1996 amendments to the Uniform Limited Liability Company Act ("ULLCA") are included in this edition.

With the exception of the original Uniform Partnership Act (1914) ("UPA"), all of the comments to all of the statutes have been reproduced in their entirety. (The comments to UPA are reproduced in edited form; an effort has been made to retain the language that plays a material role in understanding UPA and its historical context without burdening the reader with the sometimes discursive quality of some of the UPA comments.) Comments are particularly helpful when substantial changes have been made to basic, nearly universally adopted legislation, which has happened recently in both the general and limited partnership areas of the law. The comments allow the reader to identify and trace the changes that have been made from the basic acts. Also, often the philosophy behind many of the changes is described, providing another reason for making comments available to the reader. There is no substitute, however, for first concentrating on and attempting to gain control over the statutes themselves, for they, not the comments, are the primary source of law.

This edition of the supplement includes excerpts from the Restatement (Second) of Agency. Agency concepts play a significant role in the application and interpretation of the statutes reproduced below.

Permission from the National Conference of Commissioners on Uniform State Laws to reprint the uniform acts and their comments, and from the American Law Institute to reprint portions of the Restatement (Second) of Agency and the Form of Partnership Agreement, is gratefully acknowledged.

June 1997

J. Dennis Hynes

Table of Contents

PART ONE

PARTNERSHIP

UNIFORM PARTNERSHIP ACT (1914)

Editor's note: The text and Comments of the Uniform Partnership Act (1914) ("UPA") contained below are taken from volume 6 of Uniform Laws Annotated, Master Edition (1995) and are reproduced with permission of the publishers. The Comments were prepared by Dr. Wm. Draper Lewis, the draftsman of the Act. They have been edited in the interest of keeping this supplement a manageable size, but all language in the Comments that contributes materially to an understanding of UPA has been retained. The information contained immediately below on adoptions of UPA is drawn from the 1997 Cumulative Annual Pocket Part to the 1995 revision of volume 6.

UPA was approved by the National Conference of Commissioners on Uniform State Laws in 1914 and adopted in the following jurisdictions: Alabama (1972), Alaska (1917), Arizona (1954), Arkansas (1941), California (1929), Colorado (1931), Delaware (1947), District of Columbia (1962), Florida (1973), Georgia (1985), Hawaii (1973), Idaho (1920), Illinois (1917), Indiana (1950), Iowa (1971), Kansas (1972), Kentucky (1954), Maine (1973), Maryland (1916), Massachusetts (1923), Michigan (1917), Minnesota (1921), Mississippi (1977), Missouri (1949), Nebraska (1943), Nevada (1931), New Hampshire (1973), New Jersey (1919), New York (1919), North Carolina (1941), Ohio (1949), Oklahoma (1955), Oregon (1939), Pennsylvania (1915), Rhode Island (1957), South Carolina (1950), South Dakota (1923), Tennessee (1917), Texas (1962), Utah (1921), Vermont (1941), Virgin Islands (1957), Virginia (1918), Washington (1945), and Wisconsin (1915).

Louisiana never adopted UPA. Alabama, Arizona, California, Florida, Texas, and Virginia have adopted the Revised Uniform Partnership Act ("RUPA") without immediately repealing UPA. UPA has been repealed in Connecticut, Montana, New Mexico, North Dakota, West Virginia and Wyoming, with RUPA now the effective law in those jurisdictions.

PART I

PRELIMINARY PROVISIONS

PART II

NATURE OF PARTNERSHIP

3

PART III

RELATIONS OF PARTNERS TO PERSONS DEALING WITH THE PARTNERSHIP

PART IV

RELATIONS OF PARTNERS TO ONE ANOTHER

PART V

PROPERTY RIGHTS OF A PARTNER

PART VI

DISSOLUTION AND WINDING UP

PART VII

MISCELLANEOUS PROVISIONS

§ 44.   When Act Takes Effect.
§ 45.   Legislation Repealed.

PART I

PRELIMINARY PROVISIONS

§ 1.   Name of Act

This act may be cited as Uniform Partnership Act.

§ 2.   Definition of Terms

In this act, "Court" includes every court and judge having jurisdiction in the case.
"Business" includes every trade, occupation, or profession.
"Person" includes individuals, partnerships, corporations, and other associations.
"Bankrupt" includes bankrupt under the Federal Bankruptcy Act or insolvent under any state insolvent act.
"Conveyance" includes every assignment, lease, mortgage, or encumbrance.
"Real property" includes land and any interest or estate in land.

§ 3.   Interpretation of Knowledge and Notice

(1) A person has "knowledge" of a fact within the meaning of this act not only when he has actual knowledge thereof, but also when he has knowledge of such other facts as in the circumstances shows bad faith.

(2) A person has "notice" of a fact within the meaning of this act when the person who claims the benefit of the notice:

(a) States the fact to such person, or

(b) Delivers through the mail, or by other means of communication, a written statement of the fact to such person or to a proper person at his place of business or residence.

§ 4.   Rules of Construction

(1) The rule that statutes in derogation of the common law are to be strictly construed shall have no application to this act.

(2) The law of estoppel shall apply under this act.

(3) The law of agency shall apply under this act.

(4) This act shall be so interpreted and construed as to effect its general purpose to make uniform the law of those states which enact it.

(5) This act shall not be construed so as to impair the obligations of any contract existing when the act goes into effect, nor to affect any action or proceedings begun or right accrued before this act takes effect.

§ 5.   Rules for Cases Not Provided for in This Act

In any case not provided for in this act the rules of law and equity, including the law merchant, shall govern.

PART II

NATURE OF PARTNERSHIP

§ 6.   Partnership Defined

(1) A partnership is an association of two or more persons to carry on as co-owners a business for profit.

(2) But any association formed under any other statute of this state, or any statute adopted by authority, other than the authority of this state, is not a partnership under this act, unless such association would have been a partnership in this state prior to the adoption of this act; but this act shall apply to limited partnerships except in so far as the statutes relating to such partnerships are inconsistent herewith.

Comment

Subdivision (1). . . . .

The words "to carry on as co-owners a business" remove any doubt in the following case: A and B sign partnership articles and make their agreed contributions to the common fund. A refuses to carry on business as agreed. Is there a partnership to be wound up in accordance with the provisions of Part VI "Dissolution and Winding-up"? The words quoted require an affirmative answer to this question. If the words "carrying on business" had been used, in the case given, no partnership would exist, and Part VI would not apply.

The definition asserts that the associates are "co-owners" of the business. This distinguishes a partnership from an agency — an association of principal and agent. A business is a series of acts directed toward an end. Ownership involves the power of ultimate control. To state that partners are co-owners of a business is to state that they each have the power of ultimate control.

Lastly, the definition asserts that the business is for profit. Partnership is a branch of our commercial law; it has developed in connection with a particular business association, and it is, therefore, essential that the operation of the act should be confined to associations organized for profit.

. . .

§ 7.   Rules for Determining the Existence of a Partnership

In determining whether a partnership exists, these rules shall apply:

(1) Except as provided by section 16 persons who are not partners as to each other are not partners as to third persons.

(2) Joint tenancy, tenancy in common, tenancy by the entireties, joint property, common property, or part ownership does not of itself establish a partnership, whether such co-owners do or do not share any profits made by the use of the property.

(3) The sharing of gross returns does not of itself establish a partnership, whether or not the persons sharing them have a joint or common right or interest in any property from which the returns are derived.

(4) The receipt by a person of a share of the profits of a business is prima facie evidence that he is a partner in the business, but no such inference shall be drawn if such profits were received in payment:

(a) As a debt by installments or otherwise,

(b) As wages of an employee or rent to a landlord,

(c) As an annuity to a widow or representative of a deceased partner,

(d) As interest on a loan, though the amount of payment vary with the profits of the business,

(e) As the consideration for the sale of a good-will of a business or other property by installments or otherwise.

§ 8. Partnership Property

(1) All property originally brought into the partnership stock or subsequently acquired by purchase or otherwise, on account of the partnership, is partnership property.

(2) Unless the contrary intention appears, property acquired with partnership funds is partnership property.

(3) Any estate in real property may be acquired in the partnership name. Title so acquired can be conveyed only in the partnership name.

(4) A conveyance to a partnership in the partnership name, though without words of inheritance, passes the entire estate of the grantor unless a contrary intent appears.

Comment

Paragraphs (3), (4), in connection with section 10, infra, do away with existing confusions where there has been a conveyance to a partnership in the partnership name, or a conveyance by a partner in the partnership name. At present such conveyance may convey an equitable, but does not convey a legal title. To this extent paragraph (3) of this section and section 10(1), infra, change existing law.

PART III

RELATIONS OF PARTNERS TO PERSONS DEALING WITH THE PARTNERSHIP

§ 9. Partner Agent of Partnership as to Partnership Business

(1) Every partner is an agent of the partnership for the purpose of its business, and the act of every partner, including the execution in the partnership name of any instrument, for apparently carrying on in the usual way the business of the partnership of which he is a member binds the partnership, unless the partner so acting has in fact no authority to act for the partnership in the particular matter, and the person with whom he is dealing has knowledge of the fact that he has no such authority.

(2) An act of a partner which is not apparently for the carrying on of the business of the partnership in the usual way does not bind the partnership unless authorized by the other partners.

(3) Unless authorized by the other partners or unless they have abandoned the business, one or more but less than all the partners have no authority to:

(a) Assign the partnership property in trust for creditors or on the assignee's promise to pay the debts of the partnership,

(b) Dispose of the good-will of the business,

(c) Do any other act which would make it impossible to carry on the ordinary business of a partnership,

(d) Confess a judgment,

(e) Submit a partnership claim or liability to arbitration or reference.

(4) No act of a partner in contravention of a restriction on authority shall bind the partnership to persons having knowledge of the restriction.

§ 10. Conveyance of Real Property of the Partnership

(1) Where title to real property is in the partnership name, any partner may convey title to such property by a conveyance executed in the partnership name; but the partnership may recover such property unless the partner's act binds the partnership under the provisions of paragraph (1) of section 9, or unless such property has been conveyed by the grantee or a person claiming through such grantee to a holder for value without knowledge that the partner, in making the conveyance, has exceeded his authority.

(2) Where title to real property is in the name of the partnership, a conveyance executed by a partner, in his own name, passes the equitable interest of the partnership, provided the act is one within the authority of the partner under the provisions of paragraph (1) of section 9.

(3) Where title to real property is in the name of one or more but not all the partners, and the record does not disclose the right of the partnership, the partners in whose name the title stands may convey title to such property, but the partnership may recover such property if the partners' act does not bind the partnership under the provisions of paragraph (1) of section 9, unless the purchaser or his assignee, is a holder for value, without knowledge.

(4) Where the title to real property is in the name of one or more or all the partners, or in a third person in trust for the partnership, a conveyance executed by a partner in the partnership name, or in his own name, passes the equitable interest of the partnership, provided the act is one within the authority of the partner under the provisions of paragraph (1) of section 9.

(5) Where the title to real property is in the names of all the partners, a conveyance executed by all the partners passes all their rights in such property.

§ 11. Partnership Bound by Admission of Partner

An admission or representation made by any partner concerning partnership affairs within the scope of his authority as conferred by this act is evidence against the partnership.

§ 12. Partnership Charged with Knowledge of or Notice to Partner

Notice to any partner of any matter relating to partnership affairs, and the knowledge of the partner acting in the particular matter, acquired while a partner or then present to his mind, and the knowledge of any other partner who reasonably could and should have communicated it to the acting partner, operate as notice to or knowledge of the partnership, except in the case of a fraud on the partnership committed by or with the consent of that partner.

Comment

. . . .

It is not clear what the present law is when "knowledge," which is not the knowledge that may come from notice, has been obtained by a partner after the formation of the partnership, but the partner having such "knowledge" is not the one acting in the particular matter. It seems clear that in this case the partnership should be charged only when the partner having "knowledge" had reason to believe that the fact related to a matter which had some possibility of being the subject of partnership business, and then only if he was so situated that he could communicate it to the partner acting in the particular matter before such partner give binding effect to his act. The words "who reasonably could and should have communicated it to the acting partner" accomplish this result.

§ 13. Partnership Bound by Partner's Wrongful Act

Where, by any wrongful act or omission of any partner acting in the ordinary course of the business of the partnership or with the authority of his co-partners, loss or injury is caused to any person, not being a partner in the partnership, or any penalty is incurred, the partnership is liable therefor to the same extent as the partner so acting or omitting to act.

§ 14. Partnership Bound by Partner's Breach of Trust

The partnership is bound to make good the loss:

(a) Where one partner acting within the scope of his apparent authority receives money or property of a third person and misapplies it; and

(b) Where the partnership in the course of its business receives money or property of a third person and the money or property so received is misapplied by any partner while it is in the custody of the partnership.

§ 15. Nature of Partner's Liability

All partners are liable

(a) Jointly and severally for everything chargeable to the partnership under sections 13 and 14.

(b) Jointly for all other debts and obligations of the partnership; but any partner may enter into a separate obligation to perform a partnership contract.

§ 16. Partner by Estoppel

(1) When a person, by words spoken or written or by conduct, represents himself, or consents to another representing him to any one, as a partner in an existing partnership or with one or more persons not actual partners, he is liable to any such person to whom such representation has been made, who has, on the faith of such representation, given credit to the actual or apparent partnership, and if he has made such representation or consented to its being made in a public manner he is liable to such person, whether the representation has or has not been made or communicated to such person so giving credit by or with the knowledge of the apparent partner making the representation or consenting to its being made.

(a) When a partnership liability results, he is liable as though he were an actual member of the partnership.

(b) When no partnership liability results, he is liable jointly with the other persons, if any, so consenting to the contract or representation as to incur liability, otherwise separately.

(2) When a person has been thus represented to be a partner in an existing partnership, or with one or more persons not actual partners, he is an agent of the persons consenting to such representation to bind them to the same extent and in the same manner as though he were a partner in fact, with respect to persons who rely upon the representation. Where all the members of the existing partnership consent to the representation, a partnership act or obligation results; but in all other cases it is the joint act or obligation of the person acting and the persons consenting to the representation.

Comment

The section clears several doubts and confusions of our existing case law. It has been held that a person is liable if he has been held out as a partner and knows that he is being held out, unless he prevents such holding out, even if to do so he has to take legal action. (Citations omitted.) On the other hand, the weight of authority is to the effect that to be held as a partner he must consent to the holding and that consent is a matter of fact. The act as drafted follows this weight of authority and better reasoning. (Citations omitted.)

§ 17. Liability of Incoming Partner

A person admitted as a partner into an existing partnership is liable for all the obligations of the partnership arising before his admission as though he had been a partner when such obligations were incurred, except that this liability shall be satisfied only out of partnership property.

Comment

The present section eliminates the difficulty which arises when a new partner is admitted without liquidation of firm debts. The present theory of the common law is that a new partnership is formed; all the property of the partnership which existed up to the moment of the entrance of the new partner being transferred to the new partnership. The result of this theory is that if the business fails, the creditors who have extended credit after the admission of the new partner have a prior claim on the assets in the business. The inequitable character of this result has led the courts, where no notice of the change of membership is had by the creditors, to be diligent in finding an assumption of liability on the part of the new partnership of the debts of the old partnership.

. . .

. . . There is no peculiar equity in the subsequent creditors giving them a right to be preferred, as against the property employed in the business, to the existing creditors. The incoming partner partakes of the benefit of the partnership property and an established business. He has every means of obtaining full knowledge and protecting himself, because he may insist on the liquidation or settlement of existing partnership debts. The creditors have no means of protecting themselves. So as to preserve the present law as nearly as possible it is declared that the liability of the incoming partner shall be satisfied only out of partnership property. It, therefore, results that existing and subsequent creditors have equal rights as against partnership property and the separate property of all the previously existing members of the partnership, while only the subsequent creditors have rights against the separate estate of the newly admitted partner.

The section should be read in connection with section 41, infra. Both sections are based on the principle that where there has been one continuous business the fact that A has been admitted to the business, or C ceased to be connected with it, should not be allowed to cause, as at present, endless confusion as to the claims of the creditors on the property employed in the business; but that all creditors of the business, irrespective of the times when they became creditors and the exact combinations of persons then owning the business, should have equal rights in such property. The recognition of this principle solves one of the most perplexing problems of present partnership law.

PART IV

RELATIONS OF PARTNERS TO ONE ANOTHER

§ 18. Rules Determining Rights and Duties of Partners

The rights and duties of the partners in relation to the partnership shall be determined, subject to any agreement between them, by the following rules:

(a) Each partner shall be repaid his contributions, whether by way of capital or advances to the partnership property and share equally in the profits and surplus remaining after all liabilities, including those to partners, are satisfied; and must contribute towards the losses, whether of capital or otherwise, sustained by the partnership according to his share in the profits.

(b) The partnership must indemnify every partner in respect of payments made and personal liabilities reasonably incurred by him in the ordinary and proper conduct of its business, or for the preservation of its business or property.

(c) A partner, who in aid of the partnership makes any payment or advance beyond the amount of capital which he agreed to contribute, shall be paid interest from the date of the payment or advance.

(d) A partner shall receive interest on the capital contributed by him only from the date when repayment should be made.

(e) All partners have equal rights in the management and conduct of the partnership business.

(f) No partner is entitled to remuneration for acting in the partnership business, except that a surviving partner is entitled to reasonable compensation for his services in winding up the partnership affairs.

(g) No person can become a member of a partnership without the consent of all the partners.

(h) Any difference arising as to ordinary matters connected with the partnership business may be decided by a majority of the partners; but no act in contravention of any agreement between the partners may be done rightfully without the consent of all the partners.

§ 19. Partnership Books

The partnership books shall be kept, subject to any agreement between the partners, at the principal place of business of the partnership, and every partner shall at all times have access to and may inspect and copy any of them.

§ 20. Duty of Partners to Render Information

Partners shall render on demand true and full information of all things affecting the partnership to any partner or the legal representative of any deceased partner or partner under legal disability.

§ 21. Partner Accountable as a Fiduciary

(1) Every partner must account to the partnership for any benefit, and hold as trustee for it any profits derived by him without the consent of the other partners from any transaction connected with the formation, conduct, or liquidation of the partnership or from any use by him of its property.

(2) This section applies also to the representatives of a deceased partner engaged in the liquidation of the affairs of the partnership as the personal representatives of the last surviving partner.

Comment

Subdivision (1) removes a doubt in the existing law. At present it is not clear whether the obligation to account where the partner has money or other property in his hands, is or is not an obligation in the nature of a trust. For instance: A, B and C are partners; A, as a result of a transaction connected with the conduct of the partnership, has in his hands, so that it may be traced, a specific sum of money or other property. A is insolvent. Is the claim of the partnership against A a claim against him as an ordinary creditor, or is it a claim to the specific property or money in his hands? The words "and hold as trustee for the partnership any profits" indicate clearly that the partnership can claim as their own any property or money that can be traced.

§ 22. Right to an Account

Any partner shall have the right to a formal account as to partnership affairs:

(a) If he is wrongfully excluded from the partnership business or possession of its property by his co-partners,

(b) If the right exists under the terms of any agreement,

(c) As provided by section 21,

(d) Whenever other circumstances render it just and reasonable.

Comment

Ordinarily a partner is not entitled to a formal account, except on dissolution. He has equal access with his partners to the partnership books, and there is no reason why they should constantly render to him accounts in the formal sense of that word, which is the sense in which it is here used. When, however, he is excluded from the business or the possession of partnership property, without any express agreement authorizing such exclusion, he should have the right to demand a formal account from his partners, without necessarily requiring him to dissolve the partnership.

The reason for clause (d) is that there frequently arise circumstances which impose on one or more of the partners the duty of rendering a formal account to the co-partner, as where one partner is traveling for a long period of time on partnership business, and the other partners are in possession of the partnership books. These various circumstances cannot be detailed in any act. In view of the wording of clause (d), the total effect of this section is to emphasize the fact that a partner, the partnership not being dissolved, has not necessarily the right to demand formal accounts, except at particular times and under particular circumstances.

§ 23. Continuation of Partnership Beyond Fixed Term

(1) When a partnership for a fixed term or particular undertaking is continued after the termination of such term or particular undertaking without any express agreement, the rights and duties of the partners remain the same as they were at such termination, so far as is consistent with a partnership at will.

(2) A continuation of the business by the partners or such of them as habitually acted therein during the term, without any settlement or liquidation of the partnership affairs, is prima facie evidence of a continuation of the partnership.

PART V

PROPERTY RIGHTS OF A PARTNER

§ 24. Extent of Property Rights of a Partner

The property rights of a partner are (1) his rights in specific partnership property, (2) his interest in the partnership, and (3) his right to participate in the management.

§ 25. Nature of a Partner's Right in Specific Partnership Property

(1) A partner is co-owner with his partners of specific partnership property holding as a tenant in partnership.

(2) The incidents of this tenancy are such that:

(a) A partner, subject to the provisions of this act and to any agreement between the partners, has an equal right with his partners to possess specific partnership property for partnership purposes; but he has no right to possess such property for any other purpose without the consent of his partners.

(b) A partner's right in specific partnership property is not assignable except in connection with the assignment of rights of all the partners in the same property.

(c) A partner's right in specific partnership property is not subject to attachment or execution, except on a claim against the partnership. When partnership property is attached for a partnership debt the partners, or any of them, or the representatives of a deceased partner, cannot claim any right under the homestead or exemption laws.

(d) On the death of a partner his right in specific partnership property vests in the surviving partner or partners, except where the deceased was the last surviving partner, when his right in such property vests in his legal representative. Such surviving partner or partners, or the legal representative of the last surviving partner, has no right to possess the partnership property for any but a partnership purpose.

(e) A partner's right in specific partnership property is not subject to dower, curtesy, or allowances to widows, heirs, or next of kin.

Comment

Subdivision (1). One of the present principal difficulties in the administration of the law of partnerships arises out of the difficulty of determining the exact nature of the rights of a partner in specific partnership property. That the partners are co-owners of partnership property is clear; but the legal incidents attached to the right of each partner as co-owner are not clear. When the English courts in the seventeenth century first began to discuss the legal incidents of this co-ownership, they were already familiar with two other kinds of co-ownership, joint tenancy and tenancy in common. In joint tenancy on the death of one owner his right in the property passes to the other co-owners. This is known as the right of survivorship. The incident of survivorship fits in with the necessities of partnership. On the death of a partner, the other partners and not the executors of the deceased partner should have a right to wind up partnership affairs. (See clause (d), infra.) The early courts, therefore, declared that partners were joint tenants of partnership property, the consequence being that all the other legal incidents of joint tenancy were applied to partnership co-ownership. Many of these incidents, however, do not apply to the necessities of the partnership relation and produce most inequitable results. This is not to be wondered at because the legal incidents of joint tenancy grew out of a co-ownership of land not held for the purposes of business. The attempt of our courts to escape the inequitable results of applying the legal incidents of joint tenancy to partnership has produced very great confusion. Practically this confusion has had more unfortunate effect on substantive rights when the separate creditors of a partner attempt to attach and sell specific partnership property than when a partner attempts to assign specific partnership property not for a partnership purpose but for his own purposes.

The Commissioners, however, believe that the proper way to end the confusion which has arisen out of the attempt to treat partners as joint tenants, is to recognize the fact that the rights of a partner as co-owner with his partners of specific partnership property should depend on the necessities of the partnership relation. In short, that the legal incidents of the tenancy in partnership are not necessarily those of any other co-ownership.

....

Subdivision (2-b). Clause (b) asserts that the right of a partner as co-owner in specific partnership property is not separately assignable. This peculiarity of tenancy in partnership is a necessary consequence of the partnership relation. If A and B are partners and A attempts to assign all his right in partnership property, say a particular chattel, to C, and the law recognizes the possibility of such a transfer, C would pro tanto become a partner with B; for the rights of A in the chattel are to possess the chattel for a partnership purpose. But partnership is a voluntary relation. B cannot have a partner thrust upon him by A without his, B's, consent.

A cannot confer on C his, A's, right to possess and deal with the chattel for a partnership purpose. Neither can he confer any other rights which he has in the property. A partner has a beneficial interest in partnership property considered as a whole. As profits accrue, he has a right to be paid his proportion, and on the winding up of the business, after the obligations due third persons have been met, he has a right to be paid in cash his share of what remains of the partnership property. These rights considered as a whole are his interest in the partnership; and this beneficial interest he may assign in whole or fractional part, as is indicated in section 27, infra....

Subdivision (2-c). Compare this clause with section 28(1). The first sentence in this clause is similar to section 23(1) of the English Act. It is a logical consequence of clause (b). If a partner's right in specific partnership property is not assignable by voluntary assignment for a separate purpose of the assignment partner, his separate creditors should not be able to force an involuntary assignment. The beneficial rights of the separate creditors of a partner in partnership property should be no greater than the beneficial rights of their debtor. . . .

§ 26. Nature of Partner's Interest in the Partnership

A partner's interest in the partnership is his share of the profits and surplus, and the same is personal property.

§ 27. Assignment of Partner's Interest

(1) A conveyance by a partner of his interest in the partnership does not of itself dissolve the partnership, nor, as against the other partners in the absence of agreement, entitle the assignee, during the continuance of the partnership, to interfere in the management or administration of the partnership business or affairs, or to require any information or account of partnership transactions, or to inspect the

partnership books; but it merely entitles the assignee to receive in accordance with his contract the profits to which the assigning partner would otherwise be entitled.

(2) In case of a dissolution of the partnership, the assignee is entitled to receive his assignor's interest and may require an account from the date only of the last account agreed to by all the partners.

Comment

In re the subject of this paragraph [subd. 1] see [citations omitted]. These authorities on the whole state that the mere assignment dissolves the partnership. Many such assignments, however, are merely by way of collateral security for a loan, the assigning partner in no wise intending to end the partnership relation. If he neglects his personal relation the other partners may dissolve the partnership under section 31 of this act. But the mere fact of assignment without more should not be said in all cases to be an act of dissolution. The change in the existing law follows a similar change of the English law embodied in section 31 of the English Partnership Act.

§ 28. Partner's Interest Subject to Charging Order

(1) On due application to a competent court by any judgment creditor of a partner, the court which entered the judgment, order, or decree, or any other court, may charge the interest of the debtor partner with payment of the unsatisfied amount of such judgment debt with interest thereon; and may then or later appoint a receiver of his share of the profits, and of any other money due or to fall due to him in respect of the partnership, and make all other orders, directions, accounts and inquiries which the debtor partner might have made, or which the circumstances of the case may require.

(2) The interest charged may be redeemed at any time before foreclosure, or in case of a sale being directed by the court may be purchased without thereby causing a dissolution:

(a) With separate property, by any one or more of the partners, or

(b) With partnership property, by any one or more of the partners with the consent of all the partners whose interests are not so charged or sold.

(3) Nothing in this act shall be held to deprive a partner of his right, if any, under the exemption laws, as regards his interest in the partnership.

PART VI

DISSOLUTION AND WINDING UP

§ 29. Dissolution Defined

The dissolution of a partnership is the change in the relation of the partners caused by any partner ceasing to be associated in the carrying on as distinguished from the winding up of the business.

Comment

As used by the legal profession the term "dissolution" designates, not only the single act of the termination of the actual conduct of the ordinary business, but also often the series of acts thereafter until the final settlement of all partnership affairs. It is also frequently said that dissolution, although the word is used to designate only the termination of ordinary business relations, terminates the partnership, it being at the same time explained that the partnership thereafter continues to exist for the purpose of suing and being sued in the process of winding up partnership affairs. Certainty demands that this confusion should be removed if possible. In this act dissolution designates the point in time when the partners cease to carry on the business together; termination is the point in time when all the partnership affairs are wound up; winding up, the process of settling partnership affairs after dissolution.

§ 30. Partnership Not Terminated by Dissolution

On dissolution the partnership is not terminated, but continues until the winding up of partnership affairs is completed.

§ 31. Causes of Dissolution

Dissolution is caused:
(1) Without violation of the agreement between the partners,
    (a) By the termination of the definite term or particular undertaking specified in the agreement,
    (b) By the express will of any partner when no definite term or particular undertaking is specified,
    (c) By the express will of all the partners who have not assigned their interests or suffered them to be charged for their separate debts, either before or after the termination of any specified term or particular undertaking,
    (d) By the expulsion of any partner from the business bona fide in accordance with such a power conferred by the agreement between the partners;
(2) In contravention of the agreement between the partners, where the circumstances do not permit a dissolution under any other provision of this section, by the express will of any partner at any time;
(3) By any event which makes it unlawful for the business of the partnership to be carried on or for the members to carry it on in partnership;
(4) By the death of any partner;
(5) By the bankruptcy of any partner or the partnership;
(6) By decree of court under section 32.

Comment

Paragraph (2) will settle a matter on which at present considerable confusion and uncertainty exists. The paragraph as drawn allows a partner to dissolve a partnership in contravention of the agreement between the partners. This is supported by the weight of authority. (Citations omitted.)

The relation of partners is one of agency. The agency is such a personal one that equity cannot enforce it even where the agreement provides that the partnership shall continue for a definite time. The power of any partner to terminate the relation, even though in doing so he breaks a contract, should, it is submitted, be recognized.

The rights of the parties upon a dissolution in contravention of the agreement are safeguarded by section 38(2), infra.

§ 32. Dissolution by Decree of Court

(1) On application by or for a partner the court shall decree a dissolution whenever:

(a) A partner has been declared a lunatic in any judicial proceeding or is shown to be of unsound mind,

(b) A partner becomes in any other way incapable of performing his part of the partnership contract,

(c) A partner has been guilty of such conduct as tends to affect prejudicially the carrying on of the business,

(d) A partner wilfully or persistently commits a breach of the partnership agreement, or otherwise so conducts himself in matters relating to the partnership business that it is not reasonably practicable to carry on the business in partnership with him,

(e) The business of the partnership can only be carried on at a loss,

(f) Other circumstances render a dissolution equitable.

(2) On the application of the purchaser of a partner's interest under sections 28 or 29 [should read 27 or 28]:

(a) After the termination of the specified term or particular undertaking,

(b) At any time if the partnership was a partnership at will when the interest was assigned or when the charging order was issued.

§ 33. General Effect of Dissolution on Authority of Partner

Except so far as may be necessary to wind up partnership affairs or to complete transactions begun but not then finished, dissolution terminates all authority of any partner to act for the partnership,

(1) With respect to the partners,

(a) When the dissolution is not by the act, bankruptcy or death of a partner; or

(b) When the dissolution is by such act, bankruptcy or death of a partner, in cases where section 34 so requires.

(2) With respect to persons not partners, as declared in section 35.

§ 34. Right of Partner to Contribution from Co-partners after Dissolution

Where the dissolution is caused by the act, death or bankruptcy of a partner, each partner is liable to his co-partners for his share of any liability created by any partner acting for the partnership as if the partnership had not been dissolved unless

(a) The dissolution being by act of any partner, the partner acting for the partnership had knowledge of the dissolution, or

(b) The dissolution being by the death or bankruptcy of a partner, the partner acting for the partnership had knowledge or notice of the death or bankruptcy.

Comment

... "Notice" should be, it is submitted, sufficient in all cases where the fact to be notified is an ordinary business fact, as notice to third persons of the dissolution of a partnership. But it is not customary for partners to dissolve a partnership at a time not previously specified, without consultation with their co-partners. Such dissolution may or may not amount to a breach of partnership contract; but in any event, if done without consultation, it is out of the ordinary course. This fact should not deprive the partner of a right to terminate a relationship which must necessarily depend on mutual good will and confidence; but if the partner so terminating wishes to show that he should not be required by his partners to be liable for his share of the loss due to a partnership contract thereafter made by them, he should be able to prove that they had "knowledge" that he had dissolved the partnership at the time they made the contract.

. . .

§ 35. Power of Partner to Bind Partnership to Third Persons after Dissolution

(1) After dissolution a partner can bind the partnership except as provided in Paragraph (3).

(a) By any act appropriate for winding up partnership affairs or completing transactions unfinished at dissolution;

(b) By any transaction which would bind the partnership if dissolution had not taken place, provided the other party to the transaction

(I) Had extended credit to the partnership prior to dissolution and had no knowledge or notice of the dissolution; or

(II) Though he had not so extended credit, had nevertheless known of the partnership prior to dissolution, and, having no knowledge or notice of dissolution, the fact of dissolution had not been advertised in a newspaper of general circulation in the place (or in each place if more than one) at which the partnership business was regularly carried on.

(2) The liability of a partner under Paragraph (1b) shall be satisfied out of partnership assets alone when such partner had been prior to dissolution

(a) Unknown as a partner to the person with whom the contract is made; and

(b) So far unknown and inactive in partnership affairs that the business reputation of the partnership could not be said to have been in any degree due to his connection with it.

(3) The partnership is in no case bound by any act of a partner after dissolution

(a) Where the partnership is dissolved because it is unlawful to carry on the business, unless the act is appropriate for winding up partnership affairs; or

(b) Where the partner has become bankrupt; or

(c) Where the partner has no authority to wind up partnership affairs; except by a transaction with one who

(I) Had extended credit to the partnership prior to dissolution and had no knowledge or notice of his want of authority; or

(II) Had not extended credit to the partnership prior to dissolution, and, having no knowledge or notice of his want of authority, the fact of his want of authority has not been advertised in the manner provided for advertising the fact of dissolution in Paragraph (1bII).

(4) Nothing in this section shall affect the liability under Section 16 of any person who after dissolution represents himself or consents to another representing him as a partner in a partnership engaged in carrying on business.

Comment

At present in most jurisdictions it is doubtful whether, under the circumstances set forth in (b), "the other party" can bind the partnership where such party has had no knowledge or notice of the dissolution and has had business transactions with the partnership before dissolution, but these business transactions have not involved any extension of credit to the partnership.

. . .

The practical impossibility of the partners knowing, by any feasible system of bookkeeping, all the persons with whom they have had dealings, unless credit has been extended, supports the wording adopted by the Commissioners.

§ 36.   Effect of Dissolution on Partner's Existing Liability

(1) The dissolution of the partnership does not of itself discharge the existing liability of any partner.

(2) A partner is discharged from any existing liability upon dissolution of the partnership by an agreement to that effect between himself, the partnership creditor and the person or partnership continuing the business; and such agreement may be inferred from the course of dealing between the creditor having knowledge of the dissolution and the person or partnership continuing the business.

(3) Where a person agrees to assume the existing obligations of a dissolved partnership, the partners whose obligations have been assumed shall be discharged from any liability to any creditor of the partnership who, knowing of the agreement, consents to a material alteration in the nature or time of payment of such obligations.

(4) The individual property of a deceased partner shall be liable for all obligations of the partnership incurred while he was a partner but subject to the prior payment of his separate debts.

§ 37.   Right to Wind Up

Unless otherwise agreed the partners who have not wrongfully dissolved the partnership or the legal representative of the last surviving partner, not bankrupt, has the right to wind up the partnership affairs; provided, however, that any partner, his legal representative or his assignee, upon cause shown, may obtain winding up by the court.

§ 38. Rights of Partners to Application of Partnership Property

(1) When dissolution is caused in any way, except in contravention of the partnership agreement, each partner, as against his co-partners and all persons claiming through them in respect of their interests in the partnership, unless otherwise agreed, may have the partnership property applied to discharge · its liabilities, and the surplus applied to pay in cash the net amount owing to the respective partners. But if dissolution is caused by expulsion of a partner, bona fide under the partnership agreement and if the expelled partner is discharged from all partnership liabilities, either by payment or agreement under section 36(2), he shall receive in cash only the net amount due him from the partnership.

(2) When dissolution is caused in contravention of the partnership agreement the rights of the partners shall be as follows:

(a) Each partner who has not caused dissolution wrongfully shall have,

I. All the rights specified in paragraph (1) of this section, and

II. The right, as against each partner who has caused the dissolution wrongfully, to damages for breach of the agreement.

(b) The partners who have not caused the dissolution wrongfully, if they all desire to continue the business in the same name, either by themselves or jointly with others, may do so, during the agreed term for the partnership and for that purpose may possess the partnership property, provided they secure the payment by bond approved by the court, or pay to any partner who has caused the dissolution wrongfully, the value of his interest in the partnership at the dissolution, less any damages recoverable under clause (2a II) of this section, and in like manner indemnify him against all present or future partnership liabilities.

(c) A partner who has caused the dissolution wrongfully shall have:

I. If the business is not continued under the provisions of paragraph (2b) all the rights of a partner under paragraph (1), subject to clause (2a II), of this section,

II. If the business is continued under paragraph (2b) of this section the right as against his co-partners and all claiming through them in respect of their interests in the partnership, to have the value of his interest in the partnership, less any damages caused to his co-partners by the dissolution, ascertained and paid to him in cash, or the payment secured by bond approved by the court, and to be released from all existing liabilities of the partnership; but in ascertaining the value of the partner's interest the value of the good-will of the business shall not be considered.

Comment

The right given to each partner, where no agreement to the contrary has been made, to have his share of the surplus paid to him in cash makes certain an existing uncertainty. At present it is not certain whether a partner may or may not insist on a physical partition of the property remaining after third persons have been paid.

§ 39. Rights Where Partnership Is Dissolved for Fraud or Misrepresentation

Where a partnership contract is rescinded on the ground of the fraud or misrepresentation of one of the parties thereto, the party entitled to rescind is, without prejudice to any other right, entitled,

(a) To a lien on, or a right of retention of, the surplus of the partnership property after satisfying the partnership liabilities to third persons for any sum of money paid by him for the purchase of an interest in the partnership and for any capital or advances contributed by him; and

(b) To stand, after all liabilities to third persons have been satisfied, in the place of the creditors of the partnership for any payments made by him in respect of the partnership liabilities; and

(c) To be indemnified by the person guilty of the fraud or making the representation against all debts and liabilities of the partnership.

§ 40. Rules for Distribution

In settling accounts between the partners after dissolution, the following rules shall be observed, subject to any agreement to the contrary:

(a) The assets of the partnership are:

I. The partnership property,

II. The contributions of the partners necessary for the payment of all the liabilities specified in clause (b) of this paragraph.

(b) The liabilities of the partnership shall rank in order of payment, as follows:

I. Those owing to creditors other than partners,

II. Those owing to partners other than for capital and profits,

III. Those owing to partners in respect of capital,

IV. Those owing to partners in respect of profits.

(c) The assets shall be applied in order of their declaration in clause (a) of this paragraph to the satisfaction of the liabilities.

(d) The partners shall contribute, as provided by section 18(a) the amount necessary to satisfy the liabilities; but if any, but not all, of the partners are insolvent, or, not being subject to process, refuse to contribute, the other partners shall contribute their share of the liabilities, and, in the relative proportions in which they share the profits, the additional amount necessary to pay the liabilities.

(e) An assignee for the benefit of creditors or any person appointed by the court shall have the right to enforce the contributions specified in clause (d) of this paragraph.

(f) Any partner or his legal representative shall have the right to enforce the contributions specified in clause (d) of this paragraph, to the extent of the amount which he has paid in excess of his share of the liability.

(g) The individual property of a deceased partner shall be liable for the contributions specified in clause (d) of this paragraph.

(h) When partnership property and the individual properties of the partners are in possession of a court for distribution, partnership creditors shall have priority on partnership property and separate creditors on individual property, saving the rights of lien or secured creditors as heretofore.

(i) Where a partner has become bankrupt or his estate is insolvent the claims against his separate property shall rank in the following order:

I. Those owing to separate creditors,

II. Those owing to partnership creditors,

III. Those owing to partners by way of contribution.

§ 41. Liability of Persons Continuing the Business in Certain Cases

(1) When any new partner is admitted into an existing partnership, or when any partner retires and assigns (or the representative of the deceased partner assigns) his rights in partnership property to two or more of the partners, or to one or more of the partners and one or more third persons, if the business is continued without liquidation of the partnership affairs, creditors of the first or dissolved partnership are also creditors of the partnership so continuing the business.

(2) When all but one partner retire and assign (or the representative of a deceased partner assigns) their rights in partnership property to the remaining partner, who continues the business without liquidation of partnership affairs, either alone or with others, creditors of the dissolved partnership are also creditors of the person or partnership so continuing the business.

(3) When any partner retires or dies and the business of the dissolved partnership is continued as set forth in paragraphs (1) and (2) of this section, with the consent of the retired partners or the representative of the deceased partner, but without any assignment of his right in partnership property, rights of creditors of the dissolved partnership and of the creditors of the person or partnership continuing the business shall be as if such assignment had been made.

(4) When all the partners or their representatives assign their rights in partnership property to one or more third persons who promise to pay the debts and who continue the business of the dissolved partnership, creditors of the dissolved partnership are also creditors of the person or partnership continuing the business.

(5) When any partner wrongfully causes a dissolution and the remaining partners continue the business under the provisions of section 38(2b), either alone or with others, and without liquidation of the partnership affairs, creditors of the dissolved partnership are also creditors of the person or partnership continuing the business.

(6) When a partner is expelled and the remaining partners continue the business either alone or with others, without liquidation of the partnership affairs, creditors of the dissolved partnership are also creditors of the person or partnership continuing the business.

(7) The liability of a third person becoming a partner in the partnership continuing the business, under this section, to the creditors of the dissolved partnership shall be satisfied out of partnership property only.

(8) When the business of a partnership after dissolution is continued under any conditions set forth in this section the creditors of the dissolved partnership, as against the separate creditors of the retiring or deceased partner or the representative of the deceased partner, have a prior right to any claim of the retired partner or the representative of the deceased partner against the person or partnership continuing the business, on account of the retired or deceased partner's interest in the dissolved partnership or on account of any consideration promised for such interest or for his right in partnership property.

(9) Nothing in this section shall be held to modify any right of creditors to set aside any assignment on the ground of fraud.

(10) The use by the person or partnership continuing the business of the partnership name, or the name of a deceased partner as part thereof, shall not of itself

make the individual property of the deceased partner liable for any debts contracted by such person or partnership.

Comment

Subdivision (1). . . .

. . . It is universally admitted that any change in membership dissolves a partnership, and creates a new partnership. This section as drafted does not alter that rule. Neither does it alter the rule that on any change of personnel the property of the dissolved partnership becomes the property of the partnership continuing the business. At present, however, creditors of the dissolved partnership do not become creditors of the new partnership. . . .

The paragraph as drawn changes the law . . . In every case the creditors of the first partnership become creditors of the second; though, of course, they do not cease to be creditors of the first partnership. As, however, the first partnership has assigned all its property, that is of little value to such creditors, unless the assignees have promised the retiring partner an additional consideration beyond the payment of the debts. The status of such additional consideration is treated in paragraph (8), infra.

The paragraph as a whole, as well as this entire section, is based on the opinion that when there is a continuous business carried on first by A, B and C, and then by A, B, C and D, or by B or C, or by B and C, by B and D, or by C and D, or by B, C and D, without any liquidation of the affairs of A, B, C, both justice and business convenience require that all the creditors of the business, irrespective of the exact grouping of the owners at the times their respective claims had their origin, should be treated alike, all being given an equal claim on the property embarked in the business. (Compare note to section 17, supra.)

Subdivision (2). Where all the partners assign to one partner, the partnership creditors are, under this paragraph, the separate creditors of the partner continuing the business, where he continues the business alone, whether such partner promises to pay the debts of the dissolved partnership or not. If he takes one or more new partners and they continue the business with the property of the dissolved partnership, the creditors of the dissolved partnership are the creditors of the partnership continuing the business. This paragraph changes the present law to the same extent as paragraph (1).

Subdivision (3). The paragraph extends the principle of the first and second paragraphs of the section to the case where the business is continued by two or more of the partners, alone or with others, after the retirement or death of a partner without any formal assignment to them of the retired or deceased partner's rights in partnership property. The neglect of the retiring partners or of the representatives of the deceased partner should not as at present create inexorable confusion between the creditors of the first and second partnership in regard to their respective rights in the property employed in the business. Both classes of creditors should be ahead of the claim of such retired partner or the representative of the deceased partner, and both classes of creditors should also have equal rights in the property. This paragraph probably effects a change in the present law, though the same result is often now brought about by implying a promise to pay the debts of the dissolved partnership on the part of the person or partnership continuing the business.

Subdivision (4). The existing law in relation to the subject matter covered by this paragraph is so uncertain that it is not possible to say whether its adoption would modify the law. The paragraph does not apply to the case where the third person or persons do not promise to pay the debts of the dissolved partnership. In that case the creditors of the dissolved partnership have no claim on the partnership continuing the business or its property unless the assignment can be set aside as a fraud on creditors, or is affected by a Sales in Bulk Act. Where, however, there has been a promise to pay the debts of the dissolved partnership, then, the creditors of the dissolved partnership are not only creditors of the promisor or promisors which, in the United States, they would be as beneficiaries but under this paragraph, if the business of the dissolved partnership is continued by a partnership, the creditors of the dissolved partnership become creditors of the partnership continuing the business, not merely the separate or joint creditors of the partners in such partnership.

. . .

§ 42. Rights of Retiring or Estate of Deceased Partner When the Business Is Continued

When any partner retires or dies, and the business is continued under any of the conditions set forth in section 41 (1, 2, 3, 5, 6), or section 38 (2b) without any settlement of accounts as between him or his estate and the person or partnership continuing the business, unless otherwise agreed, he or his legal representative as against such persons or partnership may have the value of his interest at the date of dissolution ascertained, and shall receive as an ordinary creditor an amount equal to the value of his interest in the dissolved partnership with interest, or, at his option or at the option of his legal representative, in lieu of interest, the profits attributable to the use of his right in the property of the dissolved partnership; provided that the creditors of the dissolved partnership as against the separate creditors, or the representative of the retired or deceased partner, shall have priority on any claim arising under this section, as provided by section 41(8) of this act.

§ 43. Accrual of Actions

The right to an account of his interest shall accrue to any partner, or his legal representative, as against the winding up partners or the surviving partners or the person or partnership continuing the business, at the date of dissolution, in the absence of any agreement to the contrary.

PART VII

MISCELLANEOUS PROVISIONS

§ 44. When Act Takes Effect

This act shall take effect on the _____ day of _____ one thousand nine hundred and _____.

§ 45. Legislation Repealed

All acts or parts of acts inconsistent with this act are hereby repealed.

CONVERSION TABLE
UPA TO RUPA

UPA	RUPA
1	1002
2	101
3	102
4(2) and (3)	104(a)
4(4)	1001
4(5)	1007
5	104(a)
6	202
7	202
8	203, 204
9	301
10	302
11	none
12	102(f)
13	305(a)
14	305(b)
15	306(a)
16	308
17	306(b)
18	401
19	403(a) and (b)
20	403(c)
21	404
22	405(b)
23	406
24	none
25	501
26	502
27	503
28	504
29	801 (see also 601)
30	802
31	801 (see also 601, 602)
32	801(5)(6) (see also 601(5)(7)(iii))
33	804 (see also 603(b)(i))
34	806 (see also 702(b))
35	804 (see also 702(a))
36	703
37	803

38	602(c), 701, 807(a)
39	none
40	807
41	705 (re 41(10))
42	701(b) and (i)
43	405
44	1004
45	1005

CONVERSION TABLE
RUPA TO UPA

RUPA	UPA
101	2
102	3, 12
103	none
104	5
105	none
106	none
107	none
201	none
202	6, 7
203	8(1), 25
204	8
301	9
302	10
303	none
304	none
305	13, 14
306	15, 17
307	none
308	16
401	18
402	38(1)
403	19, 20
404	21
405(a)	none
405(b)	22, 43
406	23
501	24, 25
502	26
503	27, 32(2)
504	28
601	See 31, 32
602	See 31(2), 38(2)
603	none
701	38, 42
702	34, 35
703	35, 36
704	none
705	41(10)
801	29, 31, 32

802	30
803	37
804	33, 35
805	none
806	33(1), 34
807	38(1), 40
901	none
902	none
903	none
904	none
905	none
906	none
907	none
908	none
1001	4(4)
1002	1
1003	none
1004	44
1005	45
1006	none
1007	none

UNIFORM PARTNERSHIP ACT (1994)
WITH AMENDMENTS CONSTITUTING THE
UNIFORM LIMITED LIABILITY PARTNERSHIP ACT
(SHOWN BY ADDITION AND DELETION)

Editor's note: The Uniform Partnership Act (1994) ("RUPA") and all of its comments are reproduced below, as amended in 1996 to include limited liability partnership provisions, creating the Uniform Limited Liability Partnership Act ("ULLPA"). The 1996 amendments are indicated by underscore and strikeout. The comments are reproduced in their entirety in order to assist the reader in tracing and in understanding the rationale underlying the many changes made by RUPA to the Uniform Partnership Act (1914) and the explanation behind the limited liability changes made in 1996 to RUPA.

The 1997 Cumulative Annual Pocket Part to 6 Uniform Laws Annotated 1 (1995) states that RUPA has been adopted in the following states: Alabama (1996), Arizona (1996), California (1996), Connecticut (effective 1997), Florida (1996), Montana (1993), North Dakota (1996); Texas (1993); Virginia (1996), West Virginia (1995); and Wyoming (1994). Montana, Texas, and Wyoming adopted an earlier version of RUPA. Also, Colorado adopted RUPA in 1997, effective 1998.

PREFATORY NOTE

The National Conference of Commissioners on Uniform State Laws first considered a uniform law of partnership in 1902. Although early drafts had proceeded along the mercantile or "entity" theory of partnerships, later drafts were based on the common-law "aggregate" theory. The resulting Uniform Partnership Act ("UPA"), which embodied certain aspects of each theory, was finally approved by the Conference in 1914. The UPA governs general partnerships, and also governs limited partnerships except where the limited partnership statute is inconsistent. The UPA has been adopted in every State other than Louisiana and has been the subject of remarkably few amendments in those States over the past 80 years.

In January of 1986, an American Bar Association subcommittee issued a detailed report that recommended extensive revisions to the UPA. *See* UPA Revision Subcommittee of the Committee on Partnerships and Unincorporated Business Organizations, Section of Business Law, American Bar Association, *Should the Uniform Partnership Act Be Revised?*, 43 Bus. Law. 121 (1987) ("ABA Report"). The ABA Report recommended that the entity theory *"should be incorporated into any revision of the UPA whenever possible." Id.* at 124.

In 1987, the Conference appointed a Drafting Committee to Revise the Uniform Partnership Act and named a Reporter. The Committee held its initial meeting in January of 1988 and a first reading of the Committee's draft was begun at the Conference's 1989 Annual Meeting in Kauai, Hawaii. The first reading was completed at the 1990 Annual Meeting in Milwaukee. The second reading was begun at Naples, Florida, in 1991 and completed at San Francisco in 1992. The Revised Uniform Partnership Act (1992) was adopted unanimously by a vote of the States on August 6, 1992. The following year, in response to suggestions from various groups, including an American Bar Association subcommittee and several state bar associations, the Drafting Committee recommended numerous revisions to the Act. Those were adopted at the Charleston, South Carolina, Annual Meeting in

1993, and the Act was restyled as the Uniform Partnership Act (1993). Subsequently, a final round of changes was incorporated, and the Conference unanimously adopted the Uniform Partnership Act (1994) at its 1994 Annual Meeting in Chicago. The Revised Act was approved by the American Bar Association House of Delegates in August, 1994.

The Uniform Partnership Act (1994) ("Revised Act" or "RUPA") gives supremacy to the partnership agreement in almost all situations. The Revised Act is, therefore, largely a series of "default rules" that govern the relations among partners in situations they have not addressed in a partnership agreement. The primary focus of RUPA is the small, often informal, partnership. Larger partnerships generally have a partnership agreement addressing, and often modifying, many of the provisions of the partnership act.

The Revised Act enhances the entity treatment of partnerships to achieve simplicity for state law purposes, particularly in matters concerning title to partnership property. RUPA does not, however, relentlessly apply the entity approach. The aggregate approach is retained for some purposes, such as partners' joint and several liability.

The Drafting Committee spent significant effort on the rules governing partnership breakups. RUPA's basic thrust is to provide stability for partnerships that have continuation agreements. Under the UPA, a partnership is dissolved every time a member leaves. The Revised Act provides that there are many departures or "dissociations" that do not result in a dissolution.

Under the Revised Act, the withdrawal of a partner is a "dissociation" that results in a dissolution of the partnership only in certain limited circumstances. Many dissociations result merely in a buyout of the withdrawing partner's interest rather than a winding up of the partnership's business. RUPA defines both the substance and procedure of the buyout right.

Article 6 of the Revised Act covers partner dissociations; Article 7 covers buyouts; and Article 8 covers dissolution and the winding up of the partnership business. *See generally* Donald J. Weidner & John W. Larson, *The Revised Uniform Partnership Act: The Reporters' Overview*, 49 Bus. Law. 1 (1993).

The Revised Act also includes a more extensive treatment of the fiduciary duties of partners. Although RUPA continues the traditional rule that a partner is a fiduciary, it also makes clear that a partner is not required to be a disinterested trustee. Provision is made for the legitimate pursuit of self-interest, with a counterbalancing irreducible core of fiduciary duties.

Another significant change introduced by RUPA is provision for the public filing of statements containing basic information about a partnership, such as the agency authority of its partners. Because of the informality of many partnerships, and the inadvertence of some, mandatory filings were eschewed in favor of a voluntary regime. It was the Drafting Committee's belief, however, that filings would become routine for sophisticated partnerships and would be required by lenders and others for major transactions.

Another innovation is found in Article 9. For the first time, the merger of two or more partnerships and the conversion of partnerships to limited partnerships (and the reverse) is expressly authorized, and a "safe harbor" procedure for effecting such transactions is provided.

One final change deserves mention. Partnership law no longer governs limited partnerships pursuant to the provisions of RUPA itself. First, limited partnerships are not "partnerships" within the RUPA definition. Second, UPA Section 6(2), which provides that the UPA governs limited partnerships in cases not provided for in the Uniform Limited Partnership Act (1976) (1985) ("RULPA") has been deleted. No substantive change in result is intended, however. Section 1105 of RULPA already provides that the UPA governs in any case not provided for in RULPA, and thus the express linkage in RUPA is unnecessary. Structurally, it is more appropriately left to RULPA to determine the applicability of RUPA to limited partnerships. It is contemplated that the Conference will review the linkage question carefully, although no changes in RULPA may be necessary despite the many changes in RUPA.

In 1996 a number of amendments were made to the Uniform Partnership Act (1994) by the National Conference of Commissioners on Uniform State Laws. These included the adoption of new Article 10 (Limited Liability Partnership) and a new Article 11 (Foreign Limited Liability Partnership). The totality of these amendments constitutes the Uniform Limited Liability Partnership Act.

ARTICLE 1. GENERAL PROVISIONS

ARTICLE 2. NATURE OF PARTNERSHIP

ARTICLE 3. RELATIONS OF PARTNERS TO PERSONS DEALING WITH PARTNERSHIP

ARTICLE 4. RELATIONS OF PARTNERS TO EACH OTHER AND TO PARTNERSHIP

ARTICLE 5. TRANSFEREES AND CREDITORS OF PARTNER

ARTICLE 6. PARTNER'S DISSOCIATION

ARTICLE 7. PARTNER'S DISSOCIATION WHEN BUSINESS NOT WOUND UP

ARTICLE 8. WINDING UP PARTNERSHIP BUSINESS

ARTICLE 9. CONVERSIONS AND MERGERS

[ARTICLE] 1

GENERAL PROVISIONS

Section 101. Definitions.

(1) "Business" includes every trade, occupation, and profession.

(2) "Debtor in bankruptcy" means a person who is the subject of:

(i) an order for relief under Title 11 of the United States Code or a comparable order under a successor statute of general application; or

(ii) a comparable order under federal, state, or foreign law governing insolvency.

(3) "Distribution" means a transfer of money or other property from a partnership to a partner in the partner's capacity as a partner or to the partner's transferee.

(4) "Foreign limited liability partnership" means a partnership that:

(i) is formed under laws other than the laws of this State; and

(ii) has the status of a limited liability partnership under those laws.

(5) "Limited liability partnership" means a partnership that has filed a statement of qualification under Section 1001 and does not have a similar statement in effect in any other jurisdiction.

(4) (6) "Partnership" means an association of two or more persons to carry on as co-owners a business for profit formed under Section 202, predecessor law, or comparable law of another jurisdiction.

(5) (7) "Partnership agreement" means the agreement, whether written, oral, or implied, among the partners concerning the partnership, including amendments to the partnership agreement.

(6) (8) "Partnership at will" means a partnership in which the partners have not agreed to remain partners until the expiration of a definite term or the completion of a particular undertaking.

(7) (9) "Partnership interest" or "partner's interest in the partnership" means all of a partner's interests in the partnership, including the partner's transferable interest and all management and other rights.

(8) (10) "Person" means an individual, corporation, business trust, estate, trust, partnership, association, joint venture, government, governmental subdivision, agency, or instrumentality, or any other legal or commercial entity.

(9) (11) "Property" means all property, real, personal, or mixed, tangible or intangible, or any interest therein.

(10) (12) "State" means a State of the United States, the District of Columbia, the Commonwealth of Puerto Rico, or any territory or insular possession subject to the jurisdiction of the United States.

(11) (13) "Statement" means a statement of partnership authority under Section 303, a statement of denial under Section 304, a statement of dissociation under Section 704, a statement of dissolution under Section 805, a statement of merger under Section 907, a statement of qualification under Section 1001, a statement of foreign qualification under Section 1102, or an amendment or cancellation of any of the foregoing.

(12) (14) "Transfer" includes an assignment, conveyance, lease, mortgage, deed, and encumbrance.

Comment

These comments include the original comments to the Revised Uniform Partnership Act (RUPA or the Act) and the new comments to the Limited Liability Partnership Act Amendments to the Uniform Partnership Act (1994). The new comments regarding limited liability partnerships are integrated into the RUPA comments.

The Revised Uniform Partnership Act (RUPA or the Act) RUPA continues the definition of "business" from Section 2 of the Uniform Partnership Act (UPA).

RUPA uses the more contemporary term "debtor in bankruptcy" instead of "bankrupt." The definition is adapted from the new Georgia Partnership Act, Ga. Code Ann. § 14-8-2(1). The definition does not distinguish between a debtor whose estate is being liquidated under Chapter 7 of the Bankruptcy Code and a debtor who is being rehabilitated under Chapter 11, 12, or 13 and includes both. The filing of a voluntary petition under Section 301 of the Bankruptcy Code constitutes an order for relief, but the debtor is entitled to notice and an opportunity to be heard before the entry of an order for relief in an involuntary case under Section 303 of the Code. The term also includes a debtor who is the subject of a comparable order under state or foreign law.

The definition of "distribution" is new and adds precision to the accounting rules established in Sections 401 and 807 and related sections. Transfers to a partner in the partner's capacity as a creditor, lessor, or employee of the partnership, for example, are not "distributions."

The definition of a "foreign limited liability partnership" includes a partnership formed under the laws of another state, foreign country, or other jurisdiction provided it has the status of a limited liability partnership in the other jurisdiction. Since the scope and nature of foreign limited liability partnership liability shields may vary in different jurisdictions, the definition avoids reference to similar or comparable laws. Rather, the definition incorporates the concept of a limited liability partnership in the foreign jurisdiction, however defined in that jurisdiction. The reference to formation "under laws other than the laws of this State" makes clear that the definition includes partnerships formed in foreign countries as well as in another state.

The definition of a "limited liability partnership" makes clear that a partnership may adopt the special liability shield characteristics of a limited liability partnership simply by filing a statement of qualification under Section 1001. A partnership may file the statement in this State regardless of where formed. When coupled with the governing law provisions of Section 106(b), this definition simplifies the choice of law issues applicable to partnership with multi-state activities and contacts. Once a statement of qualification is filed, a partnership's internal affairs and the liability of its partners are determined by the law of the State where the statement is filed. See Section 106(b). The partnership may not vary this particular requirement. See Section 103(b)(9).

The reference to a "partnership" in the definition of a limited liability partnership makes clear that the RUPA definition of the term rather than the UPA concept controls for purposes of a limited liability partnership. Section 101(6) defines a "partnership" as "an association of two or more persons to carry on as co-owners a business for profit formed under Section 202, predecessor law, or comparable law of another jurisdiction." Section 202(b) further provides that "an association formed under a statute other than this [Act], a predecessor statute, or a comparable statute of another jurisdiction is not a partnership under this [Act]." This language was intended to clarify that a limited partnership is not a RUPA general partnership. It was not intended to preclude the application of any RUPA general partnership rules to limited partnerships where limited partnership law otherwise adopts the RUPA rules. See Comments to Section 202(b) and Prefatory Note.

The effect of these definitions leaves the scope and applicability of RUPA to limited partnerships to limited partnership law, not to sever the linkage between the two Acts in all cases. Certain provisions of RUPA will continue to govern limited partnerships by virtue of Revised Uniform Limited Partnership Act (RULPA) Section 1105 which provides that "in any case not provided for in this [Act] the provisions of the Uniform Partnership Act govern." The RUPA partnership definition includes partnerships formed under the UPA. Therefore, the limited liability partnership rules will govern limited partnerships "in any case not provided for" in RULPA. Since RULPA does not provide for any rules applicable to a limited partnership becoming a limited liability partnership, the limited liability partnership rules should apply to limited partnerships that file a statement of qualification.

Partner liability deserves special mention. RULPA Section 403(b) provides that a general partner of a limited partnership "has the liabilities of a partner in a partnership without limited partners." Thus limited partnership law expressly references general partnership law for general partner liability and does not separately consider the liability of such partners. The liability of a general partner of a limited partnership that becomes a LLLP would therefore be the liability of a general partner in an LLP and would be governed by Section 306. The liability of a limited partner in a LLLP is a more complicated matter. RULPA Section 303(a) separately considers the liability of a limited partner. Unless also a general partner, a limited partner is not liable for the obligations of a limited partnership unless the partner participates in the control of the business and then only to persons reasonably believing the limited partner is a general partner. Therefore, arguably limited partners in a LLLP will have the specific RULPA Section 303(a) liability shield while general partners will have a superior Section 306(c) liability shield. In order to clarify limited partner liability and other linkage issues, states that have adopted RUPA, these limited liability partnership rules, and RULPA may wish to consider an amendment to RULPA. A suggested form of such an amendment is:

§ 1107. Limited Liability Limited Partnership.

(a) A limited partnership may become a limited liability partnership by:

(1) obtaining approval of the terms and conditions of the limited partnership becoming a limited liability limited partnership by the vote necessary to amend the limited partnership agreement except, in the case of a limited partnership agreement that expressly considers contribution obligations, the vote necessary to amend those provisions;

(2) filing a statement of qualification under Section 1001(c) of the Uniform Partnership Act (1994); and

(3) complying with the name requirements of Section 1002 of the Uniform Partnership Act (1994).

(b) A limited liability limited partnership continues to be the same entity that existed before the filing of a statement of qualification under Section 1001(c) of the Uniform Partnership Act (1994).

(c) Sections 306(c) and 307(f) [sic] of the Uniform Partnership Act (1994) apply to both general and limited partners of a limited liability limited partnership.

"Partnership" is defined to mean an association of two or more persons to carry on as co-owners a business for profit formed under Section 202 (or predecessor law or comparable law of another jurisdiction), that is, a general partnership. Thus, as used in RUPA, the term "partnership" does not encompass limited partnerships, contrary to the use of the term in the UPA. Section 901(3) defines "limited partnership" for the purpose of Article 9, which deals with conversions and mergers of general and limited partnerships.

The definition of "partnership agreement" is adapted from Section 101(9) of RULPA the Revised Uniform Limited Partnership Act (RULPA). The RUPA definition is intended to include the agreement among the partners, including amendments, concerning either the affairs of the partnership or the conduct of its business. It does not include other agreements between some or all of the partners, such as a lease or loan agreement. The partnership agreement need not be written; it may be oral or inferred from the conduct of the parties.

Any partnership in which the partners have not agreed to remain partners until the expiration of a definite term or the completion of a particular undertaking is a "partnership at will." The distinction between an "at-will" partnership and a partnership for "a definite term or the completion of a particular undertaking" is important in determining the rights of dissociating and continuing partners following the dissociation of a partner. *See* Sections 601, 602, 701(b), 801(a), 802(b), and 803.

It is sometimes difficult to determine whether a partnership is at will or is for a definite term or the completion of a particular undertaking. Presumptively, every partnership is an at-will partnership. *See, e.g., Stone v. Stone*, 292 So. 2d 686 (La. 1974); *Frey v. Hauke*, 171 Neb. 852, 108 N.W.2d 228 (1961). To constitute a partnership for a term or a particular undertaking, the partners must agree (i) that the partnership will continue for a definite term or until a particular undertaking is completed and (ii) that they will remain partners until the expiration of the term or the completion of the undertaking. Both are necessary for a term partnership; if the partners have the unrestricted right, as distinguished from the power, to withdraw from a partnership formed for a term or particular undertaking, the partnership is one at will, rather than a term partnership.

To find that the partnership is formed for a definite term or a particular undertaking, there must be clear evidence of an agreement among the partners that the partnership (i) has a minimum or maximum duration or (ii) terminates at the conclusion of a particular venture whose time is indefinite but certain to occur. *See, e.g., Stainton v. Tarantino*, 637 F. Supp. 1051 (E.D. Pa. 1986) (partnership to dissolve no later than December 30, 2020); *Abel v. American Art Analog, Inc.*, 838 F.2d 691 (3d Cir. 1988) (partnership purpose to market an art book); *68th Street Apts., Inc. v. Lauricella*, 362 A.2d 78 (N.J. Super. Ct. 1976) (partnership purpose to construct an apartment building). A partnership to conduct a business which may last indefinitely, however, is an at-will partnership, even though there may be an obligation of the partnership, such as a mortgage, which must be repaid by a certain date, absent a specific agreement that no partner can rightfully withdraw until the obligation is repaid. *See, e.g., Page v. Page*, 55 Cal. 2d. 192, 359 P.2d 41 (1961) (partnership purpose to operate a linen supply business); *Frey v. Hauke, supra* (partnership purpose to contract and operate a bowling alley); *Girard Bank v. Haley*, 460 Pa. 237, 332 A.2d 443 (1975) (partnership purpose to maintain and lease buildings).

"Partnership interest" or "partner's interest in the partnership" is defined to mean all of a partner's interests in the partnership, including the partner's transferable interest and all management and other rights. A partner's "transferable interest" is a more limited concept and means only his share of the profits and losses and right to receive distributions, that is, the partner's economic interests. *See* Section 502 and Comment. Compare RULPA § 101(10) ("partnership interest" includes partner's economic interests only).

The definition of "person" is the usual definition used by the National Conference of Commissioners on Uniform State Laws (NCCUSL or the Conference). The definition includes other legal or commercial entities such as limited liability companies.

"Property" is defined broadly to include all types of property, as well as any interest in property.

The definition of "State" is the Conference's usual definition.

The definition of "statement" is new and refers to one of the various statements authorized by RUPA to enhance or limit the agency authority of a partner, to deny the authority or status of a partner, or to give notice of certain events, such as the dissociation of a partner or the dissolution of the partnership. *See* Sections 303, 304, 704, 805, and 907. Generally, Section 105 governs the execution, filing, and recording of all statements. The definition also makes clear that a statement of qualification under Section 1001 and a statement of foreign qualification under Section 1102 are considered statements. Both qualification statements are therefore subject to the execution, filing, and recordation rules of Section 105.

"Transfer" is defined broadly to include all manner of conveyances, including leases and encumbrances.

Section 102. Knowledge and Notice.

(a) A person knows a fact if the person has actual knowledge of it.

(b) A person has notice of a fact if the person:

(1) knows of it;

(2) has received a notification of it; or

(3) has reason to know it exists from all of the facts known to the person at the time in question.

(c) A person notifies or gives a notification to another by taking steps reasonably required to inform the other person in ordinary course, whether or not the other person learns of it.

(d) A person receives a notification when the notification:

(1) comes to the person's attention; or

(2) is duly delivered at the person's place of business or at any other place held out by the person as a place for receiving communications.

(e) Except as otherwise provided in subsection (f), a person other than an individual knows, has notice, or receives a notification of a fact for purposes of a particular transaction when the individual conducting the transaction knows, has notice, or receives a notification of the fact, or in any event when the fact would have been brought to the individual's attention if the person had exercised reasonable diligence. The person exercises reasonable diligence if it maintains reasonable routines for communicating significant information to the individual conducting the transaction and there is reasonable compliance with the routines. Reasonable diligence does not require an individual acting for the person to communicate information unless the communication is part of the individual's regular duties or the individual has reason to know of the transaction and that the transaction would be materially affected by the information.

(f) A partner's knowledge, notice, or receipt of a notification of a fact relating to the partnership is effective immediately as knowledge by, notice to, or receipt of a notification by the partnership, except in the case of a fraud on the partnership committed by or with the consent of that partner.

Comment

The concepts and definitions of "knowledge," "notice," and "notification" draw heavily on Section 1-201(25) to (27) of the Uniform Commercial Code (UCC). The UCC text has been altered somewhat to improve clarity and style, but in general no substantive changes are intended from the UCC concepts. "A notification" replaces the UCC's redundant phrase, "a notice or notification," throughout the Act.

A person "knows" a fact only if that person has actual knowledge of it. Knowledge is cognitive awareness. That is solely an issue of fact. This is a change from the UPA Section 3(1) definition of "knowledge" which included the concept of "bad faith" knowledge arising from other known facts.

"Notice" is a lesser degree of awareness than "knows" and is based on a person's: (i) actual knowledge; (ii) receipt of a notification; or (iii) reason to know based on actual knowledge of other facts and the circumstances at the time. The latter is the traditional concept of inquiry notice.

Generally, under RUPA, statements filed pursuant to Section 105 do not constitute constructive knowledge or notice, except as expressly provided in the Act. *See* Section 301(1) (generally requiring knowledge of limitations on partner's apparent authority). Properly recorded statements of limitation on a partner's authority, on the other hand, generally constitute constructive knowledge with respect to the transfer of real property held in the partnership name. *See* Sections 303(d)(1), 303(e), 704(b), and 805(b). The other exceptions are Sections 704(c) (statement of dissociation effective 90 days after filing) and 805(c) (statement of dissolution effective 90 days after filing).

A person "receives" a notification when (i) the notification is delivered to the person's place of business (or other place for receiving communications) or (ii) the recipient otherwise actually learns of its existence.

The sender "notifies" or gives a notification by making an effort to inform the recipient, which is reasonably calculated to do so in ordinary course, even if the recipient does not actually learn of it.

The Official Comment to UCC Section 1-201(26), on which this subsection is based, explains that "notifies" is the word used when the essential fact is the proper dispatch of the notice, not its receipt. When the essential fact is the other party's receipt of the notice, that is stated.

A notification is not required to be in writing. That is a change from UPA Section 3(2)(b). As under the UCC, the time and circumstances under which a notification may cease to be effective are not determined by RUPA.

Subsection (e) determines when an agent's knowledge or notice is imputed to an organization, such as a corporation. In general, only the knowledge or notice of the agent conducting the particular transaction is imputed to the organization. Organizations are expected to maintain reasonable internal routines to insure that important information reaches the individual agent handling the transaction. If, in the exercise of reasonable diligence on the part of the organization, the agent should have known or had notice of a fact, or received a notification of it, the organization is bound. The Official Comment to UCC Section 1-201(27) explains:

> This makes clear that reason to know, knowledge, or a notification, although "received" for instance by a clerk in Department A of an organization, is effective for a transaction conducted in Department B only from the time when it was or should have been communicated to the individual conducting that transaction.

Subsection (e) uses the phrase "person other than an individual" in lieu of the UCC term "organization."

Subsection (f) continues the rule in UPA Section 12 that a partner's knowledge or notice of a fact relating to the partnership is imputed to the partnership, except in the case of fraud on the partnership. Limited partners, however, are not "partners" within the meaning of RUPA. *See* Comment 4 to Section 202. It is anticipated that RULPA will address the issue of whether notice to a limited partner is imputed to a limited partnership.

Section 103. Effect of Partnership Agreement; Nonwaivable Provisions

(a) Except as otherwise provided in subsection (b), relations among the partners and between the partners and the partnership are governed by the partnership agreement. To the extent the partnership agreement does not otherwise provide, this [Act] governs relations among the partners and between the partners and the partnership.

(b) The partnership agreement may not:

(1) vary the rights and duties under Section 105 except to eliminate the duty to provide copies of statements to all of the partners;

(2) unreasonably restrict the right of access to books and records under Section 403(b);

(3) eliminate the duty of loyalty under Section 404(b) or 603(b)(3), but:

(i) the partnership agreement may identify specific types or categories of activities that do not violate the duty of loyalty, if not manifestly unreasonable; or

(ii) all of the partners or a number or percentage specified in the partnership agreement may authorize or ratify, after full disclosure of all material facts, a specific act or transaction that otherwise would violate the duty of loyalty;

(4) unreasonably reduce the duty of care under Section 404(c) or 603(b)(3);

(5) eliminate the obligation of good faith and fair dealing under Section 404(d), but the partnership agreement may prescribe the standards by which the performance of the obligation is to be measured, if the standards are not manifestly unreasonable;

(6) vary the power to dissociate as a partner under Section 602(a), except to require the notice under Section 601(1) to be in writing;

(7) vary the right of a court to expel a partner in the events specified in Section 601(5);

(8) vary the requirement to wind up the partnership business in cases specified in Section 801(4), (5), or (6); or

(9) vary the law applicable to a limited liability partnership under Section 106(b); or

(9) (10) restrict rights of third parties under this [Act].

Comment

1. The general rule under Section 103(a) is that relations among the partners and between the partners and the partnership are governed by the partnership agreement. *See* Section 101(5). To the extent that the partners fail to agree upon a contrary rule, RUPA provides the default rule. Only the right and duties listed in Section 103(b), and implicitly the corresponding liabilities and remedies under Section 405 are mandatory and cannot be waived or varied by agreement beyond what is authorized. Those are the only exceptions to the general principle that the provisions of RUPA with respect to the rights of the partners *inter se* are merely default rules, subject to modification by the partners. All modifications must also, of course, satisfy the general standards of contract validity. *See* Section 104.

2. Under subsection (b)(1), the partnership agreement may not vary the requirements for executing, filing, and recording statements under Section 105, except the duty to provide copies to all the partners. A statement that is not executed, filed, and recorded in accordance with the statutory requirements will not be accorded the effect prescribed in the Act, except as provided in Section 303(d).

3. Subsection (b)(2) provides that the partnership agreement may not unreasonably restrict a partner or former partner's access rights to books and records under Section 403(b). It is left to the courts to determine what restrictions are reasonable. *See* Comment 2 to Section 403. Other information rights in Section 403 can be varied or even eliminated by agreement.

4. Subsection (b)(3) through (5) are intended to ensure a fundamental core of fiduciary responsibility. Neither the fiduciary duties of loyalty or care, nor the obligation of good faith and fair dealing, may be eliminated entirely. However, the statutory requirements of each can be modified by agreement, subject to the limitation stated in subsection (b)(3) through (5).

There has always been a tension regarding the extent to which a partner's fiduciary duty of loyalty can be varied by agreement, as contrasted with the other partners' consent to a particular and known breach of duty. On the one hand, courts have been loathe to enforce agreements broadly "waiving" in advance a partner's fiduciary duty of loyalty, especially where there is unequal bargaining power information, or sophistication. For this reason, a very broad provision in a partnership agreement in effect negating any duty of loyalty, such as a provision giving a managing partner complete discretion to manage the business with no liability except for acts and omissions that constitute wilful misconduct, will not likely be enforced. *See, e.g., Labovitz v. Dolan*, 189 Ill. App. 3d 403, 136 Ill. Dec. 780, 545 N.E.2d 304 (1989). On the other hand, it is clear that the remaining partners can "consent" to a particular conflicting interest transaction or other breach of duty, after the fact, provided there is full disclosure.

RUPA attempts to provide a standard that partners can rely upon in drafting exculpatory agreements. It is not necessary that the agreement be restricted to a particular transaction. That would require bargaining over every transaction or opportunity, which would be excessively burdensome. The agreement may be drafted in terms of types or categories of activities or transactions, but it should be reasonably specific.

A provision in a real estate partnership agreement authorizing a partner who is a real estate agent to retain commissions on partnership property bought and sold by that partner would be an example of a "type or category" of activity that is not manifestly unreasonable and thus should be enforceable under the Act. Likewise, a provision authorizing that partner to buy or sell real property for his own account without prior disclosure to the other partners or without first offering it to the partnership would be enforceable as a valid category of partnership activity.

Ultimately, the courts must decide the outer limits of validity of such agreements, and context may be significant. It is intended that the risk of judicial refusal to enforce manifestly unreasonable exculpatory clauses will discourage sharp practices while accommodating the legitimate needs of the parties in structuring their relationship.

5. Subsection (b)(3)(i) permits the partners, in their partnership agreement, to identify specific types or categories of partnership activities that do not violate the duty of loyalty. A modification of the statutory standard must not, however, be manifestly unreasonable. This is intended to discourage overreaching by a partner with superior bargaining power since the courts may refuse to enforce an overly broad exculpatory clause. *See, e.g., Vlases v. Montgomery Ward & Co.*, 377 F.2d 846, 850 (3d Cir. 1967) (limitation prohibits unconscionable agreements); *PPG Industries, Inc. v. Shell Oil Co.*, 919 F.2d 17, 19 (5th Cir. 1990) (apply limitation deferentially to agreements of sophisticated parties).

Subsection (b)(3)(ii) is intended to clarify the right of partners, recognized under general law, to consent to a known past or anticipated violation of duty and to waive their legal remedies for redress of that violation. This is intended to cover situations where the conduct in question is not specifically authorized by the partnership agreement. It can also be used to validate conduct that might otherwise not satisfy the "manifestly unreasonable" standard. Clause (ii) provides that, after full disclosure of all material facts regarding a specific act or transaction that otherwise would violate the duty of loyalty, it may be authorized or ratified by the partners. That authorization or ratification must be unanimous unless a lesser number or percentage is specified for this purpose in the partnership agreement.

6. Under subsection (b)(4), the partners' duty of care may not be unreasonably reduced below the statutory standard set forth in Section 404(d), that is, to refrain from engaging in grossly negligent or reckless conduct, intentional misconduct, or a knowing violation of law.

For example, partnership agreements frequently contain provisions releasing a partner from liability for actions taken in good faith and in the honest belief that the actions are in the best interests of the partnership and indemnifying the partner against any liability incurred in connection with the business of the partnership if the partner acts in a good faith belief that he has authority to act. Many partnership agreements reach this same result by listing various activities and stating that the performance of these activities is deemed not to constitute gross negligence or wilful misconduct. These types of provisions are intended to come within the modifications authorized by subsection (b)(4). On the other hand, absolving partners of intentional misconduct is probably unreasonable. As with contractual standards of loyalty, determining the outer limit in reducing the standard of care is left to the courts.

The standard may, of course, be increased by agreement to one of ordinary care or an even higher standard of care.

7. Subsection (b)(5) authorizes the partners to determine the standards by which the performance of the obligation of good faith and fair dealing is to be measured. The language of subsection (b)(5) is based on UCC Section 1-102(3). The partners can negotiate and draft specific contract provisions tailored to their particular needs (*e.g.*, five days notice of a partners' meeting is adequate notice), but blanket waivers of the obligation are unenforceable. *See, e.g., PPG Indus., Inc. v. Shell Oil Co.*, 919 F.2d 17 (5th Cir. 1990); *First Security Bank v. Mountain View Equip. Co.*, 112 Idaho 158, 730 P.2d 1078 (Ct. App. 1986), *aff'd,* 112 Idaho 1078, 739 P.2d 377 (1987); *American Bank of Commerce v. Covolo*, 88 N.M. 405, 540 P.2d 1294 (1975).

8. Section 602(a) continues the traditional UPA Section 31(2) rule that every partner has the power to withdraw from the partnership at any time, which power cannot be bargained away. Section 103(b)(6) provides that the partnership agreement may not vary the power to dissociate as a partner under Section 602(a), except to require that the notice of withdrawal under Section 601(1) be in writing. The UPA was silent with respect to requiring a written notice of withdrawal.

9. Under subsection (b)(7), the right of a partner to seek court expulsion of another partner under Section 601(5) cannot be waived or varied (e.g., requiring a 90-day notice) by agreement. Section 601(5) refers to judicial expulsion on such grounds as misconduct, breach of duty, or impracticability.

10. Under subsection (b)(8), the partnership agreement may not vary the right of partners to have the partnership dissolved and its business wound up under Section 801(4), (5), or (6). Section 801(4) provides that the partnership must be wound up if its business is unlawful. Section 801(5) provides for judicial winding up in such circumstances as frustration of the firm's economic purpose, partner misconduct, or impracticability. Section 801(6) accords standing to transferees of an interest in the partnership to seek judicial dissolution of the partnership in specified circumstances.

11. Subsection (b)(9) makes clear that a limited liability partnership may not designate the law of a State other than the State where it filed its statement of qualification to govern its internal affairs and the liability of its partners. See Sections 101(5), 106(b), and 202(a). Therefore, the selection of a state within which to file a statement of qualification has important choice of law ramifications, particularly where the partnership was formed in another state. See Comments to Section 106(b).

11 12. Although stating the obvious, subsection (b)(9) (b)(10) provides expressly that the rights of a third party under the Act may not be restricted by an agreement among the partners to which the third party has not agreed. A non-partner who is a party to an agreement among the partners is, of course, bound. Cf. Section 703(c) (creditor joins release).

12 13. The Article 9 rules regarding conversions and mergers are not listed in Section 103(b) as mandatory. Indeed Section 908 states expressly that partnerships may be converted and merged in any other manner provided by law. The effect of compliance with Article 9 is to provide a "safe harbor" assuring the legal validity of such conversions and mergers. Although not immune from variation in the partnership agreement, noncompliance with the requirements of Article 9 in effecting

a conversion or merger is to deny that "safe harbor" validity to the transaction. In this regard, Sections 903(b) and 905(c)(2) require that the conversion or merger of a limited partnership be approved by all of the partners, notwithstanding a contrary provision in the limited partnership agreement. Thus, in effect, the agreement cannot vary the voting requirement without sacrificing the benefits of the "safe harbor."

Section 104. Supplemental Principles of Law.

(a) Unless displaced by particular provisions of this [Act], the principles of law and equity supplement this [Act].

(b) If an obligation to pay interest arises under this [Act] and the rate is not specified, the rate is that specified in [applicable statute].

Comment

The principles of law and equity supplement RUPA unless displaced by a particular provision of the Act. This broad statement combines the separate rules contained in UPA Sections 4(2), 4(3), and 5. These supplementary principles encompass not only the law of agency and estoppel and the law merchant mentioned in the UPA, but all of the other principles listed in UCC Section 1-103: the law, relative to capacity to contract, fraud, misrepresentation, duress, coercion, mistake, bankruptcy, and other common law validating or invalidating causes, such as unconscionability. No substantive change from either the UPA or the UCC is intended.

It was thought unnecessary to repeat the UPA Section 4(1) admonition that statutes in derogation of the common law are not to be strictly construed. This principle is now so well established that it is not necessary to so state in the Act. No change in the law is intended. See the Comment to RULPA Section 1101.

Subsection (b) is new. It is based on the definition of "interest" in Section 14-8-2(5) of the Georgia act and establishes the applicable rate of interest in the absence of an agreement among the partners. Adopting States can select the State's legal rate of interest or other statutory interest rate, such as the rate for judgments.

Section 105. Execution, Filing, and Recording of Statements.

(a) A statement may be filed in the office of [the Secretary of State]. A certified copy of a statement that is filed in an office in another State may be filed in the office of [the Secretary of State]. Either filing has the effect provided in this [Act] with respect to partnership property located in or transactions that occur in this State.

(b) A certified copy of a statement that has been filed in the office of the [Secretary of State] and recorded in the office for recording transfers of real property has the effect provided for recorded statements in this [Act]. A recorded statement that is not a certified copy of a statement filed in the office of the [Secretary of State] does not have the effect provided for recorded statements in this [Act].

(c) A statement filed by a partnership must be executed by at least two partners. Other statements must be executed by a partner or other person authorized by this [Act]. An individual who executes a statement as, or on behalf of, a partner or other person named as a partner in a statement shall personally declare under penalty of perjury that the contents of the statement are accurate.

(d) A person authorized by this [Act] to file a statement may amend or cancel the statement by filing an amendment or cancellation that names the partnership, identifies the statement, and states the substance of the amendment or cancellation.

(e) A person who files a statement pursuant to this section shall promptly send a copy of the statement to every nonfiling partner and to any other person named as a partner in the statement. Failure to send a copy of a statement to a partner or other person does not limit the effectiveness of the statement as to a person not a partner.

(f) The [Secretary of State] may collect a fee for filing or providing a certified copy of a statement. The [officer responsible for] recording transfers of real property may collect a fee for recording a statement.

Comment

1. Section 105 is new. It mandates the procedural rules for the execution, filing, and recording of the various "statements" (see Section 101(11)) authorized by RUPA. Section 101(13) makes clear that a statement of qualification filed by a partnership to become a limited liability partnership is included in the definition of a statement. Therefore, the execution, filing, and recording rules of this section must be followed except that the decision to file the statement of qualification must be approved by the vote of the partners necessary to amend the partnership agreement as to contribution requirements. See Section 1001(b) and comments.

No filings are mandatory under RUPA. In all cases, the filing of a statement is optional and voluntary. A system of mandatory filing and disclosure for partnerships, similar to that required for corporations and limited partnerships, was rejected for several reasons. First, RUPA is designed to accommodate the needs of small partnerships, which often have unwritten or sketchy agreements and limited resources. Furthermore, inadvertent partnerships are also governed by the Act, as the default form of business organization, in which case filing would be unlikely.

The RUPA filing provisions are, however, likely to encourage the voluntary use of partnership statements. There are a number of strong incentives for the partnership or the partners to file statements or for third parties, such as lenders or transferees of partnership property, to compel them to do so

Only statements that are executed, filed, and, if appropriate (such as the authority to transfer real property), recorded in conformity with Section 105 have the legal consequences accorded statements by RUPA. The requirements of Section 105 cannot be varied in the partnership agreement, except the duty to provide copies of statements to all the partners. *See* Section 103(b)(1).

In most States today, the filing and recording of statements requires written documents. As technology advances, alternatives suitable for filing and recording may be developed. RUPA itself does not impose any requirement that statements be in writing. It is intended that the form or medium for filing and recording be left to the general law of adopting States.

2. Section 105(a) provides for a single, central filing of all statements, as is the case with corporations, limited partnerships, and limited liability companies. The expectation is that most States will assign to the Secretary of State the responsibility of maintaining the filing system for partnership statements. Since a partnership is an

entity under RUPA, all statements should be indexed by partnership name, not by the names of the individual partners.

Partnerships transacting business in more than one State will want to file copies of statements in each State because subsection (a) limits the legal effect of filed statements to property located or transactions occurring within the state. The filing of a certified copy of a statement originally filed in another State is permitted, and indeed encouraged, in order to avoid inconsistencies between statements filed in different States.

3. Subsection (b), in effect, mandates the use of certified copies of filed statements for local recording in the real estate records by limiting the legal effect of recorded statements under the Act to those copies. The reason for recording only certified copies of filed statements is to eliminate the possibility of inconsistencies affecting the title to real property.

Subsection (c) requires that statements filed on behalf of a partnership, that is, the entity, be executed by at least two partners. Individual partners and other persons authorized by the Act to file a statement may execute it on their own behalf. To protect the partners and the partnership from unauthorized or improper filings, an individual who executes a statement as a partner must personally declare under penalty of perjury that the statement is accurate.

The amendment or cancellation of statements is authorized by subsection (d).

As a further safeguard against inaccurate or unauthorized filings, subsection (e) requires that a copy of every statement filed be sent to each partner, although the failure to do so does not limit the effectiveness of the statement. This requirement may, however, be eliminated in the partnership agreement. *See* Section 103(b)(1). Partners may also file a statement of denial under Section 304.

4. A filed statement may be amended or canceled by any person authorized by the Act to file an original statement. The amendment or cancellation must state the name of the partnership so that it can be properly indexed and found, identify the statement being amended or canceled, and the substance of the amendment or cancellation. An amendment generally has the same operative effect as an original statement. A cancellation of extraordinary authority terminates that authority. A cancellation of a limitation on authority revives a previous grant of authority. *See* Section 303(d). The subsequent filing of a statement similar in kind to a statement already of record is treated as an amendment, even if not so denominated. Any substantive conflict between filed statements operates as a cancellation of authority under Section 303.

Section 106. Governing Law ~~Governing Internal Relations~~.

(a) ~~The~~ Except as otherwise provided in subsection (b), the law of the jurisdiction in which a partnership has its chief executive office governs relations among the partners and between the partners and the partnership.

(b) The law of this State governs relations among the partners and between the partners and the partnership and the liability of partners for an obligation of a limited liability partnership.

Comment

The <u>subsection (a)</u> internal relations rule is new. *Cf.* RULPA § 901 (internal affairs governed by law of State in which limited partnership organized).

RUPA looks to the jurisdiction in which a partnership's chief executive office is located to provide the law governing the internal relations among the partners and between the partners and the partnership. The concept of the partnership's "chief executive office" is drawn from UCC Section 9-103(3)(d). It was chosen in lieu of the State of organization because no filing is necessary to form a general partnership, and thus the situs of its organization is not always clear, unlike a limited partnership, which is organized in the State where its certificate is filed.

The term "chief executive office" is not defined in the Act, nor is it defined in the UCC. Paragraph 5 of the Official Comment to UCC Section 9-103(3)(d) explains:

> "Chief executive office" ... means the place from which in fact the debtor manages the main part of his business operations.... Doubt may arise as to which is the "chief executive office" of a multi-state enterprise, but it would be rare that there could be more than two possibilities.... [The rule] will be simple to apply in most cases....

In the absence of any other clear rule for determining a partnership's legal situs, it seems convenient to use that rule for choice of law purposes as well.

The choice-of-law rule provided by ~~Section106~~ <u>subsection (a)</u> is only a default rule, and the partners may by agreement select the law of another State to govern their internal affairs, subject to generally applicable conflict of laws requirements. For example, where the partners may not resolve a particular issue by an explicit provision of the partnership agreement, such as the rights and duties set forth in Section 103(b), the law chosen will not be applied if the partners or the partnership have no substantial relationship to the chosen State or other reasonable basis for their choice or if application of the law of the chosen State would be contrary to a fundamental policy of a State that has a materially greater interest than the chosen State. *See* Restatement (Second) of Conflict of Laws § 187(2) (1971). The partners must, however, select only one State to govern their internal relations. They cannot select one State for some aspects of their internal relations and another State for others.

<u>Contrasted with the variable choice-of-law rule provided by subsection (a), the law of the State where a limited liability partnership files its statement of qualification applies to such a partnership and may not be varied by the agreement of the partners. See Section 103(b)(9). Also, a partnership that files a statement of qualification in another state is not defined as a limited liability partnership in this state. See Section 101(5). Unlike a general partnership which may be formed without any filing, a partnership may only become a limited liability partnership by filing a statement of qualification. Therefore, the situs of its organization is clear. Because it is often unclear where a general partnership is actually formed, the decision to file a statement of qualification in a particular state constitutes a choice-of-law for the partnership which cannot be altered by the partnership agreement. See Comments to Section 103(b)(9). If the partnership agreement of an existing partnership specifies the law of a particular state as its governing law, and the partnership thereafter files a</u>

statement of qualification in another state, the partnership agreement choice is no longer controlling. In such cases, the filing of a statement of qualification "amends" the partnership agreement on this limited matter. Accordingly, if a statement of qualification is revoked or canceled for a limited liability partnership, the law of the state of filing would continue to apply unless the partnership agreement thereafter altered the applicable law rule.

Section 107. Partnership Subject to Amendment or Repeal of [Act].

A partnership governed by this [Act] is subject to any amendment to or repeal of this [Act].

Comment

The reservation of power provision is new. It is adapted from Section 1.02 of the Revised Model Business Corporation Act (RMBCA) and Section 1106 of RULPA.

As explained in the Official Comment to the RMBCA, the genesis of those provisions is *Trustees of Dartmouth College v. Woodward*, 17 U.S. (4 Wheat) 518 (1819), which held that the United States Constitution prohibits the application of newly enacted statutes to existing corporations, while suggesting the efficacy of a reservation of power provision. Its purpose is to avoid any possible argument that a legal entity created pursuant to statute or its members have a contractual or vested right in any specific statutory provision and to ensure that the State may in the future modify its enabling statute as it deems appropriate and require existing entities to comply with the statutes as modified.

[ARTICLE] 2

NATURE OF PARTNERSHIP

Section 201. Partnership As Entity.
Section 202. Formation of Partnership.
Section 203. Partnership Property.
Section 204. When Property Is Partnership Property.

Section 201. Partnership as Entity.

(a) A partnership is an entity distinct from its partners.
(b) A limited liability partnership continues to be the same entity that existed before the filing of a statement of qualification under Section 1001.

Comment

RUPA embraces the entity theory of the partnership. In light of the UPA's ambivalence on the nature of partnerships, an the explicit statement provided by subsection (a) is deemed appropriate as an expression of the increased emphasis on the entity theory as the dominant model. *But see* Section 305 306 (partners' liability joint and several unless the partnership has filed a statement of qualification to become a limited liability partnership).

Giving clear expression to the entity nature of a partnership is intended to allay previous concerns stemming from the aggregate theory, such as the necessity of a deed to convey title from the "old" partnership to the "new" partnership every time there is a change of cast among the partners. Under RUPA, there is no "new" partnership just because of membership changes. That will avoid the result in cases such as *Fairway Development Co. v. Title Insurance Co.,* 621 F. Supp. 120 (N.D. Ohio 1985), which held that the "new" partnership resulting from a partner's death did not have standing to enforce a title insurance policy issued to the "old" partnership.

Subsection (b) makes clear that the explicit entity theory provided by subsection (a) applies to a partnership both before and after it files a statement of qualification to become a limited liability partnership. Thus, just as there is no "new" partnership resulting from membership changes, the filing of a statement of qualification does not create a "new" partnership. The filing partnership continues to be the same partnership entity that existed before the filing. Similarly, the amendment or cancellation of a statement of qualification under Section 105(d) or the revocation of a statement of qualification under Section 1003(c) does not terminate the partnership and create a "new" partnership. See Section 1003(d). Accordingly, a partnership remains the same entity regardless of a filing, cancellation, or revocation of a statement of qualification.

Section 202. Formation of Partnership.

(a) Except as otherwise provided in subsection (b), the association of two or more persons to carry on as co-owners a business for profit forms a partnership, whether or not the persons intend to form a partnership.

(b) An association formed under a statute other than this [Act], a predecessor statute, or a comparable statute of another jurisdiction is not a partnership under this [Act].

(c) In determining whether a partnership is formed, the following rules apply:

(1) Joint tenancy, tenancy in common, tenancy by the entireties, joint property, common property, or part ownership does not by itself establish a partnership, even if the co-owners share profits made by the use of the property.

(2) The sharing of gross returns does not by itself establish a partnership, even if the persons sharing them have a joint or common right or interest in property from which the returns are derived.

(3) A person who receives a share of the profits of a business is presumed to be a partner in the business, unless the profits were received in payment:

(i) of a debt by installments or otherwise;

(ii) for services as an independent contractor or of wages or other compensation to an employee;

(iii) of rent;

(iv) of an annuity or other retirement or health benefit to a beneficiary, representative, or designee of a deceased or retired partner;

(v) of interest or other charge on a loan, even if the amount of payment varies with the profits of the business, including a direct or indirect present or future ownership of the collateral, or rights to income, proceeds, or increase in value derived from the collateral; or

(vi) for the sale of the goodwill of a business or other property by installments or otherwise.

Comment

1. Section 202 combines UPA Sections 6 and 7. The traditional UPA Section 6(1) "definition" of a partnership is recast as an operative rule of law. No substantive change in the law is intended. The UPA "definition" has always been understood as an operative rule, as well as a definition. The addition of the phrase, "whether or not the persons intend to form a partnership," merely codifies the universal judicial construction of UPA Section 6(1) that a partnership is created by the association of persons whose intent is to carry on as co-owners a business for profit, regardless of their subjective intention to be "partners." Indeed, they may inadvertently create a partnership despite their expressed subjective intention not to do so. The new language alerts readers to this possibility.

As under the UPA, the attribute of co-ownership distinguishes a partnership from a mere agency relationship. A business is a series of acts directed toward an end. Ownership involves the power of ultimate control. To state that partners are co-owners of a business is to state that they each have the power of ultimate control. *See* Official Comment to UPA § 6(1). On the other hand, as subsection (c)(1) makes clear, passive co-ownership of property by itself, as distinguished from the carrying on of a business, does not establish a partnership.

2. Subsection (b) provides that business associations organized under other statutes are not partnerships. Those statutory associations include corporations, limited partnerships, and limited liability companies. That continues the UPA concept that general partnership is the residual form of for profit business association, existing only if another form does not.

A limited partnership is not a partnership under this definition. Nevertheless, certain provisions of RUPA will continue to govern limited partnerships because RULPA itself, in Section 1105, so requires "in any case not provided for" in RULPA. For example, the rules applicable to a limited liability partnership will generally apply to limited partnerships. See Comment to Section 101(5) (definition of a limited liability partnership). In light of ~~that section~~ RULPA Section 1105, UPA Section 6(2), which provides that limited partnerships are governed by the UPA, is redundant and has not been carried over to RUPA. It is also more appropriate that the applicability of RUPA to limited partnerships be governed exclusively by RULPA. For example, a RULPA amendment may clarify certain linkage questions regarding the application of the limited liability partnership rules to limited partnerships. See Comment to Section 101(5) for a suggested form of such an amendment.

It is not intended that RUPA change any common law rules concerning special types of associations, such as mining partnerships, which in some jurisdictions are not governed by the UPA.

Relationships that are called "joint ventures" are partnerships if they otherwise fit the definition of a partnership. An association is not classified as a partnership, however, simply because it is called a "joint venture."

An unincorporated nonprofit organization is not a partnership under RUPA, even if it qualifies as a business, because it is not a "for profit" organization.

3. Subsection (c) provides three rules of construction that apply in determining whether a partnership has been formed under subsection (a). They are largely derived from UPA Section 7, and to that extent no substantive change is intended. The sharing of profits is recast as a rebuttable presumption of a partnership, a more contemporary construction, rather than as prima facie evidence thereof. The protected categories, in which receipt of a share of the profits is not presumed to create a partnership, apply whether the profit share is a single flat percentage or a ratio which varies, for example, after reaching a dollar floor or different levels of profits.

Like its predecessor, RUPA makes no attempt to answer in every case whether a partnership is formed. Whether a relationship is more properly characterized as that of borrower and lender, employer and employee, or landlord and tenant is left to the trier of fact. As under the UPA, a person may function in both partner and nonpartner capacities.

Paragraph (3)(v) adds a new protected category to the list. It shields from the presumption a share of the profits received in payment of interest or other charges on a loan, "including a direct or indirect present or future ownership in the collateral, or rights to income, proceeds, or increase in value derived from the collateral." The quoted language is taken from Section 211 of the Uniform Land Security Interest Act. The purpose of the new language is to protect shared-appreciation mortgages, contingent or other variable or performance-related mortgages, and other equity participation arrangements by clarifying that contingent payments do not presumptively convert lending arrangements into partnerships.

4. Section 202(e) of the 1993 Act stated that partnerships formed under RUPA are general partnerships and that the partners are general partners. That section has been deleted as unnecessary. Limited partners are not "partners" within the meaning of RUPA, however.

Section 203. Partnership Property.

Property acquired by a partnership is property of the partnership and not of the partners individually.

Comment

All property acquired by a partnership, by transfer or otherwise, becomes partnership property and belongs to the partnership as an entity, rather than to the individual partners. This expresses the substantive result of UPA Sections 8(1) and 25.

Neither UPA Section 8(1) nor RUPA Section 203 provides any guidance concerning when property is "acquired by" the partnership. That problem is dealt with in Section 204.

UPA Sections 25(2)(c) and (e) also provide that partnership property is not subject to exemptions, allowances, or rights of a partner's spouse, heirs, or next of kin. Those provisions have been omitted as unnecessary. No substantive change is intended. Those exemptions and rights inure to the property of the partners, and not to partnership property.

Section 204. When Property Is Partnership Property.

(a) Property is partnership property if acquired in the name of:
(1) the partnership; or
(2) one or more partners with an indication in the instrument transferring title to the property of the person's capacity as a partner or of the existence of a partnership but without an indication of the name of the partnership.

(b) Property is acquired in the name of the partnership by a transfer to:
(1) the partnership in its name; or
(2) one or more partners in their capacity as partners in the partnership, if the name of the partnership is indicated in the instrument transferring title to the property.

(c) Property is presumed to be partnership property if purchased with partnership assets, even if not acquired in the name of the partnership or of one or more partners with an indication in the instrument transferring title to the property of the person's capacity as a partner or of the existence of a partnership.

(d) Property acquired in the name of one or more of the partners, without an indication in the instrument transferring title to the property of the person's capacity as a partner or of the existence of a partnership and without use of partnership assets is presumed to be separate property, even if used for partnership purposes.

Comment

1. Section 204 sets forth the rules for determining when property is acquired by the partnership and, hence, becomes partnership property. It is based on UPA Section 8(3), as influenced by the recent Alabama and Georgia modifications. The rules govern the acquisition of personal property, as well as real property, that is held in the partnership name. *See* Section 101(9).

2. Subsection (a) governs the circumstances under which property becomes "partnership property," and subsection (b) clarifies the circumstances under which property is acquired "in the name of the partnership." The concept of record title is emphasized, although the term itself is not used. Titled personal property, as well as all transferable interests in real property acquired in the name of the partnership, are covered by this section.

Property becomes partnership property if acquired (1) in the name of the partnership or (2) in the name of one or more of the partners with an indication in the instrument transferring title of either (i) their capacity as partners or (ii) of the existence of a partnership, even if the name of the partnership is not indicated. Property acquired "in the name of the partnership" includes property acquired in the name of one or more partners in their capacity as partners, but only if the name of the partnership is indicated in the instrument transferring title.

Property transferred to a partner is partnership property, even though the name of the partnership is not indicated, if the instrument transferring title indicates either (i) the partner's capacity as a partner or (ii) the existence of a partnership. This is consonant with the entity theory of partnership and resolves the troublesome issue of a conveyance to fewer than all the partners but which nevertheless indicates their partner status.

3. Ultimately, it is the intention of the partners that controls whether property belongs to the partnership or to one or more of the partners in their individual capacities, at least as among the partners themselves. RUPA sets forth two rebuttable presumptions that apply when the partners have failed to express their intent.

First, under subsection (c), property purchased with partnership funds is presumed to be partnership property, notwithstanding the name in which title is held. The presumption is intended to apply if partnership credit is used to obtain financing, as well as the use of partnership cash or property for payment. Unlike the rule in subsection (b), under which property is **deemed** to be partnership property if the partnership's name or the partner's capacity as a partner is disclosed in the instrument of conveyance, subsection (c) raises only a **presumption** that the property is partnership property if it is purchased with partnership assets.

That presumption is also subject to an important caveat. Under Section 302(b), partnership property held in the name of individual partners, without an indication of their capacity as partners or of the existence of a partnership, that is transferred by the partners in whose name title is held to a purchaser without knowledge that it is partnership property is free of any claims of the partnership.

Second, under subsection (d), property acquired in the name of one or more of the partners, without an indication of their capacity as partners and without use of partnership funds or credit, is presumed to be the partners' separate property, even if used for partnership purposes. In effect, it is presumed in that case that only the use of the property is contributed to the partnership.

4. Generally, under RUPA, partners and third parties dealing with partnerships will be able to rely on the record to determine whether property is owned by the partnership. The exception is property purchased with partnership funds without any reference to the partnership in the title documents. The inference concerning the partners' intent from the use of partnership funds outweighs any inference from the state of the title, subject to the overriding reliance interest in the case of a purchaser without notice of the partnership's interest. This allocation of risk should encourage the partnership to eliminate doubt about ownership by putting title in the partnership.

5. UPA Section 8(4) provides, "A transfer to a partnership in the partnership name, even without words of inheritance, passes the entire estate or interest of the grantor unless a contrary intent appears." It has been omitted from RUPA as unnecessary because modern conveyancing law deems all transfers to pass the entire estate or interest of the grantor unless a contrary intent appears.

[ARTICLE] 3

RELATIONS OF PARTNERS TO
PERSONS DEALING WITH PARTNERSHIP

Section 301. Partner Agent of Partnership.

Subject to the effect of a statement of partnership authority under Section 303:

(1) Each partner is an agent of the partnership for the purpose of its business. An act of a partner, including the execution of an instrument in the partnership name, for apparently carrying on in the ordinary course the partnership business or business of the kind carried on by the partnership binds the partnership, unless the partner had no authority to act for the partnership in the particular matter and the person with whom the partner was dealing knew or had received a notification that the partner lacked authority.

(2) An act of a partner which is not apparently for carrying on in the ordinary course the partnership business or business of the kind carried on by the partnership binds the partnership only if the act was authorized by the other partners.

Comment

1. Section 301 sets forth a partner's power, as an agent of the firm, to bind the partnership entity to third parties. The rights of the partners among themselves, including the right to restrict a partner's authority, are governed by the partnership agreement and by Section 401.

The agency rules set forth in Section 301 are subject to an important qualification. They may be affected by the filing or recording of a statement of partnership authority. The legal effect of filing or recording a statement of partnership authority is set forth in Section 303.

2. Section 301(1) retains the basic principles reflected in UPA Section 9(1). It declares that each partner is an agent of the partnership and that, by virtue of partnership status, each partner has apparent authority to bind the partnership in ordinary course transactions. The effect of Section 301(1) is to characterize a partner as a general managerial agent having both actual and apparent authority co-extensive in scope with the firm's ordinary business, at least in the absence of a contrary partnership agreement.

Section 301(1) effects two changes from UPA Section 9(1). First, it clarifies that a partner's apparent authority includes acts for carrying on in the ordinary course "business of the kind carried on by the partnership," not just the business of the particular partnership in question. The UPA is ambiguous on this point, but there is some authority for an expanded construction in accordance with the so-called

English rule. *See, e.g., Burns v. Gonzalez,* 439 S.W.2d 128, 131 (Tex. Civ. App. 1969) (dictum); *Commercial Hotel Co. v. Weeks,* 254 S.W. 521 (Tex. Civ. App. 1923). No substantive change is intended by use of the more customary phrase "carrying on in the ordinary course" in lieu of the UPA phrase "in the usual way." The UPA and the case law use both terms without apparent distinction.

The other change from the UPA concerns the allocation of risk of a partner's lack of authority. RUPA draws the line somewhat differently from the UPA.

Under UPA Section 9(1) and (4), only a person with knowledge of a restriction on a partner's authority is bound by it. Section 301(1) provides that a person who has received a notification of a partner's lack of authority is also bound. The meaning of "receives a notification" is explained in Section 102(d). Thus, the partnership may protect itself from unauthorized acts by giving a notification of a restriction on a partner's authority to a person dealing with that partner. A notification may be effective upon delivery, whether or not it actually comes to the other person's attention. To that extent, the risk of lack of authority is shifted to those dealing with partners.

On the other hand, as used in the UPA, the term "knowledge" embodies the concept of "bad faith" knowledge arising from other known facts. As used in RUPA, however, "knowledge" is limited to actual knowledge. *See* Section 102(a). Thus, RUPA does not expose persons dealing with a partner to the greater risk of being bound by a restriction based on their purported reason to know of the partner's lack of authority from all the facts they did know. Compare Section 102(b)(3) (notice).

With one exception, this result is not affected even if the partnership files a statement of partnership authority containing a limitation on a partner's authority. Section 303(f) makes clear that a person dealing with a partner is not deemed to know of such a limitation merely because it is contained in a filed statement of authority. Under Section 303(e), however, all persons are deemed to know of a limitation on the authority of a partner to transfer real property contained in a recorded statement. Thus, a recorded limitation on authority concerning real property constitutes constructive knowledge of the limitation to the whole world.

3. Section 301(2) is drawn directly from UPA Section 9(2), with conforming changes to mirror the new language of subsection (1). Subsection (2) makes it clear that the partnership is bound by a partner's actual authority, even if the partner has no apparent authority. Section 401(j) requires the unanimous consent of the partners for a grant of authority outside the ordinary course of business, unless the partnership agreement provides otherwise. Under general agency principles, the partners can subsequently ratify a partner's unauthorized act. *See* Section 104(a).

4. UPA Section 9(3) contains a list of five extraordinary acts that require unanimous consent of the partners before the partnership is bound. RUPA omits that section. That leaves it to the courts to decide the outer limits of the agency power of a partner. Most of the acts listed in UPA Section 9(3) probably remain outside the apparent authority of a partner under RUPA, such as disposing of the goodwill of the business, but elimination of a statutory rule will afford more flexibility in some situations specified in UPA Section 9(3). In particular, it seems archaic that the submission of a partnership claim to arbitration always requires unanimous consent. *See* UPA § 9(3)(e).

5. Section 301(1) fully reflects the principle embodied in UPA Section 9(4) that the partnership is not bound by an act of a partner in contravention of a restriction on his authority known to the other party.

Section 302. Transfer of Partnership Property.

(a) Partnership property may be transferred as follows:

(1) Subject to the effect of a statement of partnership authority under Section 303, partnership property held in the name of the partnership may be transferred by an instrument of transfer executed by a partner in the partnership name.

(2) Partnership property held in the name of one or more partners with an indication in the instrument transferring the property to them of their capacity as partners or of the existence of a partnership, but without an indication of the name of the partnership, may be transferred by an instrument of transfer executed by the persons in whose name the property is held.

(3) Partnership property held in the name of one or more persons other than the partnership, without an indication in the instrument transferring the property to them of their capacity as partners or of the existence of a partnership, may be transferred by an instrument of transfer executed by the persons in whose name the property is held.

(b) A partnership may recover partnership property from a transferee only if it proves that execution of the instrument of initial transfer did not bind the partnership under Section 301 and:

(1) as to a subsequent transferee who gave value for property transferred under subsection (a)(1) and (2), proves that the subsequent transferee knew or had received a notification that the person who executed the instrument of initial transfer lacked authority to bind the partnership; or

(2) as to a transferee who gave value for property transferred under subsection (a)(3), proves that the transferee knew or had received a notification that the property was partnership property and that the person who executed the instrument of initial transfer lacked authority to bind the partnership.

(c) A partnership may not recover partnership property from a subsequent transferee if the partnership would not have been entitled to recover the property, under subsection (b), from any earlier transferee of the property.

(d) If a person holds all of the partners' interests in the partnership, all of the partnership property vests in that person. The person may execute a document in the name of the partnership to evidence vesting of the property in that person and may file or record the document.

Comment

1. Section 302 replaces UPA Section 10 and provides rules for the transfer and recovery of partnership property. The language is adapted in part from Section 14-8-10 of the Georgia partnership statute.

2. Subsection (a)(1) deals with the transfer of partnership property held in the name of the partnership and subsection (a)(2) with property held in the name of one or more of the partners with an indication either of their capacity as partners or of the existence of a partnership. Subsection (a)(3) deals with partnership property held in

the name of one or more of the partners without an indication of their capacity as partners or of the existence of a partnership. Like the general agency rules in Section 301, the power of a partner to transfer partnership property under subsection (a)(1) is subject to the effect under Section 303 of the filing or recording of a statement of partnership authority. These rules are intended to foster reliance on record title.

UPA Section 10 covers only real property. Section 302, however, also governs the transfer of partnership personal property acquired by instrument and held in the name of the partnership or one or more of the partners.

3. Subsection (b) deals with the right of the partnership to recover partnership property transferred by a partner without authority. Subsection (b)(1) deals with the recovery of property held in either the name of the partnership or the name of one or more of the partners with an indication of their capacity as partners or of the existence of a partnership, while subsection (b)(2) deals with the recovery of property held in the name of one or more persons without an indication of their capacity as partners or of the existence of a partnership.

In either case, a transfer of partnership property may be avoided only if the partnership proves that it was not bound under Section 301 by the execution of the instrument of initial transfer. Under Section 301, the partnership is bound by a transfer in the ordinary course of business, unless the transferee actually knew or had received a notification of the partner's lack of authority. *See* Section 102(a) and (d). The reference to Section 301, rather than Section 301(1), is intended to clarify that a partner's actual authority is not revoked by Section 302. Compare UPA § 10(1) (refers to partner's authority under Section 9(1)).

The burden of proof is on the partnership to prove the partner's lack of authority and, in the case of a subsequent transferee, the transferee's knowledge or notification thereof. Thus, even if the transfer to the initial transferee could be avoided, the partnership may not recover the property from a subsequent purchaser or other transferee for value unless it also proves that the subsequent transferee knew or had received a notification of the partner's lack of authority with respect to the initial transfer. Since knowledge is required, rather than notice, a remote purchaser has no duty to inquire as to the authority for the initial transfer, even if he knows it was partnership property.

The burden of proof is on the transferee to show that value was given. Value, as used in this context, is synonymous with valuable consideration and means any consideration sufficient to support a simple contract.

The burden of proof on all other issues is allocated to the partnership because it is generally in a better position than the transferee to produce the evidence. Moreover, the partnership may protect itself against unauthorized transfers by ensuring that partnership real property is held in the name of the partnership and that a statement of partnership authority is recorded specifying any limitations on the partners' authority to convey real property. Under Section 303(e), transferees of real property held in the partnership name are conclusively bound by those limitations. On the other hand, transferees can protect themselves by insisting that the partnership record a statement specifying who is authorized to transfer partnership property. Under Section 303(d), transferees for value, without actual knowledge to the contrary, may rely on that grant of authority.

4. Subsection (b)(2) replaces UPA Section 10(3) and provides that partners who hold partnership property in their own names, without an indication in the record of their capacity as partners or of the existence of a partnership, may transfer good title to a transferee for value without knowledge or a notification that it was partnership property. To recover the property under this subsection, the partnership has the burden of proving that the transferee knew or had received a notification of the partnership's interest in the property, as well as of the partner's lack of authority for the initial transfer.

5. Subsection (c) is new and provides that property may not be recovered by the partnership from a remote transferee if any intermediate transferee of the property would have prevailed against the partnership. *Cf.* Uniform Fraudulent Transfer Act, §§ 8(a) (subsequent transferee from bona fide purchaser protected), 8(b)(2) (same).

6. Subsection (d) is new. The UPA does not have a provision dealing with the situation in which all of the partners' interests in the partnership are held by one person, such as a surviving partner or a purchaser of all the other partners' interests. Subsection (d) allows for clear record title, even though the partnership no longer exists as a technical matter. When a partnership becomes a sole proprietorship by reason of the dissociation of all but one of the partners, title vests in the remaining "partner," although there is no "transfer" of the property. The remaining "partner" may execute a deed or other transfer of record in the name of the non-existent partnership to evidence vesting of the property in that person's individual capacity.

7. UPA Section 10(2) provides that, where title to real property is in the partnership name, a conveyance by a partner in his own name transfers the partnership's equitable interest in the property. It has been omitted as was done in Georgia and Florida. In this situation, the conveyance is clearly outside the chain of title and so should not pass title or any interest in the property. UPA Section 10(2) dilutes, albeit slightly, the effect of record title and is, therefore, inconsistent with RUPA's broad policy of fostering reliance on the record.

UPA Section 10(4) and (5) have also been omitted. Those situations are now adequately covered by Section 302(a).

Section 303. Statement of Partnership Authority.

(a) A partnership may file a statement of partnership authority, which:

   (1) must include:

   (i) the name of the partnership;

   (ii) the street address of its chief executive office and of one office in this State, if there is one;

   (iii) the names and mailing addresses of all of the partners or of an agent appointed and maintained by the partnership for the purpose of subsection (b); and

   (iv) the names of the partners authorized to execute an instrument transferring real property held in the name of the partnership; and

   (2) may state the authority, or limitations on the authority, of some or all of the partners to enter into other transactions on behalf of the partnership and any other matter.

(b) If a statement of partnership authority names an agent, the agent shall maintain a list of the names and mailing addresses of all of the partners and make it available to any person on request for good cause shown.

(c) If a filed statement of partnership authority is executed pursuant to Section 105(c) and states the name of the partnership but does not contain all of the other information required by subsection (a), the statement nevertheless operates with respect to a person not a partner as provided in subsections (d) and (e).

(d) Except as otherwise provided in subsection (g), a filed statement of partnership authority supplements the authority of a partner to enter into transactions on behalf of the partnership as follows:

(1) Except for transfers of real property, a grant of authority contained in a filed statement of partnership authority is conclusive in favor of a person who gives value without knowledge to the contrary, so long as and to the extent that a limitation on that authority is not then contained in another filed statement. A filed cancellation of a limitation on authority revives the previous grant of authority.

(2) A grant of authority to transfer real property held in the name of the partnership contained in a certified copy of a filed statement of partnership authority recorded in the office for recording transfers of that real property is conclusive in favor of a person who gives value without knowledge to the contrary, so long as and to the extent that a certified copy of a filed statement containing a limitation on that authority is not then of record in the office for recording transfers of that real property. The recording in the office for recording transfers of that real property of a certified copy of a filed cancellation of a limitation on authority revives the previous grant of authority.

(e) A person not a partner is deemed to know of a limitation on the authority of a partner to transfer real property held in the name of the partnership if a certified copy of the filed statement containing the limitation on authority is of record in the office for recording transfers of that real property.

(f) Except as otherwise provided in subsections (d) and (e) and Sections 704 and 805, a person not a partner is not deemed to know of a limitation on the authority of a partner merely because the limitation is contained in a filed statement.

(g) Unless earlier canceled, a filed statement of partnership authority is canceled by operation of law five years after the date on which the statement, or the most recent amendment, was filed with the [Secretary of State].

Comment

1. Section 303 is new. It provides for an optional statement of partnership authority specifying the names of the partners authorized to execute instruments transferring real property held in the name of the partnership. It may also grant supplementary authority to partners, or limit their authority, to enter into other transactions on behalf of the partnership. The execution, filing, and recording of statements is governed by Section 105.

RUPA follows the lead of California and Georgia in authorizing the optional filing of statements of authority. Filing a statement of partnership authority may be deemed to satisfy the disclosure required by a State's fictitious name statute, if the State so chooses.

Section 105 provides for the central filing of statements, rather than local filing. However, to be effective in connection with the transfer of real property, a statement of partnership authority must also be recorded locally with the land records.

2. The most important goal of the statement of authority is to facilitate the transfer of real property held in the name of the partnership. A statement must specify the names of the partners authorized to execute an instrument transferring that property.

Under subsection (d)(2), a recorded grant of authority to transfer real property held in the name of the partnership is conclusive in favor of a transferee for value without actual knowledge to the contrary. A partner's authority to transfer partnership real property is affected by a recorded statement only if the property is held in the name of the partnership. A recorded statement has no effect on the partners' authority to transfer partnership real property that is held other than in the name of the partnership. In that case, by definition, the record will not indicate the name of the partnership, and thus the partnership's interest would not be disclosed by a title search. *See* Section 204. To be effective, the statement recorded with the land records must be a certified copy of the original statement filed with the secretary of state. *See* Section 105(b).

The presumption of authority created by subsection (d)(2) operates only so long as and to the extent that a limitation on the partner's authority is not contained in another recorded statement. This is intended to condition reliance on the record to situations where there is no conflict among recorded statements, amendments, or denials of authority. *See* Section 304. If the record is in conflict regarding a partner's authority, transferees must go outside the record to determine the partners' actual authority. This rule is modified slightly in the case of a cancellation of a limitation on a partner's authority, which revives the previous grant of authority.

Under subsection (e), third parties are deemed to know of a recorded limitation on the authority of a partner to transfer real property held in the partnership name. Since transferees are bound under Section 301 by knowledge of a limitation on a partner's authority, they are bound by such a recorded limitation. Of course, a transferee with actual knowledge of a limitation on a partner's authority is bound under Section 301, whether or not there is a recorded statement of limitation.

3. A statement of partnership authority may have effect beyond the transfer of real property held in the name of the partnership. Under subsection (a)(2), a statement of authority may contain any other matter the partnership chooses, including a grant of authority, or a limitation on the authority, of some or all of the partners to enter into other transactions on behalf of the partnership. Since Section 301 confers authority on all partners to act for the partnership in ordinary matters, the real import of such a provision is to grant extraordinary authority, or to limit the ordinary authority, of some or all of the partners.

The effect given to such a provision is different from that accorded a provision regarding the transfer of real property. Under subsection (d)(1), a filed grant of authority is binding on the partnership, in favor of a person who gives value without actual knowledge to the contrary, unless limited by another filed statement. That is the same rule as for statements involving real property under subsection 301(d)(2). There is, however, no counterpart to subsection (e) regarding a filed limitation of authority. To the contrary, subsection (f) makes clear that filing a limitation of authority does not operate as constructive knowledge of a partner's lack of authority with respect to non-real property transactions.

Under Section 301, only a third party who knows or has received a notification of a partner's lack of authority in an ordinary course transaction is bound. Thus, a limitation on a partner's authority to transfer personal property or to enter into other non-real property transactions on behalf of the partnership, contained in a filed statement of partnership authority, is effective only against a third party who knows or has received a notification of it. The fact of the statement being filed has no legal significance in those transactions, although the filed statement is a potential source of actual knowledge to third parties.

4. It should be emphasized that Section 303 concerns the authority of partners to bind the partnership to third persons. As among the partners, the authority of a partner to take any action is governed by the partnership agreement, or by the provisions of RUPA governing the relations among partners, and is not affected by the filing or recording of a statement of partnership authority.

5. The exercise of the option to file a statement of partnership authority imposes a further disclosure obligation on the partnership. Under subsection (a)(1), a filed statement must include the street address of its chief executive office and of an office in the State (if any), as well as the names and mailing addresses of all of the partners or, alternatively, of an agent appointed and maintained by the partnership for the purpose of maintaining such a list. If an agent is appointed, subsection (b) provides that the agent shall maintain a list of all of the partners and make it available to any person on request for good cause shown. Under subsection (c), the failure to make all of the required disclosures does not affect the statement's operative effect, however.

6. Under subsection (g), a statement of authority is canceled by operation of law five years after the date on which the statement, or the most recent amendment, was filed.

7. Section 308(c) makes clear that a person does not become a partner solely because he is named as a partner in a statement of partnership authority filed by another person. *See also* Section 304 ("person named as a partner" may file statement of denial).

8. Under certain circumstances a statement of authority can potentially affect the tax status of a partnership. Under the classification regulations in the Internal Revenue Code, centralization of management may exist if there is any limitation on the normal agency authority of partners. *See* Treas. Reg. § 301.7701-2(c). A statement of authority that simply names the partners who are authorized to execute deeds or other instruments transferring partnership real property, pursuant to Section 303(a)(1)(iv), does not create a tax classification problem because that designation has no effect on the agency power of the partners to bind the partnership by entering into the transaction. The mere execution of the instruments transferring partnership property is essentially a ministerial act and presupposes that the underlying transaction has already been approved and is binding on the partnership. If the statement of authority goes further and grants some partners more power than other partners to bind the partnership or limits the normal agency authority of one or more partners, however, a potential centralization of management issue exists. The distinction is between saying "Partner John Smith is authorized to sign deeds and other instruments conveying interests in the partnership's real property" and "Partner John Smith has the exclusive power to enter into transactions on behalf of this partnership" or "Partner John Smith cannot enter into any transaction exceeding $5,000."

Even if the statement of partnership authority contains a special grant or limitation of authority, the potential adverse tax consequences are minimal for two reasons. First, whether the particular partnership will be held to have centralized management depends on all the facts and circumstances. The statement of authority is merely one factor in the analysis. Second, even if there is centralized management, the partnership will still be taxed under Subchapter K of the Internal Revenue Code unless it also possess at least two of the three other corporate characteristics deemed important by the Regulations: (1) continuity of life, (2) limited liability, and (3) free transferability of interests; that will rarely be the case.

Section 304. Statement of Denial.

A partner or other person named as a partner in a filed statement of partnership authority or in a list maintained by an agent pursuant to Section 303(b) may file a statement of denial stating the name of the partnership and the fact that is being denied, which may include denial of a person's authority or status as a partner. A statement of denial is a limitation on authority as provided in Section 303(d) and (e).

Comment

Section 304 is new and complements Section 303. It provides partners (and persons named as partners) an opportunity to deny any fact asserted in a statement of partnership authority, including denial of a person's status as a partner or of another person's authority as a partner. A statement of denial must be executed, filed, and recorded pursuant to the requirements of Section 105.

Section 304 does not address the consequences of a denial of partnership. No adverse inference should be drawn from the failure of a person named as a partner to deny such status, however. *See* Section 308(c) (person not liable as a partner merely because named in statement as a partner).

A statement of denial operates as a limitation on a partner's authority to the extent provided in Section 303. Section 303(d) provides that a filed or recorded statement of partnership authority is conclusive, in favor of purchasers without knowledge to the contrary, so long as and to the extent that a limitation on that authority is not contained in another filed or recorded statement. A filed or recorded statement of denial operates as such a limitation on authority, thereby precluding reliance on an inconsistent grant of authority. Under Section 303(d), a filed or recorded cancellation of a statement of denial that operates as a limitation on authority revives the previous grant of authority.

Under Section 303(e), a recorded statement of denial of a partner's authority to transfer partnership real property held in the partnership name constitutes constructive knowledge of that limitation.

Section 305. Partnership Liable for Partner's Actionable Conduct.

(a) A partnership is liable for loss or injury caused to a person, or for a penalty incurred, as a result of a wrongful act or omission, or other actionable conduct, of a partner acting in the ordinary course of business of the partnership or with authority of the partnership.

(b) If, in the course of the partnership's business or while acting with authority of the partnership, a partner receives or causes the partnership to receive money or property of a person not a partner, and the money or property is misapplied by a partner, the partnership is liable for the loss.

Comment

Section 305(a), which is derived from UPA Section 13, imposes liability on the partnership for the wrongful acts of a partner acting in the ordinary course of the partnership's business or otherwise within the partner's authority. The scope of the section has been expanded by deleting from UPA Section 13, "not being a partner in the partnership." This is intended to permit a partner to sue the partnership on a tort or other theory during the term of the partnership, rather than being limited to the remedies of dissolution and an accounting. *See also* Comment 2 to Section 405.

The section has also been broadened to cover no-fault torts by the addition of the phrase, "or other actionable conduct."

The partnership is liable for the actionable conduct or omission of a partner acting in the ordinary course of its business or "with the authority of the partnership." This is intended to include a partner's apparent, as well as actual, authority, thereby bringing within Section 305(a) the situation covered in UPA Section 14(a).

The phrase in UPA Section 13, "to the same extent as the partner so acting or omitting to act" has been deleted to prevent a partnership from asserting a partner's immunity from liability. This is consistent with the general agency rule that a principal is not entitled to its agent's immunities. *See* Restatement (Second) of Agency § 217(b) (1957). The deletion is not intended to limit a partnership's contractual rights.

Section 305(b) is drawn from UPA Section 14(b), but has been edited to improve clarity. It imposes strict liability on the partnership for the misapplication of money or property received by a partner in the course of the partnership's business or otherwise within the scope of the partner's actual authority.

Section 306. Partner's Liability.

(a) Except as otherwise provided in ~~subsection~~ subsections (b) and (c), all partners are liable jointly and severally for all obligations of the partnership unless otherwise agreed by the claimant or provided by law.

(b) A person admitted as a partner into an existing partnership is not personally liable for any partnership obligation incurred before the person's admission as a partner.

(c) An obligation of a partnership incurred while the partnership is a limited liability partnership, whether arising in contract, tort, or otherwise, is solely the obligation of the partnership. A partner is not personally liable, directly or indirectly, by way of contribution or otherwise, for such a partnership obligation solely by reason of being or so acting as a partner. This subsection applies notwithstanding anything inconsistent in the partnership agreement that existed immediately before the vote required to become a limited liability partnership under Section 1001(b).

Comment

1. Section 306(a) changes the UPA rule by imposing joint and several liability on the partners for all partnership obligations where the partnership is not a limited liability partnership. Under UPA Section 15, partners' liability for torts is joint and several, while their liability for contracts is joint but not several. About ten States that have adopted the UPA already provide for joint and several liability. The UPA reference to "debts and obligations" is redundant and no change is intended by RUPA's reference solely to "obligations."

Joint and several liability under RUPA differs, however, from the classic model, which permits a judgment creditor to proceed immediately against any of the joint and several judgment debtors. Generally, Section 307(d) requires the judgment creditor to exhaust the partnership's assets before enforcing a judgment against the separate assets of a partner.

2. RUPA continues the UPA scheme of liability with respect to an incoming partner, but states the rule more clearly and simply. Under Section 306(a), an incoming partner becomes jointly and severally liable, as a partner, for all partnership obligations, except as otherwise provided in subsection (b). That subsection eliminates an incoming partner's personal liability for partnership obligations incurred before his admission as a partner. In effect, a new partner has no personal liability to existing creditors of the partnership, and only his investment in the firm is at risk for the satisfaction of existing partnership debts. That is presently the rule under UPA Sections 17 and 41(7), and no substantive change is intended. As under the UPA, a new partner's personal assets are at risk with respect to partnership liabilities incurred after his admission as a partner.

3. Subsection (c) alters classic joint and several liability of general partners for obligations of a partnership that is a limited liability partnership. Like shareholders of a corporation and members of a limited liability company, partners of a limited liability partnership are not personally liable for partnership obligations incurred while the partnership liability shield is in place solely because they are partners. As with shareholders of a corporation and members of a limited liability company, partners remain personally liable for their personal misconduct.

In cases of partner misconduct, Section 401(c) sets forth a partnership's obligation to indemnify the culpable partner where the partner's liability was incurred in the ordinary course of the partnership's business. When indemnification occurs, the assets of both the partnership and the culpable partner are available to a creditor. However, Sections 306(c), 401(b), and 807(b) make clear that a partner who is not otherwise liable under Section 306(c) is not obligated to contribute assets to the partnership in excess of agreed contributions to share the loss with the culpable partner. (See Comments to Sections 401(b) and 807(b), regarding a slight variation in the context of priority of payment of partnership obligations.) Accordingly, Section 306(c) makes clear that an innocent partner is not personally liable for specified partnership obligations, directly or indirectly, by way of contribution or otherwise.

Although the liability shield protections of Section 306(c) may be modified in part or in full in a partnership agreement (and by way of private contractual guarantees), the modifications must constitute an intentional waiver of the liability protections. See Sections 103(b), 104(a), and 902(b). Since the mere act of filing a statement of qualification reflects the assumption that the partners intend to modify the otherwise applicable partner liability rules, the final sentence of subsection (c) makes clear that the filing negates inconsistent aspects of the partnership agreement that existed immediately before the vote to approve becoming a limited liability partnership. The negation only applies to a partner's personal liability for future partnership obligations. The filing however has no effect as to previously created partner obligations to the partnership in the form of specific capital contribution requirements.

Inter se contribution agreements may erode part or all of the effects of the liability shield. For example, Section 807(f) provides that an assignee for the benefit of creditors of a partnership or a partner may enforce a partner's obligation to contribute to the partnership. The ultimate effect of such contribution obligations may make each partner jointly and severally liable for all partnership obligations — even those incurred while the partnership is a limited liability partnership. Although the final sentence of subsection (c) negates such provisions existing before a statement of qualification is filed, it will have no effect on any amendments to the partnership agreement after the statement is filed.

The connection between partner status and personal liability for partnership obligations is severed only with respect to obligations incurred while the partnership is a limited liability partnership. Partnership obligations incurred before a partnership becomes a limited liability partnership or incurred after limited liability partnership status is revoked or canceled are treated as obligations of an ordinary partnership. See Sections 1001 (filing), 1003 (revocation), and 1006 (cancellation). Obligations incurred by a partnership during the period when its statement of qualification is administratively revoked will be considered as incurred by a limited liability partnership provided the partnership's status as such is reinstated within two years under Section 1003(e). See Section 1003(f).

When an obligation is incurred is determined by other law. See Section 104(a). Under that law, and for the limited purpose of determining when partnership contract obligations are incurred, the reasonable expectations of creditors and the partners are paramount. Therefore, partnership obligations under or relating to a note, contract, or other agreement generally are incurred when the note, contract, or other agreement is made. Also, an amendment, modification, extension, or renewal of a note, contract, or other agreement should not affect or otherwise reset the time at which a partnership obligation under or relating to that note, contract, or other agreement is incurred, even as to a claim that relates to the subject matter of the amendment, modification, extension, or renewal. A note, contract, or other agreement may expressly modify these rules and fix the time a partnership obligation is incurred thereunder.

For the limited purpose of determining when partnership tort obligations are incurred, a distinction is intended between injury and the conduct causing that injury. The purpose of the distinction is to prevent unjust results. Partnership obligations under or relating to a tort generally are incurred when the tort conduct occurs rather than at the time of the actual injury or harm. This interpretation prevents a culpable partnership from engaging in wrongful conduct and then filing a statement of qualification to sever the vicarious responsibility of its partners for future injury or harm caused by conduct that occurred prior to the filing.

Section 307. Actions By and Against Partnership and Partners.

(a) A partnership may sue and be sued in the name of the partnership.

(b) An action may be brought against the partnership and, to the extent not inconsistent with Section 306, any or all of the partners in the same action or in separate actions.

(c) A judgment against a partnership is not by itself a judgment against a partner. A judgment against a partnership may not be satisfied from a partner's assets unless there is also a judgment against the partner.

(d) A judgment creditor of a partner may not levy execution against the assets of the partner to satisfy a judgment based on a claim against the partnership unless the partner is personally liable for the claim under Section 306 and:

(1) a judgment based on the same claim has been obtained against the partnership and a writ of execution on the judgment has been returned unsatisfied in whole or in part;

(2) the partnership is a debtor in bankruptcy;

(3) the partner has agreed that the creditor need not exhaust partnership assets;

(4) a court grants permission to the judgment creditor to levy execution against the assets of a partner based on a finding that partnership assets subject to execution are clearly insufficient to satisfy the judgment, that exhaustion of partnership assets is excessively burdensome, or that the grant of permission is an appropriate exercise of the court's equitable powers; or

(5) liability is imposed on the partner by law or contract independent of the existence of the partnership.

(e) This section applies to any partnership liability or obligation resulting from a representation by a partner or purported partner under Section 308.

Comment

1. Section 307 is new. Subsection (a) provides that a partnership may sue and be sued in the partnership name. That entity approach is designed to simplify suits by and against a partnership.

At common law, a partnership, not being a legal entity, could not sue or be sued in the firm name. The UPA itself is silent on this point, so in the absence of another enabling statute, it is generally necessary to join all the partners in an action against the partnership.

Most States have statutes or rules authorizing partnerships to sue or be sued in the partnership name. Many of those statutes, however, are found in the state provisions dealing with civil procedure rather than in the partnership act.

2. Subsection (b) provides that suit generally may be brought against the partnership and any or all of the partners in the same action or in separate actions. It is intended to clarify that the partners need not be named in an action against the partnership. In particular, in an action against a partnership, it is not necessary to name a partner individually in addition to the partnership. This will simplify and reduce the cost of litigation, especially in cases of small claims where there are known to be significant partnership assets and thus no necessity to collect the judgment out of the partners' assets.

Where the partnership is a limited liability partnership, the limited liability partnership rules clarify that a partner not liable for the alleged partnership obligation may not be named in the action against the partnership unless the action also seeks to establish personal liability of the partner for the obligation. See subsections (b) and (d).

3. Subsection (c) provides that a judgment against the partnership is not, standing alone, a judgment against the partners, and it cannot be satisfied from a partner's personal assets unless there is a judgment against the partner. Thus, a partner must be individually named and served, either in the action against the partnership or in a later suit, before his personal assets may be subject to levy for a claim against the partnership.

RUPA leaves it to the law of judgments, as did the UPA, to determine the collateral effects to be accorded a prior judgment for or against the partnership in a subsequent action against a partner individually. *See* Section 60 of the Second Restatement of Judgments (1982) and the Comments thereto.

4. Subsection (d) requires partnership creditors to exhaust the partnership's assets before levying on a judgment debtor partner's individual property where the partner is personally liable for the partnership obligation under Section 306. That rule respects the concept of the partnership as an entity and makes partners more in the nature of guarantors than principal debtors on every partnership debt. It is already the law in some States.

As a general rule, a final judgment against a partner cannot be enforced by a creditor against the partner's separate assets unless a writ of execution against the partnership has been returned unsatisfied. Under subsection (d), however, a creditor may proceed directly against the partner's assets if (i) the partnership is a debtor in bankruptcy (see Section 101(2)); (ii) the partner has consented; or (iii) the liability is imposed on the partner independently of the partnership. For example, a judgment creditor may proceed directly against the assets of a partner who is liable independently as the primary tortfeasor, but must exhaust the partnership's assets before proceeding against the separate assets of the other partners who are liable only as partners.

There is also a judicial override provision in subsection (d)(4). A court may authorize execution against the partner's assets on the grounds that (i) the partnership's assets are clearly insufficient; (ii) exhaustion of the partnership's assets would be excessively burdensome; or (iii) it is otherwise equitable to do so. For example, if the partners who are parties to the action have assets located in the forum State, but the partnership does not, a court might find that exhaustion of the partnership's assets would be excessively burdensome.

5. Although subsection (d) is silent with respect to pre-judgment remedies, the law of pre-judgment remedies already adequately embodies the principle that partnership assets should be exhausted before partners' assets are attached or garnished. Attachment, for example, typically requires a showing that the partnership's assets are being secreted or fraudulently transferred or are otherwise inadequate to satisfy the plaintiff's claim. A showing of some exigent circumstance may also be required to satisfy due process. *See Connecticut v. Doehr*, 501 U.S. 1, 16 (1991).

6. Subsection (e) clarifies that actions against the partnership under Section 308, involving representations by partners or purported partners, are subject to Section 307.

Section 308. Liability of Purported Partner.

(a) If a person, by words or conduct, purports to be a partner, or consents to being represented by another as a partner, in a partnership or with one or more persons not partners, the purported partner is liable to a person to whom the representation is made, if that person, relying on the representation, enters into a transaction with the actual or purported partnership. If the representation, either by the purported partner or by a person with the purported partner's consent, is made in a public manner, the purported partner is liable to a person who relies upon the purported partnership even if the purported partner is not aware of being held out as a partner to the claimant. If partnership liability results, the purported partner is liable with respect to that liability as if the purported partner were a partner. If no partnership liability results, the purported partner is liable with respect to that liability jointly and severally with any other person consenting to the representation.

(b) If a person is thus represented to be a partner in an existing partnership, or with one or more persons not partners, the purported partner is an agent of persons consenting to the representation to bind them to the same extent and in the same manner as if the purported partner were a partner, with respect to persons who enter into transactions in reliance upon the representation. If all of the partners of the existing partnership consent to the representation, a partnership act or obligation results. If fewer than all of the partners of the existing partnership consent to the representation, the person acting and the partners consenting to the representation are jointly and severally liable.

(c) A person is not liable as a partner merely because the person is named by another in a statement of partnership authority.

(d) A person does not continue to be liable as a partner merely because of a failure to file a statement of dissociation or to amend a statement of partnership authority to indicate the partner's dissociation from the partnership.

(e) Except as otherwise provided in subsections (a) and (b), persons who are not partners as to each other are not liable as partners to other persons.

Comment

Section 308 continues the basic principles of partnership by estoppel from UPA Section 16, now more accurately entitled "Liability of Purported Partner." Subsection (a) continues the distinction between representations made to specific persons and those made in a public manner. It is the exclusive basis for imposing liability as a partner on persons who are not partners in fact. As under the UPA, there is no duty of denial, and thus a person held out by another as a partner is not liable unless he actually consents to the representation. *See* the Official Comment to UPA Section 16. Also see Section 308(c) (no duty to file statement of denial) and Section 308(d) (no duty to file statement of dissociation or to amend statement of partnership authority).

Subsection (b) emphasizes that the persons being protected by Section 308 are those who enter into transactions in reliance upon a representation. If all of the partners of an existing partnership consent to the representation, a partnership obligation results. Apart from Section 308, the firm may be bound in other situations under general principles of apparent authority or ratification.

If a partnership liability results under Section 308, the creditor must exhaust the partnership's assets before seeking to satisfy the claim from the partners. *See* Section 307.

Subsections (c) and (d) are new and deal with potential negative inferences to be drawn from a failure to correct inaccurate or outdated filed statements. Subsection (c) makes clear that an otherwise innocent person is not liable as a partner for failing to deny his partnership status as asserted by a third person in a statement of partnership authority. Under Subsection (d), a partner's liability as a partner does not continue after dissociation solely because of a failure to file a statement of dissociation.

Subsection (e) is derived from UPA Section 7(1). It means that only those persons who are partners as among themselves are liable as partners to third parties for the obligations of the partnership, except for liabilities incurred by purported partners under Section 308(a) and (b).

[ARTICLE] 4

RELATIONS OF PARTNERS TO EACH OTHER
AND TO PARTNERSHIP

Section 401. Partner's Rights and Duties.
Section 402. Distributions in Kind.
Section 403. Partner's Rights and Duties with Respect to Information.
Section 404. General Standards of Partner's Conduct.
Section 405. Actions by Partnership and Partners.
Section 406. Continuation of Partnership Beyond Definite Term or Particular Undertaking.

Section 401. Partner's Rights and Duties.

(a) Each partner is deemed to have an account that is:

(1) credited with an amount equal to the money plus the value of any other property, net of the amount of any liabilities, the partner contributes to the partnership and the partner's share of the partnership profits; and

(2) charged with an amount equal to the money plus the value of any other property, net of the amount of any liabilities, distributed by the partnership to the partner and the partner's share of the partnership losses.

(b) Each partner is entitled to an equal share of the partnership profits and is chargeable with a share of the partnership losses in proportion to the partner's share of the profits.

(c) A partnership shall reimburse a partner for payments made and indemnify a partner for liabilities incurred by the partner in the ordinary course of the business of the partnership or for the preservation of its business or property.

(d) A partnership shall reimburse a partner for an advance to the partnership beyond the amount of capital the partner agreed to contribute.

(e) A payment or advance made by a partner which gives rise to a partnership obligation under subsection (c) or (d) constitutes a loan to the partnership which accrues interest from the date of the payment or advance.

(f) Each partner has equal rights in the management and conduct of the partnership business.

(g) A partner may use or possess partnership property only on behalf of the partnership.

(h) A partner is not entitled to remuneration for services performed for the partnership except for reasonable compensation for services rendered in winding up the business of the partnership.

(i) A person may become a partner only with the consent of all of the partners.

(j) A difference arising as to a matter in the ordinary course of business of a partnership may be decided by a majority of the partners. An act outside the ordinary course of business of a partnership and an amendment to the partnership agreement may be undertaken only with the consent of all of the partners.

(k) This section does not affect the obligations of a partnership to other persons under Section 301.

Comment

1. Section 401 is drawn substantially from UPA Section 18. It establishes many of the default rules that govern the relations among partners. All of these rules are, however, subject to contrary agreement of the partners as provided in Section 103.

2. Subsection (a) provides that each partner is deemed to have an account that is credited with the partner's contributions and share of the partnership profits and charged with distributions to the partner and the partner's share of partnership losses. In the absence of another system of partnership accounts, these rules establish a rudimentary system of accounts for the partnership. The rules regarding the settlement of the partners' accounts upon the dissolution and winding up of the partnership business are found in Section 807.

3. Subsection (b) establishes the default rules for the sharing of partnership profits and losses. The UPA Section 18(a) rules that profits are shared equally and that losses, whether capital or operating, are shared in proportion to each partner's share of the profits are continued. Thus, under the default rule, partners share profits per capita and not in proportion to capital contribution as do corporate shareholders or partners in limited partnerships. Compare RULPA Section 504. With respect to losses, the qualifying phrase, "whether capital or operating," has been deleted as inconsistent with contemporary partnership accounting practice and terminology; no substantive change is intended.

If partners agree to share profits other than equally, losses will be shared similarly to profits, absent agreement to do otherwise. That rule, carried over from the UPA, is predicated on the assumption that partners would likely agree to share losses on the same basis as profits, but may fail to say so. Of course, by agreement, they may share losses on a different basis from profits.

The default rules apply, as does UPA Section 18(a), where one or more of the partners contribute no capital, although there is case law to the contrary. *See, e.g.,* *Kovacik v. Reed*, 49 Cal. 2d 166, 315 P.2d 314 (1957); *Becker v. Killarney*, 177 Ill. App. 3d 793, 523 N.E.2d 467 (1988). It may seem unfair that the contributor of services, who contributes little or no capital, should be obligated to contribute toward the capital loss of the large contributor who contributed no services. In entering a partnership with such a capital structure, the partners should foresee that application of the default rule may bring about unusual results and take advantage of their power to vary by agreement the allocation of capital losses.

Subsection (b) provides that each partner "is chargeable" with a share of the losses, rather than the UPA formulation that each partner shall "contribute" to losses. Losses are charged to each partner's account as provided in subsection (a)(2). It is intended to make clear that a partner is not obligated to contribute to partnership losses before his withdrawal or the liquidation of the partnership, unless the partners agree otherwise. In effect, <u>unless related to an obligation for which the partner is not personally liable under Section 306(c),</u> a partner's negative account represents a debt to the partnership unless the partners agree to the contrary. Similarly, each partner's share of the profits is credited to his account under subsection (a)(1). Absent an agreement to the contrary, however, a partner does not have a right to receive a current distribution of the profits credited to his account, the interim distribution of profits being a matter arising in the ordinary course of business to be decided by majority vote of the partners.

<u>However, where a liability to contribute at dissolution and winding up relates to a partnership obligation governed by the limited liability rule of Section 306(c), a partner is not obligated to contribute additional assets even at dissolution and winding up. See Section 807(b). In such a case, although a partner is not personally liable for the partnership obligation, that partner's interest in the partnership remains at risk. See also Comment to Section 401(c) relating to indemnification.</u>

<u>In the case of an operating limited liability partnership, the Section 306 liability shield may be partially eroded where the limited liability partnership incurs both shielded and unshielded liabilities. Where the limited liability partnership uses its assets to pay shielded liabilities before paying unshielded liabilities, each partner's obligation to contribute to the limited liability partnership for that partner's share of the unpaid and unshielded obligations at dissolution and winding up remains intact. The same issue is less likely to occur in the context of the termination of a limited liability partnership since a partner's contribution obligation is based only on that partner's share of unshielded obligations and the partnership will ordinarily use the contributed assets to pay unshielded claims first as they were the basis of the contribution obligations. See Comments to Section 807(b).</u>

4. Subsection (c) is derived from UPA Section 18(b) and provides that the partnership shall reimburse partners for payments made and indemnify them for liabilities incurred in the ordinary course of the partnership's business or for the preservation of its business or property. Reimbursement and indemnification is an obligation of the partnership. Indemnification may create a loss toward which the partners must contribute. Although the right to indemnification is usually enforced in the settlement of accounts among partners upon dissolution and winding up of the partnership business, the right accrues when the liability is incurred and thus may be enforced during the term of the partnership in an appropriate case. *See* Section 405 and Comment. <u>A partner's right to indemnification under this Act is not affected by</u>

the partnership becoming a limited liability partnership. Accordingly, partners continue to share partnership losses to the extent of partnership assets.

5. Subsection (d) is based on UPA Section 18(c). It makes explicit that the partnership must reimburse a partner for an advance of funds beyond the amount of the partner's agreed capital contribution, thereby treating the advance as a loan.

6. Subsection (e), which is also drawn from UPA Section 18(c), characterizes the partnership's obligation under subsections (c) or (d) as a loan to the partnership which accrues interest from the date of the payment or advance. *See* Section 104(b) (default rate of interest).

7. Under subsection (f), each partner has equal rights in the management and conduct of the business. It is based on UPA Section 18(e), which has been interpreted broadly to mean that, absent contrary agreement, each partner has a continuing right to participate in the management of the partnership and to be informed about the partnership business, even if his assent to partnership business decisions is not required. There are special rules regarding the partner vote necessary to approve a partnership becoming (or canceling its status as) a limited liability partnership. See Section 1001(b).

8. Subsection (g) provides that partners may use or possess partnership property only for partnership purposes. That is the edited remains of UPA Section 25(2)(a), which deals in detail with the incidents of tenancy in partnership. That tenancy is abolished as a consequence of the entity theory of partnerships. *See* Section 501 and Comments.

9. Subsection (h) continues the UPA Section 18(f) rule that a partner is not entitled to remuneration for services performed, except in winding up the partnership. Subsection (h) deletes the UPA reference to a "surviving" partner. That means any partner winding up the business is entitled to compensation, not just a surviving partner winding up after the death of another partner. The exception is not intended to apply in the hypothetical winding up that takes place if there is a buyout under Article 7.

10. Subsection (i) continues the substance of UPA Section 18(g) that no person can become a partner without the consent of all the partners.

11. Subsection (j) continues with one important clarification of the UPA Section 18(h) scheme of allocating management authority among the partners. In the absence of an agreement to the contrary, matters arising in the ordinary course of the business may be decided by a majority of the partners. Amendments to the partnership agreement and matters outside the ordinary course of the partnership business require unanimous consent of the partners. Although the text of the UPA is silent regarding extraordinary matters, courts have generally required the consent of all partners for those matters. *See, e.g., Paciaroni v. Crane*, 408 A.2d 946 (Del. Ch. 1989); *Thomas v. Marvin E. Jewell & Co.*, 232 Neb. 261, 440 N.W.2d 437 (1989); *Duell v. Hancock*, 83 A.D.2d 762, 443 N.Y.S.2d 490 (1981).

It is not intended that subsection (j) embrace a claim for an objection to a partnership decision that is not discovered until after the fact. There is no cause of action based on that after-the-fact second-guessing.

12. Subsection (k) is new and was added to make it clear that Section 301 governs partners' agency power to bind the partnership to third persons, while Section 401 governs partners' rights among themselves.

Section 402. Distributions in Kind.

A partner has no right to receive, and may not be required to accept, a distribution in kind.

Comment

Section 402 provides that a partner has no right to demand and receive a distribution in kind and may not be required to take a distribution in kind. That continues the "in kind" rule of UPA Section 38(1). The new language is suggested by RULPA Section 605.

This section is complemented by Section 807(a) which provides that, in winding up the partnership business on dissolution, any surplus after the payment of partnership obligations must be applied to pay in cash the net amount distributable to each partner.

Section 403. Partner's Rights and Duties with Respect to Information.

(a) A partnership shall keep its books and records, if any, at its chief executive office.

(b) A partnership shall provide partners and their agents and attorneys access to its books and records. It shall provide former partners and their agents and attorneys access to books and records pertaining to the period during which they were partners. The right of access provides the opportunity to inspect and copy books and records during ordinary business hours. A partnership may impose a reasonable charge, covering the costs of labor and material, for copies of documents furnished.

(c) Each partner and the partnership shall furnish to a partner, and to the legal representative of a deceased partner or partner under legal disability:

(1) without demand, any information concerning the partnership's business and affairs reasonably required for the proper exercise of the partner's rights and duties under the partnership agreement or this [Act]; and

(2) on demand, any other information concerning the partnership's business and affairs, except to the extent the demand or the information demanded is unreasonable or otherwise improper under the circumstances.

Comment

1. Subsection (a) provides that the partnership's books and records, if any shall be kept at its chief executive office. It continues the UPA Section 19 rule, modified to include partnership records other than its "books," i.e., financial records. The concept of "chief executive office" comes from UCC Section 9-103(3)(d). See the Comment to Section 106.

Since general partnerships are often informal or even inadvertent no books and records are enumerated as mandatory, such as that found in RULPA Section 105. Any requirement in UPA Section 19 that the partnership keep books is oblique at best, since it states merely where the books shall be kept, not that they shall be kept. Under RUPA, there is no liability to either partners or third parties for the failure to keep partnership books. A partner who undertakes to keep books, however, must do so accurately and adequately.

In general, a partnership should, at a minimum, keep those books and records necessary to enable the partners to determine their share of the profits and losses, as well as their rights on withdrawal. An action for an accounting provides an adequate remedy in the event adequate records are not kept. The partnership must also maintain any books and records required by state or federal taxing or other governmental authorities.

2. Under subsection (b), partners are entitled to access to the partnership books and records. Former partners are expressly given a similar right, although limited to the books and records pertaining to the period during which they were partners. The line between partners and former partners is not a bright one for this purpose, however, and should be drawn in light of the legitimate interests of a dissociated partner in the partnership. For example, a withdrawing partner's liability is ongoing for pre-withdrawal liabilities and will normally be extended to new liabilities for at least 90 days. It is intended that a former partner be accorded access to partnership books and records as reasonably necessary to protect that partner's legitimate interests during the period his rights and liabilities are being wound down.

The right of access is limited to ordinary business hours, and the right to inspect and copy by agent or attorney is made explicit. The partnership may impose a reasonable charge for furnishing copies of documents. *Accord*, RULPA § 105(b).

A partner's right to inspect and copy the partnership's books and records is not conditioned on the partner's purpose or motive. Compare RMBCA Section 16.02(c)(1) (shareholder must have proper purpose to inspect certain corporate records). A partner's unlimited personal liability justifies an unqualified right of access to the partnership books and records. An abuse of the right to inspect and copy might constitute a violation of the obligation of good faith and fair dealing for which the other partners would have a remedy. *See* Sections 404(d) and 405.

Under Section 103(b)(2), a partner's right of access to partnership books and records may not be unreasonably restricted by the partnership agreement. Thus, to preserve a partner's core information rights despite unequal bargaining power, an agreement limiting a partner's right to inspect and copy partnership books and records is subject to judicial review. Nevertheless, reasonable restrictions on access to partnership books and records by agreement are authorized. For example, a provision in a partnership agreement denying partners access to the compensation of other partners should be upheld, absent any abuse such as fraud or duress.

3. Subsection (c) is a significant revision of UPA Section 20 and provides a more comprehensive, although not exclusive, statement of partners' rights and duties with respect to partnership information other than books and records. Both the partnership and the other partners are obligated to furnish partnership information.

Paragraph (1) is new and imposes an affirmative disclosure obligation on the partnership and partners. There is no express UPA provision imposing an affirmative obligation to disclose any information other than the partnership books. Under some circumstances, however, an affirmative disclosure duty has been inferred from other sections of the Act, as well as from the common law, such as the fiduciary duty of good faith. Under UPA Section 18(e), for example, all partners enjoy an equal right in the management and conduct of the partnership business, absent contrary agreement. That right has been construed to require that every partner be provided with ongoing information concerning the partnership business. *See* Comment 7 to Section 401. Paragraph (1) provides expressly that partners must be furnished, without demand, partnership information reasonably needed for them to exercise their rights and duties as partners. In addition, a disclosure duty may, under some circumstances, also spring from the Section 404(d) obligation of good faith and fair dealing. *See* Comment 4 to Section 404.

Paragraph (2) continues the UPA rule that partners are entitled, on demand, to any other information concerning the partnership's business and affairs. The demand may be refused if either the demand or the information demanded is unreasonable or otherwise improper. That qualification is new to the statutory formulation. The burden is on the partnership or partner from whom the information is requested to show that the demand is unreasonable or improper. The UPA admonition that the information furnished be "true and full" has been deleted as unnecessary, and no substantive change is intended.

The Section 403(c) information rights can be waived or varied by agreement of the partners, since there is no Section 103(b) limitation on the variation of those rights as there is with respect to the Section 403(b) access rights to books and records. *See* Section 103(b)(2).

Section 404. General Standards of Partner's Conduct.

(a) The only fiduciary duties a partner owes to the partnership and the other partners are the duty of loyalty and the duty of care set forth in subsections (b) and (c).

(b) A partner's duty of loyalty to the partnership and the other partners is limited to the following:

    (1) to account to the partnership and hold as trustee for it any property, profit, or benefit derived by the partner in the conduct and winding up of the partnership business or derived from a use by the partner of partnership property, including the appropriation of a partnership opportunity;

    (2) to refrain from dealing with the partnership in the conduct or winding up of the partnership business as or on behalf of a party having an interest adverse to the partnership; and

    (3) to refrain from competing with the partnership in the conduct of the partnership business before the dissolution of the partnership.

(c) A partner's duty of care to the partnership and the other partners in the conduct and winding up of the partnership business is limited to refraining from engaging in grossly negligent or reckless conduct, intentional misconduct, or a knowing violation of law.

(d) A partner shall discharge the duties to the partnership and the other partners under this [Act] or under the partnership agreement and exercise any rights consistently with the obligation of good faith and fair dealing.

(e) A partner does not violate a duty or obligation under this [Act] or under the partnership agreement merely because the partner's conduct furthers the partner's own interest.

(f) A partner may lend money to and transact other business with the partnership, and as to each loan or transaction the rights and obligations of the partner are the same as those of a person who is not a partner, subject to other applicable law.

(g) This section applies to a person winding up the partnership business as the personal or legal representative of the last surviving partner as if the person were a partner.

Comment

1. Section 404 is new. The title, "General Standards of Partner's Conduct," is drawn from RMBCA Section 8.30. Section 404 is both comprehensive and exclusive. In that regard, it is structurally different from the UPA which touches only sparingly on a partner's duty of loyalty and leaves any further development of the fiduciary duties of partners to the common law of agency. Compare UPA Sections 4(3) and 21.

Section 404 begins by stating that the **only** fiduciary duties a partner owes to the partnership and the other partners are the duties of loyalty and care set forth in subsections (b) and (c) of the Act. Those duties may not be waived or eliminated in the partnership agreement, but the agreement may identify activities and determine standards for measuring performance of the duties, if not manifestly unreasonable. *See* Sections 103(b)(3)-(5).

Section 404 continues the term "fiduciary" from UPA Section 21, which is entitled "Partner Accountable as a Fiduciary." Arguably, the term "fiduciary" is inappropriate when used to describe the duties of a partner because a partner may legitimately pursue self-interest (see Section 404(e)) and not solely the interest of the partnership and the other partners, as must a true trustee. Nevertheless, partners have long been characterized as fiduciaries. *See, e.g., Meinhard v. Salmon*, 249 N.Y. 458, 463, 164 N.E. 545, 546 (1928) (Cardozo, J.). Indeed, the law of partnership reflects the broader law of principal and agent, under which every agent is a fiduciary. *See* Restatement (Second) of Agency § 13 (1957).

2. Section 404(b) provides three specific rules that comprise a partner's duty of loyalty. Those rules are exclusive and encompass the entire duty of loyalty.

Subsection (b)(1) is based on UPA Section 21(1) and continues the rule that partnership property usurped by a partner, including the misappropriation of a partnership opportunity, is held in trust for the partnership. The express reference to the appropriation of a partnership opportunity is new, but merely codifies case law on the point. *See, e.g., Meinhard v. Salmon, supra*; *Fouchek v. Janicek*, 190 Ore. 251, 225 P.2d 783 (1950). Under a constructive trust theory, the partnership can recover any money or property in the partner's hands that can be traced to the partnership. *See, e.g., Yoder v. Hooper*, 695 P.2d 1182 (Colo. App. 1984), *aff'd*, 737 P.2d 852 (Colo. 1987); *Fortugno v. Hudson Manure Co.*, 51 N.J. Super. 482, 144 A.2d 207 (1958); *Harestad v. Weitzel*, 242 Or. 199, 536 P.2d 522 (1975). As a result, the partnership's claim is greater than that of an ordinary creditor. *See* Official Comment to UPA Section 21.

UPA Section 21(1) imposes the duty on partners to account for profits and benefits in all transactions connected with "the formation, conduct, or liquidation of the partnership." Reference to the "formation" of the partnership has been eliminated by RUPA because of concern that the duty of loyalty could be inappropriately extended to the pre-formation period when the parties are really negotiating at arm's length. *Compare Herring v. Offutt*, 295 A.2d 876 (Ct. App. Md. 1972), *with Phoenix Mutual Life Ins. Co. v. Shady Grove Plaza Limited Partnership*, 734 F. Supp. 1181 (D. Md. 1990), *aff'd*, 937 F.2d 603 (4th Cir. 1991). Once a partnership is agreed to, each partner becomes a fiduciary in the "conduct" of the business. Pre-formation negotiations are, of course, subject to the general contract obligation to deal honestly and without fraud.

Upon a partner's dissociation, Section 603(b)(3) limits the application of the duty to account for personal profits to those derived from matters arising or events occurring before the dissociation, unless the partner participates in winding up the partnership's business. Thus, after withdrawal, a partner is free to appropriate to his own benefit any new business opportunity thereafter coming to his attention, even if the partnership continues.

Subsection (b)(2) provides that a partner must refrain from dealing with the partnership as or on behalf of a party having an interest adverse to the partnership. This rule is derived from Sections 389 and 391 of the Restatement (Second) of Agency. Comment c to Section 389 explains that the rule is not based upon the harm caused to the principal, but upon avoiding a conflict of opposing interests in the mind of an agent whose duty is to act for the benefit of his principal.

Upon a partner's dissociation, Section 603(b)(3) limits the application of the duty to refrain from representing interests adverse to the partnership to the same extent as the duty to account. Thus, after withdrawal, a partner may deal with the partnership as an adversary with respect to new matters or events.

Section 404(b)(3) provides that a partner must refrain from competing with the partnership in the conduct of its business. This rule is derived from Section 393 of the Restatement (Second) of Agency and is an application of the general duty of an agent to act solely on his principal's behalf.

The duty not to compete applies only to the "conduct" of the partnership business; it does not extend to winding up the business, as do the other loyalty rules. Thus, a partner is free to compete immediately upon an event of dissolution under Section 801, unless the partnership agreement otherwise provides. A partner who dissociates without a winding up of the business resulting is also free to compete, because Section 603(b)(2) provides that the duty not to compete terminates upon dissociation. A dissociated partner is not, however, free to use confidential partnership information after dissociation. *See* Restatement (Second) of Agency § 393 cmt. e (1957). Trade secret law also may apply. *See* the Uniform Trade Secrets Act.

Under Section 103(b)(3), the partnership agreement may not "eliminate" the duty of loyalty. Section 103(b)(3)(i) expressly empowers the partners, however, to identify specific types or categories of activities that do not violate the duty of loyalty, if not manifestly unreasonable. As under UPA Section 21, the other partners may also consent to a specific act or transaction that otherwise violates one of the rules. For the consent to be effective under Section 103(b)(3)(ii), there must be full disclosure of all material facts regarding the act or transaction and the partner's conflict of interest. *See* Comment 5 to Section 103.

3. Subsection (c) is new and establishes the duty of care that partners owe to the partnership and to the other partners. There is no statutory duty of care under the

UPA, although a common law duty of care is recognized by some courts. *See, e.g., Rosenthal v. Rosenthal*, 543 A.2d 348, 352 (Me. 1988) (duty of care limited to acting in a manner that does not constitute gross negligence or wilful misconduct).

The standard of care imposed by RUPA is that of gross negligence, which is the standard generally recognized by the courts. *See, e.g., Rosenthal v. Rosenthal, supra.* Section 103(b)(4) provides that the duty of care may not be eliminated entirely by agreement, but the standard may be reasonably reduced. *See* Comment 6 to Section 103.

4. Subsection (d) is also new. It provides that partners have an obligation of good faith and fair dealing in the discharge of all their duties, including those arising under the Act, such as their fiduciary duties of loyalty and care, and those arising under the partnership agreement. The exercise of any rights by a partner is also subject to the obligation of good faith and fair dealing. The obligation runs to the partnership and to the other partners in all matters related to the conduct and winding up of the partnership business.

The obligation of good faith and fair dealing is a contract concept, imposed on the partners because of the consensual nature of a partnership. *See* Restatement (Second) of Contracts § 205 (1981). It is not characterized, in RUPA, as a fiduciary duty arising out of the partners' special relationship. Nor is it a separate and independent obligation. It is an ancillary obligation that applies whenever a partner discharges a duty or exercises a right under the partnership agreement or the Act.

The meaning of "good faith and fair dealing" is not firmly fixed under present law. "Good faith" clearly suggests a subjective element, while "fair dealing" implies an objective component. It was decided to leave the terms undefined in the Act and allow the courts to develop their meaning based on the experience of real cases. Some commentators, moreover, believe that good faith is more properly understood by what it excludes than by what it includes. *See* Robert S. Summers, *"Good Faith" in General Contract Law and the Sales Provisions of the Uniform Commercial Code*, 54 Va. L. Rev. 195, 262 (1968):

> Good faith, as judges generally use the term in matters contractual, is best understood as an "excluder" a phrase with no general meaning or meanings of its own. Instead, it functions to rule out many different forms of bad faith. It is hard to get this point across to persons used to thinking that every word must have one or more general meanings of its own must be either univocal or ambiguous.

The UCC definition of "good faith" is honesty in fact and, in the case of a merchant, the observance of reasonable commercial standards of fair dealing in the trade. *See* UCC §§ 1-201(19), 2-103(b). Those definitions were rejected as too narrow or not applicable.

In some situations the obligation of good faith includes a disclosure component. Depending on the circumstances, a partner may have an affirmative disclosure obligation that supplements the Section 403 duty to render information.

Under Section 103(b)(5), the obligation of good faith and fair dealing may not be eliminated by agreement, but the partners by agreement may determine the standards by which the performance of the obligation is to be measured, if the standards are not manifestly unreasonable. *See* Comment 7 to Section 103.

5. Subsection (e) is new and deals expressly with a very basic issue on which the UPA is silent. A partner as such is not a trustee and is not held to the same standards as a trustee. Subsection (e) makes clear that a partner's conduct is not deemed to be improper merely because it serves the partner's own individual interest.

That admonition has particular application to the duty of loyalty and the obligation of good faith and fair dealing. It underscores the partner's rights as an owner and principal in the enterprise, which must always be balanced against his duties and obligations as an agent and fiduciary. For example, a partner who, with consent, owns a shopping center may, under subsection (e), legitimately vote against a proposal by the partnership to open a competing shopping center.

6. Subsection (f) authorizes partners to lend money to and transact other business with the partnership and, in so doing, to enjoy the same rights and obligations as a nonpartner. That language is drawn from RULPA Section 107. The rights and obligations of a partner doing business with the partnership as an outsider are expressly made subject to the usual laws governing those transactions. They include, for example, rules limiting or qualifying the rights and remedies of inside creditors, such as fraudulent transfer law, equitable subordination, and the law of avoidable preferences, as well as general debtor-creditor law. The reference to "other applicable law" makes clear that subsection (f) is not intended to displace those laws, and thus they are preserved under Section 104(a).

It is unclear under the UPA whether a partner may, for the partner's own account, purchase the assets of the partnership at a foreclosure sale or upon the liquidation of the partnership. Those purchases are clearly within subsection (f)'s broad approval. It is also clear under that subsection that a partner may purchase partnership assets at a foreclosure sale, whether the partner is the mortgagee or the mortgagee is an unrelated third party. Similarly, a partner may purchase partnership property at a tax sale. The obligation of good faith requires disclosure of the partner's interest in the transaction, however.

7. Subsection (g) provides that the prescribed standards of conduct apply equally to a person engaged in winding up the partnership business as the personal or legal representative of the last surviving partner, as if the person were a partner. This is derived from UPA Section 21(2), but now embraces the duty of care and the obligation of good faith and fair dealing, as well as the duty of loyalty.

Section 405. Actions by Partnership and Partners.

(a) A partnership may maintain an action against a partner for a breach of the partnership agreement, or for the violation of a duty to the partnership, causing harm to the partnership.

(b) A partner may maintain an action against the partnership or another partner for legal or equitable relief, with or without an accounting as to partnership business, to:

(1) enforce the partner's rights under the partnership agreement;

(2) enforce the partner's rights under this [Act], including:

(i) the partner's rights under Sections 401, 403, or 404;

(ii) the partner's right on dissociation to have the partner's interest in the partnership purchased pursuant to Section 701 or enforce any other right under [Article] 6 or 7; or

(iii) the partner's right to compel a dissolution and winding up of the partnership business under Section 801 or enforce any other right under [Article] 8; or

(3) enforce the rights and otherwise protect the interests of the partner, including rights and interests arising independently of the partnership relationship.

(c) The accrual of, and any time limitation on, a right of action for a remedy under this section is governed by other law. A right to an accounting upon a dissolution and winding up does not revive a claim barred by law.

Comment

1. Section 405(a) is new and reflects the entity theory of partnership. It provides that the partnership itself may maintain an action against a partner for any breach of the partnership agreement or for the violation of any duty owed to the partnership, such as a breach of fiduciary duty.

2. Section 405(b) is the successor to UPA Section 22, but with significant changes. At common law, an accounting was generally not available before dissolution. That was modified by UPA Section 22 which specifies certain circumstances in which an accounting action is available without requiring a partner to dissolve the partnership. Section 405(b) goes far beyond the UPA rule. It provides that, during the term of the partnership, partners may maintain a variety of legal or equitable actions, including an action for an accounting, as well as a final action for an accounting upon dissolution and winding up. It reflects a new policy choice that partners should have access to the courts during the term of the partnership to resolve claims against the partnership and the other partners, leaving broad judicial discretion to fashion appropriate remedies.

Under RUPA, an accounting is not a prerequisite to the availability of the other remedies a partner may have against the partnership or the other partners. That change reflects the increased willingness courts have shown to grant relief without the requirement of an accounting, in derogation of the so-called "exclusivity rule." *See, e.g., Farney v. Hauser*, 109 Kan. 75, 79, 198 Pac. 178, 180 (1921) ("[F]or all practical purposes a partnership may be considered as a business entity"); *Auld v. Eastridge*, 86 Misc. 2d 895, 901, 382 N.Y.S.2d 897, 901 (1976) ("No purpose of justice is served by delaying the resolution here on empty procedural grounds").

Under subsection (b), a partner may bring a direct suit against the partnership or another partner for almost any cause of action arising out of the conduct of the partnership business. That eliminates the present procedural barriers to suits between partners filed independently of an accounting action. In addition to a formal account, the court may grant any other appropriate legal or equitable remedy. Since general partners are not passive investors like limited partners, RUPA does not authorize derivative actions, as does RULPA Section 1001.

Subsection (b)(3) makes it clear that a partner may recover against the partnership and the other partners for personal injuries or damage to the property of the partner caused by another partner. *See, e.g., Duffy v. Piazza Construction Co.*, 815 P.2d 267 (Wash. App. 1991); *Smith v. Hensley*, 354 S.W.2d 744 (Ky. App.). One partner's negligence is not imputed to bar another partner's action. *See, e.g., Reeves v. Harmon*, 475 P.2d 400 (Okla. 1970); *Eagle Star Ins. Co. v. Bean*, 134 F.2d 755 (9th

Cir. 1943) (fire insurance company not subrogated to claim against partners who negligently caused fire that damaged partnership property).

3. Generally, partners may limit or contract away their Section 405 remedies. They may not, however, eliminate entirely the remedies for breach of those duties that are mandatory under Section 103(b). *See* Comment 1 to Section 103.

4. Section 405(c) replaces UPA Section 43 and provides that other (i.e., non-partnership) law governs the accrual of a cause of action for which subsection (b) provides a remedy. The statute of limitations on such claims is also governed by other law, and claims barred by a statute of limitations are not revived by reason of the partner's right to an accounting upon dissolution, as they were under the UPA. The effect of those rules is to compel partners to litigate their claims during the life of the partnership or risk losing them. Because an accounting is an equitable proceeding, it may also be barred by laches where there is an undue delay in bringing the action. Under general law, the limitations periods may be tolled by a partner's fraud.

5. UPA Section 39 grants ancillary remedies to a person who rescinds his participation in a partnership because it was fraudulently induced, including the right to a lien on surplus partnership property for the amount of that person's interest in the partnership. RUPA has no counterpart provision to UPA Section 39, and leaves it to the general law of rescission to determine the rights of a person fraudulently induced to invest in a partnership. *See* Section 104(a).

Section 406. Continuation of Partnership Beyond Definite Term or Particular Undertaking.

(a) If a partnership for a definite term or particular undertaking is continued, without an express agreement, after the expiration of the term or completion of the undertaking, the rights and duties of the partners remain the same as they were at the expiration or completion, so far as is consistent with a partnership at will.

(b) If the partners, or those of them who habitually acted in the business during the term or undertaking, continue the business without any settlement or liquidation of the partnership, they are presumed to have agreed that the partnership will continue.

Comment

Section 406 continues UPA Section 23, with no substantive change. Subsection (a) provides that, if a term partnership is continued without an express agreement beyond the expiration of its term or the completion of the undertaking, the partners' rights and duties remain the same as they were, so far as is consistent with a partnership at will.

Subsection (b) provides that if the partnership is continued by the partners without any settlement or liquidation of the business, it is presumed that the partners have agreed not to wind up the business. The presumption is rebuttable. If the partnership is continued under this subsection, there is no dissolution under Section 801(2)(iii). As a partnership at will, however, the partnership may be dissolved under Section 801(1) at any time.

[ARTICLE] 5

TRANSFEREES AND CREDITORS OF PARTNER

Section 501. Partner Not Co-Owner of Partnership Property.
Section 502. Partner's Transferable Interest in Partnership.
Section 503. Transfer of Partner's Transferable Interest.
Section 504. Partner's Transferable Interest Subject to Charging Order.

Section 501. Partner Not Co-Owner of Partnership Property.

A partner is not a co-owner of partnership property and has no interest in partnership property which can be transferred, either voluntarily or involuntarily.

Comment

Section 501 provides that a partner is not a co-owner of partnership property and has no interest in partnership property that can be transferred, either voluntarily or involuntarily. Thus, the section abolishes the UPA Section 25(1) concept of tenants in partnership and reflects the adoption of the entity theory. Partnership property is owned by the entity and not by the individual partners. See also Section 203, which provides that property transferred to or otherwise acquired by the partnership is property of the partnership and not of the partners individually.

RUPA also deletes the references in UPA Sections 24 and 25 to a partner's "right in specific partnership property," although those rights are largely defined away by the detailed rules of UPA Section 25 itself. Thus, it is clear that a partner who misappropriates partnership property is guilty of embezzlement the same as a shareholder who misappropriates corporate property.

Adoption of the entity theory also has the effect of protecting partnership property from execution or other process by a partner's personal creditors. That continues the result under UPA Section 25(2)(c). Those creditors may seek a charging order under Section 504 to reach the partner's transferable interest in the partnership.

RUPA does not interfere with a partner's exemption claim in nonpartnership property. As under the UPA, disputes over whether specific property belongs to the partner or to the firm will likely arise in the context of an exemption claim by a partner.

A partner's spouse, heirs, or next of kin are not entitled to allowances or other rights in partnership property. That continues the result under UPA Section 25(2)(e).

Section 502. Partner's Transferable Interest in Partnership.

The only transferable interest of a partner in the partnership is the partner's share of the profits and losses of the partnership and the partner's right to receive distributions. The interest is personal property.

Comment

Section 502 continues the UPA Section 26 concept that a partner's only transferable interest in the partnership is the partner's share of profits and losses and right to receive distributions, that is, the partner's financial rights. The term "distribution" is defined in Section 101(3). Compare RULPA Section 101(10) ("partnership interest").

The partner's transferable interest is deemed to be personal property, regardless of the nature of the underlying partnership assets.

Under Section 503(b)(3), a transferee of a partner's transferable interest has standing to seek judicial dissolution of the partnership business.

A partner has other interests in the partnership that may not be transferred, such as the right to participate in the management of the business. Those rights are included in the broader concept of a "partner's interest in the partnership." *See* Section 101(7).

Section 503. Transfer of Partner's Transferable Interest.

(a) A transfer, in whole or in part, of a partner's transferable interest in the partnership:

(1) is permissible;

(2) does not by itself cause the partner's dissociation or a dissolution and winding up of the partnership business; and

(3) does not, as against the other partners or the partnership, entitle the transferee, during the continuance of the partnership, to participate in the management or conduct of the partnership business, to require access to information concerning partnership transactions, or to inspect or copy the partnership books or records.

(b) A transferee of a partner's transferable interest in the partnership has a right:

(1) to receive, in accordance with the transfer, distributions to which the transferor would otherwise be entitled;

(2) to receive upon the dissolution and winding up of the partnership business, in accordance with the transfer, the net amount otherwise distributable to the transferor; and

(3) to seek under Section 801(6) a judicial determination that it is equitable to wind up the partnership business.

(c) In a dissolution and winding up, a transferee is entitled to an account of partnership transactions only from the date of the latest account agreed to by all of the partners.

(d) Upon transfer, the transferor retains the rights and duties of a partner other than the interest in distributions transferred.

(e) A partnership need not give effect to a transferee's rights under this section until it has notice of the transfer.

(f) A transfer of a partner's transferable interest in the partnership in violation of a restriction on transfer contained in the partnership agreement is ineffective as to a person having notice of the restriction at the time of transfer.

Comment

1. Section 503 is derived from UPA Section 27. Subsection (a)(1) states explicitly that a partner has the right to transfer his transferable interest in the partnership. The term "transfer" is used throughout RUPA in lieu of the term "assignment." *See* Section 101(10).

Subsection (a)(2) continues the UPA Section 27(1) rule that an assignment of a partner's interest in the partnership does not of itself cause a winding up of the partnership business. Under Section 601(4)(ii), however, a partner who has transferred substantially all of his partnership interest may be expelled by the other partners.

Subsection (a)(3), which is also derived from UPA Section 27(1), provides that a transferee is not as against the other partners, entitled (i) to participate in the management or conduct of the partnership business; (ii) to inspect the partnership books or records; or (iii) to require any information concerning or an account of partnership transactions.

2. The rights of a transferee are set forth in subsection (b). Under subsection (b)(1), which is derived from UPA Section 27(1), a transferee is entitled to receive, in accordance with the terms of the assignment, any distributions to which the transferor would otherwise have been entitled under the partnership agreement before dissolution. After dissolution, the transferee is also entitled to receive, under subsection (b)(2), the net amount that would otherwise have been distributed to the transferor upon the winding up of the business.

Subsection (b)(3) confers standing on a transferee to seek a judicial dissolution and winding up of the partnership business as provided in Section 801(6), thus continuing the rule of UPA Section 32(2).

Section 504(b) accords the rights of a transferee to the purchaser at a sale foreclosing a charging order. The same rule should apply to creditors or other purchasers who acquire partnership interests by pursuing UCC remedies or statutory liens under federal or state law.

3. Subsection (c) is based on UPA Section 27(2). It grants to transferees the right to an account of partnership transactions, limited to the period since the date of the last account agreed to by all of the partners.

4. Subsection (d) is new. It makes clear that unless otherwise agreed the partner whose interest is transferred retains all of the rights and duties of a partner, other than the right to receive distributions. That means the transferor is entitled to participate in the management of the partnership and remains personally liable for all partnership obligations, unless and until he withdraws as a partner, is expelled under Section 601(4)(ii), or is otherwise dissociated under Section 601.

A divorced spouse of a partner who is awarded rights in the partner's partnership interest as part of a property settlement is entitled only to the rights of a transferee. The spouse may instead be granted a money judgment in the amount of the property award, enforceable by a charging order in the same manner as any other money judgment against a partner. In neither case, however, would the spouse become a partner by virtue of the property settlement or succeed to any of the partner's management rights. *See, e.g., Warren v. Warren,* 12 Ark. App. 260, 675 S.W.2d 371 (1984).

5. Subsection (e) is new and provides that the partnership has no duty to give effect to the transferee's rights until the partnership receives notice of the transfer. This is consistent with UCC Section 9-318(3), which provides that an "account debtor" is authorized to pay the assignor until the account debtor receives notification that the amount due or to become due has been assigned and that payment is to be

made to the assignee. It further provides that the assignee, on request, must furnish reasonable proof of the assignment.

6. Subsection (f) is new and provides that a transfer of a partner's transferable interest in the partnership in violation of a restriction on transfer contained in a partnership agreement is ineffective as to a person with timely notice of the restriction. Under Section 103(a), the partners may agree among themselves to restrict the right to transfer their partnership interests. Subsection (f) makes explicit that a transfer in violation of such a restriction is ineffective as to a transferee with notice of the restriction. *See* Section 102(b) for the meaning of "notice." RUPA leaves to general law and the UCC the issue of whether a transfer in violation of a valid restriction is effective as to a transferee without notice of the restriction.

Whether a particular restriction will be enforceable, however, must be considered in light of other law. *See* 11 U.S.C. § 541(c)(1) (property owned by bankrupt passes to trustee regardless of restrictions on transfer); UCC § 9-318(4) (agreement between account debtor and assignor prohibiting creation of security interest in a general intangible or requiring account debtor's consent is ineffective); *Battista v. Carlo*, 57 Misc. 2d 495, 293 N.Y.S.2d 227 (1968) (restriction on transfer of partnership interest subject to rules against unreasonable restraints on alienation of property) (dictum); *Tupper v. Kroc*, 88 Nev. 146, 494 P.2d. 1275 (1972) (partnership interest subject to charging order even if partnership agreement prohibits assignments). *Cf. Tu-Vu Drive-In Corp. v. Ashkins*, 61 Cal. 2d 283, 38 Cal. Rptr. 348, 391 P.2d 828 (1964) (restraints on transfer of corporate stock must be reasonable). Even if a restriction on the transfer of a partner's transferable interest in a partnership were held to be unenforceable, the transfer might be grounds for expelling the partner-transferor from the partnership under Section 601(5)(ii).

7. Other rules that apply in the case of transfers include Section 601(4)(ii) (expulsion of partner who transfers substantially all of partnership interest); Section 601(6) (dissociation of partner who makes an assignment for benefit of creditors); and Section 801(6) (transferee has standing to seek judicial winding up).

Section 504. Partner's Transferable Interest Subject to Charging Order.

(a) On application by a judgment creditor of a partner or of a partner's transferee, a court having jurisdiction may charge the transferable interest of the judgment debtor to satisfy the judgment. The court may appoint a receiver of the share of the distributions due or to become due to the judgment debtor in respect of the partnership and make all other orders, directions, accounts, and inquiries the judgment debtor might have made or which the circumstances of the case may require.

(b) A charging order constitutes a lien on the judgment debtor's transferable interest in the partnership. The court may order a foreclosure of the interest subject to the charging order at any time. The purchaser at the foreclosure sale has the rights of a transferee.

(c) At any time before foreclosure, an interest charged may be redeemed:

(1) by the judgment debtor;

(2) with property other than partnership property, by one or more of the other partners; or

(3) with partnership property, by one or more of the other partners with the consent of all of the partners whose interests are not so charged.

(d) This [Act] does not deprive a partner of a right under exemption laws with respect to the partner's interest in the partnership.

(e) This section provides the exclusive remedy by which a judgment creditor of a partner or partner's transferee may satisfy a judgment out of the judgment debtor's transferable interest in the partnership.

Comment

1. Section 504 continues the UPA Section 28 charging order as the proper remedy by which a judgment creditor of a partner may reach the debtor's transferable interest in a partnership to satisfy the judgment. Subsection (a) makes the charging order available to the judgment creditor of a transferee of a partnership interest. Under Section 503(b), the transferable interest of a partner or transferee is limited to the partner's right to receive distributions from the partnership and to seek judicial liquidation of the partnership. The court may appoint a receiver of the debtor's share of the distributions due or to become due and make all other orders that may be required.

2. Subsection (b) is new and codifies the case law under the UPA holding that a charging order constitutes a lien on the debtor's transferable interest. The lien may be foreclosed by the court at any time, and the purchaser at the foreclosure sale has the Section 503(b) rights of a transferee. For a general discussion of the charging order remedy, see I *Alan R. Bromberg & Larry E. Ribstein, Partnership* (1988), at 3:69.

3. Subsection (c) continues the UPA Section 28(2) right of the debtor or other partners to redeem the partnership interest before the foreclosure sale. Redemption by the partnership (i.e., with partnership property) requires the consent of all the remaining partners. Neither the UPA nor RUPA provide a statutory procedural framework for the redemption.

4. Subsection (d) provides that nothing in RUPA deprives a partner of his rights under the State's exemption laws. That is essentially the same as UPA Section 28(3).

5. Subsection (e) provides that the charging order is the judgment creditor's exclusive remedy. Although the UPA nowhere states that a charging order is the exclusive process for a partner's individual judgment creditor, the courts have generally so interpreted it. *See, e.g., Matter of Pischke*, 11 B.R. 913 (E.D. Va. 1981); *Baum v. Baum*, 51 Cal. 2d 610, 335 P.2d 481 (1959); *Atlantic Mobile Homes, Inc. v. LeFever*, 481 So. 2d 1002 (Fla. App. 1986).

Notwithstanding subsection (e), there may be an exception for the enforcement of family support orders. Some States have unique statutory procedures for the enforcement of support orders. In Florida, for example, a court may issue an "income deduction order" requiring any person or entity providing "income" to the obligor of a support order to remit to the obligee or a depository, as directed by the court, a specified portion of the income. Fla. Stat. § 61.1301 (1993). "Income" is broadly defined to include any form of payment to the obligor, including wages, salary, compensation as an independent contractor, dividends, interest, or other payment, regardless of source. Fla. Stat. § 61.046(4) (1993). That definition includes distributions payable to an obligor partner. A charging order under RUPA would still be necessary to reach the obligor's entire partnership interest, however.

[ARTICLE] 6

PARTNER'S DISSOCIATION

Section 601. Events Causing Partner's Dissociation.
Section 602. Partner's Power to Dissociate; Wrongful Dissociation.
Section 603. Effect of Partner's Dissociation.

Section 601. Events Causing Partner's Dissociation.

A partner is dissociated from a partnership upon the occurrence of any of the following events:

(1) the partnership's having notice of the partner's express will to withdraw as a partner or on a later date specified by the partner;

(2) an event agreed to in the partnership agreement as causing the partner's dissociation;

(3) the partner's expulsion pursuant to the partnership agreement;

(4) the partner's expulsion by the unanimous vote of the other partners if:

(i) it is unlawful to carry on the partnership business with that partner;

(ii) there has been a transfer of all or substantially all of that partner's transferable interest in the partnership, other than a transfer for security purposes, or a court order charging the partner's interest, which has not been foreclosed;

(iii) within 90 days after the partnership notifies a corporate partner that it will be expelled because it has filed a certificate of dissolution or the equivalent, its charter has been revoked, or its right to conduct business has been suspended by the jurisdiction of its incorporation, there is no revocation of the certificate of dissolution or no reinstatement of its charter or its right to conduct business; or

(iv) a partnership that is a partner has been dissolved and its business is being wound up;

(5) on application by the partnership or another partner, the partner's expulsion by judicial determination because:

(i) the partner engaged in wrongful conduct that adversely and materially affected the partnership business;

(ii) the partner willfully or persistently committed a material breach of the partnership agreement or of a duty owed to the partnership or the other partners under Section 404; or

(iii) the partner engaged in conduct relating to the partnership business which makes it not reasonably practicable to carry on the business in partnership with the partner;

(6) the partner's:

(i) becoming a debtor in bankruptcy;

(ii) executing an assignment for the benefit of creditors;

(iii) seeking, consenting to, or acquiescing in the appointment of a trustee, receiver, or liquidator of that partner or of all or substantially all of that partner's property; or

(iv) failing, within 90 days after the appointment, to have vacated or stayed the appointment of a trustee, receiver, or liquidator of the partner or of all or substantially all of the partner's property obtained without the partner's consent or acquiescence, or failing within 90 days after the expiration of a stay to have the appointment vacated;

(7) in the case of a partner who is an individual:

(i) the partner's death;

(ii) the appointment of a guardian or general conservator for the partner; or

(iii) a judicial determination that the partner has otherwise become incapable of performing the partner's duties under the partnership agreement;

(8) in the case of a partner that is a trust or is acting as a partner by virtue of being a trustee of a trust, distribution of the trust's entire transferable interest in the partnership, but not merely by reason of the substitution of a successor trustee;

(9) in the case of a partner that is an estate or is acting as a partner by virtue of being a personal representative of an estate, distribution of the estate's entire transferable interest in the partnership, but not merely by reason of the substitution of a successor personal representative; or

(10) termination of a partner who is not an individual, partnership, corporation, trust, or estate.

Comment

1. RUPA dramatically changes the law governing partnership breakups and dissolution. An entirely new concept, "dissociation," is used in lieu of the UPA term "dissolution" to denote the change in the relationship caused by a partner's ceasing to be associated in the carrying on of the business. "Dissolution" is retained but with a different meaning. *See* Section 802. The entity theory of partnership provides a conceptual basis for continuing the firm itself despite a partner's withdrawal from the firm.

Under RUPA, unlike the UPA, the dissociation of a partner does not necessarily cause a dissolution and winding up of the business of the partnership. Section 801 identifies the situations in which the dissociation of a partner causes a winding up of the business. Section 701 provides that in all other situations there is a buyout of the partner's interest in the partnership, rather than a windup of the partnership business. In those other situations, the partnership entity continues, unaffected by the partner's dissociation.

A dissociated partner remains a partner for some purposes and still has some residual rights, duties, powers, and liabilities. Although Section 601 determines when a partner is dissociated from the partnership, the consequences of the partner's dissociation do not all occur at the same time. Thus, it is more useful to think of a dissociated partner as a partner for some purposes, but as a former partner for others. For example, see Section 403(b) (former partner's access to partnership books and records). The consequences of a partner's dissociation depend on whether the partnership continues or is wound up, as provided in Articles 6, 7, and 8.

Section 601 enumerates all of the events that cause a partner's dissociation. Section 601 is similar in approach to RULPA Section 402, which lists the events resulting in a general partner's withdrawal from a limited partnership.

2. Section 601(1) provides that a partner is dissociated when the partnership has notice of the partner's express will to withdraw as a partner, unless a later date is specified by the partner. If a future date is specified by the partner, other partners may dissociate before that date; specifying a future date does not bind the others to remain as partners until that date. *See* also Section 801(2)(i).

Section 602(a) provides that a partner has the power to withdraw at any time. The power to withdraw is immutable under Section 103(b)(6), with the exception that the partners may agree the notice must be in writing. This continues the present rule that a partner has the power to withdraw at will, even if not the right. *See* UPA Section 31(2). Since no writing is required to create a partner relationship, it was felt unnecessarily formalistic, and a trap for the unwary, to require a writing to end one. If a written notification is given, Section 102(d) clarifies when it is deemed received.

RUPA continues the UPA "express will" concept, thus preserving existing case law. Section 601(1) clarifies existing law by providing that the partnership must have notice of the partner's expression of will before the dissociation is effective. See Section 102(b) for the meaning of "notice."

3. Section 601(2) provides expressly that a partner is dissociated upon an event agreed to in the partnership agreement as causing dissociation. There is no such provision in the UPA, but that result has been assumed.

4. Section 601(3) provides that a partner may be expelled by the other partners pursuant to a power of expulsion contained in the partnership agreement. That continues the basic rule of UPA Section 31(1)(d). The expulsion can be with or without cause. As under existing law, the obligation of good faith under Section 404(d) does not require prior notice, specification of cause, or an opportunity to be heard. *See Holman v. Coie*, 11 Wash. App. 195, 522 P.2d 515, *cert. denied*, 420 U.S. 984 (1974).

5. Section 601(4) empowers the partners, by unanimous vote, to expel a partner for specified causes, even if not authorized in the partnership agreement. This changes the UPA Section 31(1)(d) rule that authorizes expulsion only if provided in the partnership agreement. A partner may be expelled from a term partnership, as well as from a partnership at will. Under Section 103(a), the partnership agreement may change or abolish the partners' power of expulsion.

Subsection (4)(i) is derived from UPA Section 31(3). A partner may be expelled if it is unlawful to carry on the business with that partner. Section 801(4), on the other hand, provides that the partnership itself is dissolved and must be wound up if substantially all of the business is unlawful.

Subsection (4)(ii) provides that a partner may be expelled for transferring substantially all of his transferable interest in the partnership, other than as security for a loan. (He may, however, be expelled upon foreclosure.) This rule is derived from UPA Section 31(1)(c). To avoid the presence of an unwelcome transferee, the remaining partners may dissolve the partnership under Section 801(2)(ii), after first expelling the transferor partner. A transfer of a partner's entire interest may, in some circumstances, evidence the transferor's intention to withdraw under Section 601(1).

Subsection (4)(iii) provides for the expulsion of a corporate partner if it has filed a certificate of dissolution, its charter has been revoked, or its right to conduct business has been suspended, unless cured within 90 days after notice. This provision is derived from RULPA, Section 402(9). The cure proviso is important because charter revocation is very common in some States and partner status should not end merely because of a technical noncompliance with corporate law that can easily be cured. Withdrawal of a voluntarily filed notice of dissolution constitutes a cure.

Subsection (4)(iv) is the partnership analogue of paragraph (iii) and is suggested by RULPA Section 402(8). It provides that a partnership that is a partner may be expelled if it has been dissolved and its business is being wound up. It is intended that the right of expulsion not be triggered solely by the dissolution event, but only upon commencement of the liquidation process.

6. Section 601(5) empowers a court to expel a partner if it determines that the partner has engaged in specified misconduct. The enumerated grounds for judicial expulsion are based on the UPA Section 32(1) grounds for judicial dissolution. The application for expulsion may be brought by the partnership or any partner. The phrase "judicial determination" is intended to include an arbitration award, as well as any final court order or decree.

Subsection (5)(i) provides for the partner's expulsion if the court finds that the partner has engaged in wrongful conduct that adversely and materially affected the partnership business. That language is derived from UPA Section 32(1)(c).

Subsection (5)(ii) provides for expulsion if the court determines that the partner wilfully or persistently committed a material breach of the partnership agreement or of a duty owed to the partnership or to the other partners under Section 404. That would include a partner's breach of fiduciary duty. Paragraph (ii), together with paragraph (iii), carry forward the substance of UPA Section 32(1)(d).

Subsection (5)(iii) provides for judicial expulsion of a partner who engaged in conduct relating to the partnership business that makes it not reasonably practicable to carry on the business in partnership with that partner. Expulsion for such misconduct makes the partner's dissociation wrongful under Section 602(a)(ii) and may also support a judicial decree of dissolution under Section 801(5)(ii).

7. Section 601(6) provides that a partner is dissociated upon becoming a debtor in bankruptcy or upon taking or suffering other action evidencing the partner's insolvency or lack of financial responsibility.

Subsection (6)(i) is derived from UPA Section 31(5), which provides for dissolution upon a partner's bankruptcy. *Accord* RULPA § 402(4)(ii). There is some doubt as to whether UPA Section 31(1) is limited to so-called "straight bankruptcy" under Chapter 7 or includes other bankruptcy relief, such as Chapter 11. Under RUPA Section 101(2), however, "debtor in bankruptcy" includes a person who files a voluntary petition, or against whom relief is ordered in an involuntary case, under any chapter of the Bankruptcy Code.

Initially, upon the filing of the bankruptcy petition, the debtor partner's transferable interest in the partnership will pass to the bankruptcy trustee as property of the estate under Section 541(a)(1) of the Bankruptcy Code, notwithstanding any restrictions on transfer provided in the partnership agreement. In most Chapter 7 cases, that will result in the eventual buyout of the partner's interest.

The application of various provisions of the federal Bankruptcy Code to Section 601(6)(i) is unclear. In particular, there is uncertainty as to the validity of UPA Section 31(5), and thus its RUPA counterpart, under Sections 365(e) and 541(c)(1) of the Bankruptcy Code. Those sections generally invalidate so-called *ipso facto* laws that cause a termination or modification of the debtor's contract or property rights because of the bankruptcy filing. As a consequence, RUPA Section 601(6)(i), which provides for a partner's dissociation by operation of law upon becoming a debtor in bankruptcy, may be invalid under the Supremacy Clause. *See, e.g., In the Matter of Phillips*, 966 F.2d 926 (5th Cir. 1992); *In re Cardinal Industries, Inc.*, 105 B.R. 385 (Bankr. S.D. Ohio 1989), 116 B.R. 964 (Bankr. S.D. Ohio 1990); *In re Corky Foods Corp.*, 85 B.R. 903 (Bankr. S.D. Fla. 1988). *But see, In re Catron*, 158 B.R. 629 (E.D. Va. 1993) (partnership agreement could not be assumed by debtor under Bankruptcy Code § 365(c)(1) because other partners excused by UPA from accepting performance by or rendering performance to party other than debtor and buyout option not invalid *ipso facto* clause under Code § 365 (e)), *aff'd per curiam*, 25 F.3d 1038 (4th Cir. 1994). RUPA reflects the policy choice, as a matter of state partnership law, that a partner be dissociated upon becoming a debtor in bankruptcy.

Subsection (6)(ii) is new and provides for dissociation upon a general assignment for the benefit of a partner's creditors. The UPA says nothing about an assignment for the benefit of creditors or the appointment of a trustee, receiver, or liquidator. Subsection (6)(iii) and (iv) cover the latter and are based substantially on RULPA Section 402(4) and (5).

8. UPA Section 31(4) provides for the dissolution of a partnership upon the death of any partner, although by agreement the remaining partners may continue the partnership business. RUPA Section 601(7)(i), on the other hand, provides for dissociation upon the death of a partner who is an individual, rather than dissolution of the partnership. That changes existing law, except in those States previously adopting a similar non-uniform provision, such as California, Georgia, and Texas. Normally, under RUPA, the deceased partner's transferable interest in the partnership will pass to his estate and be bought out under Article 7.

Section 601(7)(ii) replaces UPA Section 32(1)(a) and provides for dissociation upon the appointment of a guardian or general conservator for partner who is an individual. The appointment itself operates as the event of dissociation, and no further order of the court is necessary.

Section 601(7)(iii) is based on UPA Section 32(1)(b) and provides for dissociation upon a judicial determination that an individual partner has in any other way become incapable of performing his duties under the partnership agreement. The intent is to include physical incapacity.

9. Section 601(8) is new and provides for the dissociation of a partner that is a trust, or is acting as a partner by virtue of being a trustee of a trust, upon the distribution by the trust of its entire transferable interest in the partnership, but not merely upon the substitution of a successor trustee. The provision is inspired by RULPA Section 402(7).

10. Section 601(9) is new and provides for the dissociation of a partner that is an estate, or is acting as a partner by virtue of being a personal representative of an

estate, upon the distribution of the estate's entire transferable interest in the partnership, but not merely the substitution of a successor personal representative. It is based on RULPA Section 402(10). Under Section 601(7), a partner is dissociated upon death, however, and the estate normally becomes a transferee, not a partner.

11. Section 601(10) is new and provides that a partner that is not an individual, partnership, corporation, trust, or estate is dissociated upon its termination. It is the comparable "death" analogue for other types of entity partners, such as a limited liability company.

Section 602. Partner's Power to Dissociate; Wrongful Dissociation.

(a) A partner has the power to dissociate at any time, rightfully or wrongfully, by express will pursuant to Section 601(1).

(b) A partner's dissociation is wrongful only if:

(1) it is in breach of an express provision of the partnership agreement; or

(2) in the case of a partnership for a definite term or particular undertaking, before the expiration of the term or the completion of the undertaking:

(i) the partner withdraws by express will, unless the withdrawal follows within 90 days after another partner's dissociation by death or otherwise under Section 601(6) through (10) or wrongful dissociation under this subsection;

(ii) the partner is expelled by judicial determination under Section 601(5);

(iii) the partner is dissociated by becoming a debtor in bankruptcy; or

(iv) in the case of a partner who is not an individual, trust other than a business trust, or estate, the partner is expelled or otherwise dissociated because it willfully dissolved or terminated.

(c) A partner who wrongfully dissociates is liable to the partnership and to the other partners for damages caused by the dissociation. The liability is in addition to any other obligation of the partner to the partnership or to the other partners.

Comment

1. Subsection (a) states explicitly what is implicit in UPA Section 31(2) and RUPA Section 601(1) that a partner has the power to dissociate at any time by expressing a will to withdraw, even in contravention of the partnership agreement. The phrase "rightfully or wrongfully" reflects the distinction between a partner's power to withdraw in contravention of the partnership agreement and a partner's **right** to do so. In this context, although a partner cannot be enjoined from exercising the power to dissociate, the dissociation may be wrongful under subsection (b).

2. Subsection (b) provides that a partner's dissociation is wrongful only if it results from one of the enumerated events. The significance of a wrongful dissociation is that it may give rise to damages under subsection (c) and, if it results in the dissolution of the partnership, the wrongfully dissociating partner is not entitled to participate in winding up the business under Section 804.

Under subsection (b), a partner's dissociation is wrongful if (1) it breaches an express provision of the partnership agreement or (2), in a term partnership, before the expiration of the term or the completion of the undertaking (i) the partner voluntarily withdraws by express will, except a withdrawal following **another** partner's wrongful dissociation or dissociation by death or otherwise under Section 601(6) through (10); (ii) the partner is expelled for misconduct under

Section 601(5); (iii) the partner becomes a debtor in bankruptcy (see Section 101(2)); or (iv) a partner that is an entity (other than a trust or estate) is expelled or otherwise dissociated because its dissolution or termination was willful. Since subsection (b) is merely a default rule, the partnership agreement may eliminate or expand the dissociations that are wrongful or modify the effects of wrongful dissociation.

The exception in subsection (b)(2)(i) is intended to protect a partner's reactive withdrawal from a term partnership after the premature departure of another partner, such as the partnership's rainmaker or main supplier of capital, under the same circumstances that may result in the dissolution of the partnership under Section 801(2)(i). Under that section, a term partnership is dissolved 90 days after the bankruptcy, incapacity, death (or similar dissociation of a partner that is an entity), or wrongful dissociation of any partner, unless a majority in interest (see Comment 5(i) to Section 801 for a discussion of the term "majority in interest") of the remaining partners agree to continue the partnership. Under Section 602(b)(2)(i), a partner's exercise of the right of withdrawal by express will under those circumstances is rendered "rightful," even if the partnership is continued by others, and does not expose the withdrawing partner to damages for wrongful dissociation under Section 602(c).

A partner wishing to withdraw prematurely from a term partnership for any other reason, such as another partner's misconduct, can avoid being treated as a wrongfully dissociating partner by applying to a court under Section 601(5)(iii) to have the offending partner expelled. Then, the partnership could be dissolved under Section 801(2)(i) or the remaining partners could, by unanimous vote, dissolve the partnership under Section 801(2)(ii).

3. Subsection (c) provides that a wrongfully dissociating partner is liable to the partnership and to the other partners for any damages caused by the wrongful nature of the dissociation. That liability is in addition to any other obligation of the partner to the partnership or to the other partners. For example, the partner would be liable for any damage caused by breach of the partnership agreement or other misconduct. The partnership might also incur substantial expenses resulting from a partner's premature withdrawal from a term partnership, such as replacing the partner's expertise or obtaining new financing. The wrongfully dissociating partner would be liable to the partnership for those and all other expenses and damages that are causally related to the wrongful dissociation.

Section 701(c) provides that any damages for wrongful dissociation may be offset against the amount of the buyout price due to the partner under Section 701(a), and Section 701(h) provides that a partner who wrongfully dissociates from a term partnership is not entitled to payment of the buyout price until the term expires.

Under UPA Section 38(2)(c)(II), in addition to an offset for damages, the goodwill value of the partnership is excluded in determining the value of a wrongfully dissociating partner's partnership interest. Under RUPA, however, unless the partnership's goodwill is damaged by the wrongful dissociation, the value of the wrongfully dissociating partner's interest will include any goodwill value of the partnership. If the firm's goodwill is damaged, the amount of the damages suffered by the partnership and the remaining partners will be offset against the buyout price. *See* Section 701 and Comments.

Section 603. Effect of Partner's Dissociation.

(a) If a partner's dissociation results in a dissolution and winding up of the partnership business, [Article] 8 applies; otherwise, [Article] 7 applies.

(b) Upon a partner's dissociation:

(1) the partner's right to participate in the management and conduct of the partnership business terminates, except as otherwise provided in Section 803;

(2) the partner's duty of loyalty under Section 404(b)(3) terminates; and

(3) the partner's duty of loyalty under Section 404(b)(1) and (2) and duty of care under Section 404(c) continue only with regard to matters arising and events occurring before the partner's dissociation, unless the partner participates in winding up the partnership's business pursuant to Section 803.

Comment

1. Section 603(a) is a "switching" provision. It provides that, after a partner's dissociation, the partner's interest in the partnership must be purchased pursuant to the buyout rules in Article 7 unless there is a dissolution and winding up of the partnership business under Article 8. Thus, a partner's dissociation will always result in either a buyout of the dissociated partner's interest or a dissolution and winding up of the business.

By contrast, under the UPA, every partner dissociation results in the dissolution of the partnership, most of which trigger a right to have the business wound up unless the partnership agreement provides otherwise. *See* UPA § 38. The only exception in which the remaining partners have a statutory right to continue the business is when a partner wrongfully dissolves the partnership in breach of the partnership agreement. *See* UPA § 38(2)(b).

2. Section 603(b) is new and deals with some of the internal effects of a partner's dissociation. Subsection (b)(1) makes it clear that one of the consequences of a partner's dissociation is the immediate loss of the right to participate in the management of the business, unless it results in a dissolution and winding up of the business. In that case, Section 804(a) provides that all of the partners who have not wrongfully dissociated may participate in winding up the business.

Subsection (b)(2) and (3) clarify a partner's fiduciary duties upon dissociation. No change from current law is intended. With respect to the duty of loyalty, the Section 404(b)(3) duty not to compete terminates upon dissociation, and the dissociated partner is free immediately to engage in a competitive business, without any further consent. With respect to the partner's remaining loyalty duties under Section 404(b) and duty of care under Section 404(c), a withdrawing partner has a continuing duty after dissociation, but it is limited to matters that arose or events that occurred before the partner dissociated. For example, a partner who leaves a brokerage firm may immediately compete with the firm for new clients, but must exercise care in completing on-going client transactions and must account to the firm for any fees received from the old clients on account of those transactions. As the last clause makes clear, there is no contraction of a dissociated partner's duties under subsection (b)(3) if the partner thereafter participates in the dissolution and winding up the partnership's business.

[ARTICLE] 7

PARTNER'S DISSOCIATION WHEN
BUSINESS NOT WOUND UP

Section 701. Purchase of Dissociated Partner's Interest.

(a) If a partner is dissociated from a partnership without resulting in a dissolution and winding up of the partnership business under Section 801, the partnership shall cause the dissociated partner's interest in the partnership to be purchased for a buyout price determined pursuant to subsection (b).

(b) The buyout price of a dissociated partner's interest is the amount that would have been distributable to the dissociating partner under Section 807(b) if, on the date of dissociation, the assets of the partnership were sold at a price equal to the greater of the liquidation value or the value based on a sale of the entire business as a going concern without the dissociated partner and the partnership were wound up as of that date. Interest must be paid from the date of dissociation to the date of payment.

(c) Damages for wrongful dissociation under Section 602(b), and all other amounts owing, whether or not presently due, from the dissociated partner to the partnership, must be offset against the buyout price. Interest must be paid from the date the amount owed becomes due to the date of payment.

(d) A partnership shall indemnify a dissociated partner whose interest is being purchased against all partnership liabilities, whether incurred before or after the dissociation, except liabilities incurred by an act of the dissociated partner under Section 702.

(e) If no agreement for the purchase of a dissociated partner's interest is reached within 120 days after a written demand for payment, the partnership shall pay, or cause to be paid, in cash to the dissociated partner the amount the partnership estimates to be the buyout price and accrued interest, reduced by any offsets and accrued interest under subsection (c).

(f) If a deferred payment is authorized under subsection (h), the partnership may tender a written offer to pay the amount it estimates to be the buyout price and accrued interest, reduced by any offsets under subsection (c), stating the time of payment, the amount and type of security for payment, and the other terms and conditions of the obligation.

(g) The payment or tender required by subsection (e) or (f) must be accompanied by the following:

(1) a statement of partnership assets and liabilities as of the date of dissociation;

(2) the latest available partnership balance sheet and income statement, if any;

(3) an explanation of how the estimated amount of the payment was calculated; and

(4) written notice that the payment is in full satisfaction of the obligation to purchase unless, within 120 days after the written notice, the dissociated partner commences an action to determine the buyout price, any offsets under subsection (c), or other terms of the obligation to purchase.

(h) A partner who wrongfully dissociates before the expiration of a definite term or the completion of a particular undertaking is not entitled to payment of any portion of the buyout price until the expiration of the term or completion of the undertaking, unless the partner establishes to the satisfaction of the court that earlier payment will not cause undue hardship to the business of the partnership. A deferred payment must be adequately secured and bear interest.

(i) A dissociated partner may maintain an action against the partnership, pursuant to Section 405(b)(2)(ii), to determine the buyout price of that partner's interest, any offsets under subsection (c), or other terms of the obligation to purchase. The action must be commenced within 120 days after the partnership has tendered payment or an offer to pay or within one year after written demand for payment if no payment or offer to pay is tendered. The court shall determine the buyout price of the dissociated partner's interest, any offset due under subsection (c), and accrued interest, and enter judgment for any additional payment or refund. If deferred payment is authorized under subsection (h), the court shall also determine the security for payment and other terms of the obligation to purchase. The court may assess reasonable attorney's fees and the fees and expenses of appraisers or other experts for a party to the action, in amounts the court finds equitable, against a party that the court finds acted arbitrarily, vexatiously, or not in good faith. The finding may be based on the partnership's failure to tender payment or an offer to pay or to comply with subsection (g).

Comment

1. Article 7 is new and provides for the buyout of a dissociated partner's interest in the partnership when the partner's dissociation does not result in a dissolution and winding up of its business under Article 8. *See* Section 603(a). If there is no dissolution, the remaining partners have a right to continue the business and the dissociated partner has a right to be paid the value of his partnership interest. These rights can, of course, be varied in the partnership agreement. *See* Section 103. A dissociated partner has a continuing relationship with the partnership and third parties as provided in Sections 603(b), 702, and 703. *See also* Section 403(b) (former partner's access to partnership books and records).

2. Subsection (a) provides that, if a partner's dissociation does not result in a windup of the business, the partnership shall cause the interest of the dissociating partner to be purchased for a buyout price determined pursuant to subsection (b). The buyout is mandatory. The "cause to be purchased" language is intended to accommodate a purchase by the partnership, one or more of the remaining partners, or a third party.

For federal income tax purposes, a payment to a partner for his interest can be characterized either as a purchase of the partner's interest or as a liquidating distribution. The two have different tax consequences. RUPA permits either option by providing that the payment may come from either the partnership, some or all of the continuing partners, or a third party purchaser.

3. Subsection (b) provides how the "buyout price" is to be determined. The terms "fair market value" or "fair value" were not used because they are often considered terms of art having a special meaning depending on the context, such as in tax or corporate law. "Buyout price" is a new term. It is intended that the term be developed as an independent concept appropriate to the partnership buyout situation, while drawing on valuation principles developed elsewhere.

Under subsection (b), the buyout price is the amount that would have been distributable to the dissociating partner under Section 807(b) if, on the date of dissociation, the assets of the partnership were sold at a price equal to the greater of liquidation value or going concern value without the departing partner. Liquidation value is not intended to mean distress sale value. Under general principles of valuation, the hypothetical selling price in either case should be the price that a willing and informed buyer would pay a willing and informed seller, with neither being under any compulsion to deal. The notion of a minority discount in determining the buyout price is negated by valuing the business as a going concern. Other discounts, such as for a lack of marketability or the loss of a key partner, may be appropriate, however.

Since the buyout price is based on the value of the business at the time of dissociation, the partnership must pay interest on the amount due from the date of dissociation until payment to compensate the dissociating partner for the use of his interest in the firm. Section 104(b) provides that interest shall be at the legal rate unless otherwise provided in the partnership agreement. The UPA Section 42 option of electing a share of the profits in lieu of interest has been eliminated.

UPA Section 38(2)(c)(II) provides that the good will of the business not be considered in valuing a wrongfully dissociating partner's interest. The forfeiture of good will rule is implicitly rejected by RUPA. *See* Section 602(c) and Comment 3.

The Section 701 rules are merely default rules. The partners may, in the partnership agreement, fix the method or formula for determining the buyout price and all of the other terms and conditions of the buyout right. Indeed, the very right to a buyout itself may be modified, although a provision providing for a complete forfeiture would probably not be enforceable. *See* Section 104(a).

4. Subsection (c) provides that the partnership may offset against the buyout price all amounts owing by the dissociated partner to the partnership, whether or not presently due, including any damages for wrongful dissociation under Section 602(c). This has the effect of accelerating payment of amounts not yet due from the departing partner to the partnership, including a long-term loan by the partnership to the dissociated partner. Where appropriate, the amounts not yet due should be discounted to present value. A dissociating partner, on the other hand, is not entitled to an add-on for amounts owing to him by the partnership. Thus, a departing partner who has made a long-term loan to the partnership must wait for repayment, unless the terms of the loan agreement provide for acceleration upon dissociation.

It is not intended that the partnership's right of setoff be construed to limit the amount of the damages for the partner's wrongful dissociation and any other amounts owing to the partnership to the value of the dissociated partner's interest. Those amounts may result in a net sum due to the partnership from the dissociated partner.

5. Subsection (d) follows the UPA Section 38 rule and provides that the partnership must indemnify a dissociated partner against all partnership liabilities, whether incurred before or after the dissociation, except those incurred by the dissociated partner under Section 702.

6. Subsection (e) provides that, if no agreement for the purchase of the dissociated partner's interest is reached within 120 days after the dissociated partner's written demand for payment, the partnership must pay, or cause to be paid, in cash the amount it estimates to be the buyout price, adjusted for any offsets allowed and accrued interest. Thus, the dissociating partner will receive in cash within 120 days of dissociation the undisputed minimum value of the partner's partnership interest. If the dissociated partner claims that the buyout price should be higher, suit may thereafter be brought as provided in subsection (i) to have the amount of the buyout price determined by the court. This is similar to the procedure for determining the value of dissenting shareholders' shares under RMBCA Sections 13.20-13.28.

The "cause to be paid" language of subsection (a) is repeated here to permit either the partnership, one or more of the continuing partners, or a third-party purchaser to tender payment of the estimated amount due.

7. Subsection (f) provides that, when deferred payment is authorized in the case of a wrongfully dissociating partner, a written offer stating the amount the partnership estimates to be the purchase price should be tendered within the 120-day period, even though actual payment of the amount may be deferred, possibly for many years. *See* Comment 8. The dissociated partner is entitled to know at the time of dissociation what amount the remaining partners think is due, including the estimated amount of any damages allegedly caused by the partner's wrongful dissociation that may be offset against the buyout price.

8. Subsection (g) provides that the payment of the estimated price (or tender of a written offer under subsection (f)) by the partnership must be accompanied by (1) a statement of the partnership's assets and liabilities as of the date of the partner's dissociation; (2) the latest available balance sheet and income statement, if the partnership maintains such financial statements; (3) an explanation of how the estimated amount of the payment was calculated; and (4) a written notice that the payment will be in full satisfaction of the partnership's buyout obligation unless the dissociated partner commences an action to determine the price within 120 days of the notice. Subsection (g) is based in past on the dissenters' rights provisions of RMBCA Section 13.25(b).

Those disclosures should serve to identify and narrow substantially the items of dispute between the dissociated partner and the partnership over the valuation of the partnership interest. They will also serve to pin down the parties as to their claims of partnership assets and values and as to the existence and amount of all known liabilities. *See* Comment 4. Lastly, it will force the remaining partners to consider thoughtfully the difficult and important questions as to the appropriate method of valuation under the circumstances, and in particular, whether they should use going concern or liquidation value. Simply getting that information on the record in a timely fashion should increase the likelihood of a negotiated resolution of the parties' differences during the 120-day period within which the dissociated partner must bring suit.

9. Subsection (h) replaces UPA Section 38(2)(c) and provides a somewhat different rule for payment to a partner whose dissociation before the expiration of a definite term or the completion of a particular undertaking is wrongful under Section 602(b). Under subsection (h), a wrongfully dissociating partner is not entitled to receive any portion of the buyout price before the expiration of the term or completion of the undertaking, unless the dissociated partner establishes to the satisfaction of the court that earlier payment will not cause undue hardship to the business of the partnership. In all other cases, there must be an immediate payment in cash.

10. Subsection (i) provides that a dissociated partner may maintain an action against the partnership to determine the buyout price, any offsets, or other terms of the purchase obligation. The action must be commenced within 120 days after the partnership tenders payment of the amount it estimates to be due or, if deferred payment is authorized, its written offer. This provision creates a 120-day "cooling off" period. It also allows the parties an opportunity to negotiate their differences after disclosure by the partnership of its financial statements and other required information.

If the partnership fails to tender payment of the estimated amount due (or a written offer, if deferred payment is authorized), the dissociated partner has one year after written demand for payment in which to commence suit.

If the parties fail to reach agreement, the court must determine the buyout price of the partner's interest, any offsets, including damages for wrongful dissociation, and the amount of interest accrued. If payment to a wrongfully dissociated partner is deferred, the court may also require security for payment and determine the other terms of the obligation.

Under subsection (i), attorney's fees and other costs may be assessed against any party found to have acted arbitrarily, vexatiously, or not in good faith in connection with the valuation dispute, including the partnership's failure to tender payment of the estimated price or to make the required disclosures. This provision is based in part on RMBCA Section 13.31(b).

Section 702. Dissociated Partner's Power to Bind and Liability to Partnership.

(a) For two years after a partner dissociates without resulting in a dissolution and winding up of the partnership business, the partnership, including a surviving partnership under [Article] 9, is bound by an act of the dissociated partner which would have bound the partnership under Section 301 before dissociation only if at the time of entering into the transaction the other party:

(1) reasonably believed that the dissociated partner was then a partner;

(2) did not have notice of the partner's dissociation; and

(3) is not deemed to have had knowledge under Section 303(e) or notice under Section 704(c).

(b) A dissociated partner is liable to the partnership for any damage caused to the partnership arising from an obligation incurred by the dissociated partner after dissociation for which the partnership is liable under subsection (a).

Comment

1. Section 702 deals with a dissociated partner's lingering apparent authority to bind the partnership in ordinary course partnership transactions and the partner's liability to the partnership for any loss caused thereby. It also applies to partners who withdraw incident to a merger under Article 9. *See* Section 906(e).

A dissociated partner has no actual authority to act for the partnership. *See* Section 603(b)(1). Nevertheless, in order to protect innocent third parties, Section 702(a) provides that the partnership remains bound, for two years after a partner's dissociation, by that partner's acts that would, before his dissociation, have bound the partnership under Section 301 if, and only if, the other party to the transaction reasonably believed that he was still a partner, did not have notice of the partner's dissociation, and is not deemed to have had knowledge of the dissociation under Section 303(e) or notice thereof under Section 704(c).

Under Section 301, every partner has **apparent** authority to bind the partnership by any act for carrying on the partnership business in the ordinary course, unless the other party knows that the partner has no actual authority to act for the partnership or has received a notification of the partner's lack of authority. Section 702(a) continues that general rule for two years after a partner's dissociation, subject to three modifications.

After a partner's dissociation, the general rule is modified, first, by requiring the other party to show reasonable reliance on the partner's status as a partner. Section 301 has no explicit reliance requirement, although the partnership is bound only if the partner purports to act on its behalf. Thus, the other party will normally be aware of the partnership and presumably the partner's status as such.

The second modification is that, under Section 702(a), the partnership is not bound if the third party has **notice** of the partner's dissociation, while under the general rule of Section 301 the partnership is bound unless the third party **knows** of the partner's lack of authority. Under Section 102(b), a person has "notice" of a fact if he knows or has reason to know it exists from all the facts that are known to him or he has received a notification of it. Thus, the partnership may protect itself by sending a notification of the dissociation to a third party, and a third party may, in any event, have a duty to inquire further based on what is known. That provides the partnership with greater protection from the unauthorized acts of a dissociated partner than from those of partners generally.

The third modification of the general apparent authority rule under Section 702(a) involves the effect of a statement of dissociation. Section 704(c) provides that, for the purposes of Sections 702(a)(3) and 703(b)(3), third parties are deemed to have notice of a partner's dissociation 90 days after the filing of a statement of dissociation. Thus, the filing of a statement operates as constructive notice of the dissociated partner's lack of authority after 90 days, conclusively terminating the dissociated partner's Section 702 apparent authority.

With respect to a dissociated partner's authority to transfer partnership real property, Section 303(e) provides that third parties are deemed to have knowledge of a limitation on a partner's authority to transfer real property held in the partnership name upon the proper recording of a statement containing such a limitation. Section 704(b) provides that a statement of dissociation operates as a limitation on the dissociated partner's authority for the purposes of Section 303(e). Thus, a properly recorded statement of dissociation operates as constructive knowledge of a dissociated partner's lack of authority to transfer real property held in the partnership name, effective immediately upon recording,

Under RUPA, therefore, a partnership should notify all known creditors of a partner's dissociation and may, by filing a statement of dissociation, conclusively limit to 90 days a dissociated partner's lingering agency power. Moreover, under Section 703(b), a dissociated partner's lingering liability for post-dissociation partnership liabilities may be limited to 90 days by filing a statement of dissociation. These incentives should encourage both partnerships and dissociating partners to file statements routinely. Those transacting substantial business with partnerships can protect themselves from the risk of dealing with dissociated partners, or relying on their credit, by checking the partnership records at least every 90 days.

2. Section 702(b) is a corollary to subsection (a) and provides that a dissociated partner is liable to the partnership for any loss resulting from an obligation improperly incurred by the partner under subsection (a). In effect, the dissociated partner must indemnify the partnership for any loss, meaning a loss net of any gain from the transaction. The dissociated partner is also personally liable to the third party for the unauthorized obligation.

Section 703. Dissociated Partner's Liability to Other Persons.

(a) A partner's dissociation does not of itself discharge the partner's liability for a partnership obligation incurred before dissociation. A dissociated partner is not liable for a partnership obligation incurred after dissociation, except as otherwise provided in subsection (b).

(b) A partner who dissociates without resulting in a dissolution and winding up of the partnership business is liable as a partner to the other party in a transaction entered into by the partnership, or a surviving partnership under [Article] 9, within two years after the partner's dissociation, only if the partner is liable for the obligation under Section 306 and at the time of entering into the transaction the other party:

(1) reasonably believed that the dissociated partner was then a partner;

(2) did not have notice of the partner's dissociation; and

(3) is not deemed to have had knowledge under Section 303(e) or notice under Section 704(c).

(c) By agreement with the partnership creditor and the partners continuing the business, a dissociated partner may be released from liability for a partnership obligation.

(d) A dissociated partner is released from liability for a partnership obligation if a partnership creditor, with notice of the partner's dissociation but without the partner's consent, agrees to a material alteration in the nature or time of payment of a partnership obligation.

Comment

Section 703(a) is based on UPA Section 36(1) and continues the basic rule that the departure of a partner does not of itself discharge the partner's liability to third parties for any partnership obligation incurred before dissociation. The word "obligation" is used instead of "liability" and is intended to include broadly both tort and contract liability incurred before dissociation. The second sentence states affirmatively that a dissociating partner is not liable for any partnership obligation incurred after dissociation except as expressly provided in subsection (b).

Section 703(b) is new and deals with the problem of protecting third parties who extend credit to the partnership after a partner's dissociation, believing that he is still a partner. It provides that the dissociated partner remains liable as a partner for transactions entered into by the partnership within two years after departure, if the other party does not have notice of the partner's dissociation and reasonably believes when entering the transaction that the dissociated partner is still a partner. The dissociated partner is not personally liable, however, if the other party is deemed to know of the dissociation under Section 303(e) or to have notice thereof under Section 704(c). Also, a dissociated partner is not personally liable for limited liability partnership obligations for which the partner is not personally liable under Section 306.

Section 703(b) operates similarly to Section 702(a) in that it requires reliance on the departed partner's continued partnership status, as well as lack of notice. Under Section 704(c), a statement of dissociation operates conclusively as constructive notice 90 days after filing for the purposes Section 703(b)(3) and, under Section 704(b), as constructive knowledge when recorded for the purposes of Section 303(d) and (e).

Section 703(c) continues the rule of UPA Section 36(2) that a departing partner can bargain for a contractual release from personal liability for a partnership obligation, but it requires the consent of both the creditor and the remaining partners.

Section 703(d) continues the rule of UPA Section 36(3) that a dissociated partner is released from liability for a partnership obligation if the creditor, with notice of the partner's departure, agrees to a material alteration in the nature or time of payment, without that partner's consent. This rule covers all partner dissociations and is not limited, as is the UPA rule, to situations in which a third party "agrees to assume the existing obligations of a dissolved partnership."

In general under RUPA, as a result of the adoption of the entity theory, relationships between a partnership and its creditors are not affected by the dissociation of a partner or by the addition of a new partner, unless otherwise agreed. Therefore, there is no need under RUPA, as there is under the UPA, for an elaborate provision deeming the new partnership to assume the liabilities of the old partnership. *See* UPA Section 41.

The "dual priority" rule in UPA Section 36(4) is eliminated to reflect the abolition of the "jingle rule," providing that separate debts have first claim on separate property, in order to conform to the Bankruptcy Code. *See* Comment 2 to Section 807. A deceased partner's estate, and thus all of his individual property, remains liable for partnership obligations incurred while he was a partner, however.

Section 704. Statement of Dissociation.

(a) A dissociated partner or the partnership may file a statement of dissociation stating the name of the partnership and that the partner is dissociated from the partnership.

(b) A statement of dissociation is a limitation on the authority of a dissociated partner for the purposes of Section 303(d) and (e).

(c) For the purposes of Sections 702(a)(3) and 703(b)(3), a person not a partner is deemed to have notice of the dissociation 90 days after the statement of dissociation is filed.

Comment

Section 704 is new and provides for a statement of dissociation and its effects. Subsection (a) authorizes either a dissociated partner or the partnership to file a statement of dissociation. Like other RUPA filings, the statement of dissociation is voluntary. Both the partnership and the departing partner have an incentive to file, however, and it is anticipated that those filings will become routine upon a partner's dissociation. The execution, filing, and recording of the statement is governed by Section 105.

Filing or recording a statement of dissociation has threefold significance:

(1) It is a statement of limitation on the dissociated partner's authority to the extent provided in Section 303(d) and (e). Under Section 303(d), a filed or recorded limitation on the authority of a partner destroys the conclusive effect of a prior grant of authority to the extent it contradicts the prior grant. Under Section 303(e), nonpartners are conclusively bound by a limitation on the authority of a partner to transfer real property held in the partnership name, if the statement is properly recorded in the real property records.

(2) Ninety days after the statement is filed, nonpartners are deemed to have notice of the dissociation and thus conclusively bound for purposes of cutting off the partner's apparent authority under Sections 301 and 702(a)(3).

(3) Ninety days after the statement is filed, third parties are conclusively bound for purposes of cutting off the dissociated partner's continuing liability under Section 703(b)(3) for transactions entered into by the partnership after dissociation.

Section 705. Continued Use of Partnership.

Continued use of a partnership name, or a dissociated partner's name as part thereof, by partners continuing the business does not of itself make the dissociated partner liable for an obligation of the partners or the partnership continuing the business.

Comment

Section 705 is an edited version of UPA Section 41(10) and provides that a dissociated partner is not liable for the debts of the continuing business simply because of continued use of the partnership name or the dissociated partner's name as a part thereof. That prevents forcing the business to forego the good will associated with its name.

[ARTICLE] 8

WINDING UP PARTNERSHIP BUSINESS

Section 801. Events Causing Dissolution and Winding Up of Partnership Business.
Section 802. Partnership Continues After Dissolution.
Section 803. Right to Wind Up Partnership Business.
Section 804. Partner's Power to Bind Partnership After Dissolution.
Section 805. Statement of Dissolution.
Section 806. Partner's Liability to Other Partners After Dissolution.
Section 807. Settlement of Accounts and Contributions Among Partners.

Section 801. Events Causing Dissolution and Winding Up of Partnership Business.

A partnership is dissolved, and its business must be wound up, only upon the occurrence of any of the following events:

(1) in a partnership at will, the partnership's having notice from a partner, other than a partner who is dissociated under Section 601(2) through (10), of that partner's express will to withdraw as a partner, or on a later date specified by the partner;

(2) in a partnership for a definite term or particular undertaking:

(i) the expiration of 90 days after a partner's dissociation by death or otherwise under Section 601(6) through (10) or wrongful dissociation under Section 602(b), unless before that time a majority in interest of the remaining partners, including partners who have rightfully dissociated pursuant to Section 602(b)(2)(i), agree to continue the partnership;

(ii) the express will of all of the partners to wind up the partnership business; or

(iii) the expiration of the term or the completion of the undertaking;

(3) an event agreed to in the partnership agreement resulting in the winding up of the partnership business;

(4) an event that makes it unlawful for all or substantially all of the business of the partnership to be continued, but a cure of illegality within 90 days after notice to the partnership of the event is effective retroactively to the date of the event for purposes of this section;

(5) on application by a partner, a judicial determination that:

(i) the economic purpose of the partnership is likely to be unreasonably frustrated;

(ii) another partner has engaged in conduct relating to the partnership business which makes it not reasonably practicable to carry on the business in partnership with that partner; or

(iii) It is not otherwise reasonably practicable to carry on the partnership business in conformity with the partnership agreement; or

(6) on application by a transferee of a partner's transferable interest, a judicial determination that it is equitable to wind up the partnership business:

(i) after the expiration of the term or completion of the undertaking, if the partnership was for a definite term or particular undertaking at the time of the transfer or entry of the charging order that gave rise to the transfer; or

(ii) at any time, if the partnership was a partnership at will at the time of the transfer or entry of the charging order that gave rise to the transfer.

Comment

1. Under UPA Section 29, a partnership is dissolved every time a partner leaves. That reflects the aggregate nature of the partnership under the UPA. Even if the business of the partnership is continued by some of the partners, it is technically a new partnership. The dissolution of the old partnership and creation of a new partnership causes many unnecessary problems.

Under RULPA, limited partnerships dissolve far less readily than do general partnerships under the UPA. A limited partnership does not dissolve on the withdrawal of a limited partner, nor does it necessarily dissolve on the withdrawal of a general partner. *See* RULPA § 801(4).

RUPA's move to the entity theory is driven in part by the need to prevent a technical dissolution or its consequences. Under RUPA, not every partner dissociation causes a dissolution of the partnership. Only certain departures trigger a dissolution. The basic rule is that a partnership is dissolved, and its business must be wound up, only upon the occurrence of one of the events listed in Section 801. All other dissociations result in a buyout of the partner's interest under Article 7 and a continuation of the partnership entity and business by the remaining partners. *See* Section 603(a).

With only three exceptions, the provisions of Section 801 are merely default rules and may by agreement be varied or eliminated as grounds for dissolution. The first exception is dissolution under Section 801(4) resulting from carrying on an illegal business. The other two exceptions cover the power of a court to dissolve a partnership under Section 801(5) on application of a partner and under Section 801(6) on application of a transferee. See Comments 6-8 for further explanation of these provisions.

2. Under RUPA, "dissolution" is merely the commencement of the winding up process. The partnership continues for the limited purpose of winding up the business. In effect, that means the scope of the partnership business contracts to completing work in process and taking such other actions as may be necessary to wind up the business. Winding up the partnership business entails selling its assets, paying its debts, and distributing the net balance, if any, to the partners in cash according to their interests. The partnership entity continues, and the partners are associated in the winding up of the business until winding up is completed. When the winding up is completed, the partnership entity terminates.

3. Section 801 continues two basic rules from the UPA. First, it continues the rule that any member of an **at-will** partnership has the right to force a liquidation. Second, by negative implication, it continues the rule that the partners who wish to continue the business of a **term** partnership cannot be forced to liquidate the business by a partner who withdraws prematurely in violation of the partnership agreement.

Those rules are gleaned from the separate UPA provisions governing dissolution and its consequences. Under UPA Section 31(1)(b), dissolution is caused by the express will of any partner when no definite term or particular undertaking is specified. UPA Section 38(1) provides that upon dissolution any partner has the right to have the business wound up. That is a default rule and applies only in the absence of an agreement affording the other partners a right to continue the business.

UPA Section 31(2) provides that a term partnership may be dissolved at any time, in contravention of the partnership agreement, by the express will of any partner. In that case, however, UPA Section 38(2)(b) provides that the nonbreaching partners may by unanimous consent continue the business. If the business is continued, they must buy out the breaching partner.

4. Section 801(1) provides that a partnership at will is dissolved and its business must be wound up upon the partnership's having notice of a partner's express will to withdraw as a partner, unless a later effective date is specified by the partner. A partner at will who has already been dissociated in some other manner, such as a partner who has been expelled, does not thereafter have a right to cause the partnership to be dissolved and its business wound up.

If, after dissolution, none of the partners wants the partnership wound up, Section 802(b) provides that, with the consent of all the partners, including the withdrawing partner, the remaining partners may continue the business. In that event, although there is a technical dissolution of the partnership and, at least in theory, a temporary contraction of the scope of the business, the partnership entity continues and the scope of its business is restored. *See* Section 802(b) and Comment 2.

5. Section 801(2) provides three ways in which a term partnership may be dissolved before the expiration of the term:

(i) Subsection (2)(i) provides for dissolution upon the expiration of 90 days after any partner's dissociation by death or otherwise under Section 601(6) to (10) or wrongful dissociation under Section 602(b), unless within that 90-day period a majority in interest of the remaining partners agree to continue the partnership. This reactive dissolution of a term partnership protects the remaining partners where the dissociating partner is crucial to the successful continuation of the business. The corresponding UPA Section 38(2)(b) rule requires unanimous consent of the remaining partners to continue the business, thus giving each partner an absolute right to a reactive liquidation. Under RUPA, if the partnership is continued by the majority, any dissenting partner who wants to withdraw may do so rightfully under the exception to Section 602(b)(2)(i), in which case his interest in the partnership will be bought out under Article 7. By itself, however, a partner's vote not to continue the business is not necessarily an expression of the partner's will to withdraw, and a dissenting partner may still elect to remain a partner and continue in the business.

The Section 601 dissociations giving rise to a reactive dissolution are: (6) a partner's bankruptcy or similar financial impairment; (7) a partner's death or incapacity; (8) the distribution by a trust-partner of its entire partnership interest; (9) the distribution by an estate-partner of its entire partnership interest; and (10) the termination of an entity-partner. Any dissociation during the term of the partnership that is wrongful under Section 602(b), including a partner's voluntary withdrawal, expulsion or bankruptcy, also gives rise to a reactive dissolution. Those statutory grounds may be varied by agreement or the reactive dissolution may be abolished entirely.

Under subsection (2)(i), a term partnership is dissolved 90 days after the first partner's dissociation unless within that time a majority in interest of the remaining partners have agreed to continue the partnership. Continuation under subsection (2)(i) requires the agreement of at least a majority in interest of the remaining partners. The interest and vote of a partner who dissociates rightfully under Section 602(b)(2)(i) is counted in determining whether a majority in interest agrees to continue.

Decision-making by a majority in interest is not the normal RUPA default rule. Section 401(j) requires a majority in number, rather than a majority in interest, for ordinary business decisions and unanimity for extraordinary matters and amendments to the partnership agreement. Requiring only majority approval to continue the partnership, rather than unanimity, in effect treats the decision as an ordinary business matter, thereby enhancing firm stability. At the same time, requiring a majority in interest, rather than a majority in number, satisfies Internal Revenue Service concerns regarding a partnership's continuity of life. *See* Treas. Reg. § 301.7701-2(b)(1).

"Majority in interest" is not defined in the Act, but is intended to satisfy Internal Revenue Service regulations regarding continuity of life. Under Rev. Proc. 94-46 (June 29, 1994), the "in-interest" concept refers to the partners' economic interests in both the profits and capital of the partnership.

Under Section 601(6)(i), a partner is dissociated upon becoming a debtor in bankruptcy. The bankruptcy of a partner or of the partnership is not, however, an event of dissolution under Section 801. That is a change from UPA Section 31(5). A partner's bankruptcy does, however, cause dissolution of a term partnership under Section 801(2)(i), unless a majority in interest of the remaining partners thereafter agree to continue the partnership. Affording the other partners the option of buying out the bankrupt partner's interest avoids the necessity of winding up a term partnership every time a partner becomes a debtor in bankruptcy.

Similarly, under Section 801(2)(i), the death of any partner will result in the dissolution of a term partnership, unless a majority in interest of the remaining partners agree to continue the business. In that case, the deceased partner's transferable interest in the partnership passes to his estate and must be bought out under Article 7. *See* Comment 8 to Section 601.

(ii) Section 801(2)(ii) provides that a term partnership may be dissolved and wound up at any time by the express will of all the partners. That is merely an expression of the general rule that the partnership agreement may override the statutory default rules and that the partnership agreement, like any contract, can be amended at any time by unanimous consent.

UPA Section 31(1)(c) provides that a term partnership may be wound up by the express will of all the partners whose transferable interests have not been assigned or charged for a partner's separate debts. That rule reflects the belief that the remaining partners may find transferees very intrusive. This provision has been deleted, however, because the liquidation is easily accomplished under Section 801(2)(ii) by first expelling the transferor partner under Section 601(4)(ii).

(iii) Section 801(2)(iii) is based on UPA Section 31(1)(a) and provides for winding up a term partnership upon the expiration of the term or the completion of the undertaking.

Subsection (2)(iii) must be read in conjunction with Section 406(a), if the partners continue the business after the expiration of the term or the completion of the undertaking, the partnership will be treated as a partnership at will. Moreover, if the partners continue the business without any settlement or liquidation of the partnership, under Section 406(b) they are presumed to have agreed that the partnership will continue, despite the lack of a formal agreement. The partners may also agree to ratify all acts taken since the end of the partnership's term.

6. Section 801(3) provides for dissolution upon the occurrence of an event specified in the partnership agreement as resulting in the winding up of the partnership business. The partners may, however, agree to continue the business and to ratify all acts taken since dissolution.

7. Section 801(4) continues the basic rule in UPA Section 31(3) and provides for dissolution if it is unlawful to continue the business of the partnership, unless cured. The "all or substantially all" proviso is intended to avoid dissolution for insubstantial or innocent regulatory violations. If the illegality is cured within 90 days after notice to the partnership, it is effective retroactively for purposes of this section. The requirement that an uncured illegal business be wound up cannot be varied in the partnership agreement. *See* Section 103(b)(8).

8. Section 801(5) provides for judicial dissolution on application by a partner. It is based in part on UPA Section 32(1), and the language comes in part from RULPA Section 802. A court may order a partnership dissolved upon a judicial determination that: (i) the economic purpose of the partnership is likely to be unreasonably frustrated; (ii) another partner has engaged in conduct relating to the partnership business which makes it not reasonably practicable to carry on the business in partnership with that partner; or (iii) it is not otherwise reasonably practicable to carry on the partnership business in conformity with the partnership agreement. The court's power to wind up the partnership under Section 801(5) cannot be varied in the partnership agreement. *See* Section 103(b)(8).

RUPA deletes UPA Section 32(1)(e) which provides for dissolution when the business can only be carried on at a loss. That provision might result in a dissolution contrary to the partners' expectations in a start-up or tax shelter situation, in which case "book" or "tax" losses do not signify business failure. Truly poor financial performance may justify dissolution under subsection (5)(i) as a frustration of the partnership's economic purpose.

RUPA also deletes UPA Section 32(1)(f) which authorizes a court to order dissolution of a partnership when "other circumstances render a dissolution equitable." That provision was regarded as too open-ended and, given RUPA's expanded remedies for partners, unnecessary. No significant change in result is intended, however, since the interpretation of UPA Section 32(1)(f) is comparable to the specific grounds expressed in subsection (5). *See, e.g., Karber v. Karber*, 145 Ariz. 293, 701 P.2d 1 (Ct. App. 1985) (partnership dissolved on basis of suspicion and ill will, citing UPA §§ 32(1)(d) and (f)); *Fuller v. Brough*, 159 Colo. 147, 411 P.2d 18 (1966) (not equitable to dissolve partnership for trifling causes or temporary grievances that do not render it impracticable to carry on partnership business); *Lau v. Wong*, 1 Haw. App. 217, 616 P.2d 1031 (1980) (partnership dissolved where business operated solely for benefit of managing partner).

9. Section 801(6) provides for judicial dissolution on application by a transferee of a partner's transferable interest in the partnership, including the purchaser of a partner's interest upon foreclosure of a charging order. It is based on UPA Section 32(2) and authorizes dissolution upon a judicial determination that it is

equitable to wind up the partnership business (i) after the expiration of the partnership term or completion of the undertaking or (ii) at any time, if the partnership were a partnership at will at the time of the transfer or when the charging order was issued. The requirement that the court determine that it is equitable to wind up the business is new. The rights of a transferee under this section cannot be varied in the partnership agreement. *See* Section 103(b)(8).

Section 802. Partnership Continues After Dissolution.

(a) Subject to subsection (b), a partnership continues after dissolution only for the purpose of winding up its business. The partnership is terminated when the winding up of its business is completed.

(b) At any time after the dissolution of a partnership and before the winding up of its business is completed, all of the partners, including any dissociating partner other than a wrongfully dissociating partner, may waive the right to have the partnership's business wound up and the partnership terminated. In that event:

(1) the partnership resumes carrying on its business as if dissolution had never occurred, and any liability incurred by the partnership or a partner after the dissolution and before the waiver is determined as if dissolution had never occurred; and

(2) the rights of a third party accruing under Section 804(1) or arising out of conduct in reliance on the dissolution before the third party knew or received a notification of the waiver may not be adversely affected.

Comment

1. Section 802(a) is derived from UPA Section 30 and provides that a partnership continues after dissolution only for the purpose of winding up its business, after which it is terminated. RUPA continues the concept of "termination" to mark the completion of the winding up process. Since no filing or other formality is required, the date will often be determined only by hindsight. No legal rights turn on the partnership's termination or the date thereof. Even after termination, if a previously unknown liability is asserted, all of the partners are still liable.

2. Section 802(b) makes explicit the right of the remaining partners to continue the business after an event of dissolution if all of the partners, including the dissociating partner or partners, waive the right to have the business wound up and the partnership terminated. Only those "dissociating" partners whose dissociation was the immediate cause of the dissolution must waive the right to have the business wound up. The consent of wrongfully dissociating partners is not required.

3. Upon waiver of the right to have the business wound up, Paragraph (1) of the subsection provides that the partnership entity may resume carrying on its business as if dissolution had never occurred, thereby restoring the scope of its business to normal. "Resumes" is intended to mean that acts appropriate to winding up, authorized when taken, are in effect ratified, and the partnership remains liable for those acts, as provided explicitly in paragraph (2).

If the business is continued following a waiver of the right to dissolution, any liability incurred by the partnership or a partner after the dissolution and before the waiver is to be determined as if dissolution had never occurred. That has the effect of validating transactions entered into after dissolution that might not have been appropriate for winding up the business, because, upon waiver, any liability incurred by either the partnership or a partner in those transactions will be determined under Sections 702 and 703, rather than Sections 804 and 806.

As to the liability for those transactions among the partners themselves, the partners by agreement may provide otherwise. Thus, a partner who, after dissolution, incurred an obligation appropriate for winding up, but not appropriate for continuing the business, may protect himself by conditioning his consent to the continuation of the business on the ratification of the transaction by the continuing partners.

Paragraph (2) of the subsection provides that the rights of third parties accruing under Section 804(1) before they knew (or were notified) of the waiver may not be adversely affected by the waiver. That is intended to mean the partnership is bound, notwithstanding a subsequent waiver of dissolution and resumption of its business, by a transaction entered into after dissolution that was appropriate for winding up the partnership business, even if not appropriate for continuing the business. Similarly, any rights of a third party arising out of conduct in reliance on the dissolution are protected, absent knowledge (or notification) of the waiver. Thus, for example, a partnership loan, callable upon dissolution, that has been called is not reinstated by a subsequent waiver. If the loan has not been called before the lender learns (or is notified) of the waiver, however, it may not thereafter be called because of the dissolution. On the other hand, a waiver does not reinstate a lease that is terminated by the dissolution itself.

Section 803. Right to Wind Up Partnership Business.

(a) After dissolution, a partner who has not wrongfully dissociated may participate in winding up the partnership's business, but on application of any partner, partner's legal representative, or transferee, the [designate the appropriate court], for good cause shown, may order judicial supervision of the winding up.

(b) The legal representative of the last surviving partner may wind up a partnership's business.

(c) A person winding up a partnership's business may preserve the partnership business or property as a going concern for a reasonable time, prosecute and defend actions and proceedings, whether civil, criminal, or administrative, settle and close the partnership's business, dispose of and transfer the partnership's property, discharge the partnership's liabilities, distribute the assets of the partnership pursuant to Section 807, settle disputes by mediation or arbitration, and perform other necessary acts.

Comment

Section 803(a) is drawn from UPA Section 37. It provides that the partners who have not wrongfully dissociated may participate in winding up the partnership business. Wrongful dissociation is defined in Section 602. On application of any partner, a court may for good cause judicially supervise the winding up.

Section 803(b) continues the rule of UPA Section 25(2)(d) that the legal representative of the last surviving partner may wind up the business. It makes clear that the representative of the last surviving partner will not be forced to go to court for authority to wind up the business. On the other hand, the legal representative of a deceased partner, other than the last surviving partner, has only the rights of a transferee of the deceased partner's transferable interest. *See* Comment 8 to Section 601.

Section 803(c) is new and provides further guidance on the powers of a person who is winding up the business. It is based on Delaware Laws, Title 6, Section 17-803. The powers enumerated are not intended to be exclusive.

Subsection (c) expressly authorizes the preservation of the partnership's business or property as a going concern for a reasonable time. Some courts have reached that result without benefit of statutory authority. *See, e.g., Paciaroni v. Crane*, 408 A.2d 946 (Del. Ch. 1979). An agreement to continue the partnership business in order to preserve its going-concern value until sale is not a waiver of a partner's right to have the business liquidated.

The authorization of mediation and arbitration implements Conference policy to encourage alternative dispute resolution.

A partner's fiduciary duties of care and loyalty under Section 404 extend to winding up the business, except as modified by Section 603(b).

Section 804. Partner's Power to Bind Partnership After Dissolution.

Subject to Section 805, a partnership is bound by a partner's act after dissolution that:

(1) is appropriate for winding up the partnership business; or

(2) would have bound the partnership under Section 301 before dissolution, if the other party to the transaction did not have notice of the dissolution.

Comment

Section 804 is the successor to UPA Sections 33(2) and 35, which wind down the authority of partners to bind the partnership to third persons.

Section 804(1) provides that partners have the authority to bind the partnership after dissolution in transactions that are appropriate for winding-up the partnership business. Section 804(2) provides that partners also have the power after dissolution to bind the partnership in transactions that are inconsistent with winding up. The partnership is bound in a transaction not appropriate for winding up, however, only if the partner's act would have bound the partnership under Section 301 before dissolution and the other party to the transaction did not have notice of the dissolution. *See* Section 102(b) (notice). Compare Section 301(1) (partner has apparent authority unless other party knows or has received a notification of lack of authority).

Section 804(2) attempts to balance the interests of the partners to terminate their mutual agency authority against the interests of outside creditors who have no notice of the partnership's dissolution. Even if the partnership is not bound under Section 804, the faithless partner who purports to act for the partnership after dissolution may be liable individually to an innocent third party under the law of agency. *See* Section 330 of the Restatement (Second) of Agency (agent liable for misrepresentation of authority), applicable under RUPA as provided in Section 104(a).

RUPA eliminates the special and confusing UPA rules limiting the authority of partners after dissolution. The special protection afforded by UPA Section 35(1)(b)(I) to former creditors and the lesser special protection afforded by UPA Section 35(1)(b)(II) to other parties who knew of the partnership before dissolution are both abolished. RUPA eschews these cumbersome notice provisions in favor of the general apparent authority rules of Section 301, subject to the effect of a filed or recorded statement of dissolution under Section 805. This enhances the protection of innocent third parties and imposes liability on the partnership and the partners who choose their fellow partner-agents and are in the best position to protect others by providing notice of the dissolution.

Also deleted are the special rules for unknown partners in UPA Section 35(2) and for certain causes of dissolution in UPA Section 35(3). Those, too, are inconsistent with RUPA's policy of adhering more closely to the general agency rules of Section 301.

Section 804 should be contrasted with Section 702, which winds down the power of a partner being bought out. The power of a dissociating partner is limited to transactions entered into within two years after the partner's dissociation. Section 804 has no time limitation. However, the apparent authority of partners in both situations is now subject to the filing of a statement of dissociation or dissolution, as the case may be, which operates to cut off such authority after 90 days.

Section 805. Statement of Dissolution.

(a) After dissolution, a partner who has not wrongfully dissociated may file a statement of dissolution stating the name of the partnership and that the partnership has dissolved and is winding up its business.

(b) A statement of dissolution cancels a filed statement of partnership authority for the purposes of Section 303(d) and is a limitation on authority for the purposes of Section 303(e).

(c) For the purposes of Sections 301 and 804, a person not a partner is deemed to have notice of the dissolution and the limitation on the partners' authority as a result of the statement of dissolution 90 days after it is filed.

(d) After filing and, if appropriate, recording a statement of dissolution, a dissolved partnership may file and, if appropriate, record a statement of partnership authority which will operate with respect to a person not a partner as provided in Section 303(d) and (e) in any transaction, whether or not the transaction is appropriate for winding up the partnership business.

Comment

1. Section 805 is new. Subsection (a) provides that, after an event of dissolution, any partner who has not wrongfully dissociated may file a statement of dissolution on behalf of the partnership. The filing and recording of a statement of dissolution is optional. The execution, filing, and recording of the statement is governed by Section 105. The legal consequences of filing a statement of dissolution are similar to those of a statement of dissociation under Section 704.

2. Subsection (b) provides that a statement of dissolution cancels a filed statement of partnership authority for the purposes of Section 303(d), thereby terminating any extraordinary grant of authority contained in that statement.

A statement of dissolution also operates as a limitation on authority for the purposes of Section 303(e). That section provides that third parties are deemed to know of a limitation on the authority of a partner to transfer real property held in the name of the partnership if a certified copy of the statement containing the limitation is recorded with the real estate records. In effect, a properly recorded statement of dissolution restricts the authority of all partners to real property transfers that are appropriate for winding up the business. Thus, third parties must inquire of the partnership whether a contemplated real property transfer is appropriate for winding up. After dissolution, the partnership may, however, file and record a new statement of authority that will bind the partnership under Section 303(d).

3. Subsection (c) operates in conjunction with Sections 301 and 804 to wind down partners' apparent authority after dissolution. It provides that, for purposes of those sections, 90 days after the filing of a statement of dissolution nonpartners are deemed to have notice of the dissolution and the corresponding limitation on the authority of all partners. Sections 301 and 804 provide that a partner's lack of authority is binding on persons with notice thereof. Thus, after 90 days the statement of dissolution operates as constructive notice conclusively limiting the apparent authority of partners to transactions that are appropriate for winding up the business.

4. Subsection (d) provides that, after filing and, if appropriate, recording a statement of dissolution, the partnership may file and record a new statement of partnership authority that will operate as provided in Section 303(d). A grant of authority contained in that statement is conclusive and may be relied upon by a person who gives value without knowledge to the contrary, whether or not the transaction is appropriate for winding up the partnership business. That makes the partners' record authority conclusive after dissolution, and precludes going behind the record to inquire into whether or not the transaction was appropriate for winding up.

Section 806. Partner's Liability to Other Partners After Dissolution.

(a) Except as otherwise provided in subsection (b) and Section 306, after dissolution a partner is liable to the other partners for the partner's share of any partnership liability incurred under Section 804.

(b) A partner who, with knowledge of the dissolution, incurs a partnership liability under Section 804(2) by an act that is not appropriate for winding up the partnership business is liable to the partnership for any damage caused to the partnership arising from the liability.

Comment

Section 806 is the successor to UPA Sections 33(1) and 34, which govern the rights of partners among themselves with respect to post-dissolution liability.

Subsection (a) provides that, except as provided in Section 306(a) and subsection (b), after dissolution each partner is liable to the other partners by way of contribution for his share of any partnership liability incurred under Section 804. That includes not only obligations that are appropriate for winding up the business, but also obligations that are inappropriate if within the partner's apparent authority. Consistent with other provisions of this Act, Section 806(a) makes clear that a partner does not have a contribution obligation with regard to limited liability partnership obligations for which the partner is not liable under Section 306. See Comments to Section 401(b).

Subsection (a) draws no distinction as to the cause of dissolution. Thus, as among the partners, their liability is treated alike in all events of dissolution. That is a change from UPA Section 33(1).

Subsection (b) creates an exception to the general rule in subsection (a). It provides that a partner, who with knowledge of the winding up nevertheless incurs a liability binding on the partnership by an act that is inappropriate for winding up the business, is liable to the partnership for any loss caused thereby.

Section 806 is merely a default rule and may be varied in the partnership agreement. *See* Section 103(a).

Section 807. Settlement of Accounts and Contributions Among Partners.

(a) In winding up a partnership's business, the assets of the partnership, including the contributions of the partners required by this section, must be applied to discharge its obligations to creditors, including, to the extent permitted by law, partners who are creditors. Any surplus must be applied to pay in cash the net amount distributable to partners in accordance with their right to distributions under subsection (b).

(b) Each partner is entitled to a settlement of all partnership accounts upon winding up the partnership business. In settling accounts among the partners, the profits and losses that result from the liquidation of the partnership assets must be credited and charged to the partners' accounts. The partnership shall make a distribution to a partner in an amount equal to any excess of the credits over the charges in the partner's account. A partner shall contribute to the partnership an amount equal to any excess of the charges over the credits in the partner's account but excluding from the calculation charges attributable to an obligation for which the partner is not personally liable under Section 306.

(c) If a partner fails to contribute the full amount required under subsection (b), all of the other partners shall contribute, in the proportions in which those partners share partnership losses, the additional amount necessary to satisfy the partnership obligations for which they are personally liable under Section 306. A partner or partner's legal representative may recover from the other partners any contributions the partner makes to the extent the amount contributed exceeds that partner's share of the partnership obligations for which the partner is personally liable under Section 306.

(d) After the settlement of accounts, each partner shall contribute, in the proportion in which the partner shares partnership losses, the amount necessary to satisfy partnership obligations that were not known at the time of the settlement and for which the partner is personally liable under Section 306.

(e) The estate of a deceased partner is liable for the partner's obligation to contribute to the partnership.

(f) An assignee for the benefit of creditors of a partnership or a partner, or a person appointed by a court to represent creditors of a partnership or a partner, may enforce a partner's obligation to contribute to the partnership.

Comment

1. Section 807 provides the default rules for the settlement of accounts and contributions among the partners in winding up the business. It is derived in part from UPA Sections 38(1) and 40.

2. Subsection (a) continues the rule in UPA Section 38(1) that, in winding up the business, the partnership assets must first be applied to discharge partnership liabilities to creditors. For this purpose, any required contribution by the partners is treated as an asset of the partnership. After the payment of all partnership liabilities, any surplus must be applied to pay in cash the net amount due the partners under subsection (b) by way of a liquidating distribution.

RUPA continues the "in-cash" rule of UPA Section 38(1) and is consistent with Section 402, which provides that a partner has no right to receive, and may not be required to accept, a distribution in kind, unless otherwise agreed. The in-cash rule avoids the valuation problems that afflict unwanted in-kind distributions.

The partnership must apply its assets to discharge the obligations of partners who are creditors on a parity with other creditors. *See* Section 404(f) and Comment 6. In effect, that abolishes the priority rules in UPA Section 40(b) and (c) which subordinate the payment of inside debt to outside debt. Both RULPA and the RMBCA do likewise. *See* RULPA § 804; RMBCA §§ 6.40(f), 14.05(a). Ultimately, however, a partner whose "debt" has been repaid by the partnership is personally liable, as a partner, for any outside debt remaining unsatisfied, unlike a limited partner or corporate shareholder. Accordingly, the obligation to contribute sufficient funds to satisfy the claims of outside creditors may result in the equitable subordination of inside debt when partnership assets are insufficient to satisfy all obligations to non-partners.

RUPA in effect abolishes the "dual priority" or "jingle" rule of UPA Section 40(h) and (i). Those sections gave partnership creditors priority as to partnership property and separate creditors priority as to separate property. The jingle rule has already been preempted by the Bankruptcy Code, at least as to Chapter 7 partnership liquidation proceedings. Under Section 723(c) of the Bankruptcy Code, and under RUPA, partnership creditors share pro rata with the partners' individual creditors in the assets of the partners' estates.

3. Subsection (b) provides that each partner is entitled to a settlement of all partnership accounts upon winding up. It also establishes the default rules for closing out the partners' accounts. First, the profits and losses resulting from the liquidation of the partnership assets must be credited or charged to the partners' accounts, according to their respective shares of profits and losses. Then, the partnership must make a final liquidating distribution to those partners with a positive account balance. That distribution should be in the amount of the excess of credits over the charges in the account. Any partner with a negative account balance must contribute to the partnership an amount equal to the excess of charges over the credits in the account provided the excess relates to an obligation for which the partner is

personally liable under Section 306. The partners may, however, agree that a negative account does not reflect a debt to the partnership and need not be repaid in settling the partners' accounts.

Section 807(d) makes clear that a partner's contribution obligation to a partnership in dissolution only considers the partner's share of obligations for which the partner was personally liable under Section 306 ("unshielded obligations"). See Comments to Section 401(b) (partner contribution obligation to an operating partnership). Properly determined under this Section, the total required partner contributions will be sufficient to satisfy the partnership's total unshielded obligations. In special circumstances where a partnership has both shielded and unshielded obligations and the partner required contributions are used to first pay shielded partnership obligations, the partners may be required to make further contributions to satisfy the partnership unpaid unshielded obligations. The proper resolution of this matter is left to debtor-creditor law as well as the law governing the fiduciary obligations of the partners. See Section 104(a).

RUPA eliminates the distinction in UPA Section 40(b) between the liability owing to a partner in respect of capital and the liability owing in respect of profits. Section 807(b) speaks simply of the right of a partner to a liquidating distribution. That implements the logic of RUPA Sections 401(a) and 502 under which contributions to capital and shares in profits and losses combine to determine the right to distributions. The partners may, however, agree to share "operating" losses differently from "capital" losses, thereby continuing the UPA distinction.

4. Subsection (c) continues the UPA Section 40(d) rule that solvent partners share proportionately in the shortfall caused by insolvent partners who fail to contribute their proportionate share. The partnership may enforce a partner's obligation to contribute. *See* Section 405(a). A partner is entitled to recover from the other partners any contributions in excess of that partner's share of the partnership's liabilities. *See* Section 405(b)(iii).

5. Subsection (d) provides that after settling the partners' accounts, each partner must contribute, in the proportion in which he shares losses, the amount necessary to satisfy partnership obligations that were not known at the time of the settlement. That continues the basic rule of UPA Section 40(d) and underscores that the obligation to contribute exists independently of the partnership's books of account. It specifically covers the situation of a partnership liability that was unknown when the partnership books were closed.

6. Under subsection (e), the estate of a deceased partner is liable for the partner's obligation to contribute to partnership losses. That continues the rule of UPA Section 40(g).

7. Subsection (f) provides that an assignee for the benefit of creditors of the partnership or of a partner (or other court appointed creditor representative) may enforce any partner's obligation to contribute to the partnership. That continues the rules of UPA Sections 36(4) and 40(e).

[ARTICLE] 9

CONVERSIONS AND MERGERS

Section 901. Definitions.

In this [article]:

(1) "General partner" means a partner in a partnership and a general partner in a limited partnership.

(2) "Limited partner" means a limited partner in a limited partnership.

(3) "Limited partnership" means a limited partnership created under the [State Limited Partnership Act], predecessor law, or comparable law of another jurisdiction.

(4) "Partner" includes both a general partner and a limited partner.

Comment

1. Article 9 is new. The UPA is silent with respect to the conversion or merger of partnerships, and thus it is necessary under the UPA to structure those types of transactions as asset transfers. RUPA provides specific statutory authority for conversions and mergers. It provides for continuation of the partnership entity, thereby simplifying those transactions and adding certainty to the legal consequences.

A number of States currently authorize the merger of limited partnerships, and some authorize them to merge with other business entities such as corporations and limited liability companies. A few States currently authorize the merger of a general and a limited partnership or the conversion of a general to a limited partnership.

2. As Section 908 makes clear, the requirements of Article 9 are not mandatory, and a partnership may convert or merge in any other manner provided by law. Article 9 is merely a "safe harbor." If the requirements of the article are followed, the conversion or merger is legally valid. Since most States have no other established procedure for the conversion or merger of partnerships, it is likely that the Article 9 procedures will be used in virtually all cases.

3. Article 9 does not restrict the provisions authorizing conversions and mergers to domestic partnerships. Since no filing is required for the creation of a partnership under RUPA, it is often unclear where a partnership is domiciled. Moreover, a partnership doing business in the State satisfies the definition of a partnership created under this Act since it is an association of two or more co-owners carrying on a business for profit. Even a partnership clearly domiciled in another State could easily amend its partnership agreement to provide that its internal affairs are to be governed by the laws of a jurisdiction that has enacted Article 9 of RUPA. No harm is likely to

result from extending to foreign partnerships the right to convert or merge under local law.

4. Because Article 9 deals with the conversion and merger of both general and limited partnerships, Section 901 sets forth four definitions distinguishing between the two types of partnerships solely for the purposes of Article 9. "Partner" includes both general and limited partners, and "general partner" includes general partners in both general and limited partnerships.

Section 902. Conversion of Partnership to Limited Partnership.

(a) A partnership may be converted to a limited partnership pursuant to this section.

(b) The terms and conditions of a conversion of a partnership to a limited partnership must be approved by all of the partners or by a number or percentage specified for conversion in the partnership agreement.

(c) After the conversion is approved by the partners, the partnership shall file a certificate of limited partnership in the jurisdiction in which the limited partnership is to be formed. The certificate must include:

(1) a statement that the partnership was converted to a limited partnership from a partnership;

(2) its former name; and

(3) a statement of the number of votes cast by the partners for and against the conversion and, if the vote is less than unanimous, the number or percentage required to approve the conversion under the partnership agreement.

(d) The conversion takes effect when the certificate of limited partnership is filed or at any later date specified in the certificate.

(e) A general partner who becomes a limited partner as a result of the conversion remains liable as a general partner for an obligation incurred by the partnership before the conversion takes effect. If the other party to a transaction with the limited partnership reasonably believes when entering the transaction that the limited partner is a general partner, the limited partner is liable for an obligation incurred by the limited partnership within 90 days after the conversion takes effect. The limited partner's liability for all other obligations of the limited partnership incurred after the conversion takes effect is that of a limited partner as provided in the [State Limited Partnership Act].

Comment

Section 902(a) authorizes the conversion of a "partnership" to a "limited partnership." Section 202(b) limits the usual RUPA definition of "partnership" to general partnerships. That definition is applicable to Article 9. If a limited partnership is contemplated, Article 9 uses the term "limited partnership." *See* Section 901(3).

Subsection (b) provides that the terms and conditions of the conversion must be approved by all the partners, unless the partnership agreement specifies otherwise for a conversion.

Subsection (c) provides that, after approval, the partnership must file a certificate of limited partnership which includes the requisite information concerning the conversion.

Subsection (d) provides that the conversion takes effect when the certificate is filed, unless a later effective date is specified.

Subsection (e) establishes the partners' liabilities following a conversion. A partner who becomes a limited partner as a result of the conversion remains fully liable as a general partner for any obligation arising before the effective date of the conversion, both to third parties and to other partners for contribution. Third parties who transact business with the converted partnership unaware of a partner's new status as a limited partner are protected for 90 days after the conversion. Since RULPA Section 201(a)(3) requires the certificate of limited partnership to name all of the general partners, and under RUPA Section 902(c) the certificate must also include a statement of the conversion, parties transacting business with the converted partnership can protect themselves by checking the record of the State where the limited partnership is formed (the State where the conversion takes place). A former general partner who becomes a limited partner as a result of the conversion can avoid the lingering 90-day exposure to liability as a general partner by notifying those transacting business with the partnership of his limited partner status.

Although Section 902 does not expressly provide that a partner's withdrawal upon a term partnership's conversion to a limited partnership is rightful, it was assumed that the unanimity requirement for the approval of a conversion would afford a withdrawing partner adequate opportunity to protect his interest as a condition of approval. This question is left to the partnership agreement if it provides for conversion without the approval of all the partners.

Section 903. Conversion of Limited Partnership to Partnership.

(a) A limited partnership may be converted to a partnership pursuant to this section.

(b) Notwithstanding a provision to the contrary in a limited partnership agreement, the terms and conditions of a conversion of a limited partnership to a partnership must be approved by all of the partners.

(c) After the conversion is approved by the partners, the limited partnership shall cancel its certificate of limited partnership.

(d) The conversion takes effect when the certificate of limited partnership is canceled.

(e) A limited partner who becomes a general partner as a result of the conversion remains liable only as a limited partner for an obligation incurred by the limited partnership before the conversion takes effect. ~~The~~ Except as otherwise provided in Section 306, the partner is liable as a general partner for an obligation of the partnership incurred after the conversion takes effect.

Comment

Section 903(a) authorizes the conversion of a limited partnership to a general partnership.

Subsection (b) provides that the conversion must be approved by all of the partners, even if the partnership agreement provides to the contrary. That includes all of the general and limited partners. *See* Section 901(4). The purpose of the unanimity requirement is to protect a limited partner from exposure to personal liability as a general partner without clear and knowing consent at the time of conversion. Despite a general voting provision to the contrary in the partnership agreement, conversion to a general partnership may never have been contemplated by the limited partner when the partnership investment was made.

Subsection (c) provides that, after approval of the conversion, the converted partnership must cancel its certificate of limited partnership. *See* RULPA § 203.

Subsection (d) provides that the conversion takes effect when the certificate of limited partnership is canceled.

Subsection (e) provides that a limited partner who becomes a general partner is liable as a general partner for all <u>partnership</u> obligations <u>for which a general partner would otherwise be personally liable for if</u> incurred after the effective date of the conversion, but still has only limited liability for obligations incurred before the conversion.

Section 904. Effect of Conversion; Entity Unchanged.

(a) A partnership or limited partnership that has been converted pursuant to this [article] is for all purposes the same entity that existed before the conversion.

(b) When a conversion takes effect:

(1) all property owned by the converting partnership or limited partnership remains vested in the converted entity;

(2) all obligations of the converting partnership or limited partnership continue as obligations of the converted entity; and

(3) an action or proceeding pending against the converting partnership or limited partnership may be continued as if the conversion had not occurred.

Comment

Section 904 sets forth the effect of a conversion on the partnership. Subsection (a) provides that the converted partnership is for all purposes the same entity as before the conversion.

Subsection (b) provides that upon conversion: (1) all partnership property remains vested in the converted entity; (2) all obligations remain the obligations of the converted entity; and (3) all pending legal actions may be continued as if the conversion had not occurred. The term "entity" as used in Article 9 refers to either or both general and limited partnerships as the context requires.

Under subsection (b)(1), title to partnership property remains vested in the converted partnership. As a matter of general property law, title remains vested without further act or deed and without reversion or impairment.

Section 905. Merger of Partnerships.

(a) Pursuant to a plan of merger approved as provided in subsection (c), a partnership may be merged with one or more partnerships or limited partnerships.

(b) The plan of merger must set forth:

(1) the name of each partnership or limited partnership that is a party to the merger;

(2) the name of the surviving entity into which the other partnerships or limited partnerships will merge;

(3) whether the surviving entity is a partnership or a limited partnership and the status of each partner;

(4) the terms and conditions of the merger;

(5) the manner and basis of converting the interests of each party to the merger into interests or obligations of the surviving entity, or into money or other property in whole or part; and

(6) the street address of the surviving entity's chief executive office.

(c) The plan of merger must be approved:

(1) in the case of a partnership that is a party to the merger, by all of the partners, or a number or percentage specified for merger in the partnership agreement; and

(2) in the case of a limited partnership that is a party to the merger, by the vote required for approval of a merger by the law of the State or foreign jurisdiction in which the limited partnership is organized and, in the absence of such a specifically applicable law, by all of the partners, notwithstanding a provision to the contrary in the partnership agreement.

(d) After a plan of merger is approved and before the merger takes effect, the plan may be amended or abandoned as provided in the plan.

(e) The merger takes effect on the later of:

(1) the approval of the plan of merger by all parties to the merger, as provided in subsection (c);

(2) the filing of all documents required by law to be filed as a condition to the effectiveness of the merger; or

(3) any effective date specified in the plan of merger.

Comment

Section 905 provides a "safe harbor" for the merger of a general partnership and one or more general or limited partnerships. The surviving entity may be either a general or a limited partnership.

The plan of merger must set forth the information required by subsection (b), including the status of each partner and the manner and basis of converting the interests of each party to the merger into interests or obligations of the surviving entity.

Subsection (c) provides that the plan of merger must be approved: (1) by all the partners of each general partnership that is a party to the merger, unless its partnership agreement specifically provides otherwise for mergers; and (2) by all the partners, including both general and limited partners, of each limited partnership that is a party to the merger, notwithstanding a contrary provision in its partnership agreement, unless specifically authorized by the law of the jurisdiction in which that limited partnership is organized. Like Section 903(b), the purpose of the unanimity requirement is to protect limited partners from exposure to liability as general partners without their clear and knowing consent.

Subsection (d) provides that the plan of merger may be amended or abandoned at any time before the merger takes effect, if the plan so provides.

Subsection (e) provides that the merger takes effect on the later of: (1) approval by all parties to the merger; (2) filing of all required documents; or (3) the effective date specified in the plan. The surviving entity must file all notices and documents relating to the merger required by other applicable statutes governing the entities that are parties to the merger, such as articles of merger or a certificate of limited partnership. It may also amend or cancel a statement of partnership authority previously filed by any party to the merger.

Section 906. Effect of Merger.

(a) When a merger takes effect:

(1) the separate existence of every partnership or limited partnership that is a party to the merger, other than the surviving entity, ceases;

(2) all property owned by each of the merged partnerships or limited partnerships vests in the surviving entity;

(3) all obligations of every partnership or limited partnership that is a party to the merger become the obligations of the surviving entity; and

(4) an action or proceeding pending against a partnership or limited partnership that is a party to the merger may be continued as if the merger had not occurred, or the surviving entity may be substituted as a party to the action or proceeding.

(b) The [Secretary of State] of this State is the agent for service of process in an action or proceeding against a surviving foreign partnership or limited partnership to enforce an obligation of a domestic partnership or limited partnership that is a party to a merger. The surviving entity shall promptly notify the [Secretary of State] of the mailing address of its chief executive office and of any change of address. Upon receipt of process, the [Secretary of State] shall mail a copy of the process to the surviving foreign partnership or limited partnership.

(c) A partner of the surviving partnership or limited partnership is liable for:

(1) all obligations of a party to the merger for which the partner was personally liable before the merger;

(2) all other obligations of the surviving entity incurred before the merger by a party to the merger, but those obligations may be satisfied only out of property of the entity; and

(3) except as otherwise provided in Section 306, all obligations of the surviving entity incurred after the merger takes effect, but those obligations may be satisfied only out of property of the entity if the partner is a limited partner.

(d) If the obligations incurred before the merger by a party to the merger are not satisfied out of the property of the surviving partnership or limited partnership, the general partners of that party immediately before the effective date of the merger shall contribute the amount necessary to satisfy that party's obligations to the surviving entity, in the manner provided in Section 807 or in the [Limited Partnership

Act] of the jurisdiction in which the party was formed, as the case may be, as if the merged party were dissolved.

(e) A partner of a party to a merger who does not become a partner of the surviving partnership or limited partnership is dissociated from the entity, of which that partner was a partner, as of the date the merger takes effect. The surviving entity shall cause the partner's interest in the entity to be purchased under Section 701 or another statute specifically applicable to that partner's interest with respect to a merger. The surviving entity is bound under Section 702 by an act of a general partner dissociated under this subsection, and the partner is liable under Section 703 for transactions entered into by the surviving entity after the merger takes effect.

Comment

Section 906 states the effect of a merger on the partnerships that are parties to the merger and on the individual partners.

Subsection (a) provides that when the merger takes effect: (1) the separate existence of every partnership that is a party to the merger (other than the surviving entity) ceases; (2) all property owned by the parties to the merger vests in the surviving entity; (3) all obligations of every party to the merger become the obligations of the surviving entity; and (4) all legal actions pending against a party to the merger may be continued as if the merger had not occurred or the surviving entity may be substituted as a party. Title to partnership property vests in the surviving entity without further act or deed and without reversion or impairment.

Subsection (b) makes the secretary of state the agent for service of process in any action against the surviving entity, if it is a foreign entity, to enforce an obligation of a domestic partnership that is a party to the merger. The purpose of this rule is to make it more convenient for local creditors to sue a foreign surviving entity when the credit was extended to a domestic partnership that has disappeared as a result of the merger.

Subsection (c) provides that a general partner of the surviving entity is liable for (1) all obligations for which the partner was personally liable before the merger; (2) all other obligations of the surviving entity incurred before the merger by a party to the merger, which obligations may be satisfied only out of the surviving entity's partnership property; and (3) all obligations incurred by the surviving entity after the merger, limited to the surviving entity's property in the case of limited partners <u>and also limited to obligations of the partnership for which the partner was personally liable under Section 306</u>.

This scheme of liability is similar to that of an incoming partner under Section 306(b). Only the surviving partnership itself is liable for all obligations, including obligations incurred by every constituent party before the merger. A general partner of the surviving entity is personally liable for obligations of the surviving entity incurred before the merger by the partnership of which he was a partner and those incurred by the surviving entity after the merger. Thus, a general partner of the surviving entity is liable only to the extent of his partnership interest for obligations incurred before the merger by a constituent party of which he was not a general partner.

Subsection (d) requires general partners to contribute the amount necessary to satisfy all obligations for which they were personally liable before the merger, if such obligations are not satisfied out of the partnership property of the surviving entity, in the same manner as provided in Section 807 or the limited partnership act of the applicable jurisdiction, as if the merged party were then dissolved. *See* RULPA §§ 502, 608.

Subsection (e) provides for the dissociation of a partner of a party to the merger who does not become a partner in the surviving entity. The surviving entity must buy out that partner's interest in the partnership under Section 701 or other specifically applicable statute. If the state limited partnership act has a dissenter's rights provision providing a different method of determining the amount due a dissociating limited partner, it would apply, rather than Section 701, since the two statutes should be read *in pari materia.*

Although subsection (e) does not expressly provide that a partner's withdrawal upon the merger of a term partnership is rightful, it was assumed that the unanimity requirement for the approval of a merger would afford a withdrawing partner adequate opportunity to protect his interest as a condition of approval. This question is left to the partnership agreement if it provides for merger without the approval of all the partners.

Under subsection (e), a dissociating general partner's lingering agency power is wound down, pursuant to Section 702, the same as in any other dissociation. Moreover, a dissociating general partner may be liable, under Section 703, for obligations incurred by the surviving entity for up to two years after the merger. A dissociating general partner can, however, limit to 90 days his exposure to liability by filing a statement of dissociation under Section 704.

Section 907. Statement of Merger

(a) After a merger, the surviving partnership or limited partnership may file a statement that one or more partnerships or limited partnerships have merged into the surviving entity.

(b) A statement of merger must contain:

(1) the name of each partnership or limited partnership that is a party to the merger;

(2) the name of the surviving entity into which the other partnerships or limited partnership were merged;

(3) the street address of the surviving entity's chief executive office and of an office in this State, if any; and

(4) whether the surviving entity is a partnership or a limited partnership.

(c) Except as otherwise provided in subsection (d), for the purposes of Section 302, property of the surviving partnership or limited partnership which before the merger was held in the name of another party to the merger is property held in the name of the surviving entity upon filing a statement of merger.

(d) For the purposes of Section 302 real property of the surviving partnership or limited partnership which before the merger was held in the name of another party to the merger is property held in the name of the surviving entity upon recording a certified copy of the statement of merger in the office for recording transfers of that real property.

(e) A filed and, if appropriate, recorded statement of merger, executed and declared to be accurate pursuant to Section 105(c), stating the name of a partnership or limited partnership that is a party to the merger in whose name property was held before the merger and the name of the surviving entity, but not containing all of the other information required by subsection (b), operates with respect to the partnerships or limited partnerships named to the extent provided in subsections (c) and (d).

Comment

Section 907(a) provides that the surviving entity may file a statement of merger. The execution, filing, and recording of the statement are governed by Section 105.

Subsection (b) requires the statement to contain the name of each party to the merger, the name and address of the surviving entity, and whether it is a general or limited partnership.

Subsection (c) provides that, for the purpose of the Section 302 rules regarding the transfer of partnership property, all personal and intangible property which before the merger was held in the name of a party to the merger becomes, upon the filing of the statement of merger with the secretary of state, property held in the name of the surviving entity.

Subsection (d) provides a similar rule for real property, except that real property does not become property held in the name of the surviving entity until a certified copy of the statement of merger is recorded in the office for recording transfers of that real property under local law.

Subsection (e) is a savings provision in the event a statement of merger fails to contain all of the information required by subsection (b). The statement will have the operative effect provided in subsections (c) and (d) if it is executed and declared to be accurate pursuant to Section 105(e) and correctly states the name of the party to the merger in whose name the property was held before the merger, so that it would be found by someone searching the record. Compare Section 303(c) (statement of partnership authority).

Section 908. Nonexclusive.

This [article] is not exclusive. Partnerships or limited partnerships may be converted or merged in any other manner provided by law.

Comment

Section 908 provides that Article 9 is not exclusive. It is merely a "safe harbor." Partnerships may be converted or merged in any other manner provided by statute or common law. Existing statutes in a few States already authorize the conversion or merger of general partnerships and limited partnerships. *See* Comment 1 to Section 901. Those procedures may be followed in lieu of Article 9.

[ARTICLE] 10

LIMITED LIABILITY PARTNERSHIP

Section 1001. Statement of Qualification.

(a) A partnership may become a limited liability partnership pursuant to this section.

(b) The terms and conditions on which a partnership becomes a limited liability partnership must be approved by the vote necessary to amend the partnership agreement except, in the case of a partnership agreement that expressly considers contribution obligations, the vote necessary to amend those provisions.

(c) After the approval required by subsection (b), a partnership may become a limited liability partnership by filing a statement of qualification. The statement must contain:

(1) the name of the partnership;

(2) the street address of the partnership's chief executive office and, if different, the street address of an office in this State, if any;

(3) if there is no office in this State, the name and street address of the partnership's agent for service of process who must be an individual resident of this State or any other person authorized to do business in this State;

(4) a statement that the partnership elects to be a limited liability partnership; and

(5) a deferred effective date, if any.

(d) The status of a partnership as a limited liability partnership is effective on the later of the filing of the statement or a date specified in the statement. The status remains effective, regardless of changes in the partnership, until it is canceled pursuant to Section 105(d) or revoked pursuant to Section 1003.

(e) The status of a partnership as a limited liability partnership and the liability of its partners is not affected by errors or later changes in the information required to be contained in the statement of qualification under subsection (c).

(f) The filing of a statement of qualification establishes that a partnership has satisfied all conditions precedent to the qualification of the partnership as a limited liability partnership.

(g) An amendment or cancellation of a statement of qualification is effective when it is filed or on a deferred effective date specified in the amendment or cancellation.

Comment

Any partnership may become a limited liability partnership by filing a statement of qualification. See Comments to Sections 101(6) and 202(b) regarding a limited partnership filing a statement of qualification to become a limited liability limited partnership. Section 1001 sets forth the required contents of a statement of qualification. The section also sets forth requirements for the approval of a statement of qualification, establishes the effective date of the filing (and any amendments) which remains effective until canceled or revoked, and provides that the liability of the partners of a limited liability partnership is not affected by errors or later changes in the statement information.

Subsection (b) provides that the terms and conditions on which a partnership becomes a limited liability partnership must generally be approved by the vote necessary to amend the partnership agreement. This means that the act of becoming a limited liability partnership is equivalent to an amendment of the partnership agreement. Where the partnership agreement is silent as to how it may be amended, the subsection (b) vote requires the approval of every partner. Since the limited liability partnership rules are not intended to increase the vote necessary to amend the partnership agreement, where the partnership agreement specifically sets forth an amendment process, that process may be used. Where a partnership agreement sets forth several amendment procedures depending upon the nature of the amendment, the required vote will be that necessary to amend the contribution obligations of the partners. The specific "contribution" vote is preferred because the filing of the statement directly affects partner contribution obligations. Therefore, the language "considers contribution" should be broadly interpreted to include any amendment vote that indirectly affects any partner's contribution obligation such as a partner's obligation to "indemnify" other partners.

The unanimous vote default rule reflects the significance of a partnership becoming a limited liability partnership. In general, upon such a filing each partner is released from the personal contribution obligation imposed under this Act in exchange for relinquishing the right to enforce the contribution obligations of other partners under this Act. See Comments to Sections 306(c) and 401(b). The wisdom of this bargain will depend on many factors including the relative risks of the partners' duties and the assets of the partnership.

Subsection (c) sets forth the information required in a statement of qualification. It must include the name of the partnership which must comply with Section 1002 to identify the partnership as a limited liability partnership. The statement must also include the address of the partnership's chief executive office and, if different, the street address of any other office in this State. A statement must include the name and street address of an agent for service of process only if it does not have any office in this State.

As with other statements, a statement of qualification must be filed in the office of the Secretary of State. See Sections 101(13) and 105(a). Accordingly, a statement of qualification is executed, filed, and otherwise regarded as a statement under this Act. For example, a copy of a filed statement must be sent to every nonfiling partner unless otherwise provided in the partnership agreement. See Sections 105(e) and 103(b)(1). A statement of qualification must be executed by at least two partners under penalties of perjury that the contents of the statement are accurate. See Section 105(c). A person who files the statement must promptly send a copy of the statement to every nonfiling partner but failure to send the copy does not limit the effectiveness of the filed statement to a nonpartner. Section 105(e). The filing must be accompanied by the fee required by the Secretary of State. Section 105(f).

Subsection (d) makes clear that once a statement is filed and effective, the status of the partnership as a limited liability partnership remains effective until the partnership status is either canceled or revoked "regardless of changes in the partnership." Accordingly, a partnership that dissolves but whose business is continued under a business continuation agreement retains its status as a limited liability partnership without the need to refile a new statement. Also, limited liability partnership status remains even though a partnership may be dissolved, wound up, and terminated. Even after the termination of the partnership, the former partners of a terminated partnership would not be personally liable for partnership obligations incurred while the partnership was a limited liability partnership.

Subsection (d) also makes clear that limited liability partnership status remains effective until actual cancellation under Section 1003 or revocation under Section 105(d). Ordinarily the terms and conditions of becoming a limited liability partnership must be approved by the vote necessary to amend the partnership agreement. See Sections 1001(b), 306(c), and 401(j). Since the statement of cancellation may be filed by a person authorized to file the original statement of qualification, the same vote necessary to approve the filing of the statement of qualification must be obtained to file the statement of cancellation. See Section 105(d).

Subsection (f) provides that once a statement of qualification is executed and filed under subsection (c) and Section 105, the partnership assumes the status of a limited liability partnership. This status is intended to be conclusive with regard to third parties dealing with the partnership. It is not intended to affect the rights of partners. For example, a properly executed and filed statement of qualification conclusively establishes the limited liability shield described in Section 306(c). If the partners executing and filing the statement exceed their authority, the internal abuse of authority has no effect on the liability shield with regard to third parties. Partners may challenge the abuse of authority for purposes of establishing the liability of the culpable partners but may not effect the liability shield as to third parties. Likewise, third parties may not challenge the existence of the liability shield because the decision to file the statement lacked the proper vote. As a result, the filing of the statement creates the liability shield even when the required subsection (b) vote is not obtained.

Section 1002. Name.

The name of a limited liability partnership must end with "Registered Limited Liability Partnership", "Limited Liability Partnership", "R.L.L.P.", "L.L.P.", "RLLP", or "LLP".

Comment

The name provisions are intended to alert persons dealing with a limited liability partnership of the presence of the liability shield. Because many jurisdictions have adopted the naming concept of a "registered" limited liability partnership, this aspect has been retained. These name requirements also distinguish limited partnerships and general partnerships that become limited liability partnerships because the new name must be at the end of and in addition to the general or limited partnership's regular name. See Comments to Section 101(6). Since the name identification rules of this section do not alter the regular name of the partnership, they do not disturb historic notions of apparent authority of partners in both general and limited partnerships.

Section 1003. Annual Report.

(a) A limited liability partnership, and a foreign limited liability partnership authorized to transact business in this State, shall file an annual report in the office of the [Secretary of State] which contains:

(1) the name of the limited liability partnership and the State or other jurisdiction under whose laws the foreign limited liability partnership is formed;

(2) the current street address of the partnership's chief executive office and, if different, the current street address of an office in this State, if any; and

(3) if there is no current office in this State, the name and street address of the partnership's current agent for service of process who must be an individual resident of this State or any other person authorized to do business in this State.

(b) An annual report must be filed between [January 1 and April 1] of each year following the calendar year in which a partnership files a statement of qualification or a foreign partnership becomes authorized to transact business in this State.

(c) The [Secretary of State] may administratively revoke the statement of qualification of a partnership that fails to file an annual report when due or to pay the required filing fee. The [Secretary of State] shall provide the partnership at least 60 days' written notice of intent to revoke the statement. The notice must be mailed to the partnership at its chief executive office set forth in the last filed statement of qualification or annual report. The notice must specify the annual report that has not been filed, the fee that has not been paid, and the effective date of the revocation. The revocation is not effective if the annual report is filed and the fee is paid before the effective date of the revocation.

(d) A revocation under subsection (c) only affects a partnership's status as a limited liability partnership and is not an event of dissolution of the partnership.

(e) A partnership whose statement of qualification has been administratively revoked may apply to the [Secretary of State] for reinstatement within two years after the effective date of the revocation. The application must state:

(1) the name of the partnership and the effective date of the revocation; and

(2) that the ground for revocation either did not exist or has been corrected.

(f) A reinstatement under subsection (e) relates back to and takes effect as of the effective date of the revocation, and the partnership's status as a limited liability partnership continues as if the revocation had never occurred.

Comment

Section 1003 sets forth the requirements of an annual report that must be filed by all limited liability partnerships and any foreign limited liability partnership authorized to transact business in this State. See Sections 101(5) (definition of a limited liability partnership) and 101(4) (definition of a foreign limited liability partnership). The failure of a limited liability partnership to file an annual report is a basis for the Secretary of State to administratively revoke its statement of qualification. See Section 1003(c). A foreign limited liability partnership that fails to file an annual report may not maintain an action or proceeding in this State. See Section 1103(a).

Subsection (a) generally requires that an annual report contain the same information required in a statement of qualification. Compare Sections 1001(a) and 1003(a). The differences are that the annual report requires disclosure of the state of formation of a foreign limited liability partnership but deletes the delayed effective date and limited liability partnership election statement provisions of a statement of qualification. As such, the annual report serves to update the information required in a statement of qualification. Under subsection (b), the annual report must be filed between January 1 and April 1 of each calendar year following the year in which a statement of qualification was filed or a foreign limited liability partnership becomes authorized to transact business. This timing requirement means that a limited liability partnership must make an annual filing and may not prefile multiple annual reports in a single year.

Subsection (c) sets forth the procedure for the Secretary of State to administratively revoke a partnership's statement of qualification for the failure to file an annual report when due or pay the required filing fee. The Secretary of State must provide a partnership at least 60 days' written notice of the intent to revoke the statement. The notice must be mailed to the partnership at the address of its chief executive office set forth in the last filed statement or annual report and must state the grounds for revocation as well as the effective date of revocation. The revocation is not effective if the stated problem is cured before the stated effective date.

Under subsection (d), a revocation only terminates the partnership's status as a limited liability partnership but is not an event of dissolution of the partnership itself. Where revocation occurs, a partnership may apply for reinstatement under subsection (e) within two years after the effective date of the revocation. The application must state that the grounds for revocation either did not exist or have been corrected. The Secretary of State may grant the application on the basis of the statements alone or require proof of correction. Under subsection (f), when the application is granted, the reinstatement relates back to and takes effect as of the effective date of the revocation. The relation back doctrine prevents gaps in a reinstated partner's liability shield. See Comments to Section 306(c).

[ARTICLE] 11

FOREIGN LIMITED LIABILITY PARTNERSHIP

Section 1101.   Law Governing Foreign Limited Liability Partnership.
Section 1102.   Statement of Foreign Qualification.
Section 1103.   Effect of Failure to Qualify.
Section 1104.   Activities Not Constituting Transacting Business.
Section 1105.   Acton by [Attorney General].

Section 1101. Law Governing Foreign Limited Liability Partnership.

(a) The laws under which a foreign limited liability partnership is formed govern relations among the partners and between the partners and the partnership and the liability of partners for obligations of the partnership.

(b) A foreign limited liability partnership may not be denied a statement of foreign qualification by reason of any difference between the laws under which the partnership was formed and the laws of this State.

(c) A statement of foreign qualification does not authorize a foreign limited liability partnership to engage in any business or exercise any power that a partnership may not engage in or exercise in this State as a limited liability partnership.

Comment

Section 1101 provides that the laws where a foreign limited liability partnership is formed rather than the laws of this State govern both the internal relations of the partnership and liability of its partners for the obligations of the partnership. See Section 101(4) (definition of a foreign limited liability partnership). Section 106(b) provides that the laws of this State govern the internal relations of a domestic limited liability partnership and the liability of its partners for the obligations of the partnership. See Section 101(5) (definition of a domestic limited liability partnership). A partnership may therefore choose the laws of a particular jurisdiction by filing a statement of qualification in that jurisdiction. But there are limitations on this choice.

Subsections (b) and (c) together make clear that although a foreign limited liability partnership may not be denied a statement of foreign qualification simply because of a difference between the laws of its foreign jurisdiction and the laws of this State, it may not engage in any business or exercise any power in this State that a domestic limited liability partnership may not engage in or exercise. Under subsection (e), a foreign limited liability partnership that engages in a business or exercises a power in this State that a domestic may not engage in or exercise, does so only as an ordinary partnership without the benefit of the limited liability partnership liability shield set forth in Section 306(c). In this sense, a foreign limited liability partnership is treated the same as a domestic limited liability partnership. Also, the Attorney General may maintain an action to restrain a foreign limited liability partnership from transacting an unauthorized business in this State. See Section 1105.

Section 1102. Statement of Foreign Qualification.

(a) Before transacting business in this State, a foreign limited liability partnership must file a statement of foreign qualification. The statement must contain:

(1) the name of the foreign limited liability partnership which satisfies the requirements of the State or other jurisdiction under whose laws it is formed and ends with "Registered Limited Liability Partnership", "Limited Liability Partnership", "R.L.L.P.", "L.L.P.", "RLLP", or "LLP";

(2) the street address of the partnership's chief executive office and, if different, the street address of an office in this State, if any;

(3) if there is no office in this State, the name and street address of the partnership's agent for service of process who must be an individual resident of this State or any other person authorized to do business in this State; and

(4) a deferred effective date, if any.

(b) The status of a partnership as a foreign limited liability partnership is effective on the later of the filing of the statement of foreign qualification or a date specified in the statement. The status remains effective, regardless of changes in the partnership, until it is canceled pursuant to Section 105(d) or revoked pursuant to Section 1003.

(c) An amendment or cancellation of a statement of foreign qualification is effective when it is filed or on a deferred effective date specified in the amendment or cancellation.

Comment

Section 1102 provides that a foreign limited liability partnership must file a statement of foreign qualification before transacting business in this State. The section also sets forth the information required in the statement. As with other statements, a statement of foreign qualification must be filed in the office of the Secretary of State. See Sections 101(13), 105(a), and 1001(c). Accordingly, a statement of foreign qualification is executed, filed, and otherwise regarded as a statement under this Act. See Section 101(13) (definition of a statement includes a statement of foreign qualification).

Subsection (a) generally requires the same information in a statement of foreign qualification as is required in a statement of qualification. The statement of foreign qualification must include a name that complies with the requirements for domestic limited liability partnership under Section 1002 and must include the address of the partnership's chief executive office and, if different, the street address of any other office in this State. If a foreign limited liability partnership does not have any office in this State, the statement of foreign qualification must include the name and street address of an agent for service of process.

As with a statement of qualification, a statement of foreign qualification (and amendments) is effective when filed or at a later specified filing date. Compare Sections 1102(b) and (c) with Sections 1001(e) and (h). Likewise, a statement of foreign qualification remains effective until canceled by the partnership or revoked by the Secretary of State, regardless of changes in the partnership. See Section 105(d) (statement cancellation) and Section 1003 (revocation for failure to file annual report or pay annual filing fee) and compare Sections 1102(b) and 1001(e). Statement of qualification provisions regarding the relationship or the status of a foreign partnership relative to its initial filing of a statement are governed by foreign law and are therefore omitted from this section. See Sections 1001(f) (effect of errors and omissions) and (g) (filing establishes all conditions precedent to qualification).

Section 1103. Effect of Failure to Qualify.

(a) A foreign limited liability partnership transacting business in this State may not maintain an action or proceeding in this State unless it has in effect a statement of foreign qualification.

(b) The failure of a foreign limited liability partnership to have in effect a statement of foreign qualification does not impair the validity of a contract or act of the foreign limited liability partnership or preclude it from defending an action or proceeding in this State.

(c) Limitations on personal liability of partners are not waived solely by transacting business in this State without a statement of foreign qualification.

(d) If a foreign limited liability partnership transacts business in this State without a statement of foreign qualification, the [Secretary of State] is its agent for service of process with respect to [claims for relief] arising out of the transaction of business in this State.

Comment

Section 1103 makes clear that the only consequence of a failure to file a statement of foreign qualification is that the foreign limited liability partnership will not be able to maintain an action or proceeding in this State. The partnership's contracts remain valid, it may defend an action or proceeding, personal liability of the partners is not waived, and the Secretary of State is the agent for service of process with respect to claims arising out of transacting business in this State. Sections 1103(b)-(d). Once a statement of foreign qualification is filed, the Secretary of State may revoke the statement for failure to file an annual report but the partnership has the right to cure the failure for two years. See Section 1003(c) and (e). Since the failure to file a statement of foreign qualification has no impact on the liability shield of the partners, a revocation of a statement of foreign qualification also has no impact on the liability shield created under foreign laws. Compare Sections 1103(c) and 1003(f) (revocation of the statement of qualification of a domestic limited liability partnership removes partner liability shield unless filing problems cured within two years).

Section 1104. Activities Not Constituting Transacting Business.

(a) Activities of a foreign limited liability partnership which do not constitute transacting business within the meaning of this [article] include:

(1) maintaining, defending, or settling an action or proceeding;

(2) holding meetings of its partners or carrying on any other activity concerning its internal affairs;

(3) maintaining bank accounts;

(4) maintaining offices or agencies for the transfer, exchange, and registration of the partnership's own securities or maintaining trustees or depositories with respect to those securities;

(5) selling through independent contractors;

(6) soliciting or obtaining orders, whether by mail or through employees or agents or otherwise, if the orders require acceptance outside this State before they become contracts;

(7) creating or acquiring indebtedness, mortgages, or security interests in real or personal property;

(8) securing or collecting debts or foreclosing mortgages or other security interests in property securing the debts, and holding, protecting, and maintaining property so acquired;

(9) conducting an isolated transaction that is completed within 30 days and is not one in the course of similar transactions of like nature; and

(10) transacting business in interstate commerce.

(b) For purposes of this [article], the ownership in this State of income-producing real property or tangible personal property, other than property excluded under subsection (a), constitutes transacting business in this State.

(c) This section does not apply in determining the contacts or activities that may subject a foreign limited liability partnership to service of process, taxation, or regulation under any other law of this State.

Comment

Because the Attorney General may restrain a foreign limited liability partnership from transacting an unauthorized business in this State and a foreign partnership may not maintain an action or proceeding in this State, the concept of "transacting business" in this State is important. To provide more certainty, subsection (a) sets forth ten separate categories of activities that do not constitute transacting business. Subsection (c) makes clear that the section only considers the definition of "transacting business" and has no impact on whether a foreign limited liability partnership's activities in this State subject it to service of process, taxation, or regulation under any other law of this State.

Section 1105. Action by [Attorney General].

The [Attorney General] may maintain an action to restrain a foreign limited liability partnership from transacting business in this State in violation of this [article].

Comment

Section 1105 makes clear that the Attorney General may restrain a foreign limited liability partnership from transacting an unauthorized business in this State. As a threshold matter, a foreign limited liability partnership must be "transacting business" in this State within the meaning of Section 1104. Secondly, the business transacted in this State must be that which could not be engaged in by a domestic limited liability partnership. See Section 1101(c). The fact that a foreign limited liability partnership has a statement of foreign qualification does not permit it to engage in any unauthorized business in this State or impair the power of the Attorney General to restrain the foreign partnership from engaging in the unauthorized business. See Section 1101(c).

[ARTICLE] 12 ~~10~~

MISCELLANEOUS PROVISIONS

Section 1201 ~~1001~~. Uniformity of Application and Construction.

This [Act] shall be applied and construed to effectuate its general purpose to make uniform the law with respect to the subject of this [Act] among States enacting it.

Section 1202 ~~1002~~. Short Title.

This [Act] may be cited as the Uniform Partnership Act (1994).

Section 1203 ~~1003~~. Severability Clause.

If any provision of this [Act] or its application to any person or circumstance is held invalid, the invalidity does not affect other provisions or applications of this [Act] which can be given effect without the invalid provision or application, and to this end the provisions of this [Act] are severable.

Section 1204 ~~1004~~. Effective Date.

This [Act] takes effect . . . .

Comment

The effective date of the Act established by an adopting State has operative effects under Section 1006, which defers mandatory application of the Act to existing partnerships.

Section 1205 ~~1005~~. Repeals.

Effective January 1, 199_, the following acts and parts of acts are repeated: [the State Partnership Act as amended and in effect immediately before the effective date of this Act].

Comment

This section repeals the adopting State's present general partnership act. The effective date of the repealer should not be any earlier than the date selected by that State in Section 1006(b) 1206(b) for the application of the Act to all partnerships.

Section 1206 1006. Applicability.

(a) Before January 1, 199_, this [Act] governs only a partnership formed:

(1) after the effective date of this [Act], unless that partnership is continuing the business of a dissolved partnership under [Section 41 of the prior Uniform Partnership Act]; and

(2) before the effective date of this [Act], that elects, as provided by subsection (c), to be governed by this [Act].

(b) After January 1, 199_, this [Act] governs all partnerships.

(c) Before January 1, 199_, a partnership voluntarily may elect, in the manner provided in its partnership agreement or by law for amending the partnership agreement, to be governed by this [Act]. The provisions of this [Act] relating to the liability of the partnership's partners to third parties apply to limit those partners' liability to a third party who had done business with the partnership within one year preceding the partnership's election to be governed by this [Act], only if the third party knows or has received a notification of the partnership's election to be governed by this [Act].

Comment

This section provides for a transition period in the applicability of the Act to existing partnerships, similar to that provided in the revised Texas partnership act. *See* Tex. Rev. Civ. Stat. Ann. art. 6132b-10.03 (Vernon Supp. 1994). Subsection (a) makes application of the Act mandatory for all partnerships formed after the effective date of the Act and permissive, by election, for existing partnerships. That affords existing partnerships and partners an opportunity to consider the changes effected by RUPA and to amend their partnership agreements, if appropriate.

Under subsection (b), application of the Act becomes mandatory for all partnerships, including existing partnerships that did not previously elect to be governed by it, upon a future date to be established by the adopting State. Texas, for example, deferred for five years mandatory compliance by existing partnerships.

Subsection (c) provides that an existing partnership may voluntarily elect to be governed by RUPA in the manner provided for amending its partnership agreement. Under UPA Section 18(h), that requires the consent of all the partners, unless otherwise agreed. Third parties doing business with the partnership must know or be notified of the election before RUPA's rules limiting a partner's liability become effective as to them. Those rules would include, for example, the provisions of Section 704 limiting the liability of a partner 90 days after the filing of a statement of dissociation. Without knowledge of the partnership's election, third parties would not be aware that they must check the record to ascertain the extent of a dissociated partner's personal liability.

Section 1207 ~~1007~~. Savings Clause.

This [Act] does not affect an action or proceeding commenced or right accrued before this [Act] takes effect.

Comment

This section continues the prior law after the effective date of the Act with respect to a pending action or proceeding or a right accrued at the time of the effective date. Since courts generally apply the law that exists at the time an action is commenced, in many circumstances the new law of this Act would displace the old law, but for this section.

Almost all States have general savings statutes, usually as part of their statutory construction acts. These are often very broad. Compare Uniform Statute and Rule Construction Act § 16(a) (narrow savings clause). As RUPA is remedial, the more limited savings provisions in Section 1007 are more appropriate than the broad savings provisions of the usual general savings clause. *See generally*, Comment to Uniform Statute and Rule Construction Act § 16.

Pending "action" refers to a judicial proceeding, while "proceeding" is broader and includes administrative proceedings. Although it is not always clear whether a right has "accrued," the term generally means that a cause of action has matured and is ripe for legal redress. *See, e.g., Estate of Hoover v. Iowa Dept. of Social Services*, 299 Iowa 702, 251 N.W.2d 529 (1977); *Nielsen v. State of Wisconsin*, 258 Wis. 1110, 141 N.W.2d 194 (1966). An inchoate right is not enough, and thus, for example, there is no accrued right under a contract until it is breached.

Section 1208. Effective Date.

These [Amendments] take effect . . . .

Section 1209. Repeals.

Effective January 1, 199_, the following acts and parts of acts are repealed: [the Limited Liability Partnership amendments to the State Partnership Act as amended and in effect immediately before the effective date of these [Amendments].

Section 1210. Applicability.

(a) Before January 1, 199_, these [Amendments] govern only a limited liability partnership formed:

(1) after the effective date of these [Amendments], unless that partnership is continuing the business of a dissolved limited liability partnership; and

(2) before the effective date of these [Amendments], that elects, as provided by subsection (c), to be governed by these [Amendments].

(b) After January 1, 199_, these [Amendments] govern all partnerships.

(c) Before January 1, 199_, a partnership voluntarily may elect, in the manner provided in its partnership agreement or by law for amending the partnership agreement, to be governed by these [Amendments]. The provisions of these [Amendments] relating to the liability of the partnership's partners to third parties apply to limit those partners' liability to a third party who had done business with the partnership within one year preceding the partnership's election to be governed by these [Amendments], only if the third party knows or has received a notification of the partnership's election to be governed by these [Amendments].

(d) The existing provisions for execution and filing a statement of qualification of a limited liability partnership continue until either the limited liability partnership elects to have this [Act] apply or January 1, 199_.

Section 1211. Savings Clause.

These [Amendments] do not affect an action or proceeding commenced or right accrued before these [Amendments] take effect.

PART TWO

LIMITED PARTNERSHIP

UNIFORM LIMITED PARTNERSHIP ACT (1916)

Editor's note: The text and Official Comments of the Uniform Limited Partnership Act (1916) ("ULPA") are taken from volume 6A of Uniform Laws Annotated (1995) and reproduced by permission. The information contained below on adoptions is drawn from page 28 of the 1997 Cumulative Annual Pocket Part to 6A U.L.A. The year of adoption is identified for each state. All of the Official Comments to ULPA are reproduced below.

The reader should be alert to the fact that nearly all jurisdictions have now adopted the Revised Uniform Limited Partnership Act ("RULPA"). The effect on ULPA of the adoption of RULPA varies from state to state. In Colorado, for example, ULPA remains in effect for limited partnerships formed prior to the effective date of RULPA, unless the general partner or partners of the firm elect to be governed by RULPA and file evidence of that election. Other states have repealed ULPA upon adoption of RULPA. For information about particular states, see the section entitled Action in Adopting Jurisdictions immediately following § 1104 of RULPA in 6A U.L.A. (1995).

ULPA was approved by the National Conference of Commissioners on Uniform State Laws on August 28, 1916, and adopted at one time in all states except Louisiana. At the present time it is still governing law in the following jurisdictions: Colorado (1931), Georgia (1952), Minnesota (1919), New York (1922), Oklahoma (1951), Vermont (1941), and Virgin Islands (1957). All of these jurisdictions except Vermont and the Virgin Islands subsequently have adopted RULPA, with ULPA applying only to limited partnerships formed prior to the enactment of RULPA.

---

§ 1. Limited Partnership Defined

A limited partnership is a partnership formed by two or more persons under the provisions of Section 2, having as members one or more general partners and one or more limited partners. The limited partners as such shall not be bound by the obligations of the partnership.

Official Comment

The business reason for the adoption of acts making provisions for limited or special partners is that men in business often desire to secure capital from others. There are at least three classes of contracts which can be made with those from whom the capital is secured: One, the ordinary loan on interest; another, the loan where the lender, in lieu of interest, takes a share in the profits of the business; third, those cases in which the person advancing the capital secures, besides a share in the profits, some measure of control over the business.

At first, in the absence of statutes the courts, both in this country and in England, assumed that one who is interested in a business is bound by its obligations, carrying the application of this principle so far, that a contract where the only evidence of interest was a share in the profits made one who supposed himself a lender, and who was probably unknown to the creditors at the times they extended their credits, unlimitedly liable as a partner for the obligations of those actually conducting the business.

Later decisions have much modified the earlier cases. The lender who takes a share in the profits, except possibly in one or two of our jurisdictions, does not by reason of that fact run a risk of being held as a partner. If, however, his contract falls within the third class mentioned, and he has any measure of control over the business, he at once runs serious risk of being held liable for the debts of the business as a partner; the risk increasing as he increases the amount of his control.

The first Limited Partnership Act was adopted by New York in 1822; the other commercial states, during the ensuing 30 years, following her example. Most of the statutes follow the language of the New York statute with little material alteration. These statutes were adopted, and to a considerable degree interpreted by the courts, during that period when it was generally held that any interest in a business should make the person holding the interest liable for its obligations. As a result the courts usually assume in the interpretation of these statutes two principles as fundamental.

First: That a limited (or as he is also called a special) partner is a partner in all respects like any other partner, except that to obtain the privilege of a limitation on his liability, he has conformed to the statutory requirements in respect to filing a certificate and refraining from participation in the conduct of the business.

Second: The limited partner, on any failure to follow the requirements in regard to the certificate or any participation in the conduct of his business, loses his privilege of limited liability and becomes, as far as those dealing with the business are concerned, in all respects a partner.

The courts in thus interpreting the statutes, although they made an American partnership with limited members something very different from the French Societe en Commandite from which the idea of the original statutes was derived, unquestionably carried out the intent of those responsible for their adoption. This is shown by the very wording of the statutes themselves. For instance, all the statutes require that all partners, limited and general, shall sign the certificate, and nearly all state that: "If any false statement be made in such certificate all the persons interested in such partnership shall be liable for all the engagements thereof as general partners."

The practical result of the spirit shown in the language and in the interpretation of existing statutes, coupled with the fact that a man may now lend money to a partnership and take a share in the profits in lieu of interest without running serious danger of becoming bound for partnership obligations, has, to a very great extent, deprived the existing statutory provisions for limited partners of any practical usefulness. Indeed, apparently their use is largely confined to associations in which those who conduct the business have not more than one limited partner.

One of the causes forcing business into the corporate form, in spite of the fact that the corporate form is ill suited to many business conditions, is the failure of the existing limited partnership acts to meet the desire of the owners of a business to secure necessary capital under the existing limited partnership form of business association.

The draft herewith submitted proceeds on the following assumptions:

First: No public policy requires a person who contributes to the capital of a business, acquires an interest in the profits, and some degree of control over the conduct of the business, to become bound for the obligations of the business; provided creditors have no reason to believe at the times their credits were extended that such person was so bound.

Second: That persons in business should be able, while remaining themselves liable without limit for the obligations contracted in its conduct, to associate with themselves others who contribute to the capital and acquire rights of ownership, provided that such contributors do not compete with creditors for the assets of the partnership.

The attempt to carry out these ideas has led to the incorporation into the draft submitted of certain features, not found in, or differing from, existing limited partnership acts.

First: In the draft the person who contributes the capital, though in accordance with custom called a limited partner, is not in any sense a partner. He is, however, a member of the association (see Sec. 1.).

Second: As limited partners are not partners securing limited liability by filing a certificate, the association is formed when substantial compliance, in good faith, is had with the requirements for a certificate (Sec. 2(2)). This provision eliminates the difficulties which arise from the recognition of de facto associations, made necessary by the assumption that the association is not formed unless a strict compliance with the requirements of the act is had.

Third: The limited partner not being in any sense a principal in the business, failure to comply with the requirements of the act in respect to the certificate, while it may result in the nonformation of the association, does not make him a partner or liable as such. The exact nature of his liability in such cases is set forth in Sec. 11.

Fourth: The limited partner, while not as such in any sense a partner, may become a partner as any person not a member of the association may become a partner; and, becoming a partner, may nevertheless retain his rights as limited partner; this last provision enabling the entire capital embraced in the business to be divided between the limited partners, all the general partners being also limited partners (Sec. 12).

Fifth: The limited partner is not debarred from loaning money or transacting other business with the partnership as any other non-member; provided he does not, in respect to such transactions, accept from the partnership collateral security, or receive from any partner or the partnership any payment, conveyance, or release from liability, if at the time the assets of the partnership are not sufficient to discharge its obligations to persons not general or limited partners. (Sec. 13).

Sixth: The substitution of a person as limited partner in place of an existing limited partner, or the withdrawal of a limited partner, or the addition of new limited partners, does not necessarily dissolve the association (Secs. 8, 16(2b)); no limited partner, however, can withdraw his contribution until all liabilities to creditors are paid (Sec. 16(1a)).

Seventh: As limited partners are not principals in transactions of the partnership, their liability, except for known false statements in the certificate (Sec. 6), is to the partnership, not to creditors of the partnership (Sec. 17). The general partners cannot, however, waive any liability of the limited partners to the prejudice of such creditors (Sec. 17(3)).

§ 2. Formation

(1) Two or more persons desiring to form a limited partnership shall

(a) Sign and swear to a certificate, which shall state

I. The name of the partnership,

II. The character of the business,

III. The location of the principal place of business,

IV. The name and place of residence of each member; general and limited partners being respectively designated,

V. The term for which the partnership is to exist,

VI. The amount of cash and a description of and the agreed value of the other property contributed by each limited partner,

VII. The additional contributions, if any, agreed to be made by each limited partner and the times at which or events on the happening of which they shall be made,

VIII. The time, if agreed upon, when the contribution of each limited partner is to be returned,

IX. The share of the profits or the other compensation by way of income which each limited partner shall receive by reason of his contribution,

X. The right, if given, of a limited partner to substitute an assignee as contributor in his place, and the terms and conditions of the substitution,

XI. The right, if given, of the partners to admit additional limited partners,

XII. The right, if given, of one or more of the limited partners to priority over other limited partners, as to contributions or as to compensation by way of income, and the nature of such priority,

XIII. The right, if given, of the remaining general partner or partners to continue the business on the death, retirement or insanity of a general partner, and

XIV. The right, if given, of a limited partner to demand and receive property other than cash in return for his contribution.

(b) File for record the certificate in the office of [here designate the proper office].

(2) A limited partnership is formed if there has been substantial compliance in good faith with the requirements of paragraph (1).

§ 3. Business Which May Be Carried On

A limited partnership may carry on any business which a partnership without limited partners may carry on, except [here designate the business to be prohibited].

§ 4. Character of Limited Partner's Contribution

The contributions of a limited partner may be cash or other property, but not services.

§ 5. A Name Not to Contain Surname of Limited Partner; Exceptions

(1) The surname of a limited partner shall not appear in the partnership name, unless

(a) It is also the surname of a general partner, or

(b) Prior to the time when the limited partner became such the business had been carried on under a name in which his surname appeared.

(2) A limited partner whose name appears in a partnership name contrary to the provisions of paragraph (1) is liable as a general partner to partnership creditors who extend credit to the partnership without actual knowledge that he is not a general partner.

§ 6. Liability for False Statements in Certificate

If the certificate contains a false statement, one who suffers loss by reliance on such statement may hold liable any party to the certificate who knew the statement to be false.

(a) At the time he signed the certificate, or

(b) Subsequently, but within a sufficient time before the statement was relied upon to enable him to cancel or amend the certificate, or to file a petition for its cancellation or amendment as provided in Section 25(3).

§ 7. Limited Partner Not Liable to Creditors

A limited partner shall not become liable as a general partner unless, in addition to the exercise of his rights and powers as a limited partner, he takes part in the control of the business.

§ 8. Admission of Additional Limited Partners

After the formation of a limited partnership, additional limited partners may be admitted upon filing an amendment to the original certificate in accordance with the requirements of Section 25.

§ 9. Rights, Powers and Liabilities of a General Partner

(1) A general partner shall have all the rights and powers and be subject to all the restrictions and liabilities of a partner in a partnership without limited partners, except that without the written consent or ratification of the specific act by all the limited partners, a general partner or all of the general partners have no authority to

(a) Do any act in contravention of the certificate,

(b) Do any act which would make it impossible to carry on the ordinary business of the partnership,

(c) Confess a judgment against the partnership,

(d) Possess partnership property, or assign their rights in specific partnership property, for other than a partnership purpose,

(e) Admit a person as a general partner,

(f) Admit a person as a limited partner, unless the right so to do is given in the certificate,

(g) Continue the business with partnership property on the death, retirement or insanity of a general partner, unless the right so to do is given in the certificate.

§ 10.   Rights of a Limited Partner

(1) A limited partner shall have the same rights as a general partner to

(a) Have the partnership books kept at the principal place of business of the partnership, and at all times to inspect and copy any of them.

(b) Have on demand true and full information of all things affecting the partnership, and a formal account of partnership affairs whenever circumstances render it just and reasonable, and

(c) Have dissolution and winding up by decree of court.

(2) A limited partner shall have the right to receive a share of the profits or other compensation by way of income, and to the return of his contribution as provided in Sections 15 and 16.

§ 11. Status of Person Erroneously Believing Himself a Limited Partner

A person who has contributed to the capital of a business conducted by a person or partnership erroneously believing that he has become a limited partner in a limited partnership, is not, by reason of his exercise of the rights of a limited partner, a general partner with the person or in the partnership carrying on the business, or bound by the obligations of such person or partnership; provided that on ascertaining the mistake he promptly renounces his interest in the profits of the business, or other compensation by way of income.

§ 12. One Person Both General and Limited Partner

(1) A person may be a general partner and a limited partner in the same partnership at the same time.

(2) A person who is a general, and also at the same time a limited partner, shall have all the rights and powers and be subject to all the restrictions of a general partner; except that, in respect to his contribution, he shall have the rights against the other members which he would have had if he were not also a general partner.

§ 13. Loans and Other Business Transactions with Limited Partner

(1) A limited partner also may loan money to and transact other business with the partnership, and, unless he is also a general partner, receive on account of resulting claims against the partnership, with general creditors, a pro rata share of the assets. No limited partner shall in respect to any such claim

    (a) Receive or hold as collateral security any partnership property, or

    (b) Receive from a general partner or the partnership any payment, conveyance, or release from liability, if at the time the assets of the partnership are not sufficient to discharge partnership liabilities to persons not claiming as general or limited partners,

(2) The receiving of collateral security, or a payment, conveyance, or release in violation of the provisions of paragraph (1) is a fraud on the creditors of the partnership.

§ 14. Relation of Limited Partners Inter Se

Where there are several limited partners the members may agree that one or more of the limited partners shall have a priority over other limited partners as to the return of their contributions, as to their compensation by way of income, or as to any other matter. If such an agreement is made it shall be stated in the certificate, and in the absence of such a statement all the limited partners shall stand upon equal footing.

§ 15. Compensation of Limited Partner

A limited partner may receive from the partnership the share of the profits or the compensation by way of income stipulated for in the certificate; provided, that after such payment is made, whether from the property of the partnership or that of a general partner, the partnership assets are in excess of all liabilities of the partnership except liabilities to limited partners on account of their contributions and to general partners.

§ 16. Withdrawal or Reduction of Limited Partner's Contribution

(1) A limited partner shall not receive from a general partner or out of partnership property any part of his contribution until

(a) All liabilities of the partnership, except liabilities to general partners and to limited partners on account of their contributions, have been paid or there remains property of the partnership sufficient to pay them,

(b) The consent of all members is had, unless the return of the contribution may be rightfully demanded under the provisions of paragraph (2), and

(c) The certificate is cancelled or so amended as to set forth the withdrawal or reduction.

(2) Subject to the provisions of paragraph (1) a limited partner may rightfully demand the return of his contribution

(a) On the dissolution of a partnership, or

(b) When the date specified in the certificate for its return has arrived, or

(c) After he has given six months' notice in writing to all other members, if no time is specified in the certificate either for the return of the contribution or for the dissolution of the partnership,

(3) In the absence of any statement in the certificate to the contrary or the consent of all members, a limited partner, irrespective of the nature of his contribution, has only the right to demand and receive cash in return for his contribution.

(4) A limited partner may have the partnership dissolved and its affairs wound up when

(a) He rightfully but unsuccessfully demands the return of his contribution, or

(b) The other liabilities of the partnership have not been paid, or the partnership property is insufficient for their payment as required by paragraph (1a) and the limited partner would otherwise be entitled to the return of his contribution.

§ 17. Liability of Limited Partner to Partnership

(1) A limited partner is liable to the partnership

(a) For the difference between his contribution as actually made and that stated in the certificate as having been made, and

(b) For any unpaid contribution which he agreed in the certificate to make in the future at the time and on the conditions stated in the certificate.

(2) A limited partner holds as trustee for the partnership

(a) Specific property stated in the certificate as contributed by him, but which was not contributed or which has been wrongfully returned, and

(b) Money or other property wrongfully paid or conveyed to him on account of his contribution.

(3) The liabilities of a limited partner as set forth in this section can be waived or compromised only by the consent of all members; but a waiver or compromise shall not affect the right of a creditor of a partnership who extended credit or whose claim arose after the filing and before a cancellation or amendment of the certificate, to enforce such liabilities.

(4) When a contributor has rightfully received the return in whole or in part of the capital of his contribution, he is nevertheless liable to the partnership for any sum, not in excess of such return with interest, necessary to discharge its liabilities to all creditors who extended credit or whose claims arose before such return.

§ 18. Nature of Limited Partner's Interest in Partnership

A limited partner's interest in the partnership is personal property.

§ 19. Assignment of Limited Partner's Interest

(1) A limited partner's interest is assignable.

(2) A substituted limited partner is a person admitted to all the rights of a limited partner who has died or has assigned his interest in a partnership.

(3) An assignee, who does not become a substituted limited partner, has no right to require any information or account of the partnership transactions or to inspect the partnership books; he is only entitled to receive the share of the profits or other compensation by way of income, or the return of his contribution, to which his assignor would otherwise be entitled.

(4) An assignee shall have the right to become a substituted limited partner if all the members (except the assignor) consent thereto or if the assignor, being thereunto empowered by the certificate, gives the assignee that right.

(5) An assignee becomes a substituted limited partner when the certificate is appropriately amended in accordance with Section 25.

(6) The substituted limited partner has all the rights and powers, and is subject to all the restrictions and liabilities of his assignor, except those liabilities of which he was ignorant at the time he became a limited partner and which could not be ascertained from the certificate.

(7) The substitution of the assignee as a limited partner does not release the assignor from liability to the partnership under Sections 6 and 17.

§ 20. Effect of Retirement, Death or Insanity of a General Partner

The retirement, death or insanity of a general partner dissolves the partnership, unless the business is continued by the remaining general partners

(a) Under a right so to do stated in the certificate, or

(b) With the consent of all members.

§ 21. Death of Limited Partner

(1) On the death of a limited partner his executor or administrator shall have all the rights of a limited partner for the purpose of settling his estate, and such power as the deceased had to constitute his assignee a substituted limited partner.

(2) The estate of a deceased limited partner shall be liable for all his liabilities as a limited partner.

§ 22.   Rights of Creditors of Limited Partner

(1) On due application to a court of competent jurisdiction by any judgment creditor of a limited partner, the court may charge the interest of the indebted limited partner with payment of the unsatisfied amount of the judgment debt; and may appoint a receiver, and make all other orders, directions, and inquiries which the circumstances of the case may require.

(2) The interest may be redeemed with the separate property of any general partner, but may not be redeemed with partnership property.

(3) The remedies conferred by paragraph (1) shall not be deemed exclusive of others which may exist.

(4) Nothing in this act shall be held to deprive a limited partner of his statutory exemption.

Official Comment

In those states where a creditor on beginning an action can attach debts due the defendant before he has obtained a judgment against the defendant it is recommended that paragraph (1) of this section read as follows:

"On due application to a court of competent jurisdiction by any creditor of a limited partner, the court may charge the interest of the indebted limited partner with payment of the unsatisfied amount of such claim; and may appoint a receiver, and make all other orders, directions, and inquiries which the circumstances of the case may require."

§ 23.   Distribution of Assets

(1) In settling accounts after dissolution the liabilities of the partnership shall be entitled to payment in the following order:

(a) Those to creditors, in the order of priority as provided by law, except those to limited partners on account of their contributions, and to general partners,

(b) Those to limited partners in respect to their share of the profits and other compensation by way of income on their contributions,

(c) Those to limited partners in respect to the capital of their contributions,

(d) Those to general partners other than for capital and profits,

(e) Those to general partners in respect to profits,

(f) Those to general partners in respect to capital.

(2) Subject to any statement in the certificate or to subsequent agreement, limited partners share in the partnership assets in respect to their claims for capital, and in respect to their claims for profits or for compensation by way of income on their contributions respectively, in proportion to the respective amounts of such claims.

§ 24.   When Certificate Shall Be Cancelled or Amended

(1) The certificate shall be cancelled when the partnership is dissolved or all limited partners cease to be such.

(2) A certificate shall be amended when

(a) There is a change in the name of the partnership or in the amount or character of the contribution of any limited partner,

(b) A person is substituted as a limited partner,

(c) An additional limited partner is admitted,

(d) A person is admitted as a general partner,

(e) A general partner retires, dies or becomes insane, and the business is continued under Section 20,

(f) There is a change in the character of the business of the partnership,

(g) There is a false or erroneous statement in the certificate,

(h) There is a change in the time as stated in the certificate for the dissolution of the partnership or for the return of a contribution,

(i) A time is fixed for the dissolution of the partnership, or the return of a contribution, no time having been specified in the certificate, or

(j) The members desire to make a change in any other statement in the certificate in order that it shall accurately represent the agreement between them.

§ 25. Requirements for Amendment and for Cancellation of Certificate

(1) The writing to amend a certificate shall

(a) Conform to the requirements of Section 2(1a) as far as necessary to set forth clearly the change in the certificate which it is desired to make, and

(b) Be signed and sworn to by all members, and an amendment substituting a limited partner or adding a limited or general partner shall be signed also by the member to be substituted or added, and when a limited partner is to be substituted, the amendment shall also be signed by the assigning limited partner.

(2) The writing to cancel a certificate shall be signed by all members.

(3) A person desiring the cancellation or amendment of a certificate, if any person designated in paragraphs (1) and (2) as a person who must execute the writing refuses to do so, may petition the [here designate the proper court] to direct a cancellation or amendment thereof.

(4) If the court finds that the petitioner has a right to have the writing executed by a person who refuses to do so, it shall order the [here designate the responsible official in the office designated in Section 2] in the office where the certificate is recorded to record the cancellation or amendment of the certificate; and where the certificate is to be amended, the court shall also cause to be filed for record in said office a certified copy of its decree setting forth the amendment.

(5) A certificate is amended or cancelled when there is filed for record in the office [here designate the office designated in Section 2] where the certificate is recorded

(a) A writing in accordance with the provisions of paragraph (1), or (2) or

(b) A certified copy of the order of court in accordance with the provisions of paragraph (4).

(6) After the certificate is duly amended in accordance with this section, the amended certificate shall thereafter be for all purposes the certificate provided for by this act.

§ 26. Parties to Actions

A contributor, unless he is a general partner, is not a proper party to proceedings by or against a partnership, except where the object is to enforce a limited partner's right against or liability to the partnership.

§ 27. Name of Act

This act may be cited as The Uniform Limited Partnership Act.

§ 28. Rules of Construction

(1) The rule that statutes in derogation of the common law are to be strictly construed shall have no application to this act.

(2) This act shall be so interpreted and construed as to effect its general purpose to make uniform the law of those states which enact it.

(3) This act shall not be so construed as to impair the obligations of any contract existing when the act goes into effect, nor to affect any action or proceedings begun or right accrued before this act takes effect.

§ 29. Rules for Cases Not Provided for in This Act

In any case not provided for in this act the rules of law and equity, including the law merchant, shall govern.

§ 30. Provisions for Existing Limited Partnerships

(1) A limited partnership formed under any statute of this state prior to the adoption of this act, may become a limited partnership under this act by complying with the provisions of Section 2; provided the certificate set forth

(a) The amount of the original contribution of each limited partner, and the time when the contribution was made, and

(b) That the property of the partnership exceeds the amount sufficient to discharge its liabilities to persons not claiming as general or limited partners by an amount greater than the sum of the contributions of its limited partners.

(2) A limited partnership formed under any statute of this state prior to the adoption of this act, until or unless it becomes a limited partnership under this act, shall continue to be governed by the provisions of [here insert proper reference to the existing limited partnership act or acts], except that such partnership shall not be renewed unless so provided in the original agreement.

Official Comment

Section 30 will be omitted in any state which has not a limited partnership act.

§ 31. Act (Acts) Repealed

Except as affecting existing limited partnerships to the extent set forth in Section 30, the act (acts) of [here designate the existing limited partnership act or acts] is (are) hereby repealed.

Official Comment

Section 31 will be omitted in any state which has not a limited partnership act.

REVISED UNIFORM LIMITED PARTNERSHIP ACT (1976)

Historical Note

The Revised Uniform Limited Partnership Act (RULPA) was approved by the National Conference of Commissioners on Uniform State Laws in 1976. It supersedes the original Uniform Limited Partnership Act approved by the Conference in 1916.

Editor's note: RULPA (1976) and all of its Comments are reproduced below. The 1997 Cumulative Annual Pocket Part to 6A Uniform Laws Annotated (1995) contains on pages 1-2 a list of the jurisdictions that have adopted RULPA. That list is as follows: Alabama (1984); Alaska (1993); Arizona (1982); Arkansas (1979); California (1984); Colorado (1981); Connecticut (1979); Delaware (1982); District of Columbia (1987); Florida (1987); Georgia (1988); Hawaii (1990); Idaho (1982); Illinois (1987); Indiana (1988); Iowa (1982); Kansas (1984); Kentucky (1988); Maine (1992); Maryland (1982); Massachusetts (1982); Michigan (1983); Minnesota (1980); Mississippi (1988); Missouri (1987); Montana (1981); Nebraska (1982); Nevada (1987); New Hampshire (1988); New Jersey (1985); New Mexico (1988); New York (1991); North Carolina (1986); North Dakota (1985); Ohio (1985); Oklahoma (1984); Oregon (1986); Pennsylvania (1989); Rhode Island (1986); South Carolina (1984); South Dakota (1986); Tennessee (1989); Texas (1987); Utah (1990); Virginia (1987); Washington (1982); West Virginia (1982); Wisconsin (1984) and Wyoming (1979).

In 1985 the National Conference approved a new Uniform Limited Partnership Act (1985). Later, however, the Conference decided instead to incorporate the 1985 revisions into the 1976 Act. 6A Uniform Laws Annotated (1995) handles this by reproducing the 1976 RULPA with the 1985 changes indicated by underlines for added materials and strikeovers for deleted material. A version of RULPA that contains the 1985 amendments identified by deletion and addition immediately follows this 1976 version of RULPA. Forty-four states have adopted the 1985 amendments or portions thereof. A list of those states is set forth in the introduction to the deletion and addition version of RULPA.

The reader should be alert to the fact that RULPA, although called a uniform act, has been treated by many of the adopting states as more like a model act. As a result, many states have made substantial amendments to their acts. 6A Uniform Laws Annotated (1995) describes the amendments, state by state, in notes following each section.

Commissioners' Prefatory Note

The Revised Uniform Limited Partnership Act adopted by the National Conference of Commissioners on Uniform State Laws in August, 1976, was intended to modernize the prior uniform law while retaining the special character of limited partnerships as compared with corporations. The draftsman of a limited partnership agreement has a degree of flexibility in defining the relations among the partners that is not available in the corporate form. Moreover, the relationship among partners is consensual, and requires a degree of privity that forces the general partner to seek approval of the partners (sometimes unanimous approval) under circumstances that corporate management would find unthinkable. The limited partnership was not intended to be an alternative in all cases where corporate form is undesirable for tax or other reasons, and the new Act was not intended to make it so. The new Act clarifies many ambiguities and fills interstices in the prior uniform law by adding more detailed language and mechanics. In addition, some important substantive changes and additions have been made.

Article 1 provides a list of all of the definitions used in the Act, integrates the use of limited partnership names with corporate names and provides for an office and agent for service of process in the state of organization. All of these provisions are new. Article 2 collects in one place all provisions dealing with execution and filing of certificates of limited partnership and certificates of amendment and cancellation. Articles 1 and 2 reflect an important change in the statutory scheme: recognition that the basic document in any partnership, including a limited partnership, is the partnership agreement. The certificate of limited partnership is not a constitutive document (except in the sense that it is a statutory prerequisite to creation of the limited partnership), and merely reflects matters as to which creditors should be put on notice.

Article 3 deals with the single most difficult issue facing lawyers who use the limited partnership form of organization: the powers and potential liabilities of limited partners. Section 303 lists a number of activities in which a limited partner may engage without being held to have so participated in the control of the business that he assumes the liability of a general partner. Moreover, it goes on to confine the liability of a limited partner who merely steps over the line of participation in control to persons who actually know of that participation in control. General liability for partnership debts is imposed only on those limited partners who are, in effect, "silent general partners."[1] With that exception, the provisions of the new Act that impose liability on a limited partner who has somehow permitted third parties to be misled to their detriment as to the limited partner's true status confine that liability to those who have actually been misled. The provisions relating to general partners are collected in Article 4.

Article 5, the finance section, makes some important changes from the prior uniform law. The contribution of services and promises to contribute cash, property or services are now explicitly permitted as contributions. And those who fail to perform promised services are required, in the absence of an agreement to the contrary, to pay the value of the services stated in the certificate of limited partnership.

A number of changes from the prior uniform law are made in Article 6, dealing with distributions from and the withdrawal of partners from the partnership. For example, Section 608 creates a statute of limitations on the right of a limited partnership to recover all or part of a contribution that has been returned to a limited partner, whether to satisfy creditors or otherwise.

The assignability of partnership interests is dealt with in considerable detail in Article 7. The provisions relating to dissolution appear in Article 8, which, among other things, imposes a new standard for seeking judicial dissolution of a limited partnership.

---

[1] The drafters probably meant to say "secret" general partners. Silent partners do not play an active role in the business.

One of the thorniest questions for those who operate limited partnerships in more than one state has been the status of the partnership in a state other than the state of organization. Neither existing case law nor administrative practice makes it clear whether the limited partners continue to possess their limited liability and which law governs the partnership. Article 9 deals with this problem by providing for registration of foreign limited partnerships and specifying choice-of-law rules.

Finally, Article 10 of the new Act authorizes derivative actions to be brought by limited partners.

REVISED UNIFORM LIMITED PARTNERSHIP ACT (1976)

ARTICLE 1

GENERAL PROVISIONS

ARTICLE 2

FORMATION; CERTIFICATE OF LIMITED PARTNERSHIP

ARTICLE 3

LIMITED PARTNERS

ARTICLE 4

GENERAL PARTNERS

ARTICLE 5

FINANCE

ARTICLE 6

DISTRIBUTIONS AND WITHDRAWAL

ARTICLE 7

ASSIGNMENT OF PARTNERSHIP INTERESTS

ARTICLE 8

DISSOLUTION

ARTICLE 9

FOREIGN LIMITED PARTNERSHIPS

§ 901. Law Governing.
§ 902. Registration.
§ 903. Issuance of Registration.
§ 904. Name.
§ 905. Changes and Amendments.
§ 906. Cancellation of Registration.
§ 907. Transaction of Business Without Registration.
§ 908. Action by [Appropriate Official].

ARTICLE 10

DERIVATIVE ACTIONS

§ 1001. Right of Action.
§ 1002. Proper Plaintiff.
§ 1003. Pleading.
§ 1004. Expenses.

ARTICLE 11

MISCELLANEOUS

§ 1101. Construction and Application.
§ 1102. Short Title.
§ 1103. Severability.
§ 1104. Effective Date, Extended Effective Date and Repeal.
§ 1105. Rules for Cases Not Provided for in This Act.

ARTICLE 1

GENERAL PROVISIONS

§ 101.   [Definitions]

As used in this Act, unless the context otherwise requires:

(1) "Certificate of limited partnership" means the certificate referred to in Section 201, and the certificate as amended.

(2) "Contribution" means any cash, property, services rendered, or a promissory note or other binding obligation to contribute cash or property or to perform services, which a partner contributes to a limited partnership in his capacity as a partner.

(3) "Event of withdrawal of a general partner" means an event that causes a person to cease to be a general partner as provided in Section 402.

(4) "Foreign limited partnership" means a partnership formed under the laws of any State other than this State and having as partners one or more general partners and one or more limited partners.

(5) "General partner" means a person who has been admitted to a limited partnership as a general partner in accordance with the partnership agreement and named in the certificate of limited partnership as a general partner.

(6) "Limited partner" means a person who has been admitted to a limited partnership as a limited partner in accordance with the partnership agreement and named in the certificate of limited partnership as a limited partner.

(7) "Limited partnership" and "domestic limited partnership" mean a partnership formed by 2 or more persons under the laws of this State and having one or more general partners and one or more limited partners.

(8) "Partner" means a limited or general partner.

(9) "Partnership agreement" means any valid agreement, written or oral, of the partners as to the affairs of a limited partnership and the conduct of its business.

(10) "Partnership interest" means a partner's share of the profits and losses of a limited partnership and the right to receive distributions of partnership assets.

(11) "Person" means a natural person, partnership, limited partnership (domestic or foreign), trust, estate, association, or corporation.

(12) "State" means a state, territory, or possession of the United States, the District of Columbia, or the Commonwealth of Puerto Rico.

Commissioners' Comment

The definitions in this section clarify a number of uncertainties in existing law and make certain changes.

Contribution: this definition makes it clear that a present contribution of services and a promise to make a future payment of cash, contribution of property or performance of services are permissible forms for a contribution. Accordingly, the present services or promise must be accorded a value in the certificate of limited partnership (Section 201(5)), and, in the case of a promise, that value may determine the liability of a partner who fails to honor his agreement (Section 502). Section 3 of the prior uniform law did not permit a limited partner's contribution to be in the form of services, although that inhibition did not apply to general partners.

Foreign limited partnership: the Act only deals with foreign limited partnerships formed under the laws of another "State" of the United States (see subdivision 12 of Section 101), and any adopting State that desires to deal by statute with the status of entities formed under the laws of foreign countries must make appropriate changes throughout the Act. The exclusion of such entities from the Act was not intended to suggest that their "limited partners" should not be accorded limited liability by the courts of a State adopting the Act. That question would be resolved by the choice-of-law rules of the forum State.

General partner: this definition recognizes the separate functions of the partnership agreement and the certificate of limited partnership. The partnership agreement establishes the basic grant of management power to the persons named as general partners; but because of the passive role played by the limited partners, the separate, formal step of embodying that grant of power in the certificate of limited partnership has been preserved to emphasize its importance.

Limited partner: as in the case of general partners, this definition provides for admission of limited partners through the partnership agreement and solemnization in the certificate of limited partnership. In addition, the definition makes it clear that being named in the certificate of limited partnership is a prerequisite to limited partner status. Failure to file does not, however, mean that the participant is a general partner or that he has general liability. See Sections 202(e) and 303.

Partnership agreement: the prior uniform law did not refer to the partnership agreement, assuming that all important matters affecting limited partners would be set forth in the certificate of limited partnership. Under modern practice, however, it has been common for the partners to enter into a comprehensive partnership agreement, only part of which was required to be included in the certificate of limited partnership. As reflected in Section 201, the certificate of limited partnership is confined principally to matters respecting the addition and withdrawal of partners and of capital, and other important issues are left to the partnership agreement.

Partnership interest: this definition is new and is intended to define what it is that is transferred when a partnership interest is assigned.

§ 102.   [Name]

The name of each limited partnership as set forth in its certificate of limited partnership:

(1) shall contain without abbreviation the words "limited partnership";

(2) may not contain the name of a limited partner unless (i) it is also the name of a general partner or the corporate name of a corporate general partner, or (ii) the business of the limited partnership had been carried on under that name before the admission of that limited partner;

(3) may not contain any word or phrase indicating or implying that it is organized other than for a purpose stated in its certificate of limited partnership;

(4) may not be the same as, or deceptively similar to, the name of any corporation or limited partnership organized under the laws of this State or licensed or registered as a foreign corporation or limited partnership in this State; and

(5) may not contain the following words [here insert prohibited words].

Commissioners' Comment

Subdivision (2) of Section 102 has been carried over from Section 5 of the prior uniform law with certain editorial changes. The remainder of Section 102 is new and primarily reflects the intention to integrate the registration of limited partnership names with that of corporate names. Accordingly, Section 201 provides for central, State-wide filing of certificates of limited partnership, and subdivisions (3), (4) and (5) of Section 102 contain standards to be applied by the filing officer in determining whether the certificate should be filed. Subdivision (1) requires that the proper name of a limited partnership contain the words "limited partnership" in full.

§ 103.   [Reservation of Name]

(a) The exclusive right to the use of a name may be reserved by:

(1) any person intending to organize a limited partnership under this Act and to adopt that name;

(2) any domestic limited partnership or any foreign limited partnership registered in this State which, in either case, intends to adopt that name;

(3) any foreign limited partnership intending to register in this State and adopt that name; and

(4) any person intending to organize a foreign limited partnership and intending to have it register in this State and adopt that name.

(b) The reservation shall be made by filing with the Secretary of State an application, executed by the applicant, to reserve a specified name. If the Secretary of State finds that the name is available for use by a domestic or foreign limited partnership, he shall reserve the name for the exclusive use of the applicant for a period of 120 days. Once having so reserved a name, the same applicant may not again reserve the same name until more than 60 days after the expiration of the last 120-day period for which that applicant reserved that name. The right to the exclusive use of a reserved name may be transferred to any other person by filing in the office of the Secretary of State a notice of the transfer, executed by the applicant for whom the name was reserved and specifying the name and address of the transferee.

Commissioners' Comment

Section 103 is new. The prior uniform law did not provide for registration of names.

§ 104.   [Specified Office and Agent]

Each limited partnership shall continuously maintain in this State:
(1) an office, which may but need not be a place of its business in this State, at which shall be kept the records required by Section 105 to be maintained; and
(2) an agent for service of process on the limited partnership, which agent must be an individual resident of this State, a domestic corporation, or a foreign corporation authorized to do business in this State.

Commissioners' Comment

Section 104 is new. It requires that a limited partnership have certain minimum contacts with its State of organization, i.e., an office at which the constitutive documents and basic financial information is kept and an agent for service of process.

§ 105.   [Records to Be Kept]

Each limited partnership shall keep at the office referred to in Section 104(1) the following: (1) a current list of the full name and last known business address of each partner set forth in alphabetical order, (2) a copy of the certificate of limited partnership and all certificates of amendment thereto, together with executed copies of any powers of attorney pursuant to which any certificate has been executed, (3) copies of the limited partnership's federal, state, and local income tax returns and reports, if any, for the 3 most recent years, and (4) copies of any then effective written partnership agreements and of any financial statements of the limited partnership for the 3 most recent years. Those records are subject to inspection and copying at the reasonable request, and at the expense, of any partner during ordinary business hours.

Commissioners' Comment

Section 105 is new. In view of the passive nature of the limited partner's position, it has been widely felt that limited partners are entitled to access to certain basic documents, including the certificate of limited partnership and any partnership agreement. In view of the great diversity among limited partnerships, it was thought inappropriate to require a standard form of financial report, and Section 105 does no more than require retention of tax returns and any other financial statements that are prepared. The names and addresses of the partners are made available to the general public.

§ 106.   [Nature of Business]

A limited partnership may carry on any business that a partnership without limited partners may carry on except [here designate prohibited activities].

Commissioners' Comment

Section 106 is identical to Section 3 of the prior uniform law. Many states require that certain regulated industries, such as banking, may be carried on only by entities organized pursuant to special statutes, and it is contemplated that the prohibited activities would be confined to the matters covered by those statutes.

§ 107.   [Business Transactions of Partner with the Partnership]

Except as provided in the partnership agreement, a partner may lend money to and transact other business with the limited partnership and, subject to other applicable law, has the same rights and obligations with respect thereto as a person who is not a partner.

Commissioners' Comment

Section 107 makes a number of important changes in Section 13 of the prior uniform law. Section 13, in effect, created a special fraudulent conveyance provision applicable to the making of secured loans by limited partners and the repayment by limited partnerships of loans from limited partners. Section 107 leaves that question to a State's general fraudulent conveyance statute. In addition, Section 107 eliminates the prohibition in former Section 13 against a general partner (as opposed to a limited partner) sharing pro rata with general creditors in the case of an unsecured loan. Of course, other doctrines developed under bankruptcy and insolvency laws may require the subordination of loans by partners under appropriate circumstances.

ARTICLE 2

FORMATION; CERTIFICATE OF LIMITED PARTNERSHIP

§ 201.   [Certificate of Limited Partnership]

(a) In order to form a limited partnership two or more persons must execute a certificate of limited partnership. The certificate shall be filed in the office of the Secretary of State and set forth:

(1) the name of the limited partnership;

(2) the general character of its business;

(3) the address of the office and the name and address of the agent for service of process required to be maintained by Section 104;

(4) the name and the business address of each partner (specifying separately the general partners and limited partners);

(5) the amount of cash and a description and statement of the agreed value of the other property or services contributed by each partner and which each partner has agreed to contribute in the future;

(6) the times at which or events on the happening of which any additional contributions agreed to be made by each partner are to be made;

(7) any power of a limited partner to grant the right to become a limited partner to an assignee of any part of his partnership interest, and the terms and conditions of the power;

(8) if agreed upon, the time at which or the events on the happening of which a partner may terminate his membership in the limited partnership and the amount of, or the method of determining, the distribution to which he may be entitled respecting his partnership interest, and the terms and conditions of the termination and distribution;

(9) any right of a partner to receive distributions of property, including cash from the limited partnership;

(10) any right of a partner to receive, or of a general partner to make, distributions to a partner which include a return of all or any part of the partner's contribution;

(11) any time at which or events upon the happening of which the limited partnership is to be dissolved and its affairs wound up;

(12) any right of the remaining general partners to continue the business on the happening of an event of withdrawal of a general partner; and

(13) any other matters the partners determine to include therein.

(b) A limited partnership is formed at the time of the filing of the certificate of limited partnership in the office of the Secretary of State or at any later time specified in the certificate of limited partnership if, in either case, there has been substantial compliance with the requirements of this section.

Commissioners' Comment

The matters required to be set forth in the certificate of limited partnership are not different in kind from those required by Section 2 of the prior uniform law, although certain additions and deletions have been made and the description has been revised to conform with the rest of the Act. In general, the certificate is intended to serve two functions: first, to place creditors on notice of the facts concerning the capital of the partnership and the rules regarding additional contributions to and withdrawals from the partnership; second, to clearly delineate the time at which persons become general partners and limited partners. Subparagraph (b), which is based upon the prior uniform law, has been retained to make it clear that the existence of the limited partnership depends only upon compliance with this section. Its continued existence is not dependent upon compliance with other provisions of this Act.

§ 202.   [Amendment to Certificate]

(a) A certificate of limited partnership is amended by filing a certificate of amendment thereto in the office of the Secretary of State. The certificate shall set forth:

(1) the name of the limited partnership;

(2) the date of filing of the certificate; and

(3) the amendment to the certificate.

(b) Within 30 days after the happening of any of the following events an amendment to a certificate of limited partnership reflecting the occurrence of the event or events shall be filed:

(1) a change in the amount or character of the contribution of any partner, or in any partner's obligation to make a contribution;

(2) the admission of a new partner;

(3) the withdrawal of a partner; or

(4) the continuation of the business under Section 801 after an event of withdrawal of a general partner.

(c) A general partner who becomes aware that any statement in a certificate of limited partnership was false when made or that any arrangements or other facts described have changed, making the certificate inaccurate in any respect, shall promptly amend the certificate, but an amendment to show a change of address of a limited partner need be filed only once every 12 months.

(d) A certificate of limited partnership may be amended at any time for any other proper purpose the general partners may determine.

(e) No person has any liability because an amendment to a certificate of limited partnership has not been filed to reflect the occurrence of any event referred to in subsection (b) of this Section if the amendment is filed within the 30-day period specified in subsection (b).

Commissioners' Comment

Section 202 makes substantial changes in Section 24 of the prior uniform law. Paragraph (b) lists the basic events — the addition or withdrawal of partners or capital or capital obligations — that are so central to the function of the certificate of limited partnership that they require prompt amendment. Paragraph (c) makes it clear, as it was not clear under subdivision (2)(g) of former Section 24, that the certificate of limited partnership is intended to be an accurate description of the facts to which it relates at all times and does not speak merely as of the date it is executed. Paragraph (e) provides a "safe harbor" against claims of creditors or others who assert that they have been misled by the failure to amend the certificate of limited partnership to reflect changes in any of the important facts referred to in paragraph (b); if the certificate of limited partnership is amended within 30 days of the occurrence of the event, no creditor or other person can recover for damages sustained during the interim. Additional protection is afforded by the provisions of Section 304.

§ 203.   [Cancellation of Certificate]

A certificate of limited partnership shall be cancelled upon the dissolution and the commencement of winding up of the partnership or at any other time there are no limited partners. A certificate of cancellation shall be filed in the office of the Secretary of State and set forth:

(1) the name of the limited partnership;

(2) the date of filing of its certificate of limited partnership;

(3) the reason for filing the certificate of cancellation;

(4) the effective date (which shall be a date certain) of cancellation if it is not to be effective upon the filing of the certificate; and

(5) any other information the general partners filing the certificate determine.

Commissioners' Comment

Section 203 changes Section 24 of the prior uniform law by making it clear that the certificate of cancellation should be filed upon the commencement of winding up of the limited partnership. Section 24 provided for cancellation "when the partnership is dissolved."

§ 204.   [Execution of Certificates]

(a) Each certificate required by this Article to be filed in the office of the Secretary of State shall be executed in the following manner:

(1) an original certificate of limited partnership must be signed by all partners named therein;

(2) a certificate of amendment must be signed by at least one general partner and by each other partner designated in the certificate as a new partner or whose contribution is described as having been increased; and

(3) a certificate of cancellation must be signed by all general partners;

(b) Any person may sign a certificate by an attorney-in-fact, but a power of attorney to sign a certificate relating to the admission, or increased contribution, of a partner must specifically describe the admission or increase.

(c) The execution of a certificate by a general partner constitutes an affirmation under the penalties of perjury that the facts stated therein are true.

Commissioners' Comment

Section 204 collects in one place the formal requirements for the execution of certificates which were set forth in Sections 2 and 25 of the prior uniform law. Those sections required that each certificate be signed by all partners, and there developed an unnecessarily cumbersome practice of having each limited partner sign powers of attorney to authorize the general partners to execute certificates of amendment on their behalf. Section 204 insures that each partner must sign a certificate when he becomes a partner or when the certificates reflect any increase in his obligation to make contributions. Certificates of amendment are required to be signed by only one general partner and all general partners must sign certificates of cancellation. Section 204 prohibits blanket powers of attorney for the execution of certificates in many cases, since those conditions under which a partner is required to sign have been narrowed to circumstances of special importance to that partner. The former requirement that all certificates be sworn has been confined to statements by the general partners, recognizing that the limited partner's role is a limited one.

§ 205.   [Amendment or Cancellation by Judicial Act]

If a person required by Section 204 to execute a certificate of amendment or cancellation fails or refuses to do so, any other partner, and any assignee of a partnership interest, who is adversely affected by the failure or refusal, may petition the [here designate the proper court] to direct the amendment or cancellation. If the court finds that the amendment or cancellation is proper and that any person so designated has failed or refused to execute the certificate, it shall order the Secretary of State to record an appropriate certificate of amendment or cancellation.

Commissioners' Comment

Section 205 changes subdivisions (3) and (4) of Section 25 of the prior uniform law by confining the persons who have standing to seek judicial intervention to partners and to those assignees who are adversely affected by the failure or refusal of the appropriate persons to file a certificate of amendment or cancellation.

§ 206.   [Filing in Office of Secretary of State]

(a) Two signed copies of the certificate of limited partnership and of any certificates of amendment or cancellation (or of any judicial decree of amendment or cancellation) shall be delivered to the Secretary of State. A person who executes a certificate as an agent or fiduciary need not exhibit evidence of his authority as a prerequisite to filing. Unless the Secretary of State finds that any certificate does not conform to law, upon receipt of all filing fees required by law he shall:

(1) endorse on each duplicate original the word "Filed" and the day, month, and year of the filing thereof;
(2) file one duplicate original in his office; and
(3) return the other duplicate original to the person who filed it or his representative.

(b) Upon the filing of a certificate of amendment (or judicial decree of amendment) in the office of the Secretary of State, the certificate of limited partnership shall be amended as set forth therein, and upon the effective date of a certificate of cancellation (or a judicial decree thereof), the certificate of limited partnership is cancelled.

Commissioners' Comment

Section 206 is new. In addition to providing mechanics for the central filing system, the second sentence of this section does away with the requirement, formerly imposed by some local filing officers, that persons who have executed certificates under a power of attorney exhibit executed copies of the power of attorney itself. Paragraph (b) changes subdivision (5) of Section 25 of the prior uniform law by providing that certificates of cancellation are effective upon their effective date under Section 203.

§ 207.   [Liability for False Statement in Certificate]

If any certificate of limited partnership or certificate of amendment or cancellation contains a false statement, one who suffers loss by reliance on the statement may recover damages for the loss from:

(1) any person who executes the certificate, or causes another to execute it on his behalf, and knew, and any general partner who knew or should have known, the statement to be false at the time the certificate was executed; and

(2) any general partner who thereafter knows or should have known that any arrangement or other fact described in the certificate has changed, making the statement inaccurate in any respect within a sufficient time before the statement was relied upon reasonably to have enabled that general partner to cancel or amend the certificate, or to file a petition for its cancellation or amendment under Section 205.

Commissioners' Comment

Section 207 changes Section 6 of the prior uniform law by providing explicitly for the liability of persons who sign a certificate as agent under a power of attorney and by confining the obligation to amend a certificate of limited partnership in light of future events to general partners.

§ 208.   [Notice]

The fact that a certificate of limited partnership is on file in the office of the Secretary of State is notice that the partnership is a limited partnership and the persons designated therein as limited partners are limited partners, but it is not notice of any other fact.

Commissioners' Comment

Section 208 is new. By stating that the filing of a certificate of limited partnership only results in notice of the limited liability of the limited partners, it obviates the concern that third parties may be held to have notice of special provisions set forth in the certificate. While this section is designed to preserve the limited liability of limited partners, the notice provided is not intended to change any liability of a limited partner which may be created by his action or inaction under the law of estoppel, agency, fraud, or the like.

§ 209.   [Delivery of Certificates to Limited Partners]

Upon the return by the Secretary of State pursuant to Section 206 of a certificate marked "Filed," the general partners shall promptly deliver or mail a copy of the certificate of limited partnership and each certificate to each limited partner unless the partnership agreement provides otherwise.

Commissioners' Comment

This section is new.

ARTICLE 3
LIMITED PARTNERS

§ 301.   [Admission of Additional Limited Partners]

(a) After the filing of a limited partnership's original certificate of limited partnership, a person may be admitted as an additional limited partner:

(1) in the case of a person acquiring a partnership interest directly from the limited partnership, upon the compliance with the partnership agreement or, if the partnership agreement does not so provide, upon the written consent of all partners; and

(2) in the case of an assignee of a partnership interest of a partner who has the power, as provided in Section 704, to grant the assignee the right to become a limited partner, upon the exercise of that power and compliance with any conditions limiting the grant or exercise of the power.

(b) In each case under subsection (a), the person acquiring the partnership interest becomes a limited partner only upon amendment of the certificate of limited partnership reflecting that fact.

Commissioners' Comment

Subdivision (1) of Section 301(a) adds to Section 8 of the prior uniform law an explicit recognition of the fact that unanimous consent of all partners is required for admission of new limited partners unless the partnership agreement provides otherwise. Subdivision (2) is derived from Section 19 of the prior uniform law but abandons the former terminology of "substituted limited partner."

§ 302.   [Voting]

Subject to Section 303, the partnership agreement may grant to all or a specified group of the limited partners the right to vote (on a per capita or other basis) upon any matter.

Commissioners' Comment

Section 302 is new, and must be read together with subdivision (b)(5) of Section 303. Although the prior uniform law did not speak specifically of the voting powers of limited partners, it is not uncommon for partnership agreements to grant such power to limited partners. Section 302 is designed only to make it clear that the partnership agreement may grant such power to limited partners. If such powers are granted to limited partners beyond the "safe harbor" of Section 303(b)(5), a court may hold that, under the circumstances, the limited partners have participated in "control of the business" within the meaning of Section 303(a). Section 303(c) simply means that the exercise of powers beyond the ambit of Section 303(b) is not ipso facto to be taken as taking part in the control of the business.

§ 303.   [Liability to Third Parties]

(a) Except as provided in subsection (d), a limited partner is not liable for the obligations of a limited partnership unless he is also a general partner or, in addition to the exercise of his rights and powers as a limited partner, he takes part in the control of the business. However, if the limited partner's participation in the control of the business is not substantially the same as the exercise of the powers of a general partner, he is liable only to persons who transact business with the limited partnership with actual knowledge of his participation in control.

(b) A limited partner does not participate in the control of the business within the meaning of subsection (a) solely by doing one or more of the following:

(1) being a contractor for or an agent or employee of the limited partnership or of a general partner;

(2) consulting with and advising a general partner with respect to the business of the limited partnership;

(3) acting as surety for the limited partnership;

(4) approving or disapproving an amendment to the partnership agreement; or

(5) voting on one or more of the following matters:

(i) the dissolution and winding up of the limited partnership;

(ii) the sale, exchange, lease, mortgage, pledge, or other transfer of all or substantially all of the assets of the limited partnership other than in the ordinary course of its business;

(iii) the incurrence of indebtedness by the limited partnership other than in the ordinary course of its business;

(iv) a change in the nature of the business; or

(v) the removal of a general partner.

(c) The enumeration in subsection (b) does not mean that the possession or exercise of any other powers by a limited partner constitutes participation by him in the business of the limited partnership.

(d) A limited partner who knowingly permits his name to be used in the name of the limited partnership, except under circumstances permitted by Section 102(2)(i), is liable to creditors who extend credit to the limited partnership without actual knowledge that the limited partner is not a general partner.

Commissioners' Comment

Section 303 makes several important changes in Section 7 of the prior uniform law. The first sentence of Section 303(a) carries over the basic test from former Section 7 whether the limited partner "takes part in the control of the business" in order to insure that judicial decisions under the prior uniform law remain applicable to the extent not expressly changed. The second sentence of Section 303(a) reflects a wholly new concept. Because of the difficulty of determining when the "control" line has been overstepped, it was thought it unfair to impose general partner's liability on a limited partner except to the extent that a third party had knowledge of his participation in control of the business. On the other hand, in order to avoid permitting a limited partner to exercise all of the powers of a general partner while avoiding any direct dealings with third parties, the "is not substantially the same as" test was introduced. Paragraph (b) is intended to provide a "safe harbor" by enumerating certain activities which a limited partner may carry on for the partnership without being deemed to have taken part in control of the business. Paragraph (d) is derived from Section 5 of the prior uniform law, but adds as a condition to the limited partner's liability the fact that a limited partner must have knowingly permitted his name to be used in the name of the limited partnership.

§ 304.   [Person Erroneously Believing Himself Limited Partner]

(a) Except as provided in subsection (b), a person who makes a contribution to a business enterprise and erroneously but in good faith believes that he has become a limited partner in the enterprise is not a general partner in the enterprise and is not bound by its obligations by reason of making the contribution, receiving distributions from the enterprise, or exercising any rights of a limited partner, if, on ascertaining the mistake, he:

(1) causes an appropriate certificate of limited partnership or a certificate of amendment to be executed and filed; or
(2) withdraws from future equity participation in the enterprise.

(b) A person who makes a contribution of the kind described in subsection (a) is liable as a general partner to any third party who transacts business with the enterprise (i) before the person withdraws and an appropriate certificate is filed to show withdrawal, or (ii) before an appropriate certificate is filed to show his status as a limited partner and, in the case of an amendment, after expiration of the 30-day period for filing an amendment relating to the person as a limited partner under Section 202, but in either case only if the third party actually believed in good faith that the person was a general partner at the time of the transaction.

Commissioners' Comment

Section 304 is derived from Section 11 of the prior uniform law. The "good faith" requirement has been added in the first sentence of Section 304(a). The provisions of subdivision (2) of Section 304(a) are intended to clarify an ambiguity in the prior law by providing that a person who chooses to withdraw from the enterprise in order to protect himself from liability is not required to renounce any of his then current interest in the enterprise so long as he has no further participation as an equity participant. Paragraph (b) preserves the liability of the equity participant prior to withdrawal (and after the time for appropriate amendment in the case of a limited partnership) to any third party who has transacted business with the person believing in good faith that he was a general partner.

§ 305. [Information]

Each limited partner has the right to:

(1) inspect and copy any of the partnership records required to be maintained by Section 105; and

(2) obtain from the general partners from time to time upon reasonable demand (i) true and full information regarding the state of the business and financial condition of the limited partnership, (ii) promptly after becoming available, a copy of the limited partnership's federal, state, and local income tax returns for each year, and (iii) other information regarding the affairs of the limited partnership as is just and reasonable.

Commissioners' Comment

Section 305 changes and restates the rights of limited partners to information about the partnership formerly provided by Section 10 of the prior uniform law.

ARTICLE 4

GENERAL PARTNERS

§ 401. [Admission of Additional General Partners]

After the filing of a limited partnership's original certificate of limited partnership, additional general partners may be admitted only with the specific written consent of each partner.

Commissioners' Comment

Section 401 is derived from Section 9 (1)(e) of the prior law and carries over the unwaivable requirement that all limited partners must consent to the admission of an additional general partner and that such consent must specifically identify the general partner involved.

§ 402.   [Events of Withdrawal]

Except as approved by the specific written consent of all partners at the time, a person ceases to be a general partner of a limited partnership upon the happening of any of the following events:

(1) the general partner withdraws from the limited partnership as provided in Section 602;

(2) the general partner ceases to be a member of the limited partnership as provided in Section 702;

(3) the general partner is removed as a general partner in accordance with the partnership agreement;

(4) unless otherwise provided in the certificate of limited partnership, the general partner: (i) makes an assignment for the benefit of creditors; (ii) files a voluntary petition in bankruptcy; (iii) is adjudicated a bankrupt or insolvent; (iv) files a petition or answer seeking for himself any reorganization, arrangement, composition, readjustment, liquidation, dissolution, or similar relief under any statute, law, or regulation; (v) files an answer or other pleading admitting or failing to contest the material allegations of a petition filed against him in any proceeding of this nature; or (vi) seeks, consents to, or acquiesces in the appointment of a trustee, receiver, or liquidator of the general partner or of all or any substantial part of his properties;

(5) unless otherwise provided in the certificate of limited partnership, [120] days after the commencement of any proceeding against the general partner seeking reorganization, arrangement, composition, readjustment, liquidation, dissolution, or similar relief under any statute, law, or regulation, the proceeding has not been dismissed, or if within [90] days after the appointment without his consent or acquiescence of a trustee, receiver, or liquidator of the general partner or of all or any substantial part of his properties, the appointment is not vacated or stayed, or within [90] days after the expiration of any such stay, the appointment is not vacated;

(6) in the case of a general partner who is a natural person,

    (i) his death; or

    (ii) the entry by a court of competent jurisdiction adjudicating him incompetent to manage his person or his estate;

(7) in the case of a general partner who is acting as a general partner by virtue of being a trustee of a trust, the termination of the trust (but not merely the substitution of a new trustee);

(8) in the case of a general partner that is a separate partnership, the dissolution and commencement of winding up of the separate partnership;

(9) in the case of a general partner that is a corporation, the filing of a certificate of dissolution, or its equivalent, for the corporation or the revocation of its charter; or

(10) in the case of an estate, the distribution by the fiduciary of the estate's entire interest in the partnership.

Commissioners' Comment

Section 402 expands considerably the provisions of Section 20 of the prior uniform law which provided for dissolution in the event of the retirement, death or insanity of a general partner. Subdivisions (1), (2) and (3) recognize, that the general partner's agency relationship is terminable at will, although it may result in a breach of the partnership agreement giving rise to an action for damages. Subdivisions (4) and (5) reflect a judgment that, unless the limited partners agree otherwise, they ought to have the power to rid themselves of a general partner who is in such dire financial straits that he is the subject of proceedings under the National Bankruptcy Act or a similar provision of law. Subdivisions (6) through (10) simply elaborate on the notion of death in the case of a general partner who is not a natural person. Of course, the addition of the words "and in the partnership agreement" was not intended to suggest that liabilities to third parties could be affected by provisions in the partnership agreement.

§ 403.   [General Powers and Liabilities]

Except as provided in this Act or in the partnership agreement, a general partner of a limited partnership has the rights and powers and is subject to the restrictions and liabilities of a partner in a partnership without limited partners.

Commissioners' Comment

Section 403 is derived from Section 9(1) of the prior uniform law.

§ 404.   [Contributions by a General Partner]

A general partner of a limited partnership may make contributions to the partnership and share in the profits and losses of, and in distributions from, the limited partnership as a general partner. A general partner also may make contributions to and share in profits, losses, and distributions as a limited partner. A person who is both a general partner and a limited partner has the rights and powers, and is subject to the restrictions and liabilities, of a general partner and, except as provided in the partnership agreement, also has the powers, and is subject to the restrictions, of a limited partner to the extent of his participation in the partnership as a limited partner.

Commissioners' Comment

Section 404 is derived from Section 12 of the prior uniform law and makes clear that the partnership agreement may provide that a general partner who is also a limited partner may exercise all of the powers of a limited partner.

§ 405.   [Voting]

The partnership agreement may grant to all or certain identified general partners the right to vote (on a per capita or any other basis), separately or with all or any class of the limited partners, on any matter.

Commissioners' Comment

Section 405 is new and is intended to make it clear that the Act does not require that the limited partners have any right to vote on matters as a separate class.

ARTICLE 5

FINANCE

§ 501.   [Form of Contribution]

The contribution of a partner may be in cash, property, or services rendered, or a promissory note or other obligation to contribute cash or property or to perform services.

Commissioners' Comment

As noted in the comment to Section 101, the explicit permission to make contributions of services expands Section 4 of the prior uniform law.

§ 502.   [Liability for Contributions]

(a) Except as provided in the certificate of limited partnership, a partner is obligated to the limited partnership to perform any promise to contribute cash or property or to perform services, even if he is unable to perform because of death, disability or any other reason. If a partner does not make the required contribution of property or services, he is obligated at the option of the limited partnership to contribute cash equal to that portion of the value (as stated in the certificate of limited partnership) of the stated contribution that has not been made.

(b) Unless otherwise provided in the partnership agreement, the obligation of a partner to make a contribution or return money or other property paid or distributed in violation of this Act may be compromised only by consent of all the partners. Notwithstanding the compromise, a creditor of a limited partnership who extends credit, or whose claim arises, after the filing of the certificate of limited partnership or an amendment thereto which, in either case, reflects the obligation, and before the amendment or cancellation thereof to reflect the compromise, may enforce the original obligation.

Commissioners' Comment

Although Section 17(1) of the prior uniform law required a partner to fulfill his promise to make contributions, the addition of contributions in the form of a promise to render services means that a partner who is unable to perform those services because of death or disability as well as because of an intentional default is required to pay the cash value of the services unless the certificate of limited partnership provides otherwise. Subdivision (b) is derived from Section 17(3) of the prior uniform law.

§ 503.   [Sharing of Profits and Losses]

The profits and losses of a limited partnership shall be allocated among the partners, and among classes of partners, in the manner provided in the partnership agreement. If the partnership agreement does not so provide, profits and losses shall be allocated on the basis of the value (as stated in the certificate of limited partnership) of the contributions made by each partner to the extent they have been received by the partnership and have not been returned.

Commissioners' Comment

Section 503 is new. The prior uniform law did not provide for the basis on which partners share profits and losses in the absence of agreement.

§ 504.   [Sharing of Distributions]

Distributions of cash or other assets of a limited partnership shall be allocated among the partners, and among classes of partners, in the manner provided in the partnership agreement. If the partnership agreement does not so provide, distributions shall be made on the basis of the value (as stated in the certificate of limited partnership) of the contributions made by each partner to the extent they have been received by the partnership and have not been returned.

Commissioners' Comment

Section 504 is new. The prior uniform law did not provide for the basis on which partners share distributions in the absence of agreement. This section also recognizes that partners may choose to share in distribution on a different basis than they share in profits and losses.

ARTICLE 6

DISTRIBUTIONS AND WITHDRAWAL

§ 601.   [Interim Distributions]

Except as provided in this Article, a partner is entitled to receive distributions from a limited partnership before his withdrawal from the limited partnership and before the dissolution and winding up thereof:

(1) to the extent and at the times or upon the happening of the events specified in the partnership agreement; and

(2) if any distribution constitutes a return of any part of his contribution under Section 608(b), to the extent and at the times or upon the happening of the events specified in the certificate of limited partnership.

Commissioners' Comment

Section 601 is new.

§ 602.   [Withdrawal of General Partner]

A general partner may withdraw from a limited partnership at any time by giving written notice to the other partners, but if the withdrawal violates the partnership agreement, the limited partnership may recover from the withdrawing general partner damages for breach of the partnership agreement and offset the damages against the amount otherwise distributable to him.

Commissioners' Comment

Section 602 is new but is generally derived from Section 38 of the Uniform Partnership Act.

§ 603.   [Withdrawal of Limited Partner]

A limited partner may withdraw from a limited partnership at the time or upon the happening of events specified in the certificate of limited partnership and in accordance with the partnership agreement. If the certificate does not specify the time or the events upon the happening of which a limited partner may withdraw or a definite time for the dissolution and winding up of the limited partnership, a limited partner may withdraw upon not less than 6 months' prior written notice to each general partner at his address on the books of the limited partnership at its office in this State.

Commissioners' Comment

Section 603 is derived from Section 16(c) of the prior uniform law.

§ 604.   [Distribution Upon Withdrawal]

Except as provided in this Article, upon withdrawal any withdrawing partner is entitled to receive any distribution to which he is entitled under the partnership agreement and, if not otherwise provided in the agreement, he is entitled to receive, within a reasonable time after withdrawal, the fair value of his interest in the limited partnership as of the date of withdrawal based upon his right to share in distributions from the limited partnership.

Commissioners' Comment

Section 604 is new. It fixes the distributive share of a withdrawing partner in the absence of an agreement among the partners.

§ 605.   [Distribution in Kind]

Except as provided in the certificate of limited partnership, a partner, regardless of the nature of his contribution, has no right to demand and receive any distribution from a limited partnership in any form other than cash. Except as provided in the partnership agreement, a partner may not be compelled to accept a distribution of any asset in kind from a limited partnership to the extent that the percentage of the asset distributed to him exceeds a percentage of that asset which is equal to the percentage in which he shares in distributions from the limited partnership.

Commissioners' Comment

The first sentence of Section 605 is derived from Section 16(3) of the prior uniform law. The second sentence is new, and is intended to protect a limited partner (and the remaining partners) against a distribution in kind of more than his share of particular assets.

§ 606.   [Right to Distribution]

At the time a partner becomes entitled to receive a distribution, he has the status of, and is entitled to all remedies available to, a creditor of the limited partnership with respect to the distribution.

Commissioners' Comment

Section 606 is new and is intended to make it clear that the right of a partner to receive a distribution, as between the partners, is not subject to the equity risks of the enterprise. On the other hand, since partners entitled to distributions have creditor status, there did not seem to be a need for the extraordinary remedy of Section 16(4) (a) of the prior uniform law, which granted a limited partner the right to seek dissolution of the partnership if he was unsuccessful in demanding the return of his contribution. It is more appropriate for the partner to simply sue as an ordinary creditor and obtain a judgment.

§ 607.   [Limitations on Distribution]

A partner may not receive a distribution from a limited partnership to the extent that, after giving effect to the distribution, all liabilities of the limited partnership, other than liabilities to partners on account of their partnership interests, exceed the fair value of the partnership assets.

Commissioners' Comment

Section 607 is derived from Section 16(1) (a) of the prior uniform law.

§ 608.   [Liability Upon Return of Contribution]

(a) If a partner has received the return of any part of his contribution without violation of the partnership agreement or this Act, he is liable to the limited partnership for a period of one year thereafter for the amount of the returned contribution, but only to the extent necessary to discharge the limited partnership's liabilities to creditors who extended credit to the limited partnership during the period the contribution was held by the partnership.

(b) If a partner has received the return of any part of his contribution in violation of the partnership agreement or this Act, he is liable to the limited partnership for a period of 6 years thereafter for the amount of the contribution wrongfully returned.

(c) A partner receives a return of his contribution to the extent that a distribution to him reduces his share of the fair value of the net assets of the limited partnership below the value (as set forth in the certificate of limited partnership) of his contribution which has not been distributed to him.

Commissioners' Comment

Paragraph (a) is derived from Section 17(4) of the prior uniform law, but the one-year statute of limitations has been added. Paragraph (b) is derived from Section 17(2) (b) of the prior uniform law but, again, a statute of limitations has been added. Paragraph (c) is new. The provisions of former Section 17(2) that referred to the partner holding as "trustee" any money or specific property wrongfully returned to him have been eliminated.

ARTICLE 7

ASSIGNMENT OF PARTNERSHIP INTERESTS

§ 701.   [Nature of Partnership Interest]

A partnership interest is personal property.

Commissioners' Comment

This section is derived from Section 18 of the prior uniform law.

§ 702.   [Assignment of Partnership Interest]

Except as provided in the partnership agreement, a partnership interest is assignable in whole or in part. An assignment of a partnership interest does not dissolve a limited partnership or entitle the assignee to become or to exercise any rights of a partner. An assignment entitles the assignee to receive, to the extent assigned, only the distribution to which the assignor would be entitled. Except as provided in the partnership agreement, a partner ceases to be a partner upon assignment of all his partnership interest.

Commissioners' Comment

Section 19(1) of the prior uniform law provided simply that "a limited partner's interest is assignable," raising a question whether *any* limitations on the right of assignment were permitted. While the first sentence of Section 702 recognizes that the power to assign may be restricted in the partnership agreement, there was no intention to affect in any way the usual rules regarding restraints on alienation of personal property. The second and third sentences of Section 702 are derived from Section 19(3) of the prior uniform law. The last sentence is new.

§ 703.   [Rights of Creditor]

On application to a court of competent jurisdiction by any judgment creditor of a partner, the court may charge the partnership interest of the partner with payment of the unsatisfied amount of the judgment with interest. To the extent so charged, the judgment creditor has only the rights of an assignee of the partnership interest. This Act does not deprive any partner of the benefit of any exemption laws applicable to his partnership interest.

Commissioners' Comment

Section 703 is derived from Section 22 of the prior uniform law but has not carried over some provisions that were thought to be superfluous. For example, references in Section 22(1) to specific remedies have been omitted, as has a prohibition in Section 22(2) against discharge of the lien with partnership property. Ordinary rules governing the remedies available to a creditor and the fiduciary obligations of general partners will determine those matters.

§ 704. [Right of Assignee to Become Limited Partner]

(a) An assignee of a partnership interest, including an assignee of a general partner, may become a limited partner if and to the extent that (1) the assignor gives the assignee that right in accordance with authority described in the certificate of limited partnership, or (2) all other partners consent.

(b) An assignee who has become a limited partner has, to the extent assigned, the rights and powers, and is subject to the restrictions and liabilities, of a limited partner under the partnership agreement and this Act. An assignee who becomes a limited partner also is liable for the obligations of his assignor to make and return contributions as provided in Article 6. However, the assignee is not obligated for liabilities unknown to the assignee at the time he became a limited partner and which could not be ascertained from the certificate of limited partnership.

(c) If an assignee of a partnership interest becomes a limited partner, the assignor is not released from his liability to the limited partnership under Sections 207 and 502.

Commissioners' Comment

Section 704 is derived from Section 19 of the prior uniform law, but paragraph (b) defines more narrowly than Section 19 the obligations of the assignor that are automatically assumed by the assignee.

§ 705. [Power of Estate of Deceased or Incompetent Partner]

If a partner who is an individual dies or a court of competent jurisdiction adjudges him to be incompetent to manage his person or his property, the partner's executor, administrator, guardian, conservator, or other legal representative may exercise all of the partner's rights for the purpose of settling his estate or administering his property, including any power the partner had to give an assignee the right to become a limited partner. If a partner is a corporation, trust, or other entity and is dissolved or terminated, the powers of that partner may be exercised by its legal representative or successor.

Commissioners' Comment

Section 705 is derived from Section 21(1) of the prior uniform law. Former Section 21(2), making a deceased limited partner's estate liable for his liabilities as a limited partner was deleted as superfluous, with no intention of changing the liability of the estate.

ARTICLE 8

DISSOLUTION

§ 801.   [Nonjudicial Dissolution]

A limited partnership is dissolved and its affairs shall be wound up upon the happening of the first to occur of the following:

(1) at the time or upon the happening of events specified in the certificate of limited partnership;

(2) written consent of all partners;

(3) an event of withdrawal of a general partner unless at the time there is at least one other general partner and the certificate of limited partnership permits the business of the limited partnership to be carried on by the remaining general partner and that partner does so, but the limited partnership is not dissolved and is not required to be wound up by reason of any event of withdrawal if, within 90 days after the withdrawal, all partners agree in writing to continue the business of the limited partnership and to the appointment of one or more additional general partners if necessary or desired; or

(4) entry of a decree of judicial dissolution under Section 802.

Commissioners' Comment

Section 801 merely collects in one place all of the events causing dissolution. Paragraph (3) is derived from Sections 9(1) (g) and 20 of the prior uniform law, but adds the 90-day grace period.

§ 802.   [Judicial Dissolution]

On application by or for a partner the [here designate the proper court] court may decree dissolution of a limited partnership whenever it is not reasonably practicable to carry on the business in conformity with the partnership agreement.

Commissioners' Comment

Section 802 is new.

§ 803.   [Winding Up]

Except as provided in the partnership agreement, the general partners who have not wrongfully dissolved a limited partnership or, if none, the limited partners, may wind up the limited partnership's affairs; but the [here designate the proper court] court may wind up the limited partnership's affairs upon application of any partner, his legal representative, or assignee.

Commissioners' Comment

Section 803 is new and is derived in part from Section 37 of the Uniform General Partnership Act.

§ 804.   [Distribution of Assets]

Upon the winding up of a limited partnership, the assets shall be distributed as follows:

(1) to creditors, including partners who are creditors, to the extent otherwise permitted by law, in satisfaction of liabilities of the limited partnership other than liabilities for distributions to partners under Section 601 or 604;

(2) except as provided in the partnership agreement, to partners and former partners in satisfaction of liabilities for distributions under Section 601 or 604; and

(3) except as provided in the partnership agreement, to partners *first* for the return of their contributions and *secondly* respecting their partnership interests, in the proportions in which the partners share in distributions.

Commissioners' Comment

Section 804 revises Section 23 of the prior uniform law by providing that (1) to the extent partners are also creditors, other than in respect of their interests in the partnership, they share with other creditors, (2) once the partnership's obligation to make a distribution accrues, it must be paid before any other distributions of an "equity" nature are made, and (3) general and limited partners rank on the same level except as otherwise provided in the partnership agreement.

ARTICLE 9

FOREIGN LIMITED PARTNERSHIPS

§ 901.   [Law Governing]

Subject to the Constitution of this State, (1) the laws of the state under which a foreign limited partnership is organized govern its organization and internal affairs and the liability of its limited partners, and (2) a foreign limited partnership may not be denied registration by reason of any difference between those laws and the laws of this State.

Commissioners' Comment

Section 901 is new.

§ 902.   [Registration]

Before transacting business in this State, a foreign limited partnership shall register with the Secretary of State. In order to register, a foreign limited partnership shall submit to the Secretary of State, in duplicate, an application for registration as a foreign limited partnership, signed and sworn to by a general partner and setting forth:

(1) the name of the foreign limited partnership and, if different, the name under which it proposes to register and transact business in this State;

(2) the state and date of its formation;

(3) the general character of the business it proposes to transact in this State;

(4) the name and address of any agent for service of process on the foreign limited partnership whom the foreign limited partnership elects to appoint; the agent must be

an individual resident of this State, a domestic corporation, or a foreign corporation having a place of business in, and authorized to do business in this State;

(5) a statement that the Secretary of State is appointed the agent of the foreign limited partnership for service of process if no agent has been appointed under paragraph (4) or, if appointed, the agent's authority has been revoked or if the agent cannot be found or served with the exercise of reasonable diligence;

(6) the address of the office required to be maintained in the State of its organization by the laws of that State or, if not so required, of the principal office of the foreign limited partnership; and

(7) if the certificate of limited partnership filed in the foreign limited partnership's state of organization is not required to include the names and business addresses of the partners, a list of the names and addresses.

Commissioners' Comment

Section 902 is new. It was thought that requiring a full copy of the certificate of limited partnership and all amendments thereto to be filed in each state in which the partnership does business would impose an unreasonable burden on interstate limited partnerships and that the information on file was sufficient to tell interested persons where they could write to obtain copies of these basic documents.

§ 903.   [Issuance of Registration]

(a) If the Secretary of State finds that an application for registration conforms to law and all requisite fees have been paid, he shall:

(1) endorse on the application the word "Filed," and the month, day, and year of the filing thereof;

(2) file in his office a duplicate original of the application; and

(3) issue a certificate of registration to transact business in this State.

(b) The certificate of registration, together with a duplicate original of the application, shall be returned to the person who filed the application or his representative.

§ 904.   [Name]

A foreign limited partnership may register with the Secretary of State under any name (whether or not it is the name under which it is registered in its state of organization) that includes without abbreviation the words "limited partnership" and that could be registered by a domestic limited partnership.

Commissioners' Comment

Section 904 is new.

§ 905.   [Changes and Amendments]

If any statement in the application for registration of a foreign limited partnership was false when made or any arrangements or other facts described have changed, making the application inaccurate in any respect, the foreign limited partnership shall promptly file in the office of the Secretary of State a certificate, signed and sworn to by a general partner, correcting such statement.

Commissioners' Comment

Section 905 is new.

§ 906.   [Cancellation of Registration]

A foreign limited partnership may cancel its registration by filing with the Secretary of State a certificate of cancellation signed and sworn to by a general partner. A cancellation does not terminate the authority of the Secretary of State to accept service of process on the foreign limited partnership with respect to [claims for relief] [causes of action] arising out of the transactions of business in this State.

Commissioners' Comment

Section 906 is new.

§ 907.   [Transaction of Business Without Registration]

(a) A foreign limited partnership transacting business in this State may not maintain any action, suit, or proceeding in any court of this State until it has registered in this State.

(b) The failure of a foreign limited partnership to register in this State does not impair the validity of any contract or act of the foreign limited partnership or prevent the foreign limited partnership from defending any action, suit, or proceeding in any court of this State.

(c) A limited partner of a foreign limited partnership is not liable as a general partner of the foreign limited partnership solely by reason of having transacted business in this State without registration.

(d) A foreign limited partnership, by transacting business in this State without registration, appoints the Secretary of State as its agent for service of process with respect to [claims for relief] [causes of action] arising out of the transaction of business in this State.

Commissioners' Comment

Section 907 is new.

§ 908.   [Action by [Appropriate Official]]

The [appropriate official] may bring an action to restrain a foreign limited partnership from transacting business in this State in violation of this Article.

Commissioners' Comment

Section 908 is new.

ARTICLE 10

DERIVATIVE ACTIONS

§ 1001. [Right of Action]

A limited partner may bring an action in the right of a limited partnership to recover a judgment in its favor if general partners with authority to do so have refused to bring the action or if an effort to cause those general partners to bring the action is not likely to succeed.

Commissioners' Comment

Section 1001 is new.

§ 1002. [Proper Plaintiff]

In a derivative action, the plaintiff must be a partner at the time of bringing the action and (1) at the time of the transaction of which he complains or (2) his status as a partner had devolved upon him by operation of law or pursuant to the terms of the partnership agreement from a person who was a partner at the time of the transaction.

Commissioners' Comment

Section 1002 is new.

§ 1003. [Pleading]

In a derivative action, the complaint shall set forth with particularity the effort of the plaintiff to secure initiation of the action by a general partner or the reasons for not making the effort.

Commissioners' Comment

Section 1003 is new.

§ 1004. [Expenses]

If a derivative action is successful, in whole or in part, or if anything is received by the plaintiff as a result of a judgment, compromise, or settlement of an action or claim, the court may award the plaintiff reasonable expenses, including reasonable attorney's fees, and shall direct him to remit to the limited partnership the remainder of those proceeds received by him.

Commissioners' Comment

Section 1004 is new.

ARTICLE 11

MISCELLANEOUS

§ 1101. [Construction and Application]

This Act shall be so applied and construed to effectuate its general purpose to make uniform the law with respect to the subject of this Act among states enacting it.

§ 1102. [Short Title]

This Act may be cited as the Uniform Limited Partnership Act.

§ 1103. [Severability]

If any provision of this Act or its application to any person or circumstance is held invalid, the invalidity does not affect other provisions or applications of the Act which can be given effect without the invalid provision or application, and to this end the provisions of this Act are severable.

§ 1104. [Effective Date, Extended Effective Date and Repeal]

Except as set forth below, the effective date of this Act is _____ and the following Acts [list prior limited partnership acts] are hereby repealed:

(1) The existing provisions for execution and filing of certificates of limited partnerships and amendments thereunder and cancellations thereof continue in effect until [specify time required to create central filing system], the extended effective date, and Sections 102, 103, 104, 105, 201, 202, 203, 204 and 206 are not effective until the extended effective date.

(2) Section 402, specifying the conditions under which a general partner ceases to be a member of a limited partnership, is not effective until the extended effective date, and the applicable provisions of existing law continue to govern until the extended effective date.

(3) Sections 501, 502 and 608 apply only to contributions and distributions made after the effective date of this Act.

(4) Section 704 applies only to assignments made after the effective date of this Act.

(5) Article 9, dealing with registration of foreign limited partnerships, is not effective until the extended effective date.

§ 1105. [Rules for Cases Not Provided for in This Act]

In any case not provided for in this Act the provisions of the Uniform Partnership Act govern.

REVISED UNIFORM LIMITED PARTNERSHIP ACT (1976) WITH 1985 AMENDMENTS (SHOWN BY DELETION AND ADDITION)

Historical Notes

The Revised Uniform Limited Partnership Act was approved by the National Conference of Commissioners on Uniform State Laws in 1976. It supersedes the original Uniform Limited Partnership Act approved by the National Conference in 1916.

In 1985 the National Conference initially approved a separate new Uniform Limited Partnership Act (1985). Subsequently, however, the Conference determined that the separate new act should be eliminated and that the changes therein made be incorporated instead into the existing Revised Uniform Limited Partnership Act of 1976. Accordingly, the changes have been incorporated here into the 1976 Act together with the revised prefatory note and comments. Changes in the text, prefatory note, and comments are indicated by Text for additions, Text for deletions.

Editor's Note: Volume 6A of the Uniform Laws Annotated 1-2 (1995) does not identify separately the jurisdictions that have adopted the 1985 amendments. A research assistant for the editor has compiled the following list of such jurisdictions: Alaska, Arizona, Arkansas, California, Colorado, Connecticut, Delaware, District of Columbia, Florida, Georgia, Hawaii, Idaho, Illinois, Indiana, Kansas, Kentucky, Maine, Maryland, Massachusetts, Minnesota, Mississippi, Missouri, Montana, Nebraska, Nevada, New Hampshire, New Jersey, New Mexico, New York, North Dakota, Ohio, Oklahoma, Oregon, Pennsylvania, Rhode Island, South Dakota, South Carolina, Tennessee, Texas, Utah, Virginia, Washington, West Virginia, Wisconsin, and Wyoming.

Prefatory Note

The Revised Uniform Limited Partnership Act adopted by the National Conference of Commissioners on Uniform State Laws in August, 1976, In 1976, the National Conference of Commissioners on Uniform State Laws adopted the first revision of the Uniform Limited Partnership Act, originally promulgated in 1916. The 1976 Act was intended to modernize the prior uniform law while retaining the special character of limited partnerships as compared with corporations. The draftsman of a limited partnership agreement has a degree of flexibility in defining the relations among the partners that is not available in the corporate form. Moreover, the relationship among partners is consensual, and requires a degree of privity that forces the under some circumstances may require a general partner to seek approval of the other partners (sometimes unanimous approval) under circumstances that corporate management would find unthinkable. The limited partnership was not intended to be an alternative in all cases where the corporate form is undesirable for tax or other reasons, and the ~~new~~ 1976 Act was not intended to make it so. The ~~new~~ 1976 Act ~~clarifies~~ clarified many ambiguities and ~~fills~~ filled interstices in the ~~prior uniform law~~ 1916 Act by adding more detailed language and mechanics. In addition, it effected some important substantive changes and additions ~~have been made~~ from the prior uniform law.

The Uniform Limited Partnership Act (1976) with the 1985 Amendments (the 1985 Act) follows the 1976 Act very closely in most respects. It makes almost no change in the basic structure of the 1976 Act. It does, however, differ from the 1976 Act in certain significant respects for the purpose of more effectively modernizing, improving, and establishing uniformity in the law of limited partnerships. The 1985 Act accomplishes this, without impairing the basic philosophy or values underlying the 1976 Act, by incorporating into the structure, framework, and text of the 1976 Act the best and most important improvements that have emerged in the limited partnership acts enacted recently by certain states. Most of those improvements were considered by the draftsmen of the 1976 Act but were not included in it because of uncertainties as to the possible consequences of such inclusion under applicable Federal income tax laws. Those uncertainties have since been resolved satisfactorily, and no impediment to incorporating them in the 1985 Act remains at this time.

Article 1 provides a list of all of the definitions used in the Act, integrates the use of limited partnership names with corporate names and provides for an office and agent for service of process in the state of organization. All of these provisions ~~are new~~ were innovations in the 1976 Act and were carried over from the 1976 Act to the 1985 Act. Article 2 collects in one place all provisions dealing with execution and filing of certificates of limited partnership and certificates of amendment and cancellation. When adopted in 1976, Articles 1 and 2 ~~reflect~~ reflected an important change in the prior statutory scheme: recognition that the basic document in any partnership, including a limited partnership, is the partnership agreement. The certificate of limited partnership is not a constitutive document (except in the sense that it is a statutory prerequisite to creation of the limited partnership), and merely reflects the most basic matters as to which government officials, creditors, and others dealing or considering dealing with the partnership should be put on notice. This principle is further implemented by the 1985 Act's elimination of the requirement, carried from the original 1916 Act into the 1976 Act, that the certificate of limited partnership set out the name, address, and capital contribution of each limited partner and certain other details relating to the operation of the partnership and the respective rights of the partners. The former requirement served no significant practical purpose while it imposed on limited partnerships (particularly those having large numbers of partners or doing business in more than one state) inordinate administrative and logistical burdens and expenses connected with filing and amending their certificates of limited partnership. Many of the other changes made by the 1985 Act merely reflect the elimination of that requirement.

Article 3 deals with the single most difficult issue facing lawyers who use the limited partnership form of organization: the powers and potential liabilities of limited partners. Section 303 lists a number of activities in which a limited partner may engage without being held to have so significantly participated in the control of the business that he ~~assumes~~ acquires the liability of a general partner. Moreover, it goes on to confine the liability of a limited partner who merely ~~steps over the line of~~

~~participation~~ participates in control to situations in which persons who actually know of that participation in control are misled thereby to their detriment into reasonably believing the limited partner to be a general partner. ~~General liability for partnership debts is imposed only on those limited partners who are, in effect, "silent general partners." With that exception, the provisions of the new Act that impose liability on a limited partner who has somehow permitted third parties to be misled to their detriment as to the limited partner's true status confine that liability to those who have actually been misled.~~ This "detrimental reliance" test, together with an expansion of the "laundry list" of specific activities in which limited partners may participate without incurring liability, are among the principal innovations in the 1985 Act.

The provisions relating to general partners are collected in Article 4. It differs little from the corresponding article in the 1976 Act, except that some of the 1976 Act's references to the certificate of limited partnership have been changed to refer instead to the partnership agreement. This is in recognition of the principle that the limited partnership agreement, not the certificate of limited partnership, is the primary constitutive, organizational, and governing document of a limited partnership.

Article 5, ~~the~~ dealing with finance ~~section, makes~~ , differs in some important respects from Article 5 of the 1976 Act, which itself made some important changes from the ~~prior uniform law~~ 1916 Act. The 1976 Act explicitly permitted contributions to the partnership to be made in the form of the contribution of services and promises to contribute cash, property, or services ~~are now explicitly permitted as contributions. And~~ , and provided that those who ~~fail~~ failed to perform promised services ~~are~~ were required, in the absence of an agreement to the contrary, to pay the value of the services ~~as~~ stated in the certificate of limited partnership. These important innovations of the 1976 Act are retained in substance in the 1985 Act. However, the 1985 Act substitutes the partnership agreement and the records of the limited partnership for the certificate of limited partnership as the place such agreements are to be set out and such information is to be kept. ~~A~~

Article 6 of the 1976 Act, dealing with distributions and with the withdrawal of partners from the partnership, made a number of changes from the ~~prior uniform law are made in Article 6, dealing with distributions from and the withdrawal of partners from the partnership~~ 1916 Act. For example, Section 608 ~~creates~~ created a statute of limitations ~~on~~ applicable to the right of a limited partnership to recover all or part of a contribution that ~~has~~ had been returned to a limited partner, whether to satisfy creditors or otherwise. The 1985 Act retains these features of the 1976 Act without substantive change.

~~The~~ In both the 1976 and the 1985 Acts, the assignability of partnership interests is dealt with in considerable detail in Article 7. ~~The~~ , and the provisions relating to dissolution appear in Article 8, ~~which, among other things, imposes~~. Article 8 of the 1976 Act established a new standard for seeking judicial dissolution of a limited partnership , which standard is carried forward into the 1985 Act.

~~One~~ Article 9 of the 1976 and 1985 Acts deals with one of the thorniest questions for those who operate limited partnerships in more than one state ~~has been~~ , i.e., the status of the partnership in a state other than the state of its organization. Neither ~~existing~~ case law under the 1916 Act nor administrative practice ~~makes~~ made it clear which state's law governed the partnership or whether , in that other state, the limited partners ~~continue~~ continued to possess ~~their~~ limited liability ~~and which law governs the partnership~~. Article 9 ~~deals~~ of the 1976 Act dealt with this problem by providing for registration of foreign limited partnerships and specifying choice-of-law rules. Article 9 of the 1985 Act retains all of those basic provisions and innovations of the 1976 Act.

~~Finally,~~ Article 10 of the ~~new~~ 1976 Act ~~authorizes~~ represented another significant innovation, by authorizing derivative actions to be brought by limited partners. The 1916 Act failed to address this entire concept. Article 10 of the 1985 Act clarifies certain provisions of the 1976 Act but does not make any substantive changes in the corresponding provisions of the 1976 Act.

Finally, Article 11 sets out a number of miscellaneous provisions, not the least of which are those dealing with the application of the new statute to limited partnerships in existence at the time of its enactment. Those provisions in the 1976 Act were expanded upon by the 1985 Act to give greater deference to the possible expectations, some of which may have constitutionally protected status, of partners in such limited partnerships concerning the continuing applicability to their partnerships of the law in effect when they were organized.

REVISED UNIFORM LIMITED PARTNERSHIP ACT (1976) WITH 1985 AMENDMENTS (SHOWN BY DELETION AND ADDITION)

ARTICLE 1

GENERAL PROVISIONS

ARTICLE 2

FORMATION; CERTIFICATE OF LIMITED PARTNERSHIP

ARTICLE 3

LIMITED PARTNERS

ARTICLE 4

GENERAL PARTNERS

ARTICLE 5

FINANCE

ARTICLE 6

DISTRIBUTIONS AND WITHDRAWAL

ARTICLE 7

ASSIGNMENT OF PARTNERSHIP INTERESTS

ARTICLE 8

DISSOLUTION

ARTICLE 9

FOREIGN LIMITED PARTNERSHIPS

ARTICLE 10

DERIVATIVE ACTIONS

ARTICLE 11

MISCELLANEOUS

ARTICLE 1

GENERAL PROVISIONS

§ 101. Definitions.

As used in this [Act], unless the context otherwise requires:

(1) "Certificate of limited partnership" means the certificate referred to in Section 201, and the certificate as amended or restated.

(2) "Contribution" means any cash, property, services rendered, or a promissory note or other binding obligation to contribute cash or property or to perform services, which a partner contributes to a limited partnership in his capacity as a partner.

(3) "Event of withdrawal of a general partner" means an event that causes a person to cease to be a general partner as provided in Section 402.

(4) "Foreign limited partnership" means a partnership formed under the laws of any State state other than this State and having as partners one or more general partners and one or more limited partners.

(5) "General partner" means a person who has been admitted to a limited partnership as a general partner in accordance with the partnership agreement and named in the certificate of limited partnership as a general partner.

(6) "Limited partner" means a person who has been admitted to a limited partnership as a limited partner in accordance with the partnership agreement and named in the certificate of limited partnership as a limited partner.

(7) "Limited partnership" and "domestic limited partnership" mean a partnership formed by two or more persons under the laws of this State and having one or more general partners and one or more limited partners.

(8) "Partner" means a limited or general partner.

(9) "Partnership agreement" means any valid agreement, written or oral, of the partners as to the affairs of a limited partnership and the conduct of its business.

(10) "Partnership interest" means a partner's share of the profits and losses of a limited partnership and the right to receive distributions of partnership assets.

(11) "Person" means a natural person, partnership, limited partnership (domestic or foreign), trust, estate, association, or corporation.

(12) "State" means a state, territory, or possession of the United States, the District of Columbia, or the Commonwealth of Puerto Rico.

Comment

The definitions in this section clarify a number of uncertainties in the law existing law prior to the 1976 Act, and also make certain changes in such prior law. The 1985 Act makes very few additional changes in Section 101.

Contribution: this definition makes it clear that a present contribution of services and a promise to make a future payment of cash, contribution of property or performance of services are permissible forms for a contribution. Accordingly, the present Section 502 of the 1985 Act provides that a limited partner's promise to make a contribution is enforceable only when set out in a writing signed by the limited partner. (This result is not dissimilar from that under the 1976 Act, which required all promises of future contributions to be described in the certificate of limited partnership, which was to be signed by, among others, the partners making such promises.) The property or services contributed presently or ~~promise~~ promised to be contributed in the future must be accorded a value in the ~~certificate of limited partnership (Section 201(5))~~ partnership agreement or the partnership records required to be kept pursuant to Section 105, and, in the case of a promise, that value may determine the liability of a partner who fails to honor his agreement (Section 502). Section 3 of the ~~prior uniform law~~ 1916 Act did not permit a limited partner's contribution to be in the form of services, although that inhibition did not apply to general partners.

Foreign limited partnership: the Act only deals with foreign limited partnerships formed under the laws of another ~~"State"~~ "state" of the United States (see subdivision 12 of Section 101), and any adopting ~~State~~ state that desires to deal by statute with the status of entities formed under the laws of foreign countries must make appropriate changes throughout the Act. The exclusion of such entities from the Act was not intended to suggest that their "limited partners" should not be accorded limited liability by the courts of a ~~State~~ state adopting the Act. That question would be resolved by the choice-of-law rules of the forum ~~State~~ state.

General partner: this definition recognizes the separate functions of the partnership agreement and the certificate of limited partnership. The partnership agreement establishes the basic grant of management power to the persons named as general partners; but because of the passive role played by the limited partners, the separate, formal step of ~~embodying~~ memorializing that grant of power in the certificate of limited partnership has been preserved to emphasize its importance and to provide notice of the identity of the partnership's general partners to persons dealing with the partnership.

Limited partner: ~~as in~~ unlike the ~~case of~~ definition of general partners, this definition provides for admission of limited partners through the partnership agreement ~~and solemnization in the certificate of limited partnership. In addition, the definition makes it clear that being named in the certificate of limited partnership is a prerequisite to limited partner status. Failure to file does not, however, mean that the participant is a general partner or that he has general liability. See Sections 202(e) and 303~~ alone and does not require identification of any limited partner in the certificate of limited partnership (Section 201). Under the 1916 and the 1976 Acts, being named as a limited partner in the certificate of limited partnership was a statutory requirement and, in most if not all cases, probably also a prerequisite to limited partner status. By eliminating the requirement that the certificate of limited partnership contain the name, address, and capital contribution of each limited partner, the 1985 Act all but eliminates any risk that a person intended to be a limited partner may be exposed to liability as a general partner as a result of the inadvertent omission of any of that information from the certificate of limited partnership, and also dispenses with the need to amend the certificate of limited partnership upon the admission or withdrawal of, transfer of an interest by, or change in the address or capital contribution of, any limited partner.

Partnership agreement: the ~~prior uniform law~~ 1916 Act did not refer to the partnership agreement, assuming that all important matters affecting limited partners would be set forth in the certificate of limited partnership. Under modern practice, however, it has been common for the partners to enter into a comprehensive partnership agreement, only part of which was required to be included or summarized in the certificate of limited partnership. As reflected in Section 201 of the 1985 Act, the certificate of limited partnership is confined principally to matters respecting the partnership itself and the ~~addition and withdrawal~~ identity of general partners ~~and of capital~~, and other important issues are left to the partnership agreement. Most of the information formerly provided by, but no longer required to be included in, the certificate of limited partnership is now required to be kept in the partnership records (Section 105).

Partnership interest: this definition ~~is new~~ first appeared in the 1976 Act and is intended to define what it is that is transferred when a partnership interest is assigned.

§ 102. Name.

The name of each limited partnership as set forth in its certificate of limited partnership:

(1) shall contain without abbreviation the words "limited partnership";

(2) may not contain the name of a limited partner unless (i) it is also the name of a general partner or the corporate name of a corporate general partner, or (ii) the business of the limited partnership had been carried on under that name before the admission of that limited partner;

~~(3) may not contain any word or phrase indicating or implying that it is organized other than for a purpose stated in its certificate of limited partnership;~~

~~(4)~~ (3) may not be the same as, or deceptively similar to, the name of any corporation or limited partnership organized under the laws of this State or licensed or registered as a foreign corporation or limited partnership in this State; and

~~(5)~~ (4) may not contain the following words [here insert prohibited words].

Comment

Subdivision (2) of Section 102 has been carried over from Section 5 of the ~~prior uniform law~~ 1916 Act with certain editorial changes. The remainder of Section 102 ~~is new~~ first appeared in the 1976 Act and primarily reflects the intention to integrate the registration of limited partnership names with that of corporate names. Accordingly, Section 201 provides for central, ~~State-wide~~ state-wide filing of certificates of limited partnership, and subdivisions (3)~~,~~ and (4) ~~and (5)~~ of Section 102 contain standards to be applied by the filing officer in determining whether the certificate should be filed. Subdivision (1) requires that the proper name of a limited partnership contain the words "limited partnership" in full. Subdivision (3) of the 1976 Act has been deleted, to reflect the deletion from Section 201 of any requirement that the certificate of limited partnership describe the partnership's purposes or the character of its business.

§ 103. Reservation of Name.

(a) The exclusive right to the use of a name may be reserved by:

(1) any person intending to organize a limited partnership under this [Act] and to adopt that name;

(2) any domestic limited partnership or any foreign limited partnership registered in this State which, in either case, intends to adopt that name;

(3) any foreign limited partnership intending to register in this State and adopt that name; and

(4) any person intending to organize a foreign limited partnership and intending to have it register in this State and adopt that name.

(b) The reservation shall be made by filing with the Secretary of State an application, executed by the applicant, to reserve a specified name. If the Secretary of State finds that the name is available for use by a domestic or foreign limited partnership, he [or she] shall reserve the name for the exclusive use of the applicant for a period of 120 days. Once having so reserved a name, the same applicant may not again reserve the same name until more than 60 days after the expiration of the last 120-day period for which that applicant reserved that name. The right to the exclusive use of a reserved name may be transferred to any other person by filing in the office of the Secretary of State a notice of the transfer, executed by the applicant for whom the name was reserved and specifying the name and address of the transferee.

Comment

Section 103 is new first appeared in the 1976 Act. The prior uniform law 1916 Act did not provide for registration of names.

§ 104. Specified Office and Agent.

Each limited partnership shall continuously maintain in this State:

(1) an office, which may but need not be a place of its business in this State, at which shall be kept the records required by Section 105 to be maintained; and

(2) an agent for service of process on the limited partnership, which agent must be an individual resident of this State, a domestic corporation, or a foreign corporation authorized to do business in this State.

Comment

Section 104 is new first appeared in the 1976 Act. It requires that a limited partnership have certain minimum contacts with its State of organization, i.e., an office at which the constitutive documents and basic financial information is kept and an agent for service of process.

§ 105. Records to be Kept.

(a) Each limited partnership shall keep at the office referred to in Section 104(1) the following:

(1) a current list of the full name and last known business address of each partner set forth, separately identifying the general partners (in alphabetical order) and the limited partners (in alphabetical order,);

(2) a copy of the certificate of limited partnership and all certificates of amendment thereto, together with executed copies of any powers of attorney pursuant to which any certificate has been executed,;

(3) copies of the limited partnership's federal, state and local income tax returns and reports, if any, for the three most recent years, and;

(4) copies of any then effective written partnership agreements and of any financial statements of the limited partnership for the three most recent years; and

(5) unless contained in a written partnership agreement, a writing setting out: (i) the amount of cash and a description and statement of the agreed value of the other property or services contributed by each partner and which each partner has agreed to contribute; (ii) the times at which or events on the happening of which any additional contributions agreed to be made by each partner are to be made; (iii) any right of a partner to receive, or of a general partner to make, distributions to a partner which include a return of all or any part of the partner's contribution; and (iv) any events upon the happening of which the limited partnership is to be dissolved and its affairs wound up.

(b) Those records Records kept under this section are subject to inspection and copying at the reasonable request and at the expense of any partner during ordinary business hours.

Comment

Section 105 is new first appeared in the 1976 Act. In view of the passive nature of the limited partner's position, it has been widely felt that limited partners are entitled to access to certain basic documents and information, including the certificate of limited partnership and, any partnership agreement , and a writing setting out certain important matters which, under the 1916 and 1976 Acts, were required to be set out in the certificate of limited partnership. In view of the great diversity among limited partnerships, it was thought inappropriate to require a standard form of financial report, and Section 105 does no more than require retention of tax returns and any other financial statements that are prepared. The names and addresses of the general partners are made available to the general public in the certificate of limited partnership.

§ 106. Nature of Business.

A limited partnership may carry on any business that a partnership without limited partners may carry on except [here designate prohibited activities].

Comment

Section 106 is identical to Section 3 of the ~~prior uniform law.~~ 1916 Act. Many states require that certain regulated industries, such as banking, may be carried on only by entities organized pursuant to special statutes, and it is contemplated that the prohibited activities would be confined to the matters covered by those statutes.

§ 107. Business Transactions of Partner with Partnership.

Except as provided in the partnership agreement, a partner may lend money to and transact other business with the limited partnership and, subject to other applicable law, has the same rights and obligations with respect thereto as a person who is not a partner.

Comment

Section 107 makes a number of important changes in Section 13 of the ~~prior uniform law.~~ 1916 Act. Section 13, in effect, created a special fraudulent conveyance provision applicable to the making of secured loans by limited partners and the repayment by limited partnerships of loans from limited partners. Section 107 leaves that question to a ~~State's~~ state's general fraudulent conveyance statute. In addition, Section 107 eliminates the prohibition in ~~former~~ Section 13 against a general ~~partner (as opposed to a limited partner)~~ partner's sharing pro rata with general creditors in the case of an unsecured loan. Of course, other doctrines developed under bankruptcy and insolvency laws may require the subordination of loans by partners under appropriate circumstances.

ARTICLE 2
FORMATION; CERTIFICATE OF LIMITED PARTNERSHIP

§ 201. Certificate of Limited Partnership.

(a) In order to form a limited partnership, ~~two or more persons must execute~~ a certificate of limited partnership. ~~The certificate shall be~~ must be executed and filed in the office of the Secretary of State. ~~and~~ The certificate shall set forth:

(1) the name of the limited partnership;

~~(2) the general character of its business;~~

~~(3)~~ (2) the address of the office and the name and address of the agent for service of process required to be maintained by Section 104;

~~(4)~~ (3) the name and the business address of each general partner ~~(specifying separately the general partners and limited partners)~~;

~~(5) the amount of cash and a description and statement of the agreed value of the other property or services contributed by each partner and which each partner has agreed to contribute in the future;~~

~~(6) the times at which or events on the happening of which any additional contributions agreed to be made by each partner are to be made;~~

~~(7) any power of a limited partner to grant the right to become a limited partner to an assignee of any part of his partnership interest, and the terms and conditions of the power;~~

~~(8) if agreed upon, the time at which or the events on the happening of which a partner may terminate his membership in the limited partnership and the amount of, or the method of determining, the distribution to which he may be entitled respecting his partnership interest, and the terms and conditions of the termination and distribution;~~

~~(9) any right of a partner to receive distributions of property, including cash from the limited partnership;~~

~~(10) any right of a partner to receive, or of a general partner to make, distributions to a partner which include a return of all or any part of the partner's contribution;~~

~~(11) any time at which or events upon the happening of which the limited partnership is to be dissolved and its affairs wound up;~~

~~(12) any right of the remaining general partners to continue the business on the happening of an event of withdrawal of a general partner;~~

(4) the latest date upon which the limited partnership is to dissolve; and

~~(13)~~ (5) any other matters the <u>general</u> partners determine to include therein.

(b) A limited partnership is formed at the time of the filing of the certificate of limited partnership in the office of the Secretary of State or at any later time specified in the certificate of limited partnership if, in either case, there has been substantial compliance with the requirements of this section.

Comment

The <u>1985 Act requires far fewer</u> matters ~~required~~ to be set forth in the certificate of limited partnership ~~are not different in kind from those required by~~ <u>than did</u> Section 2 of the ~~prior uniform law, although certain additions and deletions have been made and the description has been revised to conform with the rest of the Act. In general, the certificate is intended to serve two functions: first, to place creditors on notice of the~~ <u>1916 Act and Section 201 of the 1976 Act. This is in recognition of the fact that the partnership agreement, not the certificate of limited partnership, has become the authoritative and comprehensive document for most limited partnerships, and that creditors and potential creditors of the partnership do and should refer to the partnership agreement and to other information furnished to them directly by the partnership and by others, not to the certificate of limited partnership, to obtain</u> facts concerning the capital <u>and finances</u> of the partnership and ~~the rules regarding additional contributions to and withdrawals from the partnership; second, to clearly delineate the time at which persons become general partners and limited partners~~ <u>other matters of concern.</u> Subparagraph (b), which is based upon the ~~prior uniform law~~ <u>1916 Act</u>, has been retained to make it clear that the existence of the limited partnership depends only upon compliance with this section. Its continued existence is not dependent upon compliance with other provisions of this Act.

§ 202. Amendment to Certificate.

(a) A certificate of limited partnership is amended by filing a certificate of amendment thereto in the office of the Secretary of State. The certificate shall set forth:

(1) the name of the limited partnership;
(2) the date of filing the certificate; and
(3) the amendment to the certificate.

(b) Within 30 days after the happening of any of the following events, an amendment to a certificate of limited partnership reflecting the occurrence of the event or events shall be filed:

~~(1) a change in the amount or character of the contribution of any partner, or in any partner's obligation to make a contribution;~~
~~(2)~~ (1) the admission of a new general partner;
~~(3)~~ (2) the withdrawal of a general partner; or
~~(4)~~ (3) the continuation of the business under Section 801 after an event of withdrawal of a general partner.

(c) A general partner who becomes aware that any statement in a certificate of limited partnership was false when made or that any arrangements or other facts described have changed, making the certificate inaccurate in any respect, shall promptly amend the certificate~~, but an amendment to show a change of address of a limited partner need be filed only once every 12 months~~.

(d) A certificate of limited partnership may be amended at any time for any other proper purpose the general partners determine.

(e) No person has any liability because an amendment to a certificate of limited partnership has not been filed to reflect the occurrence of any event referred to in subsection (b) of this ~~Section~~ section if the amendment is filed within the 30-day period specified in subsection (b).

(f) A restated certificate of limited partnership may be executed and filed in the same manner as a certificate of amendment.

Comment

Section 202 ~~makes~~ of the 1976 Act made substantial changes in Section 24 of the ~~prior uniform law~~ 1916 Act. Further changes in this section are made by the 1985 Act. Paragraph (b) lists the basic events the addition or withdrawal of ~~partners or capital or capital obligations~~ a general partner that are so central to the function of the certificate of limited partnership that they require prompt amendment. With the elimination of the requirement that the certificate of limited partnership include the names of all limited partners and the amount and character of all capital contributions, the requirement of the 1916 and 1976 Acts that the certificate be amended upon the admission or withdrawal of limited partners or on any change in the partnership capital must also be eliminated. This change should greatly reduce the frequency and complexity of amendments to the certificate of limited partnership. Paragraph (c) makes it clear, as it was not clear under ~~subdivision (2)(g) of former~~ Section ~~24~~ 24(2)(g) of the 1916 Act, that the certificate of limited partnership is intended to be an accurate description of the facts to which it relates at all times and does not speak merely as of the date it is executed.

Paragraph (e) provides a "safe harbor" against claims of creditors or others who assert that they have been misled by the failure to amend the certificate of limited partnership to reflect changes in any of the important facts referred to in paragraph (b); if the certificate of limited partnership is amended within 30 days of the occurrence of the event, no creditor or other person can recover for damages sustained during the interim. Additional protection is afforded by the provisions of Section 304. The elimination of the requirement that the certificate of limited partnership identify all limited partners and their respective capital contributions may have rendered paragraph (e) an obsolete and unnecessary vestige. The principal, if not the sole, purpose of paragraph (e) in the 1976 Act was to protect limited partners newly admitted to a partnership from being held liable as general partners when an amendment to the certificate identifying them as limited partners and describing their contributions was not filed contemporaneously with their admission to the partnership. Such liability cannot arise under the 1985 Act because such information is not required to be stated in the certificate. Nevertheless, the 1985 Act retains paragraph (e) because it is protective of partners, shielding them from liability to the extent its provisions apply, and does not create or impose any liability.

Paragraph (f) is added in the 1985 Act to provide explicit statutory recognition of the common practice of restating an amended certificate of limited partnership. While a limited partnership seeking to amend its certificate of limited partnership may do so by recording a restated certificate which incorporates the amendment, that is by no means the only purpose or function of a restated certificate, which may be filed for the sole purpose of restating in a single integrated instrument all the provisions of a limited partnership's certificate of limited partnership which are then in effect.

§ 203. Cancellation of Certificate.

A certificate of limited partnership shall be cancelled upon the dissolution and the commencement of winding up of the partnership or at any other time there are no limited partners. A certificate of cancellation shall be filed in the office of the Secretary of State and set forth:

(1) the name of the limited partnership;

(2) the date of filing of its certificate of limited partnership;

(3) the reason for filing the certificate of cancellation;

(4) the effective date (which shall be a date certain) of cancellation if it is not to be effective upon the filing of the certificate; and

(5) any other information the general partners filing the certificate determine.

Comment

Section 203 changes Section 24 of the ~~prior uniform law~~ 1916 Act by making it clear that the certificate of cancellation should be filed upon the commencement of winding up of the limited partnership. Section 24 provided for cancellation "when the partnership is dissolved."

§ 204. Execution of Certificates.

(a) Each certificate required by this Article to be filed in the office of the Secretary of State shall be executed in the following manner:

(1) an original certificate of limited partnership must be signed by all general partners named therein;

(2) a certificate of amendment must be signed by at least one general partner and by each other general partner designated in the certificate as a new general partner or whose contribution is described as having been increased; and

(3) a certificate of cancellation must be signed by all general partners;.

(b) Any person may sign a certificate by an attorney-in-fact, but a power of attorney to sign a certificate relating to the admission, or increased contribution, of a general partner must specifically describe the admission or increase.

(c) The execution of a certificate by a general partner constitutes an affirmation under the penalties of perjury that the facts stated therein are true.

Comment

Section 204 collects in one place the formal requirements for the execution of certificates which were set forth in Sections 2 and 25 of the prior uniform law 1916 Act. Those sections required that each certificate be signed by all partners, and there developed an unnecessarily cumbersome practice of having each limited partner sign powers of attorney to authorize the general partners to execute certificates of amendment on their behalf. Section 204 insures that each partner must sign a certificate obligation to make contributions. The 1976 Act, while simplifying the execution requirements, nevertheless required that an original certificate of limited partnership be signed by all partners and a certificate of amendment by all new partners being admitted to the limited partnership. However, the certificate of limited partnership is no longer required to include the name or capital contribution of any limited partner. Therefore, while the 1985 Act still requires all general partners to sign the original certificate of limited partnership, no limited partner is required to sign any certificate. Certificates of amendment are required to be signed by only one general partner and all general partners must sign certificates of cancellation. Section 204 prohibits blanket powers of attorney for the execution of certificates in many cases, since those conditions under which a partner is required to sign have been narrowed to circumstances of special importance to that partner. The former requirement in the 1916 Act that all certificates be sworn has been confined to statements by the general partners, recognizing that the limited partner's role is a limited one was deleted in the 1976 and 1985 Acts as potentially an unfair trap for the unwary (see, e.g., Wisniewski v. Johnson, 223 Va. 141, 286 S.E.2d 223 (1982)); in its place, paragraph (c) now provides, as a matter of law, that the execution of a certificate by a general partner subjects him to the penalties of perjury for inaccuracies in the certificate.

§ 205. ~~Amendment or Cancellation~~ Execution by Judicial Act.

If a person required by Section 204 to execute ~~a~~ any certificate ~~of amendment or cancellation~~ fails or refuses to do so, any other ~~partner, and any assignee of a partnership interest,~~ person who is adversely affected by the failure or refusal, may petition the [designate the appropriate court] to direct the ~~amendment or cancellation~~ execution of the certificate. If the court finds that ~~the amendment or cancellation is proper~~ it is proper for the certificate to be executed and that any person so designated has failed or refused to execute the certificate, it shall order the Secretary of State to record an appropriate certificate ~~of amendment or cancellation.~~

Comment

Section 205 ~~changes~~ of the 1976 Act changed subdivisions (3) and (4) of Section 25 of the ~~prior uniform law~~ 1916 Act by confining the persons who have standing to seek judicial intervention to partners and to those assignees who ~~are~~ were adversely affected by the failure or refusal of the appropriate persons to file a certificate of amendment or cancellation. Section 205 of the 1985 Act reverses that restriction, and provides that any person adversely affected by a failure or refusal to file any certificate (not only a certificate of cancellation or amendment) has standing to seek judicial intervention.

§ 206. Filing in Office of Secretary of State.

(a) Two signed copies of the certificate of limited partnership and of any certificates of amendment or cancellation (or of any judicial decree of amendment or cancellation) shall be delivered to the Secretary of State. A person who executes a certificate as an agent or fiduciary need not exhibit evidence of his [or her] authority as a prerequisite to filing. Unless the Secretary of State finds that any certificate does not conform to law, upon receipt of all filing fees required by law he [or she] shall:

(1) endorse on each duplicate original the word "Filed" and the day, month, and year of the filing thereof;

(2) file one duplicate original in his [or her] office; and

(3) return the other duplicate original to the person who filed it or his [or her] representative.

(b) Upon the filing of a certificate of amendment (or judicial decree of amendment) in the office of the Secretary of State, the certificate of limited partnership shall be amended as set forth therein, and upon the effective date of a certificate of cancellation (or a judicial decree thereof), the certificate of limited partnership is cancelled.

Comment

Section 206 ~~is new.~~ first appeared in the 1976 Act. In addition to providing mechanics for the central filing system, the second sentence of this section does away with the requirement, formerly imposed by some local filing officers, that persons who have executed certificates under a power of attorney exhibit executed copies of the power of attorney itself. Paragraph (b) changes subdivision (5) of Section 25 of the ~~prior uniform law~~ 1916 Act by providing that certificates of cancellation are effective upon their effective date under Section 203.

§ 207. Liability for False Statement in Certificate.

If any certificate of limited partnership or certificate of amendment or cancellation contains a false statement, one who suffers loss by reliance on the statement may recover damages for the loss from:

(1) any person who executes the certificate, or causes another to execute it on his behalf, and knew, and any general partner who knew or should have known, the statement to be false at the time the certificate was executed; and

(2) any general partner who thereafter knows or should have known that any arrangement or other fact described in the certificate has changed, making the statement inaccurate in any respect within a sufficient time before the statement was relied upon reasonably to have enabled that general partner to cancel or amend the certificate, or to file a petition for its cancellation or amendment under Section 205.

Comment

Section 207 changes Section 6 of the ~~prior uniform law~~ 1916 Act by providing explicitly for the liability of persons who sign a certificate as agent under a power of attorney and by confining the obligation to amend a certificate of limited partnership in light of future events to general partners.

§ 208. Scope of Notice.

The fact that a certificate of limited partnership is on file in the office of the Secretary of State is notice that the partnership is a limited partnership and the persons designated therein as ~~limited~~ general partners are ~~limited~~ general partners, but it is not notice of any other fact.

Comment

Section 208 ~~is new~~ first appeared in the 1976 Act, and referred to the certificate's providing constructive notice of the status as limited partners of those so identified therein. The 1985 Act's deletion of any requirement that the certificate name limited partners required that Section 208 be modified accordingly.

By stating that the filing of a certificate of limited partnership only results in notice of the ~~limited~~ general liability of the ~~limited~~ general partners, ~~it~~ Section 208 obviates the concern that third parties may be held to have notice of special provisions set forth in the certificate. While this section is designed to preserve by implication the limited liability of limited partners, the ~~notice~~ implicit protection provided is not intended to change any liability of a limited partner which may be created by his action or inaction under the law of estoppel, agency, fraud, or the like.

§ 209. Delivery of Certificates to Limited Partners.

Upon the return by the Secretary of State pursuant to Section 206 of a certificate marked "Filed," the general partners shall promptly deliver or mail a copy of the certificate of limited partnership and each certificate of amendment or cancellation to each limited partner unless the partnership agreement provides otherwise.

Comment

This section ~~is new.~~ first appeared in the 1976 Act.

ARTICLE 3

LIMITED PARTNERS

§ 301. Admission of ~~Additional~~ Limited Partners.

(a) A person becomes a limited partner:

(1) at the time the limited partnership is formed; or
(2) at any later time specified in the records of the limited partnership for becoming a limited partner.

~~(a)~~(b) After the filing of a limited partnership's original certificate of limited partnership, a person may be admitted as an additional limited partner:

(1) in the case of a person acquiring a partnership interest directly from the limited partnership, upon compliance with the partnership agreement or, if the partnership agreement does not so provide, upon the written consent of all partners; and

(2) in the case of an assignee of a partnership interest of a partner who has the power, as provided in Section 704, to grant the assignee the right to become a limited partner, upon the exercise of that power and compliance with any conditions limiting the grant or exercise of the power.

~~(b) In each case under subsection (a), the person acquiring the partnership interest becomes a limited partner only upon amendment of the certificate of limited partnership reflecting that fact.~~

Comment

Section 301(a) is new; no counterpart was found in the 1916 or 1976 Acts. This section imposes on the partnership an obligation to maintain in its records the date each limited partner becomes a limited partner. Under the 1976 Act, one could not become a limited partner until an appropriate certificate reflecting his status as such was filed with the Secretary of State. Because the 1985 Act eliminates the need to name limited partners in the certificate of limited partnership, an alternative mechanism had to be established to evidence the fact and date of a limited partner's admission. The partnership records required to be maintained under Section 105 now serve that function, subject to the limitation that no person may become a limited partner before the partnership is formed (Section 201(b)).

Subdivision (1) of Section ~~301(a)~~ 301(b) adds to Section 8 of the ~~prior uniform law~~ 1916 Act an explicit recognition of the fact that unanimous consent of all partners is required for admission of new limited partners unless the partnership agreement provides otherwise. Subdivision (2) is derived from Section 19 of the ~~prior uniform law~~ 1916 Act but abandons the former terminology of "substituted limited partner."

§ 302. Voting.

Subject to Section 303, the partnership agreement may grant to all or a specified group of the limited partners the right to vote (on a per capita or other basis) upon any matter.

Comment

Section 302 ~~is new~~ first appeared in the 1976 Act, and must be read together with subdivision ~~(b)(5)~~ (b)(6) of Section 303. Although the ~~prior uniform law~~ 1916 Act did not speak specifically of the voting powers of limited partners, it ~~is~~ was not uncommon for partnership agreements to grant such ~~power~~ powers to limited partners. Section 302 is designed only to make it clear that the partnership agreement may grant such power to limited partners. If such powers are granted to limited partners beyond the "safe harbor" of subdivision (6) or (8) of Section ~~303(b)(5)~~ 303(b), a court may (but of course need not) hold that, under the circumstances, the limited partners have participated in "control of the business" within the meaning of Section 303(a). Section 303(c) ~~simply means~~ makes clear that the exercise of powers beyond the ambit of Section 303(b) is not ipso facto to be taken as taking part in the control of the business.

§ 303. Liability to Third Parties.

(a) Except as provided in subsection (d), a limited partner is not liable for the obligations of a limited partnership unless he [or she] is also a general partner or, in addition to the exercise of his [or her] rights and powers as a limited partner, he [or she] ~~takes part~~ participates in the control of the business. However, if the limited ~~partner's participation~~ partner participates in the control of the business ~~is not substantially the same as the exercise of the powers of a general partner~~, he [or she] is liable only to persons who transact business with the limited partnership ~~with actual knowledge of his participation in control~~ reasonably believing, based upon the limited partner's conduct, that the limited partner is a general partner.

(b) A limited partner does not participate in the control of the business within the meaning of subsection (a) solely by doing one or more of the following:

(1) being a contractor for or an agent or employee of the limited partnership or of a general partner or being an officer, director, or shareholder of a general partner that is a corporation;

(2) consulting with and advising a general partner with respect to the business of the limited partnership;

(3) acting as surety for the limited partnership or guaranteeing or assuming one or more specific obligations of the limited partnership;

(4) ~~approving or disapproving an amendment to the partnership agreement~~ taking any action required or permitted by law to bring or pursue a derivative action in the right of the limited partnership; ~~or~~

~~(5) voting on one or more of the following matters:~~

(5) requesting or attending a meeting of partners;

(6) proposing, approving, or disapproving, by voting or otherwise, one or more of the following matters:

(i) the dissolution and winding up of the limited partnership;

(ii) the sale, exchange, lease, mortgage, pledge, or other transfer of all or substantially all of the assets of the limited partnership ~~other than in the ordinary course of its business~~;

(iii) the incurrence of indebtedness by the limited partnership other than in the ordinary course of its business;

(iv) a change in the nature of the business; ~~or~~

(v) the admission or removal of a general partner~~.~~;

(vi) the admission or removal of a limited partner;

(vii) a transaction involving an actual or potential conflict of interest between a general partner and the limited partnership or the limited partners;

(viii) an amendment to the partnership agreement or certificate of limited partnership; or

(ix) matters related to the business of the limited partnership not otherwise enumerated in this subsection (b), which the partnership agreement states in writing may be subject to the approval or disapproval of limited partners;

(7) winding up the limited partnership pursuant to Section 803; or

(8) exercising any right or power permitted to limited partners under this [Act] and not specifically enumerated in this subsection (b).

(c) The enumeration in subsection (b) does not mean that the possession or exercise of any other powers by a limited partner constitutes participation by him [or her] in the business of the limited partnership.

(d) A limited partner who knowingly permits his [or her] name to be used in the name of the limited partnership, except under circumstances permitted by Section 102(2), is liable to creditors who extend credit to the limited partnership without actual knowledge that the limited partner is not a general partner.

Comment

Section 303 makes several important changes in Section 7 of the ~~prior uniform law~~ 1916 Act. The first sentence of Section 303(a) ~~carries over the basic test from former Section 7 whether the limited partner "takes part in the control of the business" in order to insure that judicial decisions under the prior uniform law remain applicable to the extent not expressly changed~~ differs from the text of Section 7 of the 1916 Act in that it speaks of participating (rather than taking part) in the control of the business; this was done for the sake of consistency with the second sentence of Section 303(a), not to change the meaning of the text. It is intended that judicial decisions interpreting the phrase "takes part in the control of the business" under the prior uniform law will remain applicable to the extent that a different result is not called for by other provisions of Section 303 and other provisions of the Act. The second sentence of Section 303(a) reflects a wholly new concept. Because in the 1976 Act that has been further modified in the 1985 Act. It was adopted partly because of the difficulty of determining when the "control" line has been overstepped, it was thought it unfair to impose general partner's liability on a limited partner except to the extent that a third party had knowledge of his participation in control of the business. On the other hand, in order to avoid permitting a limited partner to exercise all of the powers of a general partner while avoiding any direct dealings with third parties, the "is not substantially the same as" test was introduced but also (and more importantly) because of a determination that it is not sound public policy to hold a limited partner who is not also a general partner liable for the obligations of the partnership except to persons who have done business with the limited partnership reasonably believing, based on the limited partner's conduct, that he is a general partner. Paragraph (b) is intended to provide a "safe harbor" by enumerating certain activities which a limited partner may carry on for the partnership without being deemed to have taken part in control of the business. This "safe harbor" list has been expanded beyond that set out in the 1976 Act to reflect case law and statutory developments and more clearly to assure that limited partners are not subjected to general liability where such liability is inappropriate. Paragraph (d) is derived from Section 5 of the prior uniform law 1916 Act, but adds as a condition to the limited partner's liability the fact requirement that a limited partner must have knowingly permitted his name to be used in the name of the limited partnership.

§ 304. Person Erroneously Believing Himself [or Herself] Limited Partner.

(a) Except as provided in subsection (b), a person who makes a contribution to a business enterprise and erroneously but in good faith believes that he [or she] has become a limited partner in the enterprise is not a general partner in the enterprise and is not bound by its obligations by reason of making the contribution, receiving distributions from the enterprise, or exercising any rights of a limited partner, if, on ascertaining the mistake, he [or she]:

(1) causes an appropriate certificate of limited partnership or a certificate of amendment to be executed and filed; or

(2) withdraws from future equity participation in the enterprise by executing and filing in the office of the Secretary of State a certificate declaring withdrawal under this section.

(b) A person who makes a contribution of the kind described in subsection (a) is liable as a general partner to any third party who transacts business with the enterprise (i) before the person withdraws and an appropriate certificate is filed to show withdrawal, or (ii) before an appropriate certificate is filed to show his status as a limited partner and, in the case of an amendment, after expiration of the 30-day period for filing an amendment relating to the person as a limited partner under Section 202 that he [or she] is not a general partner, but in either case only if the third party actually believed in good faith that the person was a general partner at the time of the transaction.

Comment

Section 304 is derived from Section 11 of the ~~prior uniform law.~~ 1916 Act. The "good faith" requirement has been added in the first sentence of Section 304(a). The provisions of subdivision (2) of Section 304(a) are intended to clarify an ambiguity in the prior law by providing that a person who chooses to withdraw from the enterprise in order to protect himself from liability is not required to renounce any of his then current interest in the enterprise so long as he has no further participation as an equity participant. Paragraph (b) preserves the liability of the equity participant prior to withdrawal ~~(and after the time for appropriate amendment in the case of a limited partnership)~~ by such person from the limited partnership or amendment to the certificate demonstrating that such person is not a general partner to any third party who has transacted business with the person believing in good faith that he was a general partner.

Evidence strongly suggests that Section 11 of the 1916 Act and Section 304 of the 1976 Act were rarely used, and one might expect that Section 304 of the 1985 Act may never have to be used. Section 11 of the 1916 Act and Section 304 of the 1976 Act could have been used by a person who invested in a limited partnership believing he would be a limited partner but who was not identified as a limited partner in the certificate of limited partnership. However, because the 1985 Act does not require limited partners to be named in the certificate, the only situation to which Section 304 would now appear to be applicable is one in which a person intending to be a limited partner was erroneously identified as a general partner in the certificate.

§ 305. Information.

Each limited partner has the right to:

(1) inspect and copy any of the partnership records required to be maintained by Section 105; and

(2) obtain from the general partners from time to time upon reasonable demand (i) true and full information regarding the state of the business and financial condition of the limited partnership, (ii) promptly after becoming available, a copy of the limited partnership's federal, state, and local income tax returns for each year, and (iii) other information regarding the affairs of the limited partnership as is just and reasonable.

Comment

Section 305 changes and restates the rights of limited partners to information about the partnership formerly provided by Section 10 of the ~~prior uniform law.~~ 1916 Act. Its importance has increased as a result of the 1985 Act's substituting the records of the partnership for the certificate of limited partnership as the place where certain categories of information are to be kept.

Section 305, which should be read together with Section 105(b), provides a mechanism for limited partners to obtain information about the partnership useful to them in making decisions concerning the partnership and their investments in it. Its purpose is not to provide a mechanism for competitors of the partnership or others having interests or agendas adverse to the partnership's to subvert the partnership's business. It is assumed that courts will protect limited partnerships from abuses and attempts to misuse Section 305 for improper purposes.

ARTICLE 4

GENERAL PARTNERS

§ 401. Admission of Additional General Partners.

After the filing of a limited partnership's original certificate of limited partnership, additional general partners may be admitted ~~only~~ as provided in writing in the partnership agreement or, if the partnership agreement does not provide in writing for the admission of additional general partners, with the ~~specific~~ written consent of ~~each partner~~ all partners.

Comment

Section 401 is derived from, but represents a significant departure from, Section 9(1)(e) of the ~~prior law and carries over the unwaivable requirement that all limited partners must consent~~ 1916 Act and Section 401 of the 1976 Act, which required, as a condition to the admission of an additional general partner, that all limited partners consent and that such consent ~~must~~ specifically identify the general partner involved. Section 401 of the 1985 Act provides that the written partnership agreement determines the procedure for authorizing the admission of additional general partners, and that the written consent of all partners is required only when the partnership agreement fails to address the question.

§ 402. Events of Withdrawal.

Except as approved by the specific written consent of all partners at the time, a person ceases to be a general partner of a limited partnership upon the happening of any of the following events:

(1) the general partner withdraws from the limited partnership as provided in Section 602;

(2) the general partner ceases to be a member of the limited partnership as provided in Section 702;

(3) the general partner is removed as a general partner in accordance with the partnership agreement;

(4) unless otherwise provided in writing in the ~~certificate of limited~~ partnership agreement, the general partner: (i) makes an assignment for the benefit of creditors; (ii) files a voluntary petition in bankruptcy; (iii) is adjudicated a bankrupt or insolvent; (iv) files a petition or answer seeking for himself [or herself] any reorganization, arrangement, composition, readjustment, liquidation, dissolution or similar relief under any statute, law, or regulation; (v) files an answer or other pleading admitting or failing to contest the material allegations of a petition filed against him [or her] in any proceeding of this nature; or (vi) seeks, consents to, or acquiesces in the appointment of a trustee, receiver, or liquidator of the general partner or of all or any substantial part of his [or her] properties;

(5) unless otherwise provided in writing in the ~~certificate of limited~~ partnership agreement, [120] days after the commencement of any proceeding against the general partner seeking reorganization, arrangement, composition, readjustment, liquidation, dissolution or similar relief under any statute, law, or regulation, the proceeding has not been dismissed, or if within [90] days after the appointment without his [or her] consent or acquiescence of a trustee, receiver, or liquidator of the general partner or of all or any substantial part of his [or her] properties, the appointment is not vacated or stayed or within [90] days after the expiration of any such stay, the appointment is not vacated;

(6) in the case of a general partner who is a natural person,

(i) his [or her] death; or

(ii) the entry of an order by a court of competent jurisdiction adjudicating him [or her] incompetent to manage his [or her] person or his [or her] estate;

(7) in the case of a general partner who is acting as a general partner by virtue of being a trustee of a trust, the termination of the trust (but not merely the substitution of a new trustee);

(8) in the case of a general partner that is a separate partnership, the dissolution and commencement of winding up of the separate partnership;

(9) in the case of a general partner that is a corporation, the filing of a certificate of dissolution, or its equivalent, for the corporation or the revocation of its charter; or

(10) in the case of an estate, the distribution by the fiduciary of the estate's entire interest in the partnership.

Comment

Section 402 expands considerably the provisions of Section 20 of the ~~prior uniform law~~ 1916 Act, which provided for dissolution in the event of the retirement, death or insanity of a general partner. Subdivisions (1), (2) and (3) recognize that the general partner's agency relationship is terminable at will, although it may result in a breach of the partnership agreement giving rise to an action for damages. Subdivisions (4) and (5) reflect a judgment that, unless the limited partners agree otherwise, they ought to have the power to rid themselves of a general partner who is in such dire financial straits that he is the subject of proceedings under the National Bankruptcy ~~Act~~ Code or a similar provision of law. Subdivisions (6) through (10) simply elaborate on the notion of death in the case of a general partner who is not a natural person. ~~Of course, the addition of the words "and in the partnership agreement" was not intended to suggest that liabilities to third parties could be affected by provisions in the partnership agreement.~~ Subdivisions (4) and (5) differ from their counterparts in the 1976 Act, reflecting the policy underlying the 1985 revision of Section 201, that the partnership agreement, not the certificate of limited partnership, is the appropriate document for setting out most provisions relating to the respective powers, rights and obligations of the partners inter se. Although the partnership agreement need not be written, the 1985 Act provides that, to protect the partners from fraud, these and certain other particularly significant provisions must be set out in a written partnership agreement to be effective for the purposes described in the Act.

§ 403. General Powers and Liabilities.

(a) Except as provided in this [Act] or in the partnership agreement, a general partner of a limited partnership has the rights and powers and is subject to the restrictions of a partner in a partnership without limited partners.

(b) Except as provided in this [Act], a general partner of a limited partnership has the liabilities of a partner in a partnership without limited partners to persons other than the partnership and the other partners. Except as provided in this [Act] or in the partnership agreement, a general partner of a limited partnership has the liabilities of a partner in a partnership without limited partners to the partnership and to the other partners.

Comment

Section 403 is derived from Section 9(1) of the ~~prior uniform law.~~ 1916 Act.

§ 404. Contributions by General Partner.

A general partner of a limited partnership may make contributions to the partnership and share in the profits and losses of, and in distributions from, the limited partnership as a general partner. A general partner also may make contributions to and share in profits, losses, and distributions as a limited partner. A person who is both a general partner and a limited partner has the rights and powers, and is subject to the restrictions and liabilities, of a general partner and, except as provided in the partnership agreement, also has the powers, and is subject to the restrictions, of a limited partner to the extent of his [or her] participation in the partnership as a limited partner.

Comment

Section 404 is derived from Section 12 of the ~~prior uniform law~~ 1916 Act and makes clear that the partnership agreement may provide that a general partner who is also a limited partner may exercise all of the powers of a limited partner.

§ 405. Voting.

The partnership agreement may grant to all or certain identified general partners the right to vote (on a per capita or any other basis), separately or with all or any class of the limited partners, on any matter.

Comment

Section 405 ~~is new~~ first appeared in the 1976 Act and is intended to make it clear that the Act does not require that the limited partners have any right to vote on matters as a separate class.

ARTICLE 5

FINANCE

§ 501. Form of Contribution.

The contribution of a partner may be in cash, property, or services rendered, or a promissory note or other obligation to contribute cash or property or to perform services.

Comment

As noted in the comment to Section 101, the explicit permission to make contributions of services expands Section 4 of the ~~prior uniform law.~~ 1916 Act.

§ 502. Liability for Contribution.

(a) A promise by a limited partner to contribute to the limited partnership is not enforceable unless set out in a writing signed by the limited partner.

~~(a)~~(b) Except as provided in the ~~certificate of limited~~ partnership agreement, a partner is obligated to the limited partnership to perform any enforceable promise to contribute cash or property or to perform services, even if he [or she] is unable to perform because of death, disability, or any other reason. If a partner does not make the required contribution of property or services, he [or she] is obligated at the option of the limited partnership to contribute cash equal to that portion of the value, as stated in the ~~certificate of limited~~ partnership records required to be kept pursuant to Section 105, of the stated contribution which has not been made.

~~(b)~~(c) Unless otherwise provided in the partnership agreement, the obligation of a partner to make a contribution or return money or other property paid or distributed in violation of this [Act] may be compromised only by consent of all partners. Notwithstanding the compromise, a creditor of a limited partnership who extends credit~~,~~ or ~~whose claim arises,~~ otherwise acts in reliance on that obligation after the ~~filing of the certificate of limited partnership or an amendment thereto~~ partner signs a writing which~~, in either case,~~ reflects the obligation~~,~~ and before the amendment or cancellation thereof to reflect the compromise~~,~~ may enforce the original obligation.

Comment

Section 502(a) is new: it has no counterpart in the 1916 or 1976 Acts. Because, unlike the prior uniform acts, the 1985 Act does not require that promises to contribute cash, property, or services be described in the limited partnership certificate, to protect against fraud it requires instead that such important promises be in a signed writing.

Although Section 17(1) of the ~~prior uniform law~~ 1916 Act required a partner to fulfill his promise to make contributions, the addition of contributions in the form of a promise to render services means that a partner who is unable to perform those services because of death or disability as well as because of an intentional default is required to pay the cash value of the services unless the ~~certificate of limited partnership~~ partnership agreement provides otherwise.

Subdivision (b) (c) is derived from, but expands upon, Section 17(3) of the prior uniform law 1916 Act.

§ 503. Sharing of Profits and Losses.

The profits and losses of a limited partnership shall be allocated among the partners, and among classes of partners, in the manner provided in writing in the partnership agreement. If the partnership agreement does not so provide in writing, profits and losses shall be allocated on the basis of the value, as stated in the certificate of limited partnership records required to be kept pursuant to Section 105, of the contributions made by each partner to the extent they have been received by the partnership and have not been returned.

Comment

Section 503 is new first appeared in the 1976 Act. The prior uniform law 1916 Act did not provide for the basis on which partners would share profits and losses in the absence of agreement. The 1985 Act differs from its counterpart in the 1976 Act by requiring that, to be effective, the partnership agreement provisions concerning allocation of profits and losses be in writing, and by its reference to records required to be kept pursuant to Section 105, the latter reflecting the 1985 changes in Section 201.

§ 504. Sharing of Distributions.

Distributions of cash or other assets of a limited partnership shall be allocated among the partners and among classes of partners in the manner provided in writing in the partnership agreement. If the partnership agreement does not so provide in writing, distributions shall be made on the basis of the value, as stated in the certificate of limited partnership records required to be kept pursuant to Section 105, of the contributions made by each partner to the extent they have been received by the partnership and have not been returned.

Comment

Section 504 is new first appeared in the 1976 Act. The prior uniform law 1916 Act did not provide for the basis on which partners would share distributions in the absence of agreement. Section 504 also differs from its counterpart in the 1976 Act by requiring that, to be effective, the partnership agreement provisions concerning allocation of distributions be in writing, and in its reference to records required to be kept pursuant to Section 105, the latter reflecting the 1985 changes in Section 201. This section also recognizes that partners may choose to share in distribution distributions on a different basis than different from that on which they share in profits and losses.

ARTICLE 6

DISTRIBUTIONS AND WITHDRAWAL

§ 601. Interim Distributions.

Except as provided in this Article, a partner is entitled to receive distributions from a limited partnership before his [or her] withdrawal from the limited partnership and before the dissolution and winding up thereof:
— (1) to the extent and at the times or upon the happening of the events specified in the partnership agreement; and
— (2) if any distribution constitutes a return of any part of his contribution under Section 608(c), to the extent and at the times or upon the happening of the events specified in the certificate of limited partnership.

Comment

Section 601 is new first appeared in the 1976 Act. The 1976 Act provisions have been modified to reflect the 1985 changes made in Section 201.

§ 602. Withdrawal of General Partner.

A general partner may withdraw from a limited partnership at any time by giving written notice to the other partners, but if the withdrawal violates the partnership agreement, the limited partnership may recover from the withdrawing general partner damages for breach of the partnership agreement and offset the damages against the amount otherwise distributable to him [or her].

Comment

Section 602 is new first appeared in the 1976 Act, but is generally derived from Section 38 of the Uniform Partnership Act.

§ 603. Withdrawal of Limited Partner.

A limited partner may withdraw from a limited partnership at the time or upon the happening of events specified in the certificate of limited partnership and in accordance with in writing in the partnership agreement. If the certificate agreement does not specify in writing the time or the events upon the happening of which a limited partner may withdraw or a definite time for the dissolution and winding up of the limited partnership, a limited partner may withdraw upon not less than six months' prior written notice to each general partner at his [or her] address on the books of the limited partnership at its office in this State.

Comment

Section 603 is derived from Section 16(c) 16 of the prior uniform law 1916 Act. The 1976 Act provision has been modified to reflect the 1985 changes made in Section 201. This section additionally reflects the policy determination, also embodied in certain other sections of the 1985 Act, that to avoid fraud, agreements concerning certain matters of substantial importance to the partners will be enforceable only if in writing. If the partnership agreement does provide, in writing, whether a limited partner may withdraw and, if he may, when and on what terms and conditions, those provisions will control.

§ 604. Distribution Upon Withdrawal.

Except as provided in this Article, upon withdrawal any withdrawing partner is entitled to receive any distribution to which he [or she] is entitled under the partnership agreement and, if not otherwise provided in the agreement, he [or she] is entitled to receive, within a reasonable time after withdrawal, the fair value of his [or her] interest in the limited partnership as of the date of withdrawal based upon his [or her] right to share in distributions from the limited partnership.

Comment

Section 604 is new first appeared in the 1976 Act. It fixes the distributive share of a withdrawing partner in the absence of an agreement among the partners.

§ 605. Distribution in Kind.

Except as provided in writing in the certificate of limited partnership agreement, a partner, regardless of the nature of his [or her] contribution, has no right to demand and receive any distribution from a limited partnership in any form other than cash. Except as provided in writing in the partnership agreement, a partner may not be compelled to accept a distribution of any asset in kind from a limited partnership to the extent that the percentage of the asset distributed to him [or her] exceeds a percentage of that asset which is equal to the percentage in which he [or she] shares in distributions from the limited partnership.

Comment

The first sentence of Section 605 is derived from Section 16(3) of the prior uniform law; 1916 Act; it also differs from its counterpart in the 1976 Act, reflecting the 1985 changes made in Section 201. The second sentence is new first appeared in the 1976 Act, and is intended to protect a limited partner (and the remaining partners) against a distribution in kind of more than his share of particular assets.

§ 606. Right to Distribution.

At the time a partner becomes entitled to receive a distribution, he [or she] has the status of, and is entitled to all remedies available to, a creditor of the limited partnership with respect to the distribution.

Comment

Section 606 is new first appeared in the 1976 Act, and is intended to make it clear that the right of a partner to receive a distribution, as between the partners, is not subject to the equity risks of the enterprise. On the other hand, since partners entitled to distributions have creditor status, there did not seem to be a need for the extraordinary remedy of Section 16(4)(a) of the ~~prior uniform law.~~ 1916 Act, which granted a limited partner the right to seek dissolution of the partnership if he was unsuccessful in demanding the return of his contribution. It is more appropriate for the partner to simply sue as an ordinary creditor and obtain a judgment.

§ 607. Limitations on Distribution.

A partner may not receive a distribution from a limited partnership to the extent that, after giving effect to the distribution, all liabilities of the limited partnership, other than liabilities to partners on account of their partnership interests, exceed the fair value of the partnership assets.

Comment

Section 607 is derived from Section 16(1)(a) of the ~~prior uniform law.~~ 1916 Act.

§ 608. Liability Upon Return of Contribution.

(a) If a partner has received the return of any part of his [or her] contribution without violation of the partnership agreement or this [Act], he [or she] is liable to the limited partnership for a period of one year thereafter for the amount of the returned contribution, but only to the extent necessary to discharge the limited partnership's liabilities to creditors who extended credit to the limited partnership during the period the contribution was held by the partnership.

(b) If a partner has received the return of any part of his [or her] contribution in violation of the partnership agreement or this [Act], he [or she] is liable to the limited partnership for a period of six years thereafter for the amount of the contribution wrongfully returned.

(c) A partner receives a return of his [or her] contribution to the extent that a distribution to him [or her] reduces his [or her] share of the fair value of the net assets of the limited partnership below the value, as set forth in the ~~certificate of limited~~ partnership records required to be kept pursuant to Section 105, of his [or her] contribution which has not been distributed to him [or her].

Comment

Paragraph (a) is derived from Section 17(4) of the ~~prior uniform law~~ 1916 Act, but the one year statute of limitations has been added. Paragraph (b) is derived from Section 17(2)(b) of the ~~prior uniform law~~ 1916 Act but, again, a statute of limitations has been added.

Paragraph (c) ~~is new~~ first appeared in the 1976 Act. The provisions of former Section 17(2) that referred to the partner holding as "trustee" any money or specific property wrongfully returned to him have been eliminated. Paragraph (c) in the 1985 Act also differs from its counterpart in the 1976 Act to reflect the 1985 changes made in Sections 105 and 201.

ARTICLE 7

ASSIGNMENT OF PARTNERSHIP INTERESTS

§ 701. Nature of Partnership Interest.

A partnership interest is personal property.

Comment

This section is derived from Section 18 of the ~~prior uniform law.~~ 1916 Act.

§ 702. Assignment of Partnership Interest.

Except as provided in the partnership agreement, a partnership interest is assignable in whole or in part. An assignment of a partnership interest does not dissolve a limited partnership or entitle the assignee to become or to exercise any rights of a partner. An assignment entitles the assignee to receive, to the extent assigned, only the distribution to which the assignor would be entitled. Except as provided in the partnership agreement, a partner ceases to be a partner upon assignment of all his [or her] partnership interest.

Comment

Section 19(1) of the ~~prior uniform law~~ 1916 Act provided simply that "a limited partner's interest is assignable," raising a question whether any limitations on the right of assignment were permitted. While the first sentence of Section 702 recognizes that the power to assign may be restricted in the partnership agreement, there was no intention to affect in any way the usual rules regarding restraints on alienation of personal property. The second and third sentences of Section 702 are derived from Section 19(3) of the ~~prior uniform law.~~ 1916 Act. The last sentence ~~is new.~~ first appeared in the 1976 Act.

§ 703. Rights of Creditor.

On application to a court of competent jurisdiction by any judgment creditor of a partner, the court may charge the partnership interest of the partner with payment of the unsatisfied amount of the judgment with interest. To the extent so charged, the judgment creditor has only the rights of an assignee of the partnership interest. This [Act] does not deprive any partner of the benefit of any exemption laws applicable to his [or her] partnership interest.

Comment

Section 703 is derived from Section 22 of the ~~prior uniform law~~ 1916 Act but has not carried over some provisions that were thought to be superfluous. For example, references in Section 22(1) to specific remedies have been omitted, as has a prohibition in Section 22(2) against discharge of the lien with partnership property. Ordinary rules governing the remedies available to a creditor and the fiduciary obligations of general partners will determine those matters.

§ 704. Right of Assignee to Become Limited Partner.

(a) An assignee of a partnership interest, including an assignee of a general partner, may become a limited partner if and to the extent that ~~(1)~~ (i) the assignor gives the assignee that right in accordance with authority described in the ~~certificate of limited partnership~~ agreement, or ~~(2)~~ (ii) all other partners consent.

(b) An assignee who has become a limited partner has, to the extent assigned, the rights and powers, and is subject to the restrictions and liabilities, of a limited partner under the partnership agreement and this [Act]. An assignee who becomes a limited partner also is liable for the obligations of his [or her] assignor to make and return contributions as provided in ~~Article~~ Articles 5 and 6. However, the assignee is not obligated for liabilities unknown to the assignee at the time he [or she] became a limited partner ~~and which could not be ascertained from the certificate of limited partnership~~.

(c) If an assignee of a partnership interest becomes a limited partner, the assignor is not released from his [or her] liability to the limited partnership under Sections 207 and 502.

Comment

Section 704 is derived from Section 19 of the ~~prior uniform law,~~ 1916 Act, but paragraph (b) defines more narrowly than Section 19 the obligations of the assignor that are automatically assumed by the assignee. Section 704 of the 1985 Act also differs from the 1976 Act to reflect the 1985 changes made in Section 201.

§ 705. Power of Estate of Deceased or Incompetent Partner.

If a partner who is an individual dies or a court of competent jurisdiction adjudges him [or her] to be incompetent to manage his [or her] person or his [or her] property, the partner's executor, administrator, guardian, conservator, or other legal representative may exercise all the partner's rights for the purpose of settling his [or her] estate or administering his [or her] property, including any power the partner had to give an assignee the right to become a limited partner. If a partner is a corporation, trust, or other entity and is dissolved or terminated, the powers of that partner may be exercised by its legal representative or successor.

Comment

Section 705 is derived from Section 21(1) of the ~~prior uniform law.~~ 1916 Act. Former Section 21(2), making a deceased limited partner's estate liable for his liabilities as a limited partner was deleted as superfluous, with no intention of changing the liability of the estate.

ARTICLE 8

DISSOLUTION

§ 801. Nonjudicial Dissolution.

A limited partnership is dissolved and its affairs shall be wound up upon the happening of the first to occur of the following:

(1) at the time specified in the certificate of limited partnership;

(2) ~~or~~ upon the happening of events specified in writing in the ~~certificate of limited~~ partnership agreement;

~~(2)~~(3) written consent of all partners;

~~(3)~~(4) an event of withdrawal of a general partner unless at the time there is at least one other general partner and the ~~certificate of limited~~ written provisions of the partnership agreement ~~permits~~ permit the business of the limited partnership to be carried on by the remaining general partner and that partner does so, but the limited partnership is not dissolved and is not required to be wound up by reason of any event of withdrawal, if, within 90 days after the withdrawal, all partners agree in writing to continue the business of the limited partnership and to the appointment of one or more additional general partners if necessary or desired; or

~~(4)~~(5) entry of a decree of judicial dissolution under Section 802.

Comment

Section 801 merely collects in one place all of the events causing dissolution. Paragraph (3) is derived from Sections 9(1)(g) and 20 of the ~~prior uniform law,~~ 1916 Act, but adds the 90-day grace period. Section 801 also differs from its counterpart in the 1976 Act to reflect the 1985 changes made in Section 201.

§ 802. Judicial Dissolution.

On application by or for a partner the [designate the appropriate court] court may decree dissolution of a limited partnership whenever it is not reasonably practicable to carry on the business in conformity with the partnership agreement.

Comment

Section 802 ~~is new~~ first appeared in the 1976 Act.

§ 803. Winding Up.

Except as provided in the partnership agreement, the general partners who have not wrongfully dissolved a limited partnership or, if none, the limited partners, may wind up the limited partnership's affairs; but the [designate the appropriate court] court may wind up the limited partnership's affairs upon application of any partner, his [or her] legal representative, or assignee.

Comment

Section 803 ~~is new~~ first appeared in the 1976 Act, and is derived in part from Section 37 of the Uniform ~~General~~ Partnership Act.

§ 804. Distribution of Assets.

Upon the winding up of a limited partnership, the assets shall be distributed as follows:

(1) to creditors, including partners who are creditors, to the extent permitted by law, in satisfaction of liabilities of the limited partnership other than liabilities for distributions to partners under Section 601 or 604;

(2) except as provided in the partnership agreement, to partners and former partners in satisfaction of liabilities for distributions under Section 601 or 604; and

(3) except as provided in the partnership agreement, to partners first for the return of their contributions and secondly respecting their partnership interests, in the proportions in which the partners share in distributions.

Comment

Section 804 revises Section 23 of the ~~prior uniform law~~ 1916 Act by providing that (1) to the extent partners are also creditors, other than in respect of their interests in the partnership, they share with other creditors, (2) once the partnership's obligation to make a distribution accrues, it must be paid before any other distributions of an "equity" nature are made, and (3) general and limited partners rank on the same level except as otherwise provided in the partnership agreement.

ARTICLE 9

FOREIGN LIMITED PARTNERSHIPS

§ 901. Law Governing.

Subject to the Constitution of this State, (i) the laws of the state under which a foreign limited partnership is organized govern its organization and internal affairs and the liability of its limited partners, and (ii) a foreign limited partnership may not be denied registration by reason of any difference between those laws and the laws of this State.

Comment

Section 901 ~~is new.~~ first appeared in the 1976 Act.

§ 902. Registration.

Before transacting business in this State, a foreign limited partnership shall register with the Secretary of State. In order to register, a foreign limited partnership shall submit to the Secretary of State, in duplicate, an application for registration as a foreign limited partnership, signed and sworn to by a general partner and setting forth:

(1) the name of the foreign limited partnership and, if different, the name under which it proposes to register and transact business in this State;

(2) the ~~state~~ State and date of its formation;

(3) ~~the general character of the business it proposes to transact in this State;~~

~~(4)~~ (3) the name and address of any agent for service of process on the foreign limited partnership whom the foreign limited partnership elects to appoint; the agent must be an individual resident of this ~~state~~ State, a domestic corporation, or a foreign corporation having a place of business in, and authorized to do business in, this State;

~~(5)~~ (4) a statement that the Secretary of State is appointed the agent of the foreign limited partnership for service of process if no agent has been appointed under paragraph ~~(4)~~ (3) or, if appointed, the agent's authority has been revoked or if the agent cannot be found or served with the exercise of reasonable diligence;

~~(6)~~ (5) the address of the office required to be maintained in the ~~State~~ state of its organization by the laws of that ~~State~~ state or, if not so required, of the principal office of the foreign limited partnership; ~~and~~

~~(7) if the certificate of limited partnership filed in the foreign limited partnership's state of organization is not required to include the names and business addresses of the partners, a list of the names and addresses.~~

(6) the name and business address of each general partner; and

(7) the address of the office at which is kept a list of the names and addresses of the limited partners and their capital contributions, together with an undertaking by the foreign limited partnership to keep those records until the foreign limited partnership's registration in this State is cancelled or withdrawn.

Comment

Section 902 ~~is new~~ first appeared in the 1976 Act. It was thought that requiring a full copy of the certificate of limited partnership and all amendments thereto to be filed in each state in which the partnership does business would impose an unreasonable burden on interstate limited partnerships and that the information ~~on file was~~ Section 902 required to be filed would be sufficient to tell interested persons where they could write to obtain copies of those basic documents. Subdivision (3) of the 1976 Act has been omitted, and subdivisions (6) and (7) differ from their counterparts in the 1976 Act, to conform these provisions relating to the registration of foreign limited partnerships to the corresponding changes made by the Act in the provisions relating to domestic limited partnerships. The requirement that an application for registration be sworn to by a general partner is simply intended to produce the same result as is provided for in Section 204(c) with respect to certificates of domestic limited partnerships; the acceptance and endorsement by the Secretary of State (or equivalent authority) of an application which was not sworn by a general partner should be deemed a mere technical and insubstantial shortcoming, and should not result in the limited partners' being subjected to general liability for the obligations of the foreign limited partnership (See Section 907(c)).

§ 903. Issuance of Registration.

(a) If the Secretary of State finds that an application for registration conforms to law and all requisite fees have been paid, he [or she] shall:

(1) endorse on the application the word "Filed," and the month, day and year of the filing thereof;

(2) file in his [or her] office a duplicate original of the application; and

(3) issue a certificate of registration to transact business in this State.

(b) The certificate of registration, together with a duplicate original of the application, shall be returned to the person who filed the application or his [or her] representative.

Comment

Section 903 first appeared in the 1976 Act.

§ 904. Name.

A foreign limited partnership may register with the Secretary of State under any name, whether or not it is the name under which it is registered in its state of organization, that includes without abbreviation the words "limited partnership" and that could be registered by a domestic limited partnership.

Comment

Section 904 is new. first appeared in the 1976 Act.

§ 905. Changes and Amendments.

If any statement in the application for registration of a foreign limited partnership was false when made or any arrangements or other facts described have changed, making the application inaccurate in any respect, the foreign limited partnership shall promptly file in the office of the Secretary of State a certificate, signed and sworn to by a general partner, correcting such statement.

Comment

Section 905 is new. first appeared in the 1976 Act. It corresponds to the provisions of Section 202(c) relating to domestic limited partnerships.

§ 906. Cancellation of Registration.

A foreign limited partnership may cancel its registration by filing with the Secretary of State a certificate of cancellation signed and sworn to by a general partner. A cancellation does not terminate the authority of the Secretary of State to accept service of process on the foreign limited partnership with respect to [claims for relief] [causes of action] arising out of the transactions of business in this State.

Comment

Section 906 is new. first appeared in the 1976 Act.

§ 907. Transaction of Business Without Registration.

(a) A foreign limited partnership transacting business in this State may not maintain any action, suit, or proceeding in any court of this State until it has registered in this State.

(b) The failure of a foreign limited partnership to register in this State does not impair the validity of any contract or act of the foreign limited partnership or prevent the foreign limited partnership from defending any action, suit, or proceeding in any court of this State.

(c) A limited partner of a foreign limited partnership is not liable as a general partner of the foreign limited partnership solely by reason of having transacted business in this State without registration.

(d) A foreign limited partnership, by transacting business in this State without registration, appoints the Secretary of State as its agent for service of process with respect to [claims for relief] [causes of action] arising out of the transaction of business in this State.

Comment

Section 907 is new. first appeared in the 1976 Act.

§ 908. Action by [Appropriate Official].

The [designate the appropriate official] may bring an action to restrain a foreign limited partnership from transacting business in this State in violation of this Article.

Comment

Section 908 is new. first appeared in the 1976 Act.

ARTICLE 10

DERIVATIVE ACTIONS

§ 1001. Right of Action.

A limited partner may bring an action in the right of a limited partnership to recover a judgment in its favor if general partners with authority to do so have refused to bring the action or if an effort to cause those general partners to bring the action is not likely to succeed.

Comment

Section 1001 is new. first appeared in the 1976 Act.

§ 1002. Proper Plaintiff.

In a derivative action, the plaintiff must be a partner at the time of bringing the action and (i) must have been a partner at the time of the transaction of which he [or she] complains or (ii) his [or her] status as a partner had must have devolved upon him [or her] by operation of law or pursuant to the terms of the partnership agreement from a person who was a partner at the time of the transaction.

Comment

Section 1002 is new. first appeared in the 1976 Act.

§ 1003. Pleading.

In a derivative action, the complaint shall set forth with particularity the effort of the plaintiff to secure initiation of the action by a general partner or the reasons for not making the effort.

Comment

Section 1003 is new. first appeared in the 1976 Act.

§ 1004. Expenses.

If a derivative action is successful, in whole or in part, or if anything is received by the plaintiff as a result of a judgment, compromise or settlement of an action or claim, the court may award the plaintiff reasonable expenses, including reasonable attorney's fees, and shall direct him [or her] to remit to the limited partnership the remainder of those proceeds received by him [or her].

Comment

Section 1004 is new. first appeared in the 1976 Act.

ARTICLE 11

MISCELLANEOUS

§ 1101. Construction and Application.

This [Act] shall be so applied and construed to effectuate its general purpose to make uniform the law with respect to the subject of this [Act] among states enacting it.

Comment

Because the principles set out in Sections 28(1) and 29 of the 1916 Act have become so universally established, it was felt that the 1976 and 1985 Acts need not contain express provisions to the same effect. However, it is intended that the principles enunciated in those provisions of the 1916 Act also apply to this Act.

§ 1102. Short Title.

This [Act] may be cited as the Uniform Limited Partnership Act.

§ 1103. Severability.

If any provision of this [Act] or its application to any person or circumstance is held invalid, the invalidity does not affect other provisions or applications of the [Act] which can be given effect without the invalid provision or application, and to this end the provisions of this [Act] are severable.

§ 1104. Effective Date, Extended Effective Date and Repeal.

Except as set forth below, the effective date of this [Act] is _____ and the following acts [list prior existing limited partnership acts] are hereby repealed:

(1) The existing provisions for execution and filing of certificates of limited partnerships and amendments thereunder and cancellations thereof continue in effect until [specify time required to create central filing system], the extended effective date, and Sections 102, 103, 104, 105, 201, 202, 203, 204 and 206 are not effective until the extended effective date.

(2) Section 402, specifying the conditions under which a general partner ceases to be a member of a limited partnership, is not effective until the extended effective date, and the applicable provisions of existing law continue to govern until the extended effective date.

(3) Sections 501, 502 and 608 apply only to contributions and distributions made after the effective date of this [Act].

(4) Section 704 applies only to assignments made after the effective date of this [Act].

(5) Article 9, dealing with registration of foreign limited partnerships, is not effective until the extended effective date.

(6) Unless otherwise agreed by the partners, the applicable provisions of existing law governing allocation of profits and losses (rather than the provisions of Section 503), distributions to a withdrawing partner (rather than the provisions of Section 604), and distribution of assets upon the winding up of a limited partnership (rather than the provisions of Section 804) govern limited partnerships formed before the effective date of this [Act].

Comment

Subdivisions (6) and (7) did not appear in Section 1104 of the 1976 Act. They are included in the 1985 Act to ensure that the application of the Act to limited partnerships formed and existing before the Act becomes effective would not violate constitutional prohibitions against the impairment of contracts. [There is no subdivision (7) in 6A Uniform Laws Annotated 293 (1995), from which this language was taken. *Ed.*]

§ 1105. Rules for Cases Not Provided for in This [Act].

In any case not provided for in this [Act] the provisions of the Uniform Partnership Act govern.

Comment

The result provided for in Section 1105 would obtain even in its absence in a jurisdiction which had adopted the Uniform Partnership Act, by operation of Section 6 of that act.

§ 1106. Savings Clause.

The repeal of any statutory provision by this [Act] does not impair, or otherwise affect, the organization or the continued existence of a limited partnership existing at the effective date of this [Act], nor does the repeal of any existing statutory provision by this [Act] impair any contract or affect any right accrued before the effective date of this [Act].

Comment

Section 1106 did not appear in the 1976 Act. It was included in the 1985 Act to ensure that the application of the Act to limited partnerships formed and existing before the Act becomes effective would not violate constitutional prohibitions against the impairment of contracts.

PART THREE

THE LIMITED LIABILITY COMPANY

UNIFORM LIMITED LIABILITY COMPANY ACT (1995)
(AS AMENDED 1996)

Historical Notes

The Uniform Limited Liability Company Act (1995) ("ULLCA") was approved by the National Conference of Commissioners on Uniform State Laws in 1995.

Editor's note: ULLCA and all of its Comments are reproduced below. ULLCA is contained in volume 6A of Uniform Laws Annotated (1995). The 1997 Cumulative Annual Pocket Part to volume 6A lists the following states that have adopted ULLCA, all in 1996: Hawaii, South Carolina, Vermont, and West Virginia. The version of ULLCA reproduced below incorporates the amendments made to ULLCA in 1996. The amendments are shown by strikeover for deletions and underscored text for language added to the Act in 1996.

Prefatory Note

Borrowing from abroad, Wyoming initiated a national movement in 1977 by enacting this country's first limited liability company act. The movement started slowly as the Internal Revenue Service took more than ten years to announce finally that a Wyoming limited liability company would be taxed like a partnership. Since that time, every State has adopted or is considering its own distinct limited liability company act, many of which have already been amended one or more times.

The allure of the limited liability company is its unique ability to bring together in a single business organization the best features of all other business forms — properly structured, its owners obtain both a corporate-styled liability shield and the pass-through tax benefits of a partnership. General and limited partnerships do not offer their partners a corporate-styled liability shield. Corporations, including those having made a Subchapter S election, do not offer their shareholders all the pass-through tax benefits of a partnership. All state limited liability company acts contain provisions for a liability shield and partnership tax status.

Despite these two common themes, state limited liability company acts display a dazzling array of diversity. Multistate activities of businesses are widespread. Recognition of out-of-state limited liability companies varies. Unfortunately, this lack of uniformity manifests itself in basic but fundamentally important questions, such as: may a company be formed and operated by only one owner; may it be formed for purposes other than to make a profit; whether owners have the power and right to withdraw from a company and receive a distribution of the fair value of their interests; who has the apparent authority to bind the company and the limits of that authority; what are the fiduciary duties of owners and managers to a company and each other; how are the rights to manage a company allocated among its owners and managers; do the owners have the right to sue a company and its other owners in their own right as well as derivatively on behalf of the company; may general and limited partnerships be converted to limited liability companies and may limited liability companies merge with other limited liability companies and other business organizations; what is the law governing foreign limited liability companies; and are any or all of these and other rules simply default rules that may be modified by agreement or are they nonwaivable.

Practitioners and entrepreneurs struggle to understand the law governing limited liability companies organized in their own State and to understand the burgeoning law of other States. Simple questions concerning where to organize are increasingly complex. Since most state limited liability company acts are in their infancy, little if any interpretative case law exists. Even when case law develops, it will have limited precedential value because of the diversity of the state acts.

Accordingly, uniform legislation in this area of the law appeared to have become urgent.

After a Study Committee appointed by the National Conference of Commissioners in late 1991 recommended that a comprehensive project be undertaken, the Conference appointed a Drafting Committee which worked on a Uniform Limited Liability Company Act (ULLCA) from early 1992 until its adoption by the Conference at its Annual Meeting in August 1994. The Drafting Committee was assisted by a blue ribbon panel of national experts and other interested and affected parties and organizations. Many, if not all, of those assisting the Committee brought substantial experience from drafting limited liability company legislation in their own States. Many are also authors of leading treatises and articles in the field. Those represented in the drafting process included an American Bar Association (ABA) liaison, four advisors representing the three separate ABA Sections of Business Law, Taxation, and Real Property, Trust and Probate, the United States Treasury Department, the Internal Revenue Service, and many observers representing several other organizations, including the California Bar Association, the New York City Bar Association, the American College of Real Estate Lawyers, the National Association of Certified Public Accountants, the National Association of Secretaries of State, the Chicago and Lawyers Title Companies, the American Land Title Association, and several university law and business school faculty members.

The Committee met nine times and engaged in numerous national telephonic conferences to discuss policies, review over fifteen drafts, evaluate legal developments and consider comments by our many knowledgeable advisers and observers, as well as an ABA subcommittee's earlier work on a prototype. In examining virtually every aspect of each state limited liability company act, the Committee maintained a single policy vision — to draft a flexible act with a comprehensive set of default rules designed to substitute as the essence of the bargain for small entrepreneurs and others.

This Act is flexible in the sense that the vast majority of its provisions may be modified by the owners in a private agreement. To simplify, those nonwaivable provisions are set forth in a single subsection. Helped thereby, sophisticated parties will negotiate their own deal with the benefit of counsel.

The Committee also recognized that small entrepreneurs without the benefit of counsel should also have access to the Act. To that end, the great bulk of the Act sets forth default rules designed to operate a limited liability company without sophisticated agreements and to recognize that members may also modify the default rules by oral agreements defined in part by their own conduct. Uniquely, the Act combines two simple default structures which depend upon the presence of designations in the articles of organization. All default rules under the Act flow from these two designations.

First, unless the articles reflect that a limited liability company is a term company and the duration of that term, the company will be an at-will company. Generally, an at-will company dissolves more easily than a term company and its owners may demand a payment of the fair value of their interests at any time. Owners of a term company must generally wait until the expiration of the term to obtain the value of their interests. Secondly, unless the articles reflect that a company will be managed by managers, the company will be managed by its members. This designation controls whether the members or managers have apparent agency authority, management authority, the nature of fiduciary duties in the company, and important dissolution characteristics.

In January of 1995 the Executive Committee of the Conference adopted an amendment to harmonize the Act with new and important Internal Revenue Service announcements, and the amendment was ratified by the National Conference at its Annual Meeting in August of 1995. The amendment modifies the Act's dissolution provision.

The adoption of ULLCA will provide much needed consistency among the States, with flexible default rules, and multistate recognition of limited liability on the part of company owners. It will also promote the development of precedential case law.

UNIFORM LIMITED LIABILITY COMPANY ACT (1995) (AS AMENDED 1996)

[ARTICLE] 1

GENERAL PROVISIONS

[ARTICLE] 6

MEMBER'S DISSOCIATION

[ARTICLE] 7

MEMBER'S DISSOCIATION WHEN BUSINESS NOT WOUND UP

[ARTICLE] 8

WINDING UP COMPANY'S BUSINESS

[ARTICLE] 9

CONVERSIONS AND MERGERS

[ARTICLE] 10

FOREIGN LIMITED LIABILITY COMPANIES

[ARTICLE] 11

DERIVATIVE ACTIONS

[ARTICLE] 12

MISCELLANEOUS PROVISIONS

[ARTICLE] 1

GENERAL PROVISIONS

§ 101. Definitions.

In this [Act]:

(1) "Articles of organization" means initial, amended, and restated articles of organization and articles of merger. In the case of a foreign limited liability company, the term includes all records serving a similar function required to be filed in the office of the [Secretary of State] or other official having custody of company records in the State or country under whose law it is organized.

(2) "At-will company" means a limited liability company other than a term company.

(3) "Business" includes every trade, occupation, profession, and other lawful purpose, whether or not carried on for profit.

(4) "Debtor in bankruptcy" means a person who is the subject of an order for relief under Title 11 of the United States Code or a comparable order under a successor statute of general application or a comparable order under federal, state, or foreign law governing insolvency.

(5) "Distribution" means a transfer of money, property, or other benefit from a limited liability company to a member in the member's capacity as a member or to a transferee of the member's distributional interest.

(6) "Distributional interest" means all of a member's interest in distributions by the limited liability company.

(7) "Entity" means a person other than an individual.

(8) "Foreign limited liability company" means an unincorporated entity organized under laws other than the laws of this State which afford limited liability to its owners comparable to the liability under Section 303 and is not required to obtain a certificate of authority to transact business under any law of this State other than this [Act].

(9) "Limited liability company" means a limited liability company organized under this [Act].

(10) "Manager" means a person, whether or not a member of a manager-managed company, who is vested with authority under Section 301.

(11) "Manager-managed company" means a limited liability company which is so designated in its articles of organization.

(12) "Member-managed company" means a limited liability company other than a manager-managed company.

(13) "Operating agreement" means the agreement under Section 103 concerning the relations among the members, managers, and limited liability company. The term includes amendments to the agreement.

(14) "Person" means an individual, corporation, business trust, estate, trust, partnership, limited liability company, association, joint venture, government, governmental subdivision, agency, or instrumentality, or any other legal or commercial entity.

(15) "Principal office" means the office, whether or not in this State, where the principal executive office of a domestic or foreign limited liability company is located.

(16) "Record" means information that is inscribed on a tangible medium or that is stored in an electronic or other medium and is retrievable in perceivable form.

(17) "Sign" means to identify a record by means of a signature, mark, or other symbol, with intent to authenticate it.

(18) "State" means a State of the United States, the District of Columbia, the Commonwealth of Puerto Rico, or any territory or insular possession subject to the jurisdiction of the United States.

(19) "Term company" means a limited liability company in which its members have agreed to remain members until the expiration of a term specified in the articles of organization.

(20) "Transfer" includes an assignment, conveyance, deed, bill of sale, lease, mortgage, security interest, encumbrance, and gift.

Comment

Uniform Limited Liability Company Act ("ULLCA") definitions, like the rest of the Act, are a blend of terms and concepts derived from the Uniform Partnership Act ("UPA"), the Uniform Partnership Act (1994) ("UPA 1994", also previously known as the Revised Uniform Partnership Act or "RUPA"), the Revised Uniform Limited Partnership Act ("RULPA"), the Uniform Commercial Code ("UCC"), and the Model Business Corporation Act ("MBCA"), or their revisions from time to time; some are tailored specially for this Act.

"Business." A limited liability company may be organized to engage in an activity either for or not for profit. The extent to which contributions to a nonprofit company may be deductible for Federal income tax purposes is determined by federal law. Other state law determines the extent of exemptions from state and local income and property taxes.

"Debtor in bankruptcy." The filing of a voluntary petition operates immediately as an "order for relief." See Sections 601(7)(i) and 602(b)(2)(iii).

"Distribution." This term includes all sources of a member's distributions including the member's capital contributions, undistributed profits, and residual interest in the assets of the company after all claims, including those of third parties and debts to members, have been paid.

"Distributional interest." The term does not include a member's broader rights to participate in the management of the company. See Comments to Article 5.

"Foreign limited liability company." The term is not restricted to companies formed in the United States.

"Manager." The rules of agency apply to limited liability companies. Therefore, managers may designate agents with whatever titles, qualifications, and responsibilities they desire. For example, managers may designate an agent as "President."

"Manager-managed company." The term includes only a company designated as such in the articles of organization. In a manager-managed company agency authority is vested exclusively in one or more managers and not in the members. See Sections 101(10) (manager), 203(a)(6) (articles designation), and 301(b) (agency authority of members and managers).

"Member-managed limited liability company." The term includes every company not designated as "manager-managed" under Section 203(a)(6) in its articles of organization.

"Operating agreement." This agreement may be oral. Members may agree upon the extent to which their relationships are to be governed by writings.

"Principal office." The address of the principal office must be set forth in the annual report required under Section 211(a)(3).

"Record." This Act is the first Uniform Act promulgated with a definition of this term. The definition brings this Act in conformity with the present state of technology and accommodates prospective future technology in the communication and storage of information other than by human memory. Modern methods of communicating and storing information employed in commercial practices are no longer confined to physical documents.

The term includes any writing. A record need not be permanent or indestructible, but an oral or other unwritten communication must be stored or preserved on some medium to qualify as a record. Information that has not been retained other than through human memory does not qualify as a record. A record may be signed or may be created without the knowledge or intent of a particular person. Other law must be consulted to determine admissibility in evidence, the applicability of statute of frauds, and other questions regarding the use of records. Under Section 206(a), electronic filings may be permitted and even encouraged.

§ 102. Knowledge and notice.

(a) A person knows a fact if the person has actual knowledge of it.

(b) A person has notice of a fact if the person:

(1) knows the fact;

(2) has received a notification of the fact; or

(3) has reason to know the fact exists from all of the facts known to the person at the time in question.

(c) A person notifies or gives a notification of a fact to another by taking steps reasonably required to inform the other person in ordinary course, whether or not the other person knows the fact.

(d) A person receives a notification when the notification:

(1) comes to the person's attention; or

(2) is duly delivered at the person's place of business or at any other place held out by the person as a place for receiving communications.

(e) An entity knows, has notice, or receives a notification of a fact for purposes of a particular transaction when the individual conducting the transaction for the entity knows, has notice, or receives a notification of the fact, or in any event when the fact would have been brought to the individual's attention had the entity exercised reasonable diligence. An entity exercises reasonable diligence if it maintains reasonable routines for communicating significant information to the individual conducting the transaction for the entity and there is reasonable compliance with the routines. Reasonable diligence does not require an individual acting for the entity to communicate information unless the communication is part of the individual's regular duties or the individual has reason to know of the transaction and that the transaction would be materially affected by the information.

Comment

Knowledge requires cognitive awareness of a fact, whereas notice is based on a lesser degree of awareness. The Act imposes constructive knowledge under limited circumstances. See Comments to Sections 301(c), 703, and 704.

§ 103. Effect of operating agreement; nonwaivable provisions.

(a) Except as otherwise provided in subsection (b), all members of a limited liability company may enter into an operating agreement, which need not be in writing, to regulate the affairs of the company and the conduct of its business, and to govern relations among the members, managers, and company. To the extent the operating agreement does not otherwise provide, this [Act] governs relations among the members, managers, and company.

(b) The operating agreement may not:

(1) unreasonably restrict a right to information or access to records under Section 408;

(2) eliminate the duty of loyalty under Section 409(b) or 603(b)(3), but the agreement may:

(i) identify specific types or categories of activities that do not violate the duty of loyalty, if not manifestly unreasonable; and

(ii) specify the number or percentage of members or disinterested managers that may authorize or ratify, after full disclosure of all material facts, a specific act or transaction that otherwise would violate the duty of loyalty;

(3) unreasonably reduce the duty of care under Section 409(c) or 603(b)(3);

(4) eliminate the obligation of good faith and fair dealing under Section 409(d), but the operating agreement may determine the standards by which the performance of the obligation is to be measured, if the standards are not manifestly unreasonable;

(5) vary the right to expel a member in an event specified in Section 601(6);

(6) vary the requirement to wind up the limited liability company's business in a case specified in Section 801(b)(4) or (b)(5)(3) or (4); or

(7) restrict rights of a person, other than a manager, member, and transferee of a member's distributional interest, under this [Act].

Comment

The operating agreement is the essential contract that governs the affairs of a limited liability company. Since it is binding on all members, amendments must be approved by all members unless otherwise provided in the agreement. Although many agreements will be in writing, the agreement and any amendments may be oral or may be in the form of a record. Course of dealing, course of performance and usage of trade are relevant to determine the meaning of the agreement unless the agreement provides that all amendments must be in writing.

This section makes clear that the only matters an operating agreement may not control are specified in subsection (b). Accordingly, an operating agreement may modify or eliminate any rule specified in any section of this Act except matters specified in subsection (b). To the extent not otherwise mentioned in subsection (b), every section of this Act is simply a default rule, regardless of whether the language of the section appears to be otherwise mandatory. This approach eliminates the necessity of repeating the phrase "unless otherwise agreed" in each section and its commentary.

Under subsection (b)(1), an operating agreement may not unreasonably restrict the right to information or access to any records under Section 408. This does not create an independent obligation beyond Section 408 to maintain any specific records. Under subsections (b)(2) to (4), an irreducible core of fiduciary responsibilities survive any contrary provision in the operating agreement. Subsection (b)(2)(i) authorizes an operating agreement to modify, but not eliminate, the three specific duties of loyalty set forth in Section 409(b)(1) to (3) provided the modification itself is not manifestly unreasonable, a question of fact. Subsection (b)(2)(ii) preserves the common law right of the members to authorize future or ratify past violations of the duty of loyalty provided there has been a full disclosure of all material facts. The authorization or ratification must be unanimous unless otherwise provided in an operating agreement, because the authorization or ratification itself constitutes an amendment to the agreement. The authorization or ratification of specific past or future conduct may sanction conduct that would have been manifestly unreasonable under subsection (b)(2)(i).

§ 104. Supplemental principles of law.

(a) Unless displaced by particular provisions of this [Act], the principles of law and equity supplement this [Act].

(b) If an obligation to pay interest arises under this [Act] and the rate is not specified, the rate is that specified in [applicable statute].

Comment

Supplementary principles include, but are not limited to, the law of agency, estoppel, law merchant, and all other principles listed in UCC Section 1-103, including the law relative to the capacity to contract, fraud, misrepresentation, duress, coercion, mistake, bankruptcy, and other validating and invalidating clauses. Other principles such as those mentioned in UCC Section 1-205 (Course of Dealing and Usage of Trade) apply as well as course of performance. As with UPA 1994 Section 104, upon which this provision is based, no substantive change from either the UPA or the UCC is intended. Section 104(b) establishes the applicable rate of interest in the absence of an agreement among the members.

§ 105. Name.

(a) The name of a limited liability company must contain "limited liability company" or "limited company" or the abbreviation "L.L.C.", "LLC", "L.C.", or "LC". "Limited" may be abbreviated as "Ltd.", and "company" may be abbreviated as "Co.".

(b) Except as authorized by subsections (c) and (d), the name of a limited liability company must be distinguishable upon the records of the [Secretary of State] from:

(1) the name of any corporation, limited partnership, or company incorporated, organized or authorized to transact business, in this State;

(2) a name reserved or registered under Section 106 or 107;

(3) a fictitious name approved under Section 1005 for a foreign company authorized to transact business in this State because its real name is unavailable.

(c) A limited liability company may apply to the [Secretary of State] for authorization to use a name that is not distinguishable upon the records of the [Secretary of State] from one or more of the names described in subsection (b). The [Secretary of State] shall authorize use of the name applied for if:

(1) the present user, registrant, or owner of a reserved name consents to the use in a record and submits an undertaking in form satisfactory to the [Secretary of State] to change the name to a name that is distinguishable upon the records of the [Secretary of State] from the name applied for; or

(2) the applicant delivers to the [Secretary of State] a certified copy of the final judgment of a court of competent jurisdiction establishing the applicant's right to use the name applied for in this State.

(d) A limited liability company may use the name, including a fictitious name, of another domestic or foreign company which is used in this State if the other company is organized or authorized to transact business in this State and the company proposing to use the name has:

(1) merged with the other company;

(2) been formed by reorganization with the other company; or

(3) acquired substantially all of the assets, including the name, of the other company.

§ 106. Reserved name.

(a) A person may reserve the exclusive use of the name of a limited liability company, including a fictitious name for a foreign company whose name is not available, by delivering an application to the [Secretary of State] for filing. The application must set forth the name and address of the applicant and the name proposed to be reserved. If the [Secretary of State] finds that the name applied for is available, it must be reserved for the applicant's exclusive use for a nonrenewable 120-day period.

(b) The owner of a name reserved for a limited liability company may transfer the reservation to another person by delivering to the [Secretary of State] a signed notice of the transfer which states the name and address of the transferee.

Comment

A foreign limited liability company that is not presently authorized to transact business in the State may reserve a fictitious name for a nonrenewable 120-day period. When its actual name is available, a company will generally register that name under Section 107 because the registration is valid for a year and may be extended indefinitely.

§ 107. Registered name.

(a) A foreign limited liability company may register its name subject to the requirements of Section 1005, if the name is distinguishable upon the records of the [Secretary of State] from names that are not available under Section 105(b).

(b) A foreign limited liability company registers its name, or its name with any addition required by Section 1005, by delivering to the [Secretary of State] for filing an application:

(1) setting forth its name, or its name with any addition required by Section 1005, the State or country and date of its organization, and a brief description of the nature of the business in which it is engaged; and

(2) accompanied by a certificate of existence, or a record of similar import, from the State or country of organization.

(c) A foreign limited liability company whose registration is effective may renew it for successive years by delivering for filing in the office of the [Secretary of State] a renewal application complying with subsection (b) between October 1 and December 31 of the preceding year. The renewal application renews the registration for the following calendar year.

(d) A foreign limited liability company whose registration is effective may qualify as a foreign company under its name or consent in writing to the use of its name by a limited liability company later organized under this [Act] or by another foreign company later authorized to transact business in this State. The registered name terminates when the limited liability company is organized or the foreign company qualifies or consents to the qualification of another foreign company under the registered name.

§ 108. Designated office and agent for service of process.

(a) A limited liability company and a foreign limited liability company authorized to do business in this State shall designate and continuously maintain in this State:

(1) an office, which need not be a place of its business in this State; and

(2) an agent and street address of the agent for service of process on the company.

(b) An agent must be an individual resident of this State, a domestic corporation, another limited liability company, or a foreign corporation or foreign company authorized to do business in this State.

Comment

Limited liability companies organized under Section 202 or authorized to transact business under Section 1004 are required to designate and continuously maintain an office in the State. Although the designated office need not be a place of business, it most often will be the only place of business of the company. The company must also designate an agent for service of process within the State and the agent's street address. The agent's address need not be the same as the company's designated office address. The initial office and agent designations must be set forth in the articles of organization, including the address of the designated office. See Section 203(a)(2) to (3). The current office and agent designations must be set forth in the company's annual report. See Section 211(a)(2). See also Section 109 (procedure for changing the office or agent designations), Section 110 (procedure for an agent to resign), and Section 111(b) (the filing officer is the service agent for the company if it fails to maintain its own service agent).

§ 109. Change of designated office or agent for service of process.

A limited liability company may change its designated office or agent for service of process by delivering to the [Secretary of State] for filing a statement of change which sets forth:

(1) the name of the company;

(2) the street address of its current designated office;

(3) if the current designated office is to be changed, the street address of the new designated office;

(4) the name and address of its current agent for service of process; and

(5) if the current agent for service of process or street address of that agent is to be changed, the new address or the name and street address of the new agent for service of process.

§ 110. Resignation of agent for service of process.

(a) An agent for service of process of a limited liability company may resign by delivering to the [Secretary of State] for filing a record of the statement of resignation.

(b) After filing a statement of resignation, the [Secretary of State] shall mail a copy to the designated office and another copy to the limited liability company at its principal office.

(c) An agency is terminated on the 31st day after the statement is filed in the office of the [Secretary of State].

§ 111. Service of process.

(a) An agent for service of process appointed by a limited liability company or a foreign limited liability company is an agent of the company for service of any process, notice, or demand required or permitted by law to be served upon the company.

(b) If a limited liability company or foreign limited liability company fails to appoint or maintain an agent for service of process in this State or the agent for service of process cannot with reasonable diligence be found at the agent's address, the [Secretary of State] is an agent of the company upon whom process, notice, or demand may be served.

(c) Service of any process, notice, or demand on the [Secretary of State] may be made by delivering to and leaving with the [Secretary of State], the [Assistant Secretary of State], or clerk having charge of the limited liability company department of the [Secretary of State's] office duplicate copies of the process, notice, or demand. If the process, notice, or demand is served on the [Secretary of State], the [Secretary of State] shall forward one of the copies by registered or certified mail, return receipt requested, to the company at its designated office. Service is effected under this subsection at the earliest of:

(1) the date the company receives the process, notice, or demand;

(2) the date shown on the return receipt, if signed on behalf of the company; or

(3) five days after its deposit in the mail, if mailed postpaid and correctly addressed.

(d) The [Secretary of State] shall keep a record of all processes, notices, and demands served pursuant to this section and record the time of and the action taken regarding the service.

(e) This section does not affect the right to serve process, notice, or demand in any manner otherwise provided by law.

Comment

Service of process on a limited liability company and a foreign company authorized to transact business in the State must be made on the company's agent for service of process whose name and address should be on file with the filing office. If for any reason a company fails to appoint or maintain an agent for service of process or the agent cannot be found with reasonable diligence at the agent's address, the filing officer will be deemed the proper agent.

§ 112. Nature of business and powers.

(a) A limited liability company may be organized under this [Act] for any lawful purpose, subject to any law of this State governing or regulating business.

(b) Unless its articles of organization provide otherwise, a limited liability company has the same powers as an individual to do all things necessary or convenient to carry on its business or affairs, including power to:

(1) sue and be sued, and defend in its name;

(2) purchase, receive, lease, or otherwise acquire, and own, hold, improve, use, and otherwise deal with real or personal property, or any legal or equitable interest in property, wherever located;

(3) sell, convey, mortgage, grant a security interest in, lease, exchange, and otherwise encumber or dispose of all or any part of its property;

(4) purchase, receive, subscribe for, or otherwise acquire, own, hold, vote, use, sell, mortgage, lend, grant a security interest in, or otherwise dispose of and deal in and with, shares or other interests in or obligations of any other entity;

(5) make contracts and guarantees, incur liabilities, borrow money, issue its notes, bonds, and other obligations, which may be convertible into or include the option to purchase other securities of the limited liability company, and secure any of its obligations by a mortgage on or a security interest in any of its property, franchises, or income;

(6) lend money, invest and reinvest its funds, and receive and hold real and personal property as security for repayment;

(7) be a promoter, partner, member, associate, or manager of any partnership, joint venture, trust, or other entity;

(8) conduct its business, locate offices, and exercise the powers granted by this [Act] within or without this State;

(9) elect managers and appoint officers, employees, and agents of the limited liability company, define their duties, fix their compensation, and lend them money and credit;

(10) pay pensions and establish pension plans, pension trusts, profit sharing plans, bonus plans, option plans, and benefit or incentive plans for any or all of its current or former members, managers, officers, employees, and agents;

(11) make donations for the public welfare or for charitable, scientific, or educational purposes; and

(12) make payments or donations, or do any other act, not inconsistent with law, that furthers the business of the limited liability company.

Comment

A limited liability company may be organized for any lawful purpose unless the State has specifically prohibited a company from engaging in a specific activity. For example, many States require that certain regulated industries, such as banking and insurance, be conducted only by organizations that meet the special requirements. Also, many States impose restrictions on activities in which a limited liability company may engage. For example, the practice of certain professionals is often subject to special conditions. A limited liability company has the power to engage in and perform important and necessary acts related to its operation and function. A company's power to enter into a transaction is distinguishable from the authority of an agent to enter into the transaction. See Section 301 (agency rules).

[ARTICLE] 2

ORGANIZATION

§ 201. Limited liability company as legal entity.

A limited liability company is a legal entity distinct from its members.

Comment

A limited liability company is legally distinct from its members who are not normally liable for the debts, obligations, and liabilities of the company. See Section 303. Accordingly, members are not proper parties to suits against the company unless an object of the proceeding is to enforce members' rights against the company or to enforce their liability to the company.

§ 202. Organization.

(a) One or more persons may organize a limited liability company, consisting of one or more members, by delivering articles of organization to the office of the [Secretary of State] for filing.

(b) Unless a delayed effective date is specified, the existence of a limited liability company begins when the articles of organization are filed.

(c) The filing of the articles of organization by the [Secretary of State] is conclusive proof that the organizers satisfied all conditions precedent to the creation of a limited liability company.

Comment

Any person may organize a limited liability company by performing the ministerial act of signing and filing the articles of organization. The person need not be a member. As a matter of flexibility, a company may be organized and operated with only one member to enable sole proprietors to obtain the benefit of a liability shield. The effect of organizing or operating a company with one member on the Federal tax classification of the company is determined by federal law.

The existence of a company begins when the articles are filed. Therefore, the filing of the articles of organization is conclusive as to the existence of the limited liability shield for persons who enter into transactions on behalf of the company. Until the articles are filed, a firm is not organized under this Act and is not a "limited liability company" as defined in Section 101(9). In that case, the parties' relationships are not governed by this Act unless they have expressed a contractual intent to be bound by the provisions of the Act. Third parties would also not be governed by the provisions of this Act unless they have expressed a contractual intent to extend a limited liability shield to the members of the would-be limited liability company.

§ 203. Articles of organization.

(a) Articles of organization of a limited liability company must set forth:

(1) the name of the company;

(2) the address of the initial designated office;

(3) the name and street address of the initial agent for service of process;

(4) the name and address of each organizer;

(5) whether the company is to be a term company and, if so, the term specified;

(6) whether the company is to be manager-managed, and, if so, the name and address of each initial manager; and

(7) whether one or more of the members of the company are to be liable for its debts and obligations under Section 303(c).

(b) Articles of organization of a limited liability company may set forth:

(1) provisions permitted to be set forth in an operating agreement; or

(2) other matters not inconsistent with law.

(c) Articles of organization of a limited liability company may not vary the nonwaivable provisions of Section 103(b). As to all other matters, if any provision of an operating agreement is inconsistent with the articles of organization:

(1) the operating agreement controls as to managers, members, and members' transferees; and

(2) the articles of organization control as to persons, other than managers, members and their transferees, who reasonably rely on the articles to their detriment.

Comment

The articles serve primarily a notice function and generally do not reflect the substantive agreement of the members regarding the business affairs of the company. Those matters are generally reserved for an operating agreement which may be unwritten. Under Section 203(b), the articles may contain provisions permitted to be set forth in an operating agreement. Where the articles and operating agreement conflict, the operating agreement controls as to members but the articles control as to third parties. The articles may also contain any other matter not inconsistent with law. The most important is a Section 301(c) limitation on the authority of a member or manager to transfer interests in the company's real property.

A company will be at-will unless it is designated as a term company and the duration of its term is specified in its articles under Section 203(a)(5). The duration of a term company may be specified in any manner which sets forth a specific and final date for the dissolution of the company. For example, the period specified may be in the form of "50 years from the date of filing of the articles" or "the period ending on January 1, 2020." Mere specification of a particular undertaking of an uncertain business duration is not sufficient unless the particular undertaking is within a longer fixed period. An example of this type of designation would include "2020 or until the building is completed, whichever occurs first." When the specified period is incorrectly specified, the company will be an at-will company. Notwithstanding the correct specification of a term in the articles, a company will be an at-will company among the members under Section 203(c)(1) if an operating agreement so provides. A term company that continues after the expiration of its term specified in its articles will also be an at-will company.

A term company possesses several important default rule characteristics that differentiate it dramatically from an at-will company. An operating agreement may alter any of these rules. Any dissociation of an at-will member dissolves a member-managed company unless a specified percentage of the remaining members agree to continue the business of the company. Before the expiration of its term, only specified dissociation events (excluding voluntary withdrawal) of a term member will dissolve a member-managed company unless a specified percentage of the remaining members agree to continue the business of the company. See Comments to Sections 601 and 801(b)(3). Also, even if the dissociation of an at-will member does not result in a dissolution of a member-managed company, the dissociated member is entitled to have the company purchase that member's interest for its fair value. Unless the company earlier dissolves, a term member must generally await the expiration of the agreed term to withdraw the fair value of the interest. See Comments to Section 701(a).

A company will be member-managed unless it is designated as manager-managed under Section 203(a)(6). Absent further designation in the articles, a company will be a member-managed at-will company. The designation of a limited liability company as either member or manager-managed is important because it defines who are agents and have the apparent authority to bind the company under Section 301 and determines whether the dissociation of members who are not managers will threaten dissolution of the company. In a member-managed company, the members have the agency authority to bind the company. In a manager-managed company only the managers have that authority. The effect of the agency structure of a company on the Federal tax classification of the company is determined by federal law. The agency designation relates only to agency and does not preclude members of a manager-managed company from participating in the actual management of company business. See Comments to Section 404(b).

In a member-managed company, the dissociation of any member will cause the company to dissolve unless a specified percentage of the remaining members agree to continue the business of the company. In a manager-managed company, only the dissociation of any member who is also a manager threatens dissolution of the company. Only where there are no members who are also managers will the dissociation of members who are not managers threaten dissolution of a manager-managed company. See Comments to Section 801.

§ 204. Amendment or restatement of articles of organization.

(a) Articles of organization of a limited liability company may be amended at any time by delivering articles of amendment to the [Secretary of State] for filing. The articles of amendment must set forth the:

(1) name of the limited liability company;

(2) date of filing of the articles of organization; and

(3) amendment to the articles.

(b) A limited liability company may restate its articles of organization at any time. Restated articles of organization must be signed and filed in the same manner as articles of amendment. Restated articles of organization must be designated as such in the heading and state in the heading or in an introductory paragraph the limited liability company's present name and, if it has been changed, all of its former names and the date of the filing of its initial articles of organization.

Comment

An amendment to the articles requires the consent of all the members unless an operating agreement provides for a lesser number. See Section 404(c)(3).

§ 205. Signing of records.

(a) Except as otherwise provided in this [Act], a record to be filed by or on behalf of a limited liability company in the office of the [Secretary of State] must be signed in the name of the company by a:

(1) manager of a manager-managed company;

(2) member of a member-managed company;

(3) person organizing the company, if the company has not been formed; or

(4) fiduciary, if the company is in the hands of a receiver, trustee, or other court-appointed fiduciary.

(b) A record signed under subsection (a) must state adjacent to the signature the name and capacity of the signer.

(c) Any person may sign a record to be filed under subsection (a) by an attorney-in-fact. Powers of attorney relating to the signing of records to be filed under subsection (a) by an attorney-in-fact need not be filed in the office of the [Secretary of State] as evidence of authority by the person filing but must be retained by the company.

Comment

Both a writing and a record may be signed. An electronic record is signed when a person adds a name to the record with the intention to authenticate the record. See Sections 101(16) ("record" definition) and 10l(17) ("signed" definition). Other provisions of this Act also provide for the filing of records with the filing office but do not require signing by the persons specified in clauses (1) to (3). Those specific sections prevail.

§ 206. Filing in office of [Secretary of State].

(a) Articles of organization or any other record authorized to be filed under this [Act] must be in a medium permitted by the [Secretary of State] and must be delivered to the office of the [Secretary of State]. Unless the [Secretary of State] determines that a record fails to comply as to form with the filing requirements of this [Act], and if all filing fees have been paid, the [Secretary of State] shall file the record and send a receipt for the record and the fees to the limited liability company or its representative.

(b) Upon request and payment of a fee, the [Secretary of State] shall send to the requester a certified copy of the requested record.

(c) Except as otherwise provided in subsection (d) and Section 207(c), a record accepted for filing by the [Secretary of State] is effective:

(1) at the time of filing on the date it is filed, as evidenced by the [Secretary of State's] date and time endorsement on the original record; or

(2) at the time specified in the record as its effective time on the date it is filed.

(d) A record may specify a delayed effective time and date, and if it does so the record becomes effective at the time and date specified. If a delayed effective date but no time is specified, the record is effective at the close of business on that date. If a delayed effective date is later than the 90th day after the record is filed, the record is effective on the 90th day.

Comment

The definition and use of the term "record" permits filings with the filing office under this Act to conform to technological advances that have been adopted by the filing office. However, since Section 206(a) provides that the filing "must be in a medium permitted by the [Secretary of State]", the Act simply conforms to filing changes as they are adopted.

§ 207. Correcting filed record.

(a) A limited liability company or foreign limited liability company may correct a record filed by the [Secretary of State] if the record contains a false or erroneous statement or was defectively signed.

(b) A record is corrected:

(1) by preparing articles of correction that:

(i) describe the record, including its filing date, or attach a copy of it to the articles of correction;

(ii) specify the incorrect statement and the reason it is incorrect or the manner in which the signing was defective; and

(iii) correct the incorrect statement or defective signing; and

(2) by delivering the corrected record to the [Secretary of State] for filing.

(c) Articles of correction are effective retroactively on the effective date of the record they correct except as to persons relying on the uncorrected record and adversely affected by the correction. As to those persons, articles of correction are effective when filed.

§ 208. Certificate of existence or authorization.

(a) A person may request the [Secretary of State] to furnish a certificate of existence for a limited liability company or a certificate of authorization for a foreign limited liability company.

(b) A certificate of existence for a limited liability company must set forth:

(1) the company's name;

(2) that it is duly organized under the laws of this State, the date of organization, whether its duration is at-will or for a specified term, and, if the latter, the period specified;

(3) if payment is reflected in the records of the [Secretary of State] and if nonpayment affects the existence of the company, that all fees, taxes, and penalties owed to this State have been paid;

(4) whether its most recent annual report required by Section 211 has been filed with the [Secretary of State];

(5) that articles of termination have not been filed; and

(6) other facts of record in the office of the [Secretary of State] which may be requested by the applicant.

(c) A certificate of authorization for a foreign limited liability company must set forth:

(1) the company's name used in this State;

(2) that it is authorized to transact business in this State;

(3) if payment is reflected in the records of the [Secretary of State] and if nonpayment affects the authorization of the company, that all fees, taxes, and penalties owed to this State have been paid;

(4) whether its most recent annual report required by Section 211 has been filed with the [Secretary of State];

(5) that a certificate of cancellation has not been filed; and

(6) other facts of record in the office of the [Secretary of State] which may be requested by the applicant.

(d) Subject to any qualification stated in the certificate, a certificate of existence or authorization issued by the [Secretary of State] may be relied upon as conclusive evidence that the domestic or foreign limited liability company is in existence or is authorized to transact business in this State.

§ 209. Liability for false statement in filed record.

If a record authorized or required to be filed under this [Act] contains a false statement, one who suffers loss by reliance on the statement may recover damages for the loss from a person who signed the record or caused another to sign it on the person's behalf and knew the statement to be false at the time the record was signed.

§ 210. Filing by judicial act.

If a person required by Section 205 to sign any record fails or refuses to do so, any other person who is adversely affected by the failure or refusal may petition the [designate the appropriate court] to direct the signing of the record. If the court finds that it is proper for the record to be signed and that a person so designated has failed or refused to sign the record, it shall order the [Secretary of State] to sign and file an appropriate record.

§ 211. Annual report for [Secretary of State].

(a) A limited liability company, and a foreign limited liability company authorized to transact business in this State, shall deliver to the [Secretary of State] for filing an annual report that sets forth:

(1) the name of the company and the State or country under whose law it is organized;

(2) the address of its designated office and the name and address of its agent for service of process in this State;

(3) the address of its principal office; and

(4) the names and business addresses of any managers.

(b) Information in an annual report must be current as of the date the annual report is signed on behalf of the limited liability company.

(c) The first annual report must be delivered to the [Secretary of State] between [January 1 and April 1] of the year following the calendar year in which a limited liability company was organized or a foreign company was authorized to transact business. Subsequent annual reports must be delivered to the [Secretary of State] between [January 1 and April 1] of the ensuing calendar years.

(d) If an annual report does not contain the information required in subsection (a), the [Secretary of State] shall promptly notify the reporting limited liability company or foreign limited liability company and return the report to it for correction. If the report is corrected to contain the information required in subsection (a) and delivered to the [Secretary of State] within 30 days after the effective date of the notice, it is timely filed.

Comment

Failure to deliver the annual report within 60 days after its due date is a primary ground for administrative dissolution of the company under Section 809. See Comments to Sections 809 to 812.

[ARTICLE] 3

RELATIONS OF MEMBERS AND MANAGERS TO PERSONS DEALING WITH LIMITED LIABILITY COMPANY

§ 301. Agency of members and managers.

(a) Subject to subsections (b) and (c):

(1) Each member is an agent of the limited liability company for the purpose of its business, and an act of a member, including the signing of an instrument in the company's name, for apparently carrying on in the ordinary course the company's business or business of the kind carried on by the company binds the company, unless the member had no authority to act for the company in the particular matter and the person with whom the member was dealing knew or had notice that the member lacked authority.

(2) An act of a member which is not apparently for carrying on in the ordinary course the company's business or business of the kind carried on by the company binds the company only if the act was authorized by the other members.

(b) Subject to subsection (c), in a manager-managed company:

(1) A member is not an agent of the company for the purpose of its business solely by reason of being a member. Each manager is an agent of the company for the purpose of its business, and an act of a manager, including the signing of an instrument in the company's name, for apparently carrying on in the ordinary course the company's business or business of the kind carried on by the company binds the company, unless the manager had no authority to act for the company in the particular matter and the person with whom the manager was dealing knew or had notice that the manager lacked authority.

(2) An act of a manager which is not apparently for carrying on in the ordinary course the company's business or business of the kind carried on by the company binds the company only if the act was authorized under Section 404.

(c) Unless the articles of organization limit their authority, any member of a member-managed company or manager of a manager-managed company may sign and deliver any instrument transferring or affecting the company's interest in real property. The instrument is conclusive in favor of a person who gives value without knowledge of the lack of the authority of the person signing and delivering the instrument.

Comment

Members of a member-managed and managers of manager-managed company, as agents of the firm, have the apparent authority to bind a company to third parties. Members of a manager-managed company are not as such agents of the firm and do not have the apparent authority, as members, to bind a company. Members and managers with apparent authority possess actual authority by implication unless the actual authority is restricted in an operating agreement. Apparent authority extends to acts for carrying on in the ordinary course the company's business and business of the kind carried on by the company. Acts beyond this scope bind the company only where supported by actual authority created before the act or ratified after the act.

Ordinarily, restrictions on authority in an operating agreement do not affect the apparent authority of members and managers to bind the company to third parties without notice of the restriction. However, the restriction may make a member or manager's conduct wrongful and create liability to the company for the breach. This rule is subject to three important exceptions. First, under Section 301(c), a limitation reflected in the articles of organization on the authority of any member or manager to sign and deliver an instrument affecting an interest in company real property is effective when filed, even to persons without knowledge of the agent's lack of authority. The effect of such a limitation on authority on the Federal tax classification of the company is determined by federal law. Secondly, under Section 703, a dissociated member's apparent authority terminates two years after dissociation, even to persons without knowledge of the dissociation. Thirdly, under Section 704, a dissociated member's apparent authority may be terminated earlier than the two years by filing a statement of dissociation. The statement is effective 90 days after filing, even to persons without knowledge of the filing. Together, these three provisions provide constructive knowledge to the world of the lack of apparent authority of an agent to bind the company.

§ 302. Limited liability company liable for member's or manager's actionable conduct.

A limited liability company is liable for loss or injury caused to a person, or for a penalty incurred, as a result of a wrongful act or omission, or other actionable conduct, of a member or manager acting in the ordinary course of business of the company or with authority of the company.

Comment

Since a member of a manager-managed company is not as such an agent, the acts of the member are not imputed to the company unless the member is acting under actual or apparent authority created by circumstances other than membership status.

§ 303. Liability of members and managers.

(a) Except as otherwise provided in subsection (c), the debts, obligations, and liabilities of a limited liability company, whether arising in contract, tort, or otherwise, are solely the debts, obligations, and liabilities of the company. A member or manager is not personally liable for a debt, obligation, or liability of the company solely by reason of being or acting as a member or manager.

(b) The failure of a limited liability company to observe the usual company formalities or requirements relating to the exercise of its company powers or management of its business is not a ground for imposing personal liability on the members or managers for liabilities of the company.

(c) All or specified members of a limited liability company are liable in their capacity as members for all or specified debts, obligations, or liabilities of the company if:

(1) a provision to that effect is contained in the articles of organization; and

(2) a member so liable has consented in writing to the adoption of the provision or to be bound by the provision.

Comment

A member or manager, as an agent of the company, is not liable for the debts, obligations, and liabilities of the company simply because of the agency. A member or manager is responsible for acts or omissions to the extent those acts or omissions would be actionable in contract or tort against the member or manager if that person were acting in an individual capacity. Where a member or manager delegates or assigns the authority or duty to exercise appropriate company functions, the member or manager is ordinarily not personally liable for the acts or omissions of the officer, employee, or agent if the member or manager has complied with the duty of care set forth in Section 409(c).

Under Section 303(c), the usual liability shield may be waived, in whole or in part, provided the waiver is reflected in the articles of organization and the member has consented in writing to be bound by the waiver. The importance and unusual nature of the waiver consent requires that the consent be evidenced by a writing and not merely an unwritten record. See Comments to Section 205. The effect of a waiver on the Federal tax classification of the company is determined by federal law.

[ARTICLE] 4

RELATIONS OF MEMBERS TO EACH OTHER
AND TO LIMITED LIABILITY COMPANY

§ 401. Form of contribution.

A contribution of a member of a limited liability company may consist of tangible or intangible property or other benefit to the company, including money, promissory notes, services performed, or other agreements to contribute cash or property, or contracts for services to be performed.

Comment

Unless otherwise provided in an operating agreement, admission of a member and the nature and valuation of a would-be member's contribution are matters requiring the consent of all of the other members. See Section 404(c)(7). An agreement to contribute to a company is controlled by the operating agreement and therefore may not be created or modified without amending that agreement through the unanimous consent of all the members, including the member to be bound by the new contribution terms. See 404(c)(1).

§ 402. Member's liability for contributions.

(a) A member's obligation to contribute money, property, or other benefit to, or to perform services for, a limited liability company is not excused by the member's death, disability, or other inability to perform personally. If a member does not make the required contribution of property or services, the member is obligated at the option of the company to contribute money equal to the value of that portion of the stated contribution which has not been made.

(b) A creditor of a limited liability company who extends credit or otherwise acts in reliance on an obligation described in subsection (a), and without notice of any compromise under Section 404(c)(5), may enforce the original obligation.

Comment

An obligation need not be in writing to be enforceable. Given the informality of some companies, a writing requirement may frustrate reasonable expectations of members based on a clear oral agreement. Obligations may be compromised with the consent of all of the members under Section 404(c)(5), but the compromise is generally effective only among the consenting members. Company creditors are bound by the compromise only as provided in Section 402(b).

§ 403. Member's and manager's rights to payments and reimbursement.

(a) A limited liability company shall reimburse a member or manager for payments made and indemnify a member or manager for liabilities incurred by the member or manager in the ordinary course of the business of the company or for the preservation of its business or property.

(b) A limited liability company shall reimburse a member for an advance to the company beyond the amount of contribution the member agreed to make.

(c) A payment or advance made by a member which gives rise to an obligation of a limited liability company under subsection (a) or (b) constitutes a loan to the company upon which interest accrues from the date of the payment or advance.

(d) A member is not entitled to remuneration for services performed for a limited liability company, except for reasonable compensation for services rendered in winding up the business of the company.

Comment

The presence of a liability shield will ordinarily prevent a member or manager from incurring personal liability on behalf of the company in the ordinary course of the company's business. Where a member of a member-managed or a manager of a manager-managed company incurs such liabilities, Section 403(a) provides that the company must indemnify the member or manager where that person acted in the ordinary course of the company's business or the preservation of its property. A member or manager is therefore entitled to indemnification only if the act was within the member or manager's actual authority, a member or manager is therefore not entitled to indemnification for conduct that violates the duty of care set forth in Section 409(c) or for tortious conduct against a third party. Since members of a manager-managed company do not possess the apparent authority to bind the company, it would be more unusual for such a member to incur a liability for indemnification in the ordinary course of the company's business.

§ 404. Management of limited liability company.

(a) In a member-managed company:

(1) each member has equal rights in the management and conduct of the company's business; and

(2) except as otherwise provided in subsection (c) or in Section 801(b)(3)(i), any matter relating to the business of the company may be decided by a majority of the members.

(b) In a manager-managed company:

(1) each manager has equal rights in the management and conduct of the company's business;

(2) except as otherwise provided in subsection (c) or in Section 801(b)(3)(i), any matter relating to the business of the company may be exclusively decided by the manager or, if there is more than one manager, by a majority of the managers; and

(3) a manager:

(i) must be designated, appointed, elected, removed, or replaced by a vote, approval, or consent of a majority of the members; and

(ii) holds office until a successor has been elected and qualified, unless the manager sooner resigns or is removed.

(c) The only matters of a member or manager-managed company's business requiring the consent of all of the members are:

(1) the amendment of the operating agreement under Section 103;

(2) the authorization or ratification of acts or transactions under Section 103(b)(2)(ii) which would otherwise violate the duty of loyalty;

(3) an amendment to the articles of organization under Section 204;

(4) the compromise of an obligation to make a contribution under Section 402(b);

(5) the compromise, as among members, of an obligation of a member to make a contribution or return money or other property paid or distributed in violation of this [Act];

(6) the making of interim distributions under Section 405(a), including the redemption of an interest;

(7) the admission of a new member;

(8) the use of the company's property to redeem an interest subject to a charging order;

(9) the consent to dissolve the company under Section 801(b)(2);

(10) a waiver of the right to have the company's business wound up and the company terminated under Section 802(b);

(11) the consent of members to merge with another entity under Section 904(c)(1); and

(12) the sale, lease, exchange, or other disposal of all, or substantially all, of the company's property with or without goodwill.

(d) Action requiring the consent of members or managers under this [Act] may be taken without a meeting.

(e) A member or manager may appoint a proxy to vote or otherwise act for the member or manager by signing an appointment instrument, either personally or by the member's or manager's attorney-in-fact.

Comment

In a member-managed company, each member has equal rights in the management and conduct of the company's business unless otherwise provided in an operating agreement. For example, an operating agreement may allocate voting rights based upon capital contributions rather than the subsection (a) per capita rule. Also, member disputes as to any matter relating to the company's business may be resolved by a majority of the members unless the matter relates to a matter specified either in subsection (c) (unanimous consent required) or in Section 801(b)(3)(i) (special consent required). Regardless of how the members allocate management rights, each member is an agent of the company with the apparent authority to bind the company in the ordinary course of its business. See Comments to Section 301(a). A member's right to participate in management terminates upon dissociation. See Section 603(b)(1).

In a manager-managed company, the members, unless also managers, have no rights in the management and conduct of the company's business unless otherwise provided in an operating agreement. If there is more than one manager, manager disputes as to any matter relating to the company's business may be resolved by a majority of the managers unless the matter relates to a matter specified either in subsection (c) (unanimous member consent required) or Section 801(b)(3)(i) (special consent required). Managers must be designated, appointed, or elected by a majority of the members. A manager need not be a member and is an agent of the company with the apparent authority to bind the company in the ordinary course of its business. See Sections 101(10) and 301(b).

To promote clarity and certainty, subsection (c) specifies those exclusive matters requiring the unanimous consent of the members, whether the company is member- or manager-managed. For example, interim distributions, including redemptions, may not be made without the unanimous consent of all the members. Unless otherwise agreed, all other company matters are to be determined under the majority of members or managers rules of subsections (a) and (b).

§ 405. Sharing of and right to distributions.

(a) Any distributions made by a limited liability company before its dissolution and winding up must be in equal shares.

(b) A member has no right to receive, and may not be required to accept, a distribution in kind.

(c) If a member becomes entitled to receive a distribution, the member has the status of, and is entitled to all remedies available to, a creditor of the limited liability company with respect to the distribution.

Comment

Recognizing the informality of many limited liability companies, this section creates a simple default rule regarding interim distributions. Any interim distributions made must be in equal shares and approved by all members. See Section 404(c)(6). The rule assumes that: profits will be shared equally; some distributions will constitute a return of contributions that should be shared equally rather than a distribution of profits; and property contributors should have the right to veto any distribution that threatens their return of contributions on liquidation. In the simple case where the members make equal contributions of property or equal contributions of services, those assumptions avoid the necessity of maintaining a complex capital account or determining profits. Where some members contribute services and others property, the unanimous vote necessary to approve interim distributions protects against unwanted distributions of contributions to service contributors. Consistently, Section 408(a) does not require the company to maintain a separate account for each member, the Act does not contain a default rule for allocating profits and losses, and Section 806(b) requires that liquidating distributions to members be made in equal shares after the return of contributions not previously returned. See Comments to Section 806(b).

Section 405(c) governs distributions declared or made when the company was solvent. Section 406 governs distributions declared or made when the company is insolvent.

§ 406. Limitations on distributions.

(a) A distribution may not be made if:

(1) the limited liability company would not be able to pay its debts as they become due in the ordinary course of business; or

(2) the company's total assets would be less than the sum of its total liabilities plus the amount that would be needed, if the company were to be dissolved, wound

up, and terminated at the time of the distribution to satisfy the preferential rights upon dissolution, winding up, and termination of members whose preferential rights are superior to those receiving the distribution.

(b) A limited liability company may base a determination that a distribution is not prohibited under subsection (a) on financial statements prepared on the basis of accounting practices and principles that are reasonable in the circumstances or on a fair valuation or other method that is reasonable in the circumstances.

(c) Except as otherwise provided in subsection (e), the effect of a distribution under subsection (a) is measured:

(1) in the case of distribution by purchase, redemption, or other acquisition of a distributional interest in a limited liability company, as of the date money or other property is transferred or debt incurred by the company; and

(2) in all other cases, as of the date the:

(i) distribution is authorized if the payment occurs within 120 days after the date of authorization; or

(ii) payment is made if it occurs more than 120 days after the date of authorization.

(d) A limited liability company's indebtedness to a member incurred by reason of a distribution made in accordance with this section is at parity with the company's indebtedness to its general, unsecured creditors.

(e) Indebtedness of a limited liability company, including indebtedness issued in connection with or as part of a distribution, is not considered a liability for purposes of determinations under subsection (a) if its terms provide that payment of principal and interest are made only if and to the extent that payment of a distribution to members could then be made under this section. If the indebtedness is issued as a distribution, each payment of principal or interest on the indebtedness is treated as a distribution, the effect of which is measured on the date the payment is made.

Comment

This section establishes the validity of company distributions, which in turn determines the potential liability of members and managers for improper distributions under Section 407. Distributions are improper if the company is insolvent under subsection (a) at the time the distribution is measured under subsection (c). In recognition of the informality of many limited liability companies, the solvency determination under subsection (b) may be made on the basis of a fair valuation or other method reasonable under the circumstances.

The application of the equity insolvency and balance sheet tests present special problems in the context of the purchase, redemption, or other acquisition of a company's distributional interests. Special rules establish the time of measurement of such transfers. Under Section 406(c)(1), the time for measuring the effect of a distribution to purchase a distributional interest is the date of payment. The company may make payment either by transferring property or incurring a debt to transfer property in the future. In the latter case, subsection (c)(1) establishes a clear rule that the legality of the distribution is tested when the debt is actually incurred, not later when the debt is actually paid. Under Section 406(e), indebtedness is not considered a liability for purposes of subsection (a) if the terms of the indebtedness itself provide that payments can be made only if and to the extent that a payment of a distribution could then be made under this section. The effect makes the holder of the indebtedness junior to all other creditors but senior to members in their capacity as members.

§ 407. Liability for unlawful distributions.

(a) A member of a member-managed company or a member or manager of a manager-managed company who votes for or assents to a distribution made in violation of Section 406, the articles of organization, or the operating agreement is personally liable to the company for the amount of the distribution which exceeds the amount that could have been distributed without violating Section 406, the articles of organization, or the operating agreement if it is established that the member or manager did not perform the member's or manager's duties in compliance with Section 409.

(b) A member of a manager-managed company who knew a distribution was made in violation of Section 406, the articles of organization, or the operating agreement is personally liable to the company, but only to the extent that the distribution received by the member exceeded the amount that could have been properly paid under Section 406.

(c) A member or manager against whom an action is brought under this section may implead in the action all:

(1) other members or managers who voted for or assented to the distribution in violation of subsection (a) and may compel contribution from them; and

(2) members who received a distribution in violation of subsection (b) and may compel contribution from the member in the amount received in violation of subsection (b).

(d) A proceeding under this section is barred unless it is commenced within two years after the distribution.

Comment

Whenever members or managers fail to meet the standards of conduct of Section 409 and vote for or assent to an unlawful distribution, they are personally liable to the company for the portion of the distribution that exceeds the maximum amount that could have been lawfully distributed. The recovery remedy under this section extends only to the company, not the company's creditors. Under subsection (a), members and managers are not liable for an unlawful distribution provided their vote in favor of the distribution satisfies the duty of care of Section 409(c).

Subsection (a) creates personal liability in favor of the company against members or managers who approve an unlawful distribution for the entire amount of a distribution that could not be lawfully distributed. Subsection (b) creates personal liability against only members who knowingly received the unlawful distribution, but only in the amount measured by the portion of the actual distribution received that was not lawfully made. Members who both vote for or assent to an unlawful distribution and receive a portion or all of the distribution will be liable, at the election of the company, under either but not both subsections.

A member or manager who is liable under subsection (a) may seek contribution under subsection (c)(1) from other members and managers who also voted for or assented to the same distribution and may also seek recoupment under subsection (c)(2) from members who received the distribution, but only if they accepted the payments knowing they were unlawful.

The two-year statute of limitations of subsection (d) is measured from the date of the distribution. The date of the distribution is determined under Section 406(c).

§ 408. Member's right to information.

(a) A limited liability company shall provide members and their agents and attorneys access to its records, if any, at the company's principal office or other reasonable locations specified in the operating agreement. The company shall provide former members and their agents and attorneys access for proper purposes to records pertaining to the period during which they were members. The right of access provides the opportunity to inspect and copy records during ordinary business hours. The company may impose a reasonable charge, limited to the costs of labor and material, for copies of records furnished.

(b) A limited liability company shall furnish to a member, and to the legal representative of a deceased member or member under legal disability:

(1) without demand, information concerning the company's business or affairs reasonably required for the proper exercise of the member's rights and performance of the member's duties under the operating agreement or this [Act]; and

(2) on demand, other information concerning the company's business or affairs, except to the extent the demand or the information demanded is unreasonable or otherwise improper under the circumstances.

(c) A member has the right upon written demand given to the limited liability company to obtain at the company's expense a copy of any written operating agreement.

Comment

Recognizing the informality of many limited liability companies, subsection (a) does not require a company to maintain any records. In general, a company should maintain records necessary to enable members to determine their share of profits and losses and their rights on dissociation. If inadequate records are maintained to determine those and other critical rights, a member may maintain an action for an accounting under Section 410(a). Normally, a company will maintain at least records required by state or federal authorities regarding tax and other filings.

The obligation to furnish access includes the obligation to insure that all records, if any, are accessible in intelligible form. For example, a company that switches computer systems has an obligation either to convert the records from the old system or retain at least one computer capable of accessing the records from the old system.

The right to inspect and copy records maintained is not conditioned on a member or former member's purpose or motive. However, an abuse of the access and copy right may create a remedy in favor of the other members as a violation of the requesting member or former member's obligation of good faith and fair dealing. See Section 409(d).

Although a company is not required to maintain any records under subsection (a), it is nevertheless subject to a disclosure duty to furnish specified information under subsection (b)(1). A company must therefore furnish to members, without demand, information reasonably needed for members to exercise their rights and duties as members. A member's exercise of these duties justifies an unqualified right of access to the company's records. The member's right to company records may not be unreasonably restricted by the operating agreement. See Section 103(b)(1).

§ 409. General standards of member's and manager's conduct.

(a) The only fiduciary duties a member owes to a member-managed company and its other members are the duty of loyalty and the duty of care imposed by subsections (b) and (c).

(b) A member's duty of loyalty to a member-managed company and its other members is limited to the following:

(1) to account to the company and to hold as trustee for it any property, profit, or benefit derived by the member in the conduct or winding up of the company's business or derived from a use by the member of the company's property, including the appropriation of a company's opportunity;

(2) to refrain from dealing with the company in the conduct or winding up of the company's business as or on behalf of a party having an interest adverse to the company; and

(3) to refrain from competing with the company in the conduct of the company's business before the dissolution of the company.

(c) A member's duty of care to a member-managed company and its other members in the conduct of and winding up of the company's business is limited to refraining from engaging in grossly negligent or reckless conduct, intentional misconduct, or a knowing violation of law.

(d) A member shall discharge the duties to a member-managed company and its other members under this [Act] or under the operating agreement and exercise any rights consistently with the obligation of good faith and fair dealing.

(e) A member of a member-managed company does not violate a duty or obligation under this [Act] or under the operating agreement merely because the member's conduct furthers the member's own interest.

(f) A member of a member-managed company may lend money to and transact other business with the company. As to each loan or transaction, the rights and obligations of the member are the same as those of a person who is not a member, subject to other applicable law.

(g) This section applies to a person winding up the limited liability company's business as the personal or legal representative of the last surviving member as if the person were a member.

(h) In a manager-managed company:

(1) a member who is not also a manager owes no duties to the company or to the other members solely by reason of being a member;

(2) a manager is held to the same standards of conduct prescribed for members in subsections (b) through (f);

(3) a member who pursuant to the operating agreement exercises some or all of the rights of a manager in the management and conduct of the company's business is held to the standards of conduct in subsections (b) through (f) to the extent that the member exercises the managerial authority vested in a manager by this [Act]; and

(4) a manager is relieved of liability imposed by law for violation of the standards prescribed by subsections (b) through (f) to the extent of the managerial authority delegated to the members by the operating agreement.

Comment

Under subsections (a), (c), and (h), members and managers, and their delegatees, owe to the company and to the other members and managers only the fiduciary duties of loyalty and care set forth in subsections (b) and (c) and the obligation of good faith and fair dealing set forth in subsection (d). An operating agreement may not waive or eliminate the duties or obligation, but may, if not manifestly unreasonable, identify activities and determine standards for measuring the performance of them. See Section 103(b)(2) to (4).

Upon a member's dissociation, the duty to account for personal profits under subsection (b)(1), the duty to refrain from acting as or representing adverse interests under subsection (b)(2), and the duty of care under subsection (c) are limited to those derived from matters arising or events occurring before the dissociation unless the member participates in winding up the company's business. Also, the duty not to compete terminates upon dissociation. See Section 603(b)(3) and (b)(2). However, a dissociated member is not free to use confidential company information after dissociation. For example, a dissociated member of a company may immediately compete with the company for new clients but must exercise care in completing ongoing client transactions and must account to the company for any fees from the old clients on account of those transactions. Subsection (c) adopts a gross negligence standard for the duty of care, the standard actually used in most partnerships and corporations.

Subsection (b)(2) prohibits a member from acting adversely or representing an adverse party to the company. The rule is based on agency principles and seeks to avoid the conflict of opposing interests in the mind of the member agent whose duty is to act for the benefit of the principal company. As reflected in subsection (f), the rule does not prohibit the member from dealing with the company other than as an adversary. A member may generally deal with the company under subsection (f) when the transaction is approved by the company.

Subsection (e) makes clear that a member does not violate the obligation of good faith under subsection (d) merely because the member's conduct furthers that member's own interest. For example, a member's refusal to vote for an interim distribution because of negative tax implications to that member does not violate that member's obligation of good faith to the other members. Likewise, a member may vote against a proposal by the company to open a shopping center that would directly compete with another shopping center in which the member owns an interest.

§ 410. Actions by members.

(a) A member may maintain an action against a limited liability company or another member for legal or equitable relief, with or without an accounting as to the company's business, to enforce:

(1) the member's rights under the operating agreement;

(2) the member's rights under this [Act]; and

(3) the rights and otherwise protect the interests of the member, including rights and interests arising independently of the member's relationship to the company.

(b) The accrual, and any time limited for the assertion, of a right of action for a remedy under this section is governed by other law. A right to an accounting upon a dissolution and winding up does not revive a claim barred by law.

Comment

During the existence of the company, members have under this section access to the courts to resolve claims against the company and other members, leaving broad judicial discretion to fashion appropriate legal remedies. A member pursues only that member's claim against the company or another member under this section. Article 11 governs a member's derivative pursuit of a claim on behalf of the company.

A member may recover against the company and the other members under subsection (a)(3) for personal injuries or damage to the member's property caused by another member. One member's negligence is therefore not imputed to bar another member's action.

§ 411. Continuation of term company after expiration of specified term.

(a) If a term company is continued after the expiration of the specified term, the rights and duties of the members and managers remain the same as they were at the expiration of the term except to the extent inconsistent with rights and duties of members and managers of an at-will company.

(b) If the members in a member-managed company or the managers in a manager-managed company continue the business without any winding up of the business of the company, it continues as an at-will company.

Comment

A term company will generally dissolve upon the expiration of its term unless either its articles are amended before the expiration of the original specified term to provide for an additional specified term or the members or managers simply continue the company as an at-will company under this section. Amendment of the articles specifying an additional term requires the unanimous consent of the members. See Section 404(c)(3). Therefore, any member has the right to block the amendment. Absent an amendment to the articles, a company may only be continued under subsection (b) as an at-will company. The decision to continue a term company as an at-will company does not require the unanimous consent of the members and is treated as an ordinary business matter with disputes resolved by a simple majority vote of either the members or managers. See Section 404. In that case, subsection (b) provides that the members' conduct amends or becomes part of an operating agreement to "continue" the company as an at-will company. The amendment to the operating agreement does not alter the rights of creditors who suffer detrimental reliance because the company does not liquidate after the expiration of its specified term. See Section 203(c)(2).

Preexisting operating-agreement provisions continue to control the relationship of the members under subsection (a) except to the extent inconsistent with the rights and duties of members of an at-will company with an operating agreement containing the same provisions. However, the members could agree in advance that, if the company's business continues after the expiration of its specified term, the company continues as a company with a new specified term or that the provisions of its operating agreement survive the expiration of the specified term.

[ARTICLE] 5

TRANSFEREES AND CREDITORS OF MEMBER

§ 501. Member's distributional interest.

(a) A member is not a co-owner of, and has no transferable interest in, property of a limited liability company.

(b) A distributional interest in a limited liability company is personal property and, subject to Sections 502 and 503, may be transferred in whole or in part.

(c) An operating agreement may provide that a distributional interest may be evidenced by a certificate of the interest issued by the limited liability company and, subject to Section 503, may also provide for the transfer of any interest represented by the certificate.

Comment

Members have no property interest in property owned by a limited liability company. A distributional interest is personal property and is defined under Section 101(6) as a member's interest in distributions only and does not include the member's broader rights to participate in management under Section 404 and to inspect company records under Section 408.

Under Section 405(a), distributions are allocated in equal shares unless otherwise provided in an operating agreement. Whenever it is desirable to allocate distributions in proportion to contributions rather than per capita, certification may be useful to reduce valuation issues. The effect of certification on the Federal tax classification of the company is determined by federal law.

§ 502. Transfer of distributional interest.

A transfer of a distributional interest does not entitle the transferee to become or to exercise any rights of a member. A transfer entitles the transferee to receive, to the extent transferred, only the distributions to which the transferor would be entitled.

Comment

Under Sections 501(b) and 502, the only interest a member may freely transfer is that member's distributional interest. A member's transfer of part, all, or substantially all of a distributional interest will threaten the dissolution of the company under Section 801(b)(3)(i) only if the transfer constitutes an event of dissociation. See Section 601(3). Member dissociation has defined dissolution consequences under Section 801(b)(3)(i) depending upon whether the company is an at-will or term company and whether it is member- or manager-managed. Only the transfer of all or substantially all of a member's distributional interest constitutes or may constitute a member dissociation. A transfer of less than substantially all of a member's distributional interest is not an event of dissociation. A member ceases to be a member upon the transfer of all that member's distributional interest and that transfer is also an event of dissociation under Section 601(3). Relating the event of dissociation to the member's transfer of all of the member's distributional interest avoids the need for the company to track potential future dissociation events associated with a member no longer financially interested in the company. Also, all the remaining members may expel a member upon the transfer of "substantially all" the member's distributional interest. The expulsion is an event of dissociation under Section 601(5)(ii).

§ 503. Rights of transferee.

(a) A transferee of a distributional interest may become a member of a limited liability company if and to the extent that the transferor gives the transferee the right in accordance with authority described in the operating agreement or all other members consent.

(b) A transferee who has become a member, to the extent transferred, has the rights and powers, and is subject to the restrictions and liabilities, of a member under the operating agreement of a limited liability company and this [Act]. A transferee who becomes a member also is liable for the transferor member's obligations to make contributions under Section 402 and for obligations under Section 407 to return unlawful distributions, but the transferee is not obligated for the transferor member's liabilities unknown to the transferee at the time the transferee becomes a member.

(c) Whether or not a transferee of a distributional interest becomes a member under subsection (a), the transferor is not released from liability to the limited liability company under the operating agreement or this [Act].

(d) A transferee who does not become a member is not entitled to participate in the management or conduct of the limited liability company's business, require access to information concerning the company's transactions, or inspect or copy any of the company's records.

(e) A transferee who does not become a member is entitled to:

(1) receive, in accordance with the transfer, distributions to which the transferor would otherwise be entitled;

(2) receive, upon dissolution and winding up of the limited liability company's business:

(i) in accordance with the transfer, the net amount otherwise distributable to the transferor;

(ii) a statement of account only from the date of the latest statement of account agreed to by all the members;

(3) seek under Section 801(b)(6)(5) a judicial determination that it is equitable to dissolve and wind up the company's business.

(f) A limited liability company need not give effect to a transfer until it has notice of the transfer.

Comment

The only interest a member may freely transfer is the member's distributional interest. A transferee may acquire the remaining rights of a member only by being admitted as a member of the company by all of the remaining members. The effect of these default rules and any modifications on the Federal tax classification of the company is determined by federal law.

A transferee not admitted as a member is not entitled to participate in management, require access to information, or inspect or copy company records. The only rights of a transferee are to receive the distributions the transferor would otherwise be entitled, receive a limited statement of account, and seek a judicial dissolution under Section 801(b)(6).

Subsection (e) sets forth the rights of a transferee of an existing member. Although the rights of a dissociated member to participate in the future management of the company parallel the rights of a transferee, a dissociated member retains additional rights that accrued from that person's membership such as the right to enforce Article 7 purchase rights. See and compare Sections 603(b)(1) and 801(b)(5) and Comments.

§ 504. Rights of creditor.

(a) On application by a judgment creditor of a member of a limited liability company or of a member's transferee, a court having jurisdiction may charge the distributional interest of the judgment debtor to satisfy the judgment. The court may appoint a receiver of the share of the distributions due or to become due to the judgment debtor and make all other orders, directions, accounts, and inquiries the judgment debtor might have made or which the circumstances may require to give effect to the charging order.

(b) A charging order constitutes a lien on the judgment debtor's distributional interest. The court may order a foreclosure of a lien on a distributional interest subject to the charging order at any time. A purchaser at the foreclosure sale has the rights of a transferee.

(c) At any time before foreclosure, a distributional interest in a limited liability company which is charged may be redeemed:

(1) by the judgment debtor;

(2) with property other than the company's property, by one or more of the other members; or

(3) with the company's property, but only if permitted by the operating agreement.

(d) This [Act] does not affect a member's right under exemption laws with respect to the member's distributional interest in a limited liability company.

(e) This section provides the exclusive remedy by which a judgment creditor of a member or a transferee may satisfy a judgment out of the judgment debtor's distributional interest in a limited liability company.

Comment

A charging order is the only remedy by which a judgment creditor of a member or a member's transferee may reach the distributional interest of a member or member's transferee. Under Section 503(e), the distributional interest of a member or transferee is limited to the member's right to receive distributions from the company and to seek judicial liquidation of the company.

[ARTICLE] 6

MEMBER'S DISSOCIATION

§ 601. Events causing member's dissociation.

A member is dissociated from a limited liability company upon the occurrence of any of the following events:

(1) the company's having notice of the member's express will to withdraw upon the date of notice or on a later date specified by the member;

(2) an event agreed to in the operating agreement as causing the member's dissociation;

(3) upon transfer of all of a member's distributional interest, other than a transfer for security purposes or a court order charging the member's distributional interest which has not been foreclosed;

(4) the member's expulsion pursuant to the operating agreement;

(5) the member's expulsion by unanimous vote of the other members if:

(i) it is unlawful to carry on the company's business with the member;

(ii) there has been a transfer of substantially all of the member's distributional interest, other than a transfer for security purposes or a court order charging the member's distributional interest which has not been foreclosed;

(iii) within 90 days after the company notifies a corporate member that it will be expelled because it has filed a certificate of dissolution or the equivalent, its charter has been revoked, or its right to conduct business has been suspended by the jurisdiction of its incorporation, the member fails to obtain a revocation of the certificate of dissolution or a reinstatement of its charter or its right to conduct business; or

(iv) a partnership or a limited liability company that is a member has been dissolved and its business is being wound up;

(6) on application by the company or another member, the member's expulsion by judicial determination because the member:

(i) engaged in wrongful conduct that adversely and materially affected the company's business;

(ii) willfully or persistently committed a material breach of the operating agreement or of a duty owed to the company or the other members under Section 409; or

(iii) engaged in conduct relating to the company's business which makes it not reasonably practicable to carry on the business with the member;

(7) the member's:

(i) becoming a debtor in bankruptcy;

(ii) executing an assignment for the benefit of creditors;

(iii) seeking, consenting to, or acquiescing in the appointment of a trustee, receiver, or liquidator of the member or of all or substantially all of the member's property; or

(iv) failing, within 90 days after the appointment, to have vacated or stayed the appointment of a trustee, receiver, or liquidator of the member or of all or substantially all of the member's property obtained without the member's consent or acquiescence, or failing within 90 days after the expiration of a stay to have the appointment vacated;

(8) in the case of a member who is an individual:

(i) the member's death;

(ii) the appointment of a guardian or general conservator for the member; or

(iii) a judicial determination that the member has otherwise become incapable of performing the member's duties under the operating agreement;

(9) in the case of a member that is a trust or is acting as a member by virtue of being a trustee of a trust, distribution of the trust's entire rights to receive distributions from the company, but not merely by reason of the substitution of a successor trustee;

(10) in the case of a member that is an estate or is acting as a member by virtue of being a personal representative of an estate, distribution of the estate's entire rights to receive distributions from the company, but not merely the substitution of a successor personal representative; or

(11) termination of the existence of a member if the member is not an individual, estate, or trust other than a business trust.

Comment

The term "dissociation" refers to the change in the relationships among the dissociated member, the company and the other members caused by a member's ceasing to be associated in the carrying on of the company's business. Member dissociation for any reason from a member-managed at-will company will cause a dissolution of the company under Section 801(b)(3) unless a specified percentage of the remaining members agree to continue the business of the company. If the dissociation does not dissolve the company, the dissociated member's distributional interest must be immediately purchased by the company under Article 7. Member dissociation from a member-managed term company, but only for the reasons specified in paragraphs (7) to (11), will cause a dissolution of the company under Section 801(b)(3) unless a specified percentage of the remaining members agree to continue the business of the company. Member dissociations specified in paragraphs (1) to (6) do not threaten dissolution under Section 801(b)(3) of a member-managed term company. If the dissociation does not dissolve the company, it is not required to purchase the dissociated member's distributional interest until the expiration of the specified term that existed on the date of the member's dissociation. If an at-will company or a term company is manager-managed, only the dissociation of a member who is also a manager or, if there is none, any member specified above threatens dissolution. The effect on the Federal tax classification of the company creating a member-manager with a minimal interest in the company is determined by federal law.

A member may be expelled from the company under paragraph (5)(ii) by the unanimous vote of the other members upon a transfer of "substantially all" of the member's distributional interest other than for a transfer as security for a loan. A transfer of "all" of the member's distributional interest is an event of dissociation under paragraph (3).

Although a member is dissociated upon death, the effect of the dissociation where the company does not dissolve depends upon whether the company is at-will or term and whether manager-managed. Only the decedent's distributional interest transfers to the decedent's estate which does not acquire the decedent member's management rights. See Section 603(b)(1). Unless otherwise agreed, if the company was at-will, the estate's distributional interest must be purchased by the company at fair value determined at the date of death. However, if a term company, the estate and its transferees continue only as the owner of the distributional interest with no management rights until the expiration of the specified term that existed on the date of death. At the expiration of that term, the company must purchase the interest of a dissociated member if the company continues for an additional term by amending its articles or simply continues as an at-will company. See Sections 411 and 701(a)(2) and Comments. Before that time, the estate and its transferees have the right to make application for a judicial dissolution of the company under Section 801(b)(5) as successors in interest to a dissociated member. See Comments to Sections 801, 411, and 701. Where the members have allocated management rights on the basis of contributions rather than simply the number of members, a member's death will result in a transfer of management rights to the remaining members on a proportionate basis. This transfer of rights may be avoided by a provision in an operating agreement extending the Section 701(a)(1) at-will purchase right to a decedent member of a term company.

§ 602. Member's power to dissociate; wrongful dissociation.

(a) Unless otherwise provided in the operating agreement, a member has the power to dissociate from a limited liability company at any time, rightfully or wrongfully, by express will pursuant to Section 601(1).

(b) If the operating agreement has not eliminated a member's power to dissociate, the member's dissociation from a limited liability company is wrongful only if:

    (1) it is in breach of an express provision of the agreement; or

    (2) before the expiration of the specified term of a term company:

        (i) the member withdraws by express will;

        (ii) the member is expelled by judicial determination under Section 601(6);

        (iii) the member is dissociated by becoming a debtor in bankruptcy; or

        (iv) in the case of a member who is not an individual, trust other than a business trust, or estate, the member is expelled or otherwise dissociated because it willfully dissolved or terminated its existence.

(c) A member who wrongfully dissociates from a limited liability company is liable to the company and to the other members for damages caused by the dissociation. The liability is in addition to any other obligation of the member to the company or to the other members.

(d) If a limited liability company does not dissolve and wind up its business as a result of a member's wrongful dissociation under subsection (b), damages sustained by the company for the wrongful dissociation must be offset against distributions otherwise due the member after the dissociation.

Comment

A member has the power to withdraw from both an at-will company and a term company although the effects of the withdrawal are remarkably different. See Comments to Section 601. At a minimum, the exercise of a power to withdraw enables members to terminate their continuing duties of loyalty and care. See Section 603(b)(2) to (3).

A member's power to withdraw by express will may be eliminated by an operating agreement. The effect of such a provision on the Federal tax classification of the company is determined by federal law. An operating agreement may eliminate a member's power to withdraw by express will to promote the business continuity of an at-will company by removing the threat of dissolution and to eliminate the member's right to force the company to purchase the member's distributional interest. See Sections 801(b)(3) and 701(a)(1). However, such a member retains the ability to seek a judicial dissolution of the company. See Section 801(b)(5).

If a member's power to withdraw by express will is not eliminated in an operating agreement, the withdrawal may nevertheless be made wrongful under subsection (b). All dissociations, including withdrawal by express will, may be made wrongful under subsection (b)(l) in both an at-will and term company by the inclusion of a provision in an operating agreement. Even where an operating agreement does not eliminate the power to withdraw by express will or make any dissociation wrongful, the disscoiation of a member of a term company for the reasons specified under subsection (b)(2) is wrongful. The member is liable to the company and other members for damages caused by a wrongful dissociation under subsection (c) and, under subsection (d), the damages may be offset against all distributions otherwise due the member after the dissociation. Section 701(f) provides a similar rule permitting damages for wrongful dissociation to be offset against any company purchase of the member's distributional interest.

§ 603. Effect of member's dissociation.

(a) ~~If under Section 801 a member's dissociation from a limited liability company results in a dissolution and winding up of the company's business, [Article] 8 applies. If a member's dissociation from the company does not result in a dissolution and winding up of the company's business under Section 801~~ Upon a member's dissociation:

(1) in an at-will company, the company must cause the dissociated member's distributional interest to be purchased under [Article] 7; and

(2) in a term company:

(i) if the company dissolves and winds up its business on or before the expiration of its specified term, [Article] 8 applies to determine the dissociated member's rights to distributions; and

(ii) if the company does not dissolve and wind up its business on or before the expiration of its specified term, the company must cause the dissociated member's distributional interest to be purchased under [Article] 7 on the date of the expiration of the term specified at the time of the member's dissociation.

(b) Upon a member's dissociation from a limited liability company:

(1) the member's right to participate in the management and conduct of the company's business terminates, except as otherwise provided in Section 803, and the member ceases to be a member and is treated the same as a transferee of a member;

(2) the member's duty of loyalty under Section 409(b)(3) terminates; and

(3) the member's duty of loyalty under Section 409(b)(1) and (2) and duty of care under Section 409(c) continue only with regard to matters arising and events occurring before the member's dissociation, unless the member participates in winding up the company's business pursuant to Section 803.

Comment

Dissociation from an at-will company that does not dissolve the company causes the dissociated member's distributional interest to be immediately purchased under Article 7. See Comments to Sections 602 and 603. Dissociation from a term company that does not dissolve the company does not cause the dissociated member's distributional interest to be purchased under Article 7 until the expiration of the specified term that existed on the date of dissociation.

Subsection (b)(1) provides that a dissociated member forfeits the right to participate in the future conduct of the company's business. Dissociation does not however forfeit that member's right to enforce the Article 7 rights that accrue by reason of the dissociation. Similarly, where dissociation occurs by death, the decedent member's successors in interest may enforce that member's Article 7 rights. See and compare Comments to Section 503(e).

Dissociation terminates the member's right to participate in management, including the member's actual authority to act for the company under Section 301, and begins the two-year period after which a member's apparent authority conclusively ends. See Comments to Section 703. Dissociation also terminates a member's continuing duties of loyalty and care, except with regard to continuing transactions, to the company and other members unless the member participates in winding up the company's business. See Comments to Section 409.

[ARTICLE] 7

MEMBER'S DISSOCIATION WHEN BUSINESS NOT WOUND UP

§ 701. Company purchase of distributional interest.

(a) A limited liability company shall purchase a distributional interest of a:

(1) member of an at-will company for its fair value determined as of the date of the member's dissociation if the member's dissociation does not result in a dissolution and winding up of the company's business under Section 801; or

(2) member of a term company for its fair value determined as of the date of the expiration of the specified term that existed on the date of the member's dissociation if the expiration of the specified term does not result in a dissolution and winding up of the company's business under Section 801.

(b) A limited liability company must deliver a purchase offer to the dissociated member whose distributional interest is entitled to be purchased not later than 30 days after the date determined under subsection (a). The purchase offer must be accompanied by:

(1) a statement of the company's assets and liabilities as of the date determined under subsection (a);

(2) the latest available balance sheet and income statement, if any; and

(3) an explanation of how the estimated amount of the payment was calculated.

(c) If the price and other terms of a purchase of a distributional interest are fixed or are to be determined by the operating agreement, the price and terms so fixed or determined govern the purchase unless the purchaser defaults. If a default occurs, the dissociated member is entitled to commence a proceeding to have the company dissolved under Section 801~~(b)(5)~~(4)(iv).

(d) If an agreement to purchase the distributional interest is not made within 120 days after the date determined under subsection (a), the dissociated member, within another 120 days, may commence a proceeding against the limited liability company to enforce the purchase. The company at its expense shall notify in writing all of the remaining members, and any other person the court directs, of the commencement of the proceeding. The jurisdiction of the court in which the proceeding is commenced under this subsection is plenary and exclusive.

(e) The court shall determine the fair value of the distributional interest in accordance with the standards set forth in Section 702 together with the terms for the purchase. Upon making these determinations, the court shall order the limited liability company to purchase or cause the purchase of the interest.

(f) Damages for wrongful dissociation under Section 602(b), and all other amounts owing, whether or not currently due, from the dissociated member to a limited liability company, must be offset against the purchase price.

Comment

This section sets forth default rules regarding an otherwise mandatory company purchase of a distributional interest. Even though a dissociated member's rights to participate in the future management of the company are equivalent to those of a transferee of a member, the dissociation does not forfeit that member's right to enforce the Article 7 purchase right. Similarly, if the dissociation occurs by reason of death, the decedent member's successors in interest may enforce the Article 7 rights. See Comments to Sections 503(e) and 603(b)(1).

An at-will company must purchase a dissociated member's distributional interest under subsection (a)(l) when that member's dissociation does not result in a dissolution of the company. The purchase price is equal to the fair value of the interest determined as of the date of dissociation. Any damages for wrongful dissociation must be offset against the purchase price.

Dissociation from a term company does not require an immediate purchase of the member's interest but certain types of dissociation may cause the dissolution of the company. See Section 801(b)(3). A term company must only purchase the dissociated member's distributional interest under subsection (a)(2) on the expiration of the specified term that existed on the date of the member's dissociation. The purchase price is equal to the fair value of the interest determined as of the date of the expiration of that specified term. Any damages for wrongful dissociation must be offset against the purchase price.

The valuation dates differ between subsections (a)(l) and (a)(2) purchases. The former is valued on the date of member dissociation whereas the latter is valued on the date of the expiration of the specified term that existed on the date of dissociation. A subsection (a)(2) dissociated member therefore assumes the risk of loss between the date of dissociation and the expiration of the then stated specified term. See Comments to Section 801 (dissociated member may file application to dissolve company under Section 801 (b)(6)).

The default valuation standard is fair value. See Comments to Section 702. An operating agreement may fix a method or formula for determining the purchase price and the terms of payment. The purchase right may be modified. For example, an operating agreement may eliminate a member's power to withdraw from an at-will company which narrows the dissociation events contemplated under subsection (a)(l). See Comments to Section 602(a). However, a provision in an operating agreement providing for complete forfeiture of the purchase right may be unenforceable where the power to dissociate has not also been eliminated. See Section 104(a).

The company must deliver a purchase offer to the dissociated member within 30 days after the date determined under subsection (a). The offer must be accompanied by information designed to enable the dissociated member to evaluate the fairness of the offer. The subsection (b)(3) explanation of how the offer price was calculated need not be elaborate. For example, a mere statement of the basis of the calculation, such as "book value," may be sufficient.

The company and the dissociated member must reach an agreement on the purchase price and terms within 120 days after the date determined under subsection (a). Otherwise, the dissociated member may file suit within another 120 days to enforce the purchase under subsection (d). The court will then determine the fair value and terms of purchase under subsection (e). See Section 702. The member's lawsuit is not available under subsection (c) if the parties have previously agreed to price and terms in an operating agreement.

§ 702. Court action to determine fair value of distributional interest.

(a) In an action brought to determine the fair value of a distributional interest in a limited liability company, the court shall:

(1) determine the fair value of the interest, considering among other relevant evidence the going concern value of the company, any agreement among some or all of the members fixing the price or specifying a formula for determining value of distributional interests for any other purpose, the recommendations of any appraiser appointed by the court, and any legal constraints on the company's ability to purchase the interest;

(2) specify the terms of the purchase, including, if appropriate, terms for installment payments, subordination of the purchase obligation to the rights of the company's other creditors, security for a deferred purchase price, and a covenant not to compete or other restriction on a dissociated member; and

(3) require the dissociated member to deliver an assignment of the interest to the purchaser upon receipt of the purchase price or the first installment of the purchase price.

(b) After the dissociated member delivers the assignment, the dissociated member has no further claim against the company, its members, officers, or managers, if any, other than a claim to any unpaid balance of the purchase price and a claim under any agreement with the company or the remaining members that is not terminated by the court.

(c) If the purchase is not completed in accordance with the specified terms, the company is to be dissolved upon application under Section 801(b)(5)(iv). If a limited liability company is so dissolved, the dissociated member has the same rights and priorities in the company's assets as if the sale had not been ordered.

(d) If the court finds that a party to the proceeding acted arbitrarily, vexatiously, or not in good faith, it may award one or more other parties their reasonable expenses, including attorney's fees and the expenses of appraisers or other experts, incurred in the proceeding. The finding may be based on the company's failure to make an offer to pay or to comply with Section 701(b).

(e) Interest must be paid on the amount awarded from the date determined under Section 701(a) to the date of payment.

Comment

The default valuation standard is fair value. Under this broad standard, a court is free to determine the fair value of a distributional interest on a fair market, liquidation, or any other method deemed appropriate under the circumstances. A fair market value standard is not used because it is too narrow, often inappropriate, and assumes a fact not contemplated by this section — a willing buyer and a willing seller.

The court has discretion under subsection (a)(2) to include in its order any conditions the court deems necessary to safeguard the interests of the company and the dissociated member or transferee. The discretion may be based on the financial and other needs of the parties.

If the purchase is not consummated or the purchaser defaults, the dissociated member or transferee may make application for dissolution of the company under subsection (c). The court may deny the petition for good cause but the proceeding affords the company an opportunity to be heard on the matter and avoid dissolution. See Comments to Section 801(b)(5).

The power of the court to award all costs and attorney's fees incurred in the suit under subsection (d) is an incentive for both parties to act in good faith. See Section 701(c).

§ 703. Dissociated member's power to bind limited liability company.

For two years after a member dissociates without the dissociation resulting in a dissolution and winding up of a limited liability company's business, the company, including a surviving company under [Article] 9, is bound by an act of the dissociated member which would have bound the company under Section 301 before dissociation only if at the time of entering into the transaction the other party:

(1) reasonably believed that the dissociated member was then a member;

(2) did not have notice of the member's dissociation; and

(3) is not deemed to have had notice under Section 704.

Comment

A dissociated member of a member-managed company does not have actual authority to act for the company. See Section 603(b)(1). Under Section 301(a), a dissociated member of a member-managed company has apparent authority to bind the company in ordinary course transactions except as to persons who knew or had notice of the dissociation. This section modifies that rule by requiring the person to show reasonable reliance on the member's status as a member provided a Section 704 statement has not been filed within the previous 90 days. See also Section 804 (power to bind after dissolution).

§ 704. Statement of dissociation.

(a) A dissociated member or a limited liability company may file in the office of the [Secretary of State] a statement of dissociation stating the name of the company and that the member is dissociated from the company.

(b) For the purposes of Sections 301 and 703, a person not a member is deemed to have notice of the dissociation 90 days after the statement of dissociation is filed.

[ARTICLE] 8

WINDING UP COMPANY'S BUSINESS

§ 801. Events causing dissolution and winding up of company's business.

(a) In this section, "future distributions" means the total distributions that, as of the date of dissociation, are reasonably estimated to be made to the remaining members if the company were continued until the projected date of its termination, reduced by the amount of distributions that would have been made to the remaining members if the business of the company were dissolved and wound up on the date of dissociation.

(b) A limited liability company is dissolved, and its business must be wound up, upon the occurrence of any of the following events:

(1) an event specified in the operating agreement;

(2) consent of the number or percentage of members specified in the operating agreement;

(3) dissociation of a member who is also a manager or, if none, a member of an at will company, and dissociation of a member who is also a manager or, if none, a member of a term company but only if the dissociation was for a reason provided in Section 601(7) through (11) and occurred before the expiration of the specified term, but the company is not dissolved and required to be wound up by reason of the dissociation if:

(i) within 90 days after the dissociation, the business of the company is continued by the agreement of:

(A) the remaining members that would be entitled to receive a majority of any distributions that would be made to them assuming the business of the company were dissolved and wound up on the date of the dissociation; and

~~(B) the remaining members that would be entitled to receive a majority of any future distributions that would be made to them assuming the business of the company were continued after the date of the dissociation; or~~

~~(ii) the business of the company is continued under a right to continue stated in the operating agreement;~~

~~(4)~~ an event that makes it unlawful for all or substantially all of the business of the company to be continued, but any cure of illegality within 90 days after notice to the company of the event is effective retroactively to the date of the event for purposes of this section;

~~(5)~~(4) on application by a member or a dissociated member, upon entry of a judicial decree that:

(i) the economic purpose of the company is likely to be unreasonably frustrated;

(ii) another member has engaged in conduct relating to the company's business that makes it not reasonably practicable to carry on the company's business with that member;

(iii) it is not otherwise reasonably practicable to carry on the company's business in conformity with the articles of organization and the operating agreement;

(iv) the company failed to purchase the petitioner's distributional interest as required by Section 701; or

(v) the managers or members in control of the company have acted, are acting, or will act in a manner that is illegal, oppressive, fraudulent, or unfairly prejudicial to the petitioner; or

~~(6)~~(5) on application by a transferee of a member's interest, a judicial determination that it is equitable to wind up the company's business:

(i) after the expiration of the specified term, if the company was for a specified term at the time the applicant became a transferee by member dissociation, transfer, or entry of a charging order that gave rise to the transfer; or

(ii) at any time, if the company was at will at the time the applicant became a transferee by member dissociation, transfer, or entry of a charging order that gave rise to the transfer.

Comment

The dissolution rules of this section are mostly default rules and may be modified by an operating agreement. However, an operating agreement may not modify or eliminate the dissolution events specified in subsection ~~(b)(4)~~(3) (illegal business) or subsection ~~(b)(5)~~(4) (member application). See Section 103(b)(6).

~~The relationship between member dissociation and company dissolution is set forth under subsection (b)(3). In order for member dissociation to cause the dissolution of a company, the dissociation must be recognized as one that triggers a dissolution vote and a specified percentage of the remaining members must fail to agree within 90 days after the dissociation to avoid dissolution under subsection (b)(3)(i). See Comments to Section 601. The means of voting and standard for avoiding dissolution may be modified in an operating agreement and would constitute a "right to continue" recognized under subsection (b)(3)(ii). The~~

~~effect on the Federal tax classification of the company altering the specified percentage vote is determined by federal law.~~

~~Decision making under this Act is normally by a majority in number of the members or managers for ordinary matters and unanimity for specified extraordinary matters. See Section 404(a) to (c). The majority of members holding requisite distributions rights varies this rule and is used only in subsection (b)(3)(i). Under this Act, distributions are shared on a per capita basis. See Comments to Section 405. Therefore, under the default rule, a majority in number would also be a majority of members holding requisite distributions rights unless the company has in excess of one hundred members.~~

A member or dissociated member whose interest is not required to be purchased by the company under Section 701 may make application under subsection ~~(b)(5)~~(4) for the involuntary dissolution of both an at-will company and a term company. A transferee may make application under subsection ~~(b)(6)~~(5). A transferee's application right, but not that of a member or dissociated member, may be modified by an operating agreement. See Section 103(b)(6). A dissociated member is not treated as a transferee for purposes of an application under subsections ~~(b)(5) and~~ ~~(b)(6)~~(4) and ~~(b)~~(5). See Section 603(b)(1). For example, this affords reasonable protection to a dissociated member of a term company to make application under subsection ~~(b)~~(4) before the expiration of the term that existed at the time of dissociation. For purposes of a subsection ~~(b)(5)~~(4) application, a dissociated member includes a successor in interest, e.g., surviving spouse. See Comments to Section 601.

In the case of applications under subsections ~~(b)(5) and (b)(6)~~(4) and ~~(b)~~(5), the applicant has the burden of proving either the existence of one or more of the circumstances listed under subsection ~~(b)(5)~~(4) or that it is equitable to wind up the company's business under subsection ~~(b)(6)~~(5). Proof of the existence of one or more of the circumstances in subsection ~~(b)(5)~~(4), may be the basis of a subsection ~~(b)(6)~~(5) application. Even where the burden of proof is met, the court has the discretion to order relief other than the dissolution of the company. Examples include an accounting, a declaratory judgment, a distribution, the purchase of the distributional interest of the applicant or another member, or the appointment of a receiver. See Section 410.

A court has the discretion to dissolve a company under subsection ~~(b)(5)~~(4)(i) when the company has a very poor financial record that is not likely to improve. In this instance, dissolution is an alternative to placing the company in bankruptcy. A court may dissolve a company under subsections ~~(b)(5)(ii), (b)(5)(iii), and~~ ~~(b)(5)~~(4)(ii), ~~(b)~~(4)(iii), and ~~(b)~~(4)(iv) for serious and protracted misconduct by one or more members. Subsection ~~(b)(5)~~(4)(v) provides a specific remedy for an improper squeeze-out of a member.

In determining whether and what type of relief to order under subsections ~~(b)~~(4) and ~~(b)~~(5) ~~and (b)(6)~~ involuntary dissolution suits, a court should take into account other rights and remedies of the applicant. For example, a court should not grant involuntary dissolution of an at-will company if the applicant member has the right to dissociate and force the company to purchase that member's distributional interest under Sections 701 and 702. In other cases, involuntary dissolution or some other remedy such as a buy-out might be appropriate where, for example, one or more members have (i) engaged in fraudulent or unconscionable conduct, (ii) improperly expelled a member seeking an unfair advantage of a provision in an operating agreement that provides for a significantly lower price on expulsion than would be payable in the event of voluntary dissociation, or (iii) engaged in serious misconduct and the applicant member is a member of a term company and would not have a right to have the company purchase that member's distributional interest upon dissociation until the expiration of the company's specified term.

§ 802. Limited liability company continues after dissolution.

(a) Subject to subsection (b), a limited liability company continues after dissolution only for the purpose of winding up its business.

(b) At any time after the dissolution of a limited liability company and before the winding up of its business is completed, the members, including a dissociated member whose dissociation caused the dissolution, may unanimously waive the right to have the company's business wound up and the company terminated. In that case:

(1) the limited liability company resumes carrying on its business as if dissolution had never occurred and any liability incurred by the company or a member after the dissolution and before the waiver is determined as if the dissolution had never occurred; and

(2) the rights of a third party accruing under Section 804(a) or arising out of conduct in reliance on the dissolution before the third party knew or received a notification of the waiver are not adversely affected.

Comment

The liability shield continues in effect for the winding up period because the legal existence of the company continues under subsection (a). The company is terminated on the filing of articles of termination. See Section 805.

§ 803. Right to wind up limited liability company's business.

(a) After dissolution, a member who has not wrongfully dissociated may participate in winding up a limited liability company's business, but on application of any member, member's legal representative, or transferee, the [designate the appropriate court], for good cause shown, may order judicial supervision of the winding up.

(b) A legal representative of the last surviving member may wind up a limited liability company's business.

(c) A person winding up a limited liability company's business may preserve the company's business or property as a going concern for a reasonable time, prosecute and defend actions and proceedings, whether civil, criminal, or administrative, settle and close the company's business, dispose of and transfer the company's property, discharge the company's liabilities, distribute the assets of the company pursuant to Section 806, settle disputes by mediation or arbitration, and perform other necessary acts.

§ 804. Member's or manager's power and liability as agent after dissolution.

(a) A limited liability company is bound by a member's or manager's act after dissolution that:

(1) is appropriate for winding up the company's business; or

(2) would have bound the company under Section 301 before dissolution, if the other party to the transaction did not have notice of the dissolution.

(b) A member or manager who, with knowledge of the dissolution, subjects a limited liability company to liability by an act that is not appropriate for winding up the company's business is liable to the company for any damage caused to the company arising from the liability.

Comment

After dissolution, members and managers continue to have the authority to bind the company that they had prior to dissolution provided that the third party did not have notice of the dissolution. See Section 102(b) (notice defined). Otherwise, they have only the authority appropriate for winding up the company's business. See Section 703 (agency power of member after dissociation).

§ 805. Articles of termination.

(a) At any time after dissolution and winding up, a limited liability company may terminate its existence by filing with the [Secretary of State] articles of termination stating:

(1) the name of the company;

(2) the date of the dissolution; and

(3) that the company's business has been wound up and the legal existence of the company has been terminated.

(b) The existence of a limited liability company is terminated upon the filing of the articles of termination, or upon a later effective date, if specified in the articles of termination.

Comment

The termination of legal existence also terminates the company's liability shield. See Comments to Section 802 (liability shield continues in effect during winding up). It also ends the company's responsibility to file an annual report. See Section 211.

§ 806. Distribution of assets in winding up limited liability company's business.

(a) In winding up a limited liability company's business, the assets of the company must be applied to discharge its obligations to creditors, including members who are creditors. Any surplus must be applied to pay in money the net amount distributable to members in accordance with their right to distributions under subsection (b).

(b) Each member is entitled to a distribution upon the winding up of the limited liability company's business consisting of a return of all contributions which have not previously been returned and a distribution of any remainder in equal shares.

§ 807. Known claims against dissolved limited liability company.

(a) A dissolved limited liability company may dispose of the known claims against it by following the procedure described in this section.

(b) A dissolved limited liability company shall notify its known claimants in writing of the dissolution. The notice must:

(1) specify the information required to be included in a claim;

(2) provide a mailing address where the claim is to be sent;

(3) state the deadline for receipt of the claim, which may not be less than 120 days after the date the written notice is received by the claimant; and

(4) state that the claim will be barred if not received by the deadline.·

(c) A claim against a dissolved limited liability company is barred if the requirements of subsection (b) are met, and:

(1) the claim is not received by the specified deadline; or

(2) in the case of a claim that is timely received but rejected by the dissolved company, the claimant does not commence a proceeding to enforce the claim within 90 days after the receipt of the notice of the rejection.

(d) For purposes of this section, "claim" does not include a contingent liability or a claim based on an event occurring after the effective date of dissolution.

Comment

A known claim will be barred when the company provides written notice to a claimant that a claim must be filed with the company no later than at least 120 days after receipt of the written notice and the claimant fails to file the claim. If the claim is timely received but is rejected by the company, the claim is nevertheless barred unless the claimant files suit to enforce the claim within 90 days after the receipt of the notice of rejection. A claim described in subsection (d) is not a "known" claim and is governed by Section 808. This section does not extend any other applicable statutes of limitation. See Section 104. Depending on the management of the company, members or managers must discharge or make provision for discharging all of the company's known liabilities before distributing the remaining assets to the members. See Sections 806(a), 406, and 407.

§ 808. Other claims against dissolved limited liability company.

(a) A dissolved limited liability company may publish notice of its dissolution and request persons having claims against the company to present them in accordance with the notice.

(b) The notice must:

(1) be published at least once in a newspaper of general circulation in the [county] in which the dissolved limited liability company's principal office is located or, if none in this State, in which its designated office is or was last located;

(2) describe the information required to be contained in a claim and provide a mailing address where the claim is to be sent; and

(3) state that a claim against the limited liability company is barred unless a proceeding to enforce the claim is commenced within five years after publication of the notice.

(c) If a dissolved limited liability company publishes a notice in accordance with subsection (b), the claim of each of the following claimants is barred unless the claimant commences a proceeding to enforce the claim against the dissolved company within five years after the publication date of the notice:

(1) a claimant who did not receive written notice under Section 807;

(2) a claimant whose claim was timely sent to the dissolved company but not acted on; and

(3) a claimant whose claim is contingent or based on an event occurring after the effective date of dissolution.

(d) A claim not barred under this section may be enforced:

(1) against the dissolved limited liability company, to the extent of its undistributed assets; or

(2) if the assets have been distributed in liquidation, against a member of the dissolved company to the extent of the member's proportionate share of the claim or the company's assets distributed to the member in liquidation, whichever is less, but a member's total liability for all claims under this section may not exceed the total amount of assets distributed to the member.

Comment

An unknown claim will be barred when the company publishes notice requesting claimants to file claims with the company and stating that claims will be barred unless the claimant files suit to enforce the claim within five years after the date of publication. The procedure also bars known claims where the claimant either did not receive written notice described in Section 807 or received notice, mailed a claim, but the company did not act on the claim.

Depending on the management of the company, members or managers must discharge or make provision for discharging all of the company's known liabilities before distributing the remaining assets to the members. See Comment to Section 807. This section does not contemplate that a company will postpone member distributions until all unknown claims are barred under this section. In appropriate cases, the company may purchase insurance or set aside funds permitting a distribution of the remaining assets. Where winding up distributions have been made to members, subsection (d)(2) authorizes recovery against those members. However, a claimant's recovery against a member is limited to the lesser of the member's proportionate share of the claim or the amount received in the distribution. This section does not extend any other applicable statutes of limitation. See Section 104.

§ 809. Grounds for administrative dissolution.

The [Secretary of State] may commence a proceeding to dissolve a limited liability company administratively if the company does not:

(1) pay any fees, taxes, or penalties imposed by this [Act] or other law within 60 days after they are due; or

(2) deliver its annual report to the [Secretary of State] within 60 days after it is due.

Comment

Administrative dissolution is an effective enforcement mechanism for a variety of statutory obligations under this Act and it avoids the more expensive judicial dissolution process. When applicable, administrative dissolution avoids wasteful attempts to compel compliance by a company abandoned by its members.

§ 810. Procedure for and effect of administrative dissolution.

(a) If the [Secretary of State] determines that a ground exists for administratively dissolving a limited liability company, the [Secretary of State] shall enter a record of the determination and serve the company with a copy of the record.

(b) If the company does not correct each ground for dissolution or demonstrate to the reasonable satisfaction of the [Secretary of State] that each ground determined by the [Secretary of State] does not exist within 60 days after service of the notice, the [Secretary of State] shall administratively dissolve the company by signing a certification of the dissolution that recites the ground for dissolution and its effective date. The [Secretary of State] shall file the original of the certificate and serve the company with a copy of the certificate.

(c) A company administratively dissolved continues its existence but may carry on only business necessary to wind up and liquidate its business and affairs under Section 802 and to notify claimants under Sections 807 and 808.

(d) The administrative dissolution of a company does not terminate the authority of its agent for service of process.

Comment

A company's failure to comply with a ground for administrative dissolution may simply occur because of oversight. Therefore, subsections (a) and (b) set forth a mandatory notice by the filing officer to the company of the ground for dissolution and a 60 day grace period for correcting the ground.

§ 811. Reinstatement following administrative dissolution.

(a) A limited liability company administratively dissolved may apply to the [Secretary of State] for reinstatement within two years after the effective date of dissolution. The application must:

(1) recite the name of the company and the effective date of its administrative dissolution;

(2) state that the ground for dissolution either did not exist or have [sic] been eliminated;

(3) state that the company's name satisfies the requirements of Section 105; and

(4) contain a certificate from the [taxing authority] reciting that all taxes owed by the company have been paid.

(b) If the [Secretary of State] determines that the application contains the information required by subsection (a) and that the information is correct, the [Secretary of State] shall cancel the certificate of dissolution and prepare a certificate of reinstatement that recites this determination and the effective date of reinstatement, file the original of the certificate, and serve the company with a copy of the certificate.

(c) When reinstatement is effective, it relates back to and takes effect as of the effective date of the administrative dissolution and the company may resume its business as if the administrative dissolution had never occurred.

§ 812. Appeal from denial of reinstatement.

(a) If the [Secretary of State] denies a limited liability company's application for reinstatement following administrative dissolution, the [Secretary of State] shall serve the company with a record that explains the reason or reasons for denial.

(b) The company may appeal the denial of reinstatement to the [name appropriate] court within 30 days after service of the notice of denial is perfected. The company appeals by petitioning the court to set aside the dissolution and attaching to the petition copies of the [Secretary of State's] certificate of dissolution, the company's application for reinstatement, and the [Secretary of State's] notice of denial.

(c) The court may summarily order the [Secretary of State] to reinstate the dissolved company or may take other action the court considers appropriate.

(d) The court's final decision may be appealed as in other civil proceedings.

[ARTICLE] 9

CONVERSIONS AND MERGERS

§ 901. Definitions.

In this [article]:

(1) "Corporation" means a corporation under [the State Corporation Act], a predecessor law, or comparable law of another jurisdiction.

(2) "General partner" means a partner in a partnership and a general partner in a limited partnership.

(3) "Limited partner" means a limited partner in a limited partnership.

(4) "Limited partnership" means a limited partnership created under [the State Limited Partnership Act], a predecessor law, or comparable law of another jurisdiction.

(5) "Partner" includes a general partner and a limited partner.

(6) "Partnership" means a general partnership under [the State Partnership Act], a predecessor law, or comparable law of another jurisdiction.

(7) "Partnership agreement" means an agreement among the partners concerning the partnership or limited partnership.

(8) "Shareholder" means a shareholder in a corporation.

Comment

Section 907 makes clear that the provisions of Article 9 are not mandatory. Therefore, a partnership or a limited liability company may convert or merge in any other manner provided by law. However, if the requirements of Article 9 are followed, the conversion or merger is legally valid. Article 9 is not restricted to domestic business entities.

§ 902. Conversion of partnership or limited partnership to limited liability company.

(a) A partnership or limited partnership may be converted to a limited liability company pursuant to this section.

(b) The terms and conditions of a conversion of a partnership or limited partnership to a limited liability company must be approved by all of the partners or by a number or percentage of the partners required for conversion in the partnership agreement.

(c) An agreement of conversion must set forth the terms and conditions of the conversion of the interests of partners of a partnership or of a limited partnership, as the case may be, into interests in the converted limited liability company or the cash or other consideration to be paid or delivered as a result of the conversion of the interests of the partners, or a combination thereof.

(d) After a conversion is approved under subsection (b), the partnership or limited partnership shall file articles of organization in the office of the [Secretary of State] which satisfy the requirements of Section 203 and contain:

(1) a statement that the partnership or limited partnership was converted to a limited liability company from a partnership or limited partnership, as the case may be;

(2) its former name;

(3) a statement of the number of votes cast by the partners entitled to vote for and against the conversion and, if the vote is less than unanimous, the number or percentage required to approve the conversion under subsection (b); and

(4) in the case of a limited partnership, a statement that the certificate of limited partnership is to be canceled as of the date the conversion took effect.

(e) In the case of a limited partnership, the filing of articles of organization under subsection (d) cancels its certificate of limited partnership as of the date the conversion took effect.

(f) A conversion takes effect when the articles of organization are filed in the office of the [Secretary of State] or at any later date specified in the articles of organization.

(g) A general partner who becomes a member of a limited liability company as a result of a conversion remains liable as a partner for an obligation incurred by the partnership or limited partnership before the conversion takes effect.

(h) A general partner's liability for all obligations of the limited liability company incurred after the conversion takes effect is that of a member of the company. A limited partner who becomes a member as a result of a conversion remains liable only to the extent the limited partner was liable for an obligation incurred by the limited partnership before the conversion takes effect.

Comment

Subsection (b) makes clear that the terms and conditions of the conversion of a general or limited partnership to a limited liability company must be approved by all of the partners unless the partnership agreement specifies otherwise.

§ 903. Effect of conversion; entity unchanged.

(a) A partnership or limited partnership that has been converted pursuant to this [article] is for all purposes the same entity that existed before the conversion.

(b) When a conversion takes effect:

(1) all property owned by the converting partnership or limited partnership vests in the limited liability company;

(2) all debts, liabilities, and other obligations of the converting partnership or limited partnership continue as obligations of the limited liability company;

(3) an action or proceeding pending by or against the converting partnership or limited partnership may be continued as if the conversion had not occurred;

(4) except as prohibited by other law, all of the rights, privileges, immunities, powers, and purposes of the converting partnership or limited partnership vest in the limited liability company; and

(5) except as otherwise provided in the agreement of conversion under Section 902(c), all of the partners of the converting partnership continue as members of the limited liability company.

Comment

A conversion is not a conveyance or transfer and does not give rise to claims of reverter or impairment of title based on a prohibited conveyance or transfer. Under subsection (b)(1), title to all partnership property, including real estate, vests in the limited liability company as a matter of law without reversion or impairment.

§ 904. Merger of entities.

(a) Pursuant to a plan of merger approved under subsection (c), a limited liability company may be merged with or into one or more limited liability companies, foreign limited liability companies, corporations, foreign corporations, partnerships, foreign partnerships, limited partnerships, foreign limited partnerships, or other domestic or foreign entities.

(b) A plan of merger must set forth:

(1) the name of each entity that is a party to the merger;

(2) the name of the surviving entity into which the other entities will merge;

(3) the type of organization of the surviving entity;

(4) the terms and conditions of the merger;

(5) the manner and basis for converting the interests of each party to the merger into interests or obligations of the surviving entity, or into money or other property in whole or in part; and

(6) the street address of the surviving entity's principal place of business.

(c) A plan of merger must be approved:

(1) in the case of a limited liability company that is a party to the merger, by all of the members or by a number or percentage of members specified in the operating agreement;

(2) in the case of a foreign limited liability company that is a party to the merger, by the vote required for approval of a merger by the law of the State or foreign jurisdiction in which the foreign limited liability company is organized;

(3) in the case of a partnership or domestic limited partnership that is a party to the merger, by the vote required for approval of a conversion under Section 902(b); and

(4) in the case of any other entities that are parties to the merger, by the vote required for approval of a merger by the law of this State or of the State or foreign jurisdiction in which the entity is organized and, in the absence of such a requirement, by all the owners of interests in the entity.

(d) After a plan of merger is approved and before the merger takes effect, the plan may be amended or abandoned as provided in the plan.

(e) The merger is effective upon the filing of the articles of merger with the [Secretary of State], or at such later date as the articles may provide.

Comment

This section sets forth a "safe harbor" for cross-entity mergers of limited liability companies with both domestic and foreign: corporations, general and limited partnerships, and other limited liability companies. Subsection (c) makes clear that the terms and conditions of the plan of merger must be approved by all of the partners unless applicable state law specifies otherwise for the merger.

§ 905. Articles of merger.

(a) After approval of the plan of merger under Section 904(c), unless the merger is abandoned under Section 904(d), articles of merger must be signed on behalf of each limited liability company and other entity that is a party to the merger and delivered to the [Secretary of State] for filing. The articles must set forth:

(1) the name and jurisdiction of formation or organization of each of the limited liability companies and other entities that are parties to the merger;

(2) for each limited liability company that is to merge, the date its articles of organization were filed with the [Secretary of State];

(3) that a plan of merger has been approved and signed by each limited liability company and other entity that is to merge;

(4) the name and address of the surviving limited liability company or other surviving entity;

(5) the effective date of the merger;

(6) if a limited liability company is the surviving entity, such changes in its articles of organization as are necessary by reason of the merger;

(7) if a party to a merger is a foreign limited liability company, the jurisdiction and date of filing of its initial articles of organization and the date when its application for authority was filed by the [Secretary of State] or, if an application has not been filed, a statement to that effect; and

(8) if the surviving entity is not a limited liability company, an agreement that the surviving entity may be served with process in this State and is subject to liability in any action or proceeding for the enforcement of any liability or obligation of any limited liability company previously subject to suit in this State which is to merge, and for the enforcement, as provided in this [Act], of the right of members of any limited liability company to receive payment for their interest against the surviving entity.

(b) If a foreign limited liability company is the surviving entity of a merger, it may not do business in this State until an application for that authority is filed with the [Secretary of State].

(c) The surviving limited liability company or other entity shall furnish a copy of the plan of merger, on request and without cost, to any member of any limited liability company or any person holding an interest in any other entity that is to merge.

(d) Articles of merger operate as an amendment to the limited liability company's articles of organization.

§ 906. Effect of merger.

(a) When a merger takes effect:

(1) the separate existence of each limited liability company and other entity that is a party to the merger, other than the surviving entity, terminates;

(2) all property owned by each of the limited liability companies and other entities that are party to the merger vests in the surviving entity;

(3) all debts, liabilities, and other obligations of each limited liability company and other entity that is party to the merger become the obligations of the surviving entity;

(4) an action or proceeding pending by or against a limited liability company or other party to a merger may be continued as if the merger had not occurred or the surviving entity may be substituted as a party to the action or proceeding; and

(5) except as prohibited by other law, all the rights, privileges, immunities, powers, and purposes of every limited liability company and other entity that is a party to a merger vest in the surviving entity.

(b) The [Secretary of State] is an agent for service of process in an action or proceeding against the surviving foreign entity to enforce an obligation of any party to a merger if the surviving foreign entity fails to appoint or maintain an agent designated for service of process in this State or the agent for service of process cannot with reasonable diligence be found at the designated office. Upon receipt of process, the [Secretary of State] shall send a copy of the process by registered or certified mail, return receipt requested, to the surviving entity at the address set forth in the articles of merger. Service is effected under this subsection at the earliest of:

(1) the date the company receives the process, notice, or demand;

(2) the date shown on the return receipt, if signed on behalf of the company; or

(3) five days after its deposit in the mail, if mailed postpaid and correctly addressed.

(c) A member of the surviving limited liability company is liable for all obligations of a party to the merger for which the member was personally liable before the merger.

(d) Unless otherwise agreed, a merger of a limited liability company that is not the surviving entity in the merger does not require the limited liability company to wind up its business under this [Act] or pay its liabilities and distribute its assets pursuant to this [Act].

(e) Articles of merger serve as articles of dissolution for a limited liability company that is not the surviving entity in the merger.

§ 907. [Article] not exclusive.

This [article] does not preclude an entity from being converted or merged under other law.

[ARTICLE] 10

FOREIGN LIMITED LIABILITY COMPANIES

§ 1001. Law governing foreign limited liability companies.

(a) The laws of the State or other jurisdiction under which a foreign limited liability company is organized govern its organization and internal affairs and the liability of its managers, members, and their transferees.

(b) A foreign limited liability company may not be denied a certificate of authority by reason of any difference between the laws of another jurisdiction under which the foreign company is organized and the laws of this State.

(c) A certificate of authority does not authorize a foreign limited liability company to engage in any business or exercise any power that a limited liability company may not engage in or exercise in this State.

Comment

The law where a foreign limited liability company is organized, rather than this Act, governs that company's internal affairs and the liability of its owners. Accordingly, any difference between the laws of the foreign jurisdiction and this Act will not constitute grounds for denial of a certificate of authority to transact business in this State. However, a foreign limited liability company transacting business in this State by virtue of a certificate of authority is limited to the business and powers that a limited liability company may lawfully pursue and exercise under Section 112.

§ 1002. Application for certificate of authority.

(a) A foreign limited liability company may apply for a certificate of authority to transact business in this State by delivering an application to the [Secretary of State] for filing. The application must set forth:

(1) the name of the foreign company or, if its name is unavailable for use in this State, a name that satisfies the requirements of Section 1005;

(2) the name of the State or country under whose law it is organized;

(3) the street address of its principal office;

(4) the address of its initial designated office in this State;

(5) the name and street address of its initial agent for service of process in this State;

(6) whether the duration of the company is for a specified term and, if so, the period specified;

(7) whether the company is manager-managed, and, if so, the name and address of each initial manager; and

(8) whether the members of the company are to be liable for its debts and obligations under a provision similar to Section 303(c).

(b) A foreign limited liability company shall deliver with the completed application a certificate of existence or a record of similar import authenticated by the secretary of state or other official having custody of company records in the State or country under whose law it is organized.

Comment

As with articles of organization, the application must be signed and filed with the filing office. See Sections 105, 107 (name registration), 205, 206, 209 (liability for false statements), and 1005.

§ 1003. Activities not constituting transacting business.

(a) Activities of a foreign limited liability company that do not constitute transacting business in this State within the meaning of this [article] include:

(1) maintaining, defending, or settling an action or proceeding;

(2) holding meetings of its members or managers or carrying on any other activity concerning its internal affairs;

(3) maintaining bank accounts;

(4) maintaining offices or agencies for the transfer, exchange, and registration of the foreign company's own securities or maintaining trustees or depositories with respect to those securities;

(5) selling through independent contractors;

(6) soliciting or obtaining orders, whether by mail or through employees or agents or otherwise, if the orders require acceptance outside this State before they become contracts;

(7) creating or acquiring indebtedness, mortgages, or security interests in real or personal property;

(8) securing or collecting debts or enforcing mortgages or other security interests in property securing the debts, and holding, protecting, and maintaining property so acquired;

(9) conducting an isolated transaction that is completed within 30 days and is not one in the course of similar transactions of a like manner; and

(10) transacting business in interstate commerce.

(b) For purposes of this [article], the ownership in this State of income-producing real property or tangible personal property, other than property excluded under subsection (a), constitutes transacting business in this State.

(c) This section does not apply in determining the contacts or activities that may subject a foreign limited liability company to service of process, taxation, or regulation under any other law of this State.

§ 1004. Issuance of certificate of authority.

Unless the [Secretary of State] determines that an application for a certificate of authority fails to comply as to form with the filing requirements of this [Act], the [Secretary of State], upon payment of all filing fees, shall file the application and send a receipt for it and the fees to the limited liability company or its representative.

§ 1005.   Name of foreign limited liability company.

(a) If the name of a foreign limited liability company does not satisfy the requirements of Section 105, the company, to obtain or maintain a certificate of authority to transact business in this State, must use a fictitious name to transact business in this State if its real name is unavailable and it delivers to the [Secretary of State] for filing a copy of the resolution of its managers, in the case of a manager-managed company, or of its members, in the case of a member-managed company, adopting the fictitious name.

(b) Except as authorized by subsections (c) and (d), the name, including a fictitious name to be used to transact business in this State, of a foreign limited liability company must be distinguishable upon the records of the [Secretary of State] from:

(1) the name of any corporation, limited partnership, or company incorporated, organized, or authorized to transact business in this State;

(2) a name reserved or registered under Section 106 or 107; and

(3) the fictitious name of another foreign limited liability company authorized to transact business in this State.

(c) A foreign limited liability company may apply to the [Secretary of State] for authority to use in this State a name that is not distinguishable upon the records of the [Secretary of State] from a name described in subsection (b). The [Secretary of State] shall authorize use of the name applied for if:

(1) the present user, registrant, or owner of a reserved name consents to the use in a record and submits an undertaking in form satisfactory to the [Secretary of State] to change its name to a name that is distinguishable upon the records of the [Secretary of State] from the name of the foreign applying limited liability company; or

(2) the applicant delivers to the [Secretary of State] a certified copy of a final judgment of a court establishing the applicant's right to use the name applied for in this State.

(d) A foreign limited liability company may use in this State the name, including the fictitious name, of another domestic or foreign entity that is used in this State if the other entity is incorporated, organized, or authorized to transact business in this State and the foreign limited liability company:

(1) has merged with the other entity;

(2) has been formed by reorganization of the other entity; or

(3) has acquired all or substantially all of the assets, including the name, of the other entity.

(e) If a foreign limited liability company authorized to transact business in this State changes its name to one that does not satisfy the requirements of Section 105, it may not transact business in this State under the name as changed until it adopts a name satisfying the requirements of Section 105 and obtains an amended certificate of authority.

§ 1006. Revocation of certificate of authority.

(a) A certificate of authority of a foreign limited liability company to transact business in this State may be revoked by the [Secretary of State] in the manner provided in subsection (b) if:

  (1) the company fails to:

    (i) pay any fees, taxes, and penalties owed to this State;

    (ii) deliver its annual report required under Section 211 to the [Secretary of State] within 60 days after it is due;

    (iii) appoint and maintain an agent for service of process as required by this [article]; or

    (iv) file a statement of a change in the name or business address of the agent as required by this [article]; or

  (2) a misrepresentation has been made of any material matter in any application, report, affidavit, or other record submitted by the company pursuant to this [article].

(b) The [Secretary of State] may not revoke a certificate of authority of a foreign limited liability company unless the [Secretary of State] sends the company notice of the revocation, at least 60 days before its effective date, by a record addressed to its agent for service of process in this State, or if the company fails to appoint and maintain a proper agent in this State, addressed to the office required to be maintained by Section 108. The notice must specify the cause for the revocation of the certificate of authority. The authority of the company to transact business in this State ceases on the effective date of the revocation unless the foreign limited liability company cures the failure before that date.

§ 1007. Cancellation of authority.

A foreign limited liability company may cancel its authority to transact business in this State by filing in the office of the [Secretary of State] a certificate of cancellation. Cancellation does not terminate the authority of the [Secretary of State] to accept service of process on the company for [claims for relief] arising out of the transactions of business in this State.

§ 1008. Effect of failure to obtain certificate of authority.

(a) A foreign limited liability company transacting business in this State may not maintain an action or proceeding in this State unless it has a certificate of authority to transact business in this State.

(b) The failure of a foreign limited liability company to have a certificate of authority to transact business in this State does not impair the validity of a contract or act of the company or prevent the foreign limited liability company from defending an action or proceeding in this State.

(c) Limitations on personal liability of managers, members, and their transferees are not waived solely by transacting business in this State without a certificate of authority.

(d) If a foreign limited liability company transacts business in this State without a certificate of authority, it appoints the [Secretary of State] as its agent for service of process for [claims for relief] arising out of the transaction of business in this State.

§ 1009. Action by [Attorney General].

The [Attorney General] may maintain an action to restrain a foreign limited liability company from transacting business in this State in violation of this [article].

[ARTICLE] 11

DERIVATIVE ACTIONS

§ 1101. Right of action.

A member of a limited liability company may maintain an action in the right of the company if the members or managers having authority to do so have refused to commence the action or an effort to cause those members or managers to commence the action is not likely to succeed.

Comment

A member may bring an action on behalf of the company when the members or managers having the authority to pursue the company recovery refuse to do so or an effort to cause them to pursue the recovery is not likely to succeed. See Comments to Section 411(a) (personal action of member against company or another member).

§ 1102. Proper plaintiff.

In a derivative action for a limited liability company, the plaintiff must be a member of the company when the action is commenced; and:

(1) must have been a member at the time of the transaction of which the plaintiff complains; or

(2) the plaintiff's status as a member must have devolved upon the plaintiff by operation of law or pursuant to the terms of the operating agreement from a person who was a member at the time of the transaction.

§ 1103. Pleading.

In a derivative action for a limited liability company, the complaint must set forth with particularity the effort of the plaintiff to secure initiation of the action by a member or manager or the reasons for not making the effort.

Comment

There is no obligation of the company or its members or managers to respond to a member demand to bring an action to pursue a company recovery. However, if a company later decides to commence the demanded action or assume control of the derivative litigation, the member's right to commence or control the proceeding ordinarily ends.

§ 1104. Expenses.

If a derivative action for a limited liability company is successful, in whole or in part, or if anything is received by the plaintiff as a result of a judgment, compromise, or settlement of an action or claim, the court may award the plaintiff reasonable expenses, including reasonable attorney's fees, and shall direct the plaintiff to remit to the limited liability company the remainder of the proceeds received.

[ARTICLE] 12

MISCELLANEOUS PROVISIONS

§ 1201. Uniformity of application and construction.

This [Act] shall be applied and construed to effectuate its general purpose to make uniform the law with respect to the subject of this [Act] among States enacting it.

§ 1202. Short title.

This [Act] may be cited as the Uniform Limited Liability Company Act (1995).

§ 1203. Severability clause.

If any provision of this [Act] or its application to any person or circumstance is held invalid, the invalidity does not affect other provisions or applications of this [Act] which can be given effect without the invalid provision or application, and to this end the provisions of this [Act] are severable.

§ 1204. Effective date.

This [Act] takes effect [_____].

§ 1205. Transitional provisions.

(a) Before January 1, 199_, this [Act] governs only a limited liability company organized:

(1) after the effective date of this [Act], unless the company is continuing the business of a dissolved limited liability company under [Section of the existing Limited Liability Company Act]; and

(2) before the effective date of this [Act], which elects, as provided by subsection (c), to be governed by this [Act].

(b) On and after January 1, 199_, this [Act] governs all limited liability companies.

(c) Before January 1, 199_, a limited liability company voluntarily may elect, in the manner provided in its operating agreement or by law for amending the operating agreement, to be governed by this [Act].

Comment

Under subsection (a)(1), the application of the Act is mandatory for all companies formed after the effective date of the Act determined under Section 1204. Under subsection (a)(2), the application of the Act is permissive, by election under subsection (c), for existing companies for a period of time specified in subsection (b) after which application becomes mandatory. This affords existing companies and their members an opportunity to consider the changes effected by this Act and to amend their operating agreements, if appropriate. If no election is made, the Act becomes effective after the period specified in subsection (b). The period specified by adopting States may vary, but a period of five years is a common period in similar cases.

§ 1206. Savings clause.

This [Act] does not affect an action or proceeding commenced or right accrued before the effective date of this [Act].

PART FOUR
SAMPLE AGREEMENT

GENERAL PARTNERSHIP AGREEMENT
FOR PROFESSIONAL PRACTICE

The following form agreement is reproduced from M. Volz, C. Trower, D. Reiss, The Drafting of Partnership Agreements 215-28 (7th ed. 1986). The Volz book also contains on pages 65-85 a form of general partnership agreement for nonprofessional partnerships which goes into more detail on questions of management, assignment and transfer of a partner's interest, accounting concepts, and other matters.

General Partnership Agreement of
[Insert Name]

This is a General Partnership Agreement, made and entered into on _____, 19__, by and between [list partners' full names] (the "Partners").

SECTION 1
FORMATION OF PARTNERSHIP

The Partners hereby form a partnership (the "Partnership") pursuant to the [name of state] Uniform Partnership Act. The rights and duties of the Partners shall be as provided in that Act except as modified by this Agreement.

SECTION 2
NAME

The business of the Partnership shall be conducted under the name "[insert name]" or such other name as the Partners shall hereafter designate by majority vote.

SECTION 3
BUSINESS OF THE PARTNERSHIP

The business of the Partnership is to engage in the practice of [medicine] [law] [public accountancy] under the laws of the State of [insert state's name] and in accordance with the [Principles of Medical Ethics of the American Medical Association] [Code of Professional Responsibility] [Accounting Standards]. The principal office of the business shall be at _____.

SECTION 4
TERM

The term of the Partnership shall begin on the date set forth above and shall continue until dissolved by an act or event specified in this Agreement or by law as one effecting dissolution.

SECTION 5
NAMES AND ADDRESS OF PARTNERS

The name and address of the Partners are
[Insert the names and addresses where partners wish to be contacted about partnership-related business.]

SECTION 6
CAPITAL AND CONTRIBUTIONS

6.01. Initial Capital. The initial contributions of the Partners shall be equal and shall be made in cash and in such amount as may be determined by a vote of [75 per cent of the Partners] [Partners having at least 75 per cent of the aggregate Partnership Percentages], and shall be paid in the manner determined by the vote, all as reflected on Annex A from time to time.

6.02. Additional Capital. Future contributions to capital, made by the Partners in accordance with their Partnership Percentages, shall be made upon determination by a vote of [75 per cent of the Partners] [Partners having at least 75 per cent of the aggregate Partnership Percentages], and shall be reflected on Annex A when made.

6.03. Interest on Capital Contributions. No Partner shall be paid interest on any Capital Contribution.

SECTION 7
DISTRIBUTIONS

Partnership cash accounts (the "Cash Accounts") shall be set up on the Partnership's books for each Partner. Each Partner's Cash Account shall be credited with his proportionate share (in accordance with his Partnership Percentage) of all cash revenues of the Partnership from business operations during any period, and shall be charged with his proportionate share of (1) all principal and interest payments on any indebtedness of the Partnership, and (2) all cash expenses incurred incident to the operations of the Partnership's business. Each Partner may make withdrawals from his Cash Account from time to time, including withdrawals in anticipation of partnership revenues, and all these withdrawals shall be charged against his Cash Account; *provided, however,* that no Partner shall be permitted to make withdrawals that would cause his Cash Account to have a negative balance of more than $_____ at any time, and any Partner with a negative balance in his Cash Account determined upon closing the books at the end of the Partnership's fiscal year shall, within 15 days, repay the deficit to the Partnership. Any deficit balance in a Cash Account that is not paid within 15 days of the end of the Partnership's fiscal year, shall bear interest at an annual rate equal to ____ per cent, until repaid in full.[1]

---

[1] Many professional partnership agreements include an "Income" or "Drawing" account, which serves as a subset of the partnership capital account in the sense that all current taxable income and losses are booked to that account to determine distributions. Cash Account as defined above is preferable to the Drawing Account when the parties wish cash withdrawls from the partnership to

SECTION 8
ALLOCATION OF PROFITS AND LOSSES
FOR TAX PURPOSES

All taxable income and tax losses of the Partnership as determined for federal income tax purposes shall be allocated among the Partners in proportion to their respective Partnership Percentages.

SECTION 9
PARTNERSHIP PERCENTAGES

The initial Partnership Percentages of each Partner shall be as follows:

Name	Initial Partnership Percentage
[insert]	[insert]

Immediately after the end of the first fiscal year of the Partnership, and at the end of each year thereafter, the Partnership Percentages shall be adjusted as follows: (1) 70 per cent of a Partner's Partnership Percentage for the immediately preceding year, plus (2) the percentage that a Partner's billings [collections] bears to the total billings [collections] of all of the Partners, *multiplied by* 30 per cent. The Partnership Percentage so calculated shall apply to the next succeeding fiscal year of the Partnership.

SECTION 10
MANAGEMENT

All of the Partners shall participate in the conduct of the Partnership's business and each Partner shall devote his entire time thereto. No Partner shall, directly or indirectly, engage in any other business or occupation without the consent of the other Partners. Notwithstanding the preceding sentence, nothing here shall prohibit any Partner from investing in or trading in securities, bonds, commodities, or other forms of investment for his own benefit. In matters relating to the management of the Partnership's business, a decision [by the majority of the Partners] [of the Partners owning a majority of the Partnership Percentages] shall be binding upon the Partnership except when a higher majority is otherwise required by this Agreement. The following specific actions may not be taken without the consent of

---

be governed by actual cash-flow, as opposed to profits and losses computed for tax purposes, which profits and losses would take into account noncash expenses, such as depreciation, and would not take into account nondeductible cash expenses such as repayment of loans. In the unusual situation in which partners will share tax items in different percentages than cash is to be withdrawn from the partnership, the income or drawing account that takes into account current shares of profits and losses and which is closed at the end of each year to the partner's capital account may be necessary to prevent a partner from creating a negative capital account balance because his shares of profits and losses for tax purposes are lower than his agreed share of cash distributions.

[__ per cent of the Partners] [Partners having Partnership Percentages aggregating __ per cent]:

(1) Except with respect to agreements and instruments in the usual and ordinary course of business of the Partnership, execute any agreement or instrument in writing to bind the Partnership or contract any debt on account of the Partnership.

(2) Pledge any property of the Partnership for the purpose of securing a loan.

(3) Lend any money of the Partnership.

(4) Assign any part of his interest in the Partnership or enter into an agreement as a result of which any person may become interested with him in the Partnership.

(5) Sell any capital assets of the Partnership.

SECTION 11
BANKING AND BOOKS OF ACCOUNT

11.01. Books and Records. All funds of the Partnership shall be deposited in its name in such accounts as shall be designated by the Partners. All withdrawals from these accounts may be made upon checks signed by any Partner except that withdrawals of more than $_____ shall require the signature of two Partners. Complete records and books of account shall be kept in which shall be entered fully and accurately all transactions and other matters about the Partnership's business as are usually entered into records and books of account maintained by persons engaged in businesses of a like character, including a Capital Account and a Drawing Account for each Partner. The books shall be kept on a cash basis. The books and records shall at all times be maintained at the principal place of business of the Partnership and each Partner shall at all times have access thereto.

11.02. Fiscal Year. The fiscal year of the Partnership shall end on the thirty-first day of December in each year.

11.03. Capital Account. Each Partner's Capital Account shall be initially equal to the cash and the adjusted basis (net of liabilities assumed or to which the property is subject) of any property he contributes to the Partnership, and during the term of the Partnership shall be (A) *increased* by (1) the amount of taxable income allocated to the Partner and (2) the amount of any additional cash or the adjusted basis (net of liabilities assumed or to which the property is subject) of any property contributed by the Partner or paid to his Cash Account, and (B) decreased by (1) the amount of tax losses allocated to the Partner and (2) the amount of cash and the adjusted basis (net of liabilities assumed or to which the property is subject) of any property distributed to the Partner, whether from his Cash Account or otherwise.

SECTION 12
PARTNERSHIP EXPENSES

12.01. Insurance. The Partnership will purchase and pay for as a partnership expense a partnership malpractice insurance policy with limits of not less than $_____, and similar insurance policies of coverages on each individual Partner. Each Partner agrees to purchase and individually pay for automobile liability insurance coverage with policy limits of not less than $_____ for personal injury and $_____ property damage. The Partnership will purchase and pay for as

Partnership expense public liability insurance, fire insurance on Partnership property, and employee bonds, all with those policy limits as shall be agreed upon by the Partners.

12.02. Other Expenses. Except as otherwise specifically provided herein, all operating and professional expenses of the Partnership (including, without limitation, rent, repairs, furnishings, [drugs, medical supplies,] office salaries, professional fees, and depreciation on equipment) shall be paid by the Partnership. Each Partner shall furnish his own automobile and shall purchase and shall pay individually the entire cost of maintaining and operating the automobile, including the cost of automobile insurance in the amount provided by Section 12.01.

12.03. Individual Expenses. Each Partner shall pay individually his dues to professional associations, his subscriptions for professional books and publications, his expenses for attending professional meetings, and his professional entertainment expenses, charitable contributions, and club dues, and shall at all times pay and satisfy his own personal debts.

SECTION 13
VACATIONS AND EDUCATION

Each Partner shall be entitled to ____ weeks of vacation in each calendar year, but there shall be no carryover of unused vacation time from one year to another. An additional ____ weeks of time off from Partnership duties will be allowed to permit attendance at [medical] [legal] [accounting] meetings and continuing education courses.

SECTION 14
NEGLIGENCE AND INDEMNIFICATION

Except to the extent that the Partnership is insured against liability, a Partner guilty of negligence or wrongdoing shall reimburse the Partnership for damages sustained by it as a result of negligence or wrongdoing. The Partnership shall indemnify and hold harmless all Partners from and against any loss, expense, damage, or injury suffered or sustained by him by reason of any act, omissions, or alleged acts or omissions arising out of his activities on behalf of the Partnership or in furtherance of the interests of the Partnership, including but not limited to any judgment, award, settlement, reasonable attorneys' fees, and other costs or expenses incurred in connection with the defense of any actual or threatened action, proceeding, or claim, if the acts, omissions, or alleged acts or omissions upon which the actual or threatened action, proceeding, or claims are based on or for a purpose reasonably believed to be in the best interests of the Partnership, and were not performed or admitted fraudulently or in bad faith or as a result of negligence by the Partner. Any of this indemnification shall be first from the assets of the Partnership and then from all Partners and borne among them in accordance with their Partnership Percentages.

SECTION 15
DISSOLUTION

The withdrawal, retirement, bankruptcy, expulsion, or death of any but one of only two Partners shall not require a winding up of the Partnership (unless the remaining Partners vote to dissolve) and shall have no effect upon the continuance of the Partnership's business. He or his estate shall have no rights in or against the Partnership or the remaining Partners except for those payments as may be due under the provisions of this Agreement. The Partnership may be dissolved at any time by [vote of 75 per cent of the Partners] [vote of Partners having 75 per cent of the Partnership Percentages], in which event the Partners shall proceed with reasonable promptness to liquidate the business and assets of the Partnership. Upon dissolution and winding up, the assets of the Partnership shall be used and distributed in the following order:

(1) To creditors in the order of priority provided by law except liabilities to the Partners in their capacity as Partners.

(2) To the Partners for loans, if any, made by them to the Partnership and to the Partners for any expenses of the Partnership paid by them, to the extent they are entitled to reimbursement.

(3) To the Partners in proportion to their respective Capital Accounts (which accounts have been determined after allocation of all taxable income and tax losses incident to the dissolution) until they have received an amount equal to their Capital Accounts immediately prior to the distribution.

(4) To the Partners in accordance with their Partnership Percentages.

SECTION 16
WITHDRAWAL, RETIREMENT, AND DEATH

16.01. Withdrawal. Any Partner may voluntarily withdraw from the Partnership at the end of any month, provided that he has given at least 30 days prior written notice of the withdrawal to the other Partners. A Partner shall withdraw from the Partnership (1) upon suspension or revocation of his right to practice [medicine] [law] [accountancy], (2) upon vote of [75 per cent of the Partners] [Partners having 75 per cent or more of the Partnership Percentages], (3) at his bankruptcy, as defined in Section 17.02, or (4) if by reason of illness or any other cause, a Partner is unable to carry on his duties for a continuous period of more than six months. Upon withdrawal of a Partner, he shall be paid the Buy-Out Amount, in the time and in the manner described in Section 16.05. A withdrawing Partner shall be entitled to take with him all [papers] [records] pertaining to the affairs of those [clients] [patients] whose business he has personally carried on or supervised unless any client requests a different disposition of those [papers] [records]. At the time of this withdrawal, the Partnership shall bill for all services rendered to those [clients] [patients] who elect to continue with the withdrawing Partner unless the withdrawing Partner consents that the amount of the bill (reduced by the withdrawing Partner's Partnership Percentage) may be deducted from the payments otherwise required to be made to him. If payment for services in any manner handled for any client who elects to continue with the withdrawing Partner is contingent upon results, the withdrawing Partner shall account to the other Partners for their proportionate shares of the value of the work in process up to the date of withdrawal, if and when the withdrawing Partner receives payment for these services. No withdrawing Partner shall be entitled to a distribution of any of the equipment or library of the Partnership.

16.02. Retirement. Each Partner shall retire at the end of the year in which he attains age _____. Upon retirement, the Partnership shall purchase and the retiring Partner shall sell the retiring Partner's interest in the Partnership for an amount equal to the Buy-Out Amount. Payment for the interest shall be made at the time and in the manner specified in Section 16.05.

16.03. Death. Upon the death of a Partner, the Partnership shall purchase and the legal representative of the deceased Partner shall sell the deceased Partner's interest in the Partnership for an amount equal to the Buy-Out Amount. Payment for the interest shall be made at the time and in the manner specified in Section 16.05.

16.04. Buy-Out Amount. The Buy-Out Amount shall be computed as of the effective date of withdrawal, death, or retirement of a Partner (the "Effective Date") and shall be equal to (1) his Capital Account, *plus* (2) the accounts receivable of the Partnership as of the Effective Date, reduced by the percentage that expenses bore to total accounts receivable during the immediately preceding fiscal year of the Partnership, and multiplied by that Partner's Partnership Percentage, *plus* (3) that Partner's share (in accordance with his Partnership Percentage) of work in progress at the Effective Date, *plus* (4) the amount in his Drawing Account. The Buy-Out Amount shall be deemed a payment with respect to Partnership property under Section 736(b) of the [Internal Revenue] Code to the extent of his Capital Account, and the remainder a distributive share under Section 736(a).

16.05. Payments — Time and Manner. The Buy-Out Amount shall be paid to the Partner or his representative within ____ days after the Effective Date, except that any amounts due with respect to work in progress received subsequent to the Effective Date shall be paid within 30 days after their receipt by the continuing Partnership (and those amounts received within ____ months of the Effective Date shall constitute full payment for work in progress).

16.06. Use of Name. The Partnership shall have the right to continue to use the name of any deceased or retiring Partner in the Partnership name, but shall have no right and shall not be required to use the name of any Partner who has withdrawn and continued the practice of [law] [medicine] [accountancy].

16.07. Adjustment of Partnership Percentages. Upon the withdrawal, death, or retirement of any Partner pursuant to this Section 16, the remaining Partners' Partnership Percentages shall be increased in total by an amount equal to the withdrawing, retiring, or deceased Partner's Partnership Percentage, and among the remaining Partners in accordance with their respective Partnership Percentages prior to the withdrawal, death, or retirement.

SECTION 17
MISCELLANEOUS

17.01. Additional Partners. Additional Partners shall be admitted by the vote of not less than [75 per cent of the Partners] [Partners having 75 per cent or more of the Partnership Percentages]. Each additional Partner, before being admitted as a Partner, shall first agree in writing to be bound by the terms of this Partnership Agreement.

17.02. Bankruptcy Defined. For purposes of this Agreement, the "bankruptcy" of a Partner shall be deemed to have occurred 60 days after the happening of any of the following: (1) the filing of an application by a Partner for, or a consent to, the appointment of a trustee of the Partner's assets, (2) the filing by a Partner of a voluntary petition in bankruptcy or the filing of a pleading in any court of record admitting in writing the Partner's inability to pay the Partner's debts as they become due, (3) the making by a Partner of a general assignment for the benefit of creditors, (4) the filing by a Partner of an answer admitting the material allegations of, or consenting to, or defaulting in answering a bankruptcy petition filed against the Partner in any bankruptcy proceeding, or (5) the entry of an order, judgment, or decree by any court of competent jurisdiction adjudicating a Partner a bankrupt, or appointing a trustee of the Partner's assets, and that order, judgment, or decree continuing unstayed and in effect for the period of 60 days.

17.03. Fees and Billings. All professional fees, salaries, and other compensation of any Partner arising out of the practice of [medicine] [law] [accountancy] including, without limitation, [fees for office calls, house calls, and consultations, hospital services and teaching] [fees or salaries for teaching, for serving on boards of directors, planning committees, and so forth] belong to the Partnership.

17.04. Amendment. This Partnership Agreement may be amended at any time and from time to time by a vote of [75 per cent of the Partners] [Partners having 75 per cent or more of the aggregate Partnership Percentages].

17.05. Entire Agreement. This Agreement constitutes the entire agreement among the parties. It supersedes any prior agreement or understanding among them, and it may not be modified or amended in any manner other than as set forth herein.

17.06. Governing Law. This Agreement and the rights of the parties hereunder shall be governed by and interpreted in accordance with the laws of _____.

17.07. Effect. Except as otherwise specifically provided herein, this Agreement shall be binding upon and inure to the benefit of the parties and their legal representatives, heirs, administrators, executors, successors, and assigns.

17.08. Pronouns and Number. Wherever from the context it appears appropriate, each term stated in either the singular or the plural shall include the singular and the plural, and pronouns stated in either the masculine, feminine, or neuter shall include the masculine, feminine, or neuter.

17.09. Captions. Captions and section headings contained in this Agreement are inserted only as a matter of convenience and in no way define, limit, or extend the scope or intent of this Agreement or any provision hereof.

17.10. Partial Enforceability. If any provision of this Agreement or the application of any provision to any person or circumstance shall be held invalid, the remainder of this Agreement, or the application of that provision to persons or circumstances other than those to which it is held invalid, shall not be affected thereby.

17.11. Counterparts. This Agreement may be executed in several counterparts, each of which shall be deemed an original but all of which shall constitute one and the same instrument.

IN WITNESS WHEREOF, the undersigned have executed this Agreement as of _____, 19__.

_____
[Partner's signature]

_____
[Partner's signature]

_____
[Partner's signature]

PART FIVE

SELECTED EXCERPTS FROM
RESTATEMENT (SECOND) OF AGENCY

SELECTED EXCERPTS FROM
RESTATEMENT (SECOND) OF AGENCY

§ 1. Agency; Principal; Agent.

(1) Agency is the fiduciary relation which results from the manifestation of consent by one person to another that the other shall act on his behalf and subject to his control, and consent by the other so to act.

(2) The one for whom action is to be taken is the principal.

(3) The one who is to act is the agent.

§ 2. Master; Servant; Independent Contractor.

(1) A master is a principal who employs an agent to perform service in his affairs and who controls or has the right to control the physical conduct of the other in the performance of the service.

(2) A servant is an agent employed by a master to perform service in his affairs whose physical conduct in the performance of the service is controlled or is subject to the right of control by the master.

(3) An independent contractor is a person who contracts with another to do something for him but who is not controlled by the other nor subject to the other's right to control with respect to his physical conduct in the performance of the undertaking. He may or may not be an agent.

§ 6. Power.

A power is an ability on the part of a person to produce a change in a given legal relation by doing or not doing a given act.

Comment:

a. The word "power" denotes not a physical or mental quality but a legal attribute, the ability to change legal relations. This ability may be rightfully exercised, as where an agent makes an authorized contract; or it may be wrongfully exercised, as where an agent, having apparent authority so to do, makes an unauthorized contract.

§ 7. Authority.

Authority is the power of the agent to affect the legal relations of the principal by acts done in accordance with the principal's manifestations of consent to him.

§ 8. Apparent authority.

Apparent authority is the power to affect the legal relations of another person by transactions with third persons, professedly as agent for the other, arising from and in accordance with the other's manifestations to such third persons.

§ 8A. Inherent agency power.

Inherent agency power is a term used in the restatement of this subject to indicate the power of an agent which is derived not from authority, apparent authority or estoppel, but solely from the agency relation and exists for the protection of persons harmed by or dealing with a servant or other agent.

§ 8B. Estoppel; change of position.

(1) A person who is not otherwise liable as a party to a transaction purported to be done on his account, is nevertheless subject to liability to persons who have changed their positions because of their belief that the transaction was entered into by or for him, if

(a) he intentionally or carelessly caused such belief, or

(b) knowing of such belief and that others might change their positions because of it, he did not take reasonable steps to notify them of the facts.

(2) An owner of property who represents to third persons that another is the owner of the property or who permits the other so to represent, or who realizes that third persons believe that another is the owner of the property, and that he could easily inform the third persons of the facts, is subject to the loss of the property if the other disposes of it to third persons who, in ignorance of the facts, purchase the property or otherwise change their position with reference to it.

(3) Change of position, as the phrase is used in the restatement of this subject, indicates payment of money, expenditure of labor, suffering a loss or subjection to legal liability.

§ 12. Agent is a holder of a power.

An agent or apparent agent holds a power to alter the legal relations between the principal and third persons and between the principal and himself.

§ 13. Agent as a fiduciary.

An agent is a fiduciary with respect to matters within the scope of the agency.

Comment:

a. The agreement to act on behalf of the principal causes the agent to be a fiduciary, that is, a person having a duty, created by his undertaking, to act primarily for the benefit of another in matters connected with his undertaking. Among the agent's fiduciary duties to the principal is the duty to account for profits arising out of the employment, the duty not to act as, or on account of, an adverse party without the principal's consent, the duty not to compete with the principal on his own account or for another in matters relating to the subject matter of the agency, and the duty to deal fairly with the principal in all transactions between them.

§ 14. Control by principal.

A principal has the right to control the conduct of the agent with respect to matters entrusted to him.

Comment:

a. The right of control by the principal may be exercised by prescribing what the agent shall or shall not do before the agent acts, or at the time when he acts, or at both times. The principal's right of control is continuous and continues as long as the agency relation exists, even though the principal agreed that he would not exercise it. Thus, the agent is subject to a duty not to act contrary to the principal's directions, although the principal has agreed not to give such directions.

§ 26. Creation of authority; general rule.

Except for the execution of instruments under seal or for the performance of transactions required by statute to be authorized in a particular way, authority to do an act can be created by written or spoken words or other conduct of the principal which, reasonably interpreted, causes the agent to believe that the principal desires him to so act on the principal's account.

§ 27. Creation of apparent authority; general rule.

Except for the execution of instruments under seal or for the conduct of transactions required by statute to be authorized in a particular way, apparent authority to do an act is created as to a third person by written or spoken words or any other conduct of the principal which, reasonably interpreted, causes the third person to believe that the principal consents to have the act done on his behalf by the person purporting to act for him.

§ 43. Acquiescence by principal in agent's conduct.

(1) Acquiescence by the principal in conduct of an agent whose previously conferred authorization reasonably might include it, indicates that the conduct was authorized; if clearly not included in the authorization, acquiescence in it indicates affirmance.

(2) Acquiescence by the principal in a series of acts by the agent indicates authorization to perform similar acts in the future.

§ 82. Ratification.

Ratification is the affirmance by a person of a prior act which did not bind him but which was done or professedly done on his account, whereby the act, as to some or all persons, is given effect as if originally authorized by him.

§ 219. When master is liable for torts of his servants.

(1) A master is subject to liability for the torts of his servants committed while acting in the scope of their employment.

(2) A master is not subject to liability for the torts of his servants acting outside the scope of their employment, unless:

    (a) the master intended the conduct or the consequences, or

    (b) the master was negligent or reckless, or

    (c) the conduct violated a non-delegable duty of the master, or

    (d) the servant purported to act or to speak on behalf of the principal and there was reliance upon apparent authority, or he was aided in accomplishing the tort by the existence of the agency relation.

§ 228. General statement of scope of employment.

(1) Conduct of a servant is within the scope of employment if, but only if:

    (a) it is of the kind he is employed to perform;

    (b) it occurs substantially within the authorized time and space limits;

    (c) it is actuated, at least in part, by a purpose to serve the master, and

    (d) if force is intentionally used by the servant against another, the use of force is not unexpectable by the master.

(2) Conduct of a servant is not within the scope of employment if it is different in kind from that authorized, far beyond the authorized time or space limits, or too little actuated by a purpose to serve the master.

§ 235. Conduct not for purpose of serving master.

An act of a servant is not within the scope of employment if it is done with no intention to perform it as a part of or incident to a service on account of which he is employed.

§ 388. Duty to account for profits arising out of employment.

Unless otherwise agreed, an agent who makes a profit in connection with transactions conducted by him on behalf of the principal is under a duty to give such profit to the principal.

§ 389. Acting as adverse party without principal's consent.

Unless otherwise agreed, an agent is subject to a duty not to deal with his principal as an adverse party in a transaction connected with his agency without the principal's knowledge.

Comment:

c. The rule stated in this Section is not based upon the existence of harm to the principal in the particular case. It exists to prevent a conflict of opposing interests in the minds of agents whose duty it is to act solely for the benefit of their principals. The rule applies, therefore, even though the transaction between the principal and the agent is beneficial to the principal.

§ 390. Acting as adverse party with principal's consent.

An agent who, to the knowledge of the principal, acts on his own account in a transaction in which he is employed has a duty to deal fairly with the principal and to disclose to him all facts which the agent knows or should know would reasonably affect the principal's judgment, unless the principal has manifested that he knows such facts or that he does not care to know them.

Comment:

c. . . . If the agent is one upon whom the principal naturally would rely for advice, the fact that the agent discloses that he is acting as an adverse party does not relieve him from the duty of giving the principal impartial advice based upon a carefully formed judgment as to the principal's interests. If he cannot or does not wish to do so, he has a duty to see that the principal secures the advice of a competent and disinterested third person.

§ 395. Using or disclosing confidential information.

Unless otherwise agreed, an agent is subject to a duty to the principal not to use or to communicate information confidentially given him by the principal or acquired by him during the course of or on account of his agency or in violation of his duties as agent, in competition with or to the injury of the principal, on his own account or on behalf of another, although such information does not relate to the transaction in which he is then employed, unless the information is a matter of general knowledge.

Comment:

b. The rule stated in this Section applies not only to those communications which are stated to be confidential, but also to information which the agent should know his principal would not care to have revealed to others or used in competition with him.

§ 396. Using confidential information after termination of agency.

Unless otherwise agreed, after the termination of the agency, the agent:

(a) has no duty not to compete with the principal;

(b) has a duty to the principal not to use or to disclose to third persons, on his own account or on account of others, in competition with the principal or to his injury, trade secrets, written lists of names, or other similar confidential matters given to him only for the principal's use or acquired by the agent in violation of duty. The agent is entitled to use general information concerning the method of business of the principal and the names of the customers retained in his memory, if not acquired in violation of his duty as agent;

(c) has a duty to account for his profits made by the sale or use of trade secrets and other confidential information, whether or not in competition with the principal;

(d) has a duty to the principal not to take advantage of a still subsisting confidential relation created during the prior agency relation.